THE SOVIET ARMY
1918 to the Present

THE
SOVIET ARMY

1918 to the Present

ALBERT SEATON
JOAN SEATON

THE BODLEY HEAD
LONDON

British Library Cataloguing
in Publication Data
Seaton, Albert
The Soviet army, 1918 to the present.
1. Union of Soviet Socialist Republics—
Armi ía—History
I. Title II. Seaton, Joan
355'.00947 UA772
ISBN 0 370 30535 3

© Albert Seaton and Joan Seaton 1986
Printed in Great Britain for
The Bodley Head Ltd
32 Bedford Square, London WC1B 3EL
by The Bath Press, Avon
Set in Linotron 202 Plantin
by Wyvern Typesetting Ltd, Bristol
First published 1986

They just slavishly follow the example of Germany, whose military system they have adopted.

British Military Attaché Wellesley
in St Petersburg in 1878

German views and methods go through theirs like a continuous red thread.

German Military Attaché Köstring
in Moscow in 1931

The universal conviction in Russia that the Russian is the world's bravest soldier . . . he just lacks German technique and guidance.

Wollenberg, a Red Army commander
c. 1931

We want to take over everything that was good and worthy from the old imperial army and continue to use it in the Red Army.

Major-General Count Ignatev
in Moscow in 1937

The Soviet Army has borrowed everything that was progressive from the pre-revolutionary combat past of the Russian people.

Marshal of the Soviet Union Grechko
in Moscow in 1975

CONTENTS

Acknowledgements   viii
List of Illustrations   ix
List of Maps   xi
Introduction   1
1 The Tsarist Heritage   4
2 The Birth of the Red Army   26
3 The Years of Military Doubt and Indecision   57
4 The Race Against Time   90
5 The Second World War   117
6 The Pre-Nuclear Army   148
7 The Rocket Age   178
8 Plus ça Change   203
9 The Eighties   225
Appendix A: Soviet Tank Models   234
Appendix B: Soviet Armoured Cars, APCs and ACVs
    (Infantry)   237
Appendix C: Soviet Anti-Tank Weapons   239
Appendix D: Soviet Ground Artillery   241
Appendix E: Soviet Ground Forces Tactical Surface-to-
    Surface Rocket Missiles and Anti-Aircraft
    Weapons   244
Appendix F: Soviet Small-Arms and Infantry Weapons   247
Source Notes   249
Bibliography   264
Index   272

ACKNOWLEDGEMENTS

The sources of the illustrations are as follows: Illustration Nos 1, 2 and 3 from *L'Armée Russe d'après photographies instantanées exécutées par de Jongh frères* by d'Almeida and de Jongh: No.13 from *Velikaia Otechestvennaia Voina Sovetskogo Soiuza (Kratkaia Istoriia):*Nos 17 and 19 from *Armiia Sovetskaia:* Nos 32 and 33 from *50 Let Vooruzhennykh Sil SSSR*: and all others from *Piat'desiat Let Sovetskikh Vooruzhennykh Sil Fotodokumenty*

The Appendices in this book covering Soviet AFVs, rocketry, guns and small-arms have been based on information contained in, *inter alia*:

Arndt's *Waffen und Gerät der Sowjetischen Landstreitkräfte*
Barker and Walter's *Russian Infantry Weapons of WWII*
Isby's *Weapons and Tactics of the Soviet Army*
Mayer's *The Russian War Machine 1917-1945*
Perrett's *Fighting Vehicles of the Red Army*
Rotmistrov's *Istoriia Voennogo Iskusstva*
Soviet Military Power 1983 and 1984
Soviet Military Review
The US Handbook of the Soviet Armed Forces 1978
Voenno-Istoricheskii Zhurnal

Gratitude is expressed to Mr George Kennan and to the Harriet Wasserman Literary Agency, New York, for kind permission to use, in the Introduction of this book, the quotation from the article that appeared on p. 57 of *The New Yorker* of 25 February 1985.

LIST OF ILLUSTRATIONS

following page 96

1. An NCO of the imperial Preobrazhensky foot-guard in field service order
2. A soldier of the imperial Moskovsky grenadiers in winter field service order
3. Members of the imperial corps of pages (officer aspirants from the aristocracy) in a variety of uniforms
4. Armed civilians forming a Red Guard street patrol in St Petersburg, 1917
5. Stalin when commissar of the South Front (1918)
6. A January 1927 meeting of the Revolutionary Military Council
7. The five 1935 Marshals of the Soviet Union
8. Red Army cavalry with a Maxim machine-gun mounted on an open carriage (the *tachanka*)
9. A column of 1937 Vickers-based T 26 with machine-guns mounted in twin turrets

following page 128

10. A 45mm anti-tank gun in action in the streets of Rostov on Don in 1942
11. Red Army artillery moving through Kiev at the end of 1943; the gun is a 76mm 1939-pattern field piece
12. Cavalry of 3 Ukrainian Front in March 1944 taking artillery ammunition forward
13. Red Army infantry supported by open-topped armoured SU 76 tank-destroyers (on T 70 chassis) in East Prussia in April 1945
14. Crews of 76mm guns M 42 in Hungary, March 1945
15. Red Army sappers and pioneers building a bridge over the Oder in 1945
16. T 34 tanks on the Pacific coast, August 1945
17. Marshals of the Soviet Union Konev, Vasilevsky, Zhukov, Rokossovsky, Meretskov, Tolbukhin, Malinovsky and Govorov, and army generals Eremenko and Bagramian

following page 192

18. Reconnaissance amphibians (6x6 Zil-485 [BAV]) swimming a river in 1956
19. Manoeuvres (about 1958): assault infantry carried on a T 54 tank with APCs (6x6 BTR 152) in the background
20. A 240mm M 53 heavy mortar in firing position (1965)
21. Artillery 'donkey's ears' observation and ranging optical equipment
22. One of the first strategic rockets on its testing stand
23. A *Scud* intermediate-range tactical guided rocket missile on a self-propelled tracked transporter
24. Parachutists making a descent by statichute from the rear-exit, probably from a four-engined transport (AN-12 *Cub*)
25. An Mi-4 *Hound* helicopter co-operating with a T 54 tank detachment (1965)

following page 224

26. A road-truck with rail-rollers, towing a section of a bridge into position (1965)
27. A mechanical BTM trench-digger made up of a ETR-409 trenching-machine mounted on an artillery tractor
28. T 55 A tanks on the Moscow parade
29. Airborne forces *Frog* mobile surface-to-surface rocket-launchers being unloaded from an An-22 *Cock* air transport
30. An SA-2 *Guideline* on its transporter
31. Air defence controllers
32. The SA-4 *Ganef* surface-to-air missile in service with the ground forces
33. An SS-X-14 (sometimes called *Scamp*) intermediate missile on a tracked transporter

LIST OF MAPS

(pages xii to xv)

1 Western Russia 1921
2 Russia and Siberia 1921
3 Western Russia 1946
4 USSR 1946

Cartographer: Linda McFie

MAP I WESTERN RUSSIA

MAP 1
WESTERN RUSSIA 1921

Scale 1 : 20,000,000
304 miles = 1 inch

MAP 2 RUSSIA AND SIBERIA

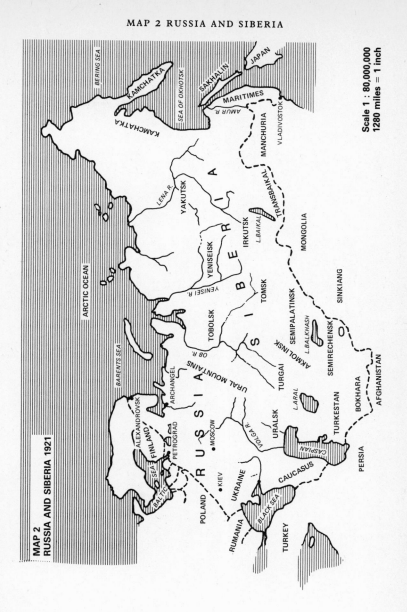

MAP 2
RUSSIA AND SIBERIA 1921

Scale 1 : 80,000,000
1280 miles = 1 inch

MAP 3 WESTERN RUSSIA

MAP 3
WESTERN RUSSIA 1946

Scale 1 : 20,000,000
304 miles = 1 inch

MAP 4 USSR 1946

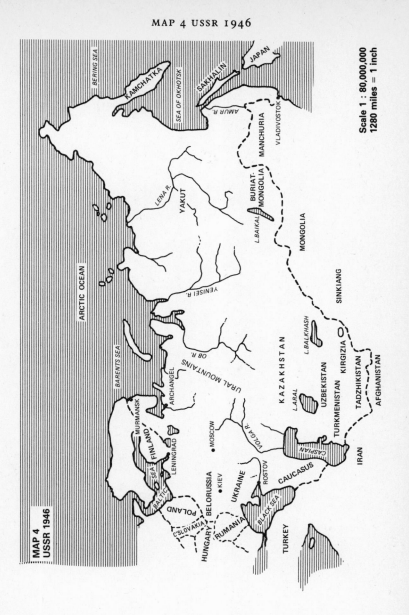

Introduction

In the period between the two world wars the Soviet Russian-language press was not widely read in the western world outside of the foreign offices and military departments in Washington, London and Paris. There, a few dedicated officials, to use the words of one of them, Mr George Kennan, 'noted the subtle changes that occurred from day to day – changes that every sophisticated Russian knew how to decipher and to interpret, as the officials themselves, in time, were equally able to do.' When, however, Mr George Kennan began this work in the thirties, he said that he was appalled 'at the propaganda that pervaded every page of the official Soviet literature – at the unabashed use of obvious falsehood, at the hypocrisy and, above all, at the savage intolerance shown towards everything that is not Soviet.'* All this is entirely true of the Soviet press today.

Russian-language military history literature is designed both to instruct and to misinform Soviet youth, not only as to the realities of the present world situation but also as to the whole course of European and world history over the last three hundred years. For the Soviet leadership has for many years been teaching its peoples that nearly all world progress over the last century or more originated with communism: and where this origin must obviously predate the October 1917 revolution, Russia, even imperial Russia, must be given the credit and the merit. This is carried to such grotesque lengths in the rewriting of history, that present-day Soviet officers, men of some intelligence and education, are taught that modern naval expertise began in Russia, that the English Lord Nelson stole his ideas from an eighteenth-century Russian admiral named Ushakov, that there was apparently no battle of Waterloo since Napoleon was destroyed in 1812 and 1813,

*The New Yorker, 25 February 1985, p. 57 (© Copyright 1985 by George F. Kennan).

that all military inventions, radio, radar, the tank, the tank-destroyer, rocketry, the jet engine and so on, originated in Russia, and that the Soviet Union, largely by its own efforts, defeated not only Nazi Germany but also imperialistic Japan.

The Soviet Russian-language press is now read widely in the western world, principally in universities that have Russian departments, and a number of these departments sponsor organizations that publish works in English on Soviet military subjects, unofficial publications of a type unknown before the war. And, although their authors are academics and not soldiers, their descriptions of current events and trends are, in the main, very good, some even excellent. Yet even the very good and the excellent are sometimes forced to rely, *faute de mieux*, on Soviet accounts to fill in historical or background gaps, since these western authors often lack independent knowledge or sources against which the Soviet claims can be checked: in these instances, in our view, a very false picture sometimes emerges in the western-published works on Russian history. For, as the Russo-Polish General Denikin once said, anyone who draws 'historic material' from Soviet sources risks refraction from the false Soviet mirror.

To give an example. Some respected western authorities on the Soviet Army apparently regard the Red Army between the two world wars as being one of the leading, if not the leading, exponent on armoured warfare; the present-day Moscow leadership certainly says so. But this ignores the reality of the times for, in truth, the situation in the thirties was very much otherwise. The Soviet armed forces at that time had no soldiers of genius or experience and the Red Army was an indifferent imitation of the German Army; for it was exactly what the German, French, American and British military attachés in Moscow judged it to be, a distinctly second-rate force. Stalin, himself, in one of his franker moments, told western dignitaries in 1943 that the Red Army had done very badly against the Finns in 1939, and that in 1941, in spite of extensive reorganization, 'it could not be said that the Red Army was in the first class;' but, added Stalin, it had improved steadily since 1941 and by 1943 was 'genuinely a good army'.* And that was the situation in a nutshell. The Red Army, like the tsarist army, learned all its lessons from the Germans, partly in peace but mainly in war, and it is a debt that the present-day Soviet

*Sherwood, *The White House Papers of Harry Hopkins*, Vol. 2, pp. 784–7.

Army still owes to the German tank philosophers of the thirties. And if one has an insight into the mentality of the one army, one understands the working of the other. Without this knowledge one is in danger of being led astray.

When the Red Army was first formed it consisted in its entirety of ground forces. The twenties saw the establishment of the Red Air Force, but this remained a component part of the Red Army very much as most of the Soviet Air Force remains part of the Soviet Army today. In the year 1935 came the founding of an air defence organization that was eventually to become the PVO home air defence command made up of air force and anti-aircraft artillery. Other post Second World War changes have been the forming of an all-service supply and equipment troop organization known as Rear Services, and, in 1960, the setting up of a separate strategic rocket forces command. All of these commands and organizations, the ground forces, the air forces, the strategic rocket forces command, the PVO and the Rear Services, jointly form part of the Soviet Army today. In this book, however, we have been obliged to confine ourselves mainly to the development of the Soviet Army ground forces.

As this book is intended for the general reader we have tried to keep the text clear of military and other specialist technicalities, and have avoided the use of Russian and German terms. There are several recognized ways of transliterating Russian words and names, all of them very different: in our bibliography we have used the Library of Congress method. Elsewhere we have shown them in the form that will be most readily understood by the English-speaking reader.

All dates are shown in accordance with the old-style calendar until 31 January 1918. The next day in Russia was 14 February (new style).

A.S. and J.W.S.

CHAPTER ONE

The Tsarist Heritage

The first permanent Russian Army dated back to Ivan the Terrible's *streltsy*, a force of forty regiments of archers and musketeers. But as these *streltsy* showed that they had little fighting value during the times of the troubles at the beginning of the seventeenth century, they were relegated to second-class militia, their place as first-line troops being taken, from 1642 onwards, by a regular army on the western pattern, under German, Swedish and Livonian officers and non-commissioned officers who formed the cadre of the new force of mounted infantry (dragoon) and foot regiments. Of these 1642 regiments, the Moskovsky was to stay in service until 1792, while the Butyrsky became 13 Erivansky grenadier that was to remain on the Russian Army lists until 1917.

When Peter the Great came to the throne in 1689, the first-line army was largely made up of foreign volunteers of which the German element was the most numerous. The mutiny and the suppression of the *streltsy* militia between 1697–9 led to the reorganization of the first-line volunteer and largely foreign standing army into a *Russian conscript force*; Peter had copied the example of Frederick William, the Great Elector of Brandenburg, who, between the years of 1640 and 1688, had rid himself of paid mercenaries and had raised instead a national Prussian Army, officered by the Prussian noble and educated classes.

The recruits for Peter's new army came almost entirely from Russian conscripts who served for life, these making up two dragoon and twenty-seven infantry regiments that were grouped into three field corps under generals named Weide, Repnin and Galovin. Peter ordered the Russian bureaucratic nobility, largely created by himself to replace the old order of boyar aristocracy, to serve as officers: yet, in

4

spite of this, many of the more senior posts continued to be held by foreigners or by Russians of foreign extraction, for, of the twenty-seven infantry regiments, twenty-two had commanders with German names, while four of the remaining five had non-Russian names. The two dragoon colonels were Schneewanz and Goltz, and Goltz's regiment was still in existence in 1917 as 1 Moskovsky dragoons. Generally, however, Peter's new regiments were known not by the names of their colonels but by the towns or provinces in which they were raised, and many of them had these same titles, together with a regimental number of seniority, until 1917. Other 1917 imperial regiments that could claim roots from this time were the Sumsky, the Kharovsky, the Iziumsky, the Akhtirsky, the Chernigovsky, the Seversky and the Kievsky, originally Cossack regiments that formed the border defence against the Tatars; these, and the first Russian guard regiments of the Preobrazhensky and the Semenovsky that dated from 1689 and 1691, were among the oldest regiments in what was to become the imperial army.[1]

The Russian Army still had no national identity, however, and it continued to be developed on the Prussian and the Swedish pattern. During the reigns of Peter's successors the German influence ousted the Swedish, in that more Prussian organizations and methods were introduced together with German commanders and staff officers. The Prussian Frederick William I and his son Frederick the Great had been much admired in St Petersburg, and Prussian prestige had suffered little there during the Napoleonic Wars, even though Prussia had been defeated repeatedly by the French.

In the eighteenth century the officers in the Russian Army were drawn from foreign volunteers (either adventuring gentlemen of fortune or professional soldiers), and from the Russian bureaucratic hereditary nobility. This hereditary nobility covered, however, a very wide class, from the very wealthy to the very poor: it might have come from the old aristocracy and might have rank and titles, being immensely rich with vast estates; on the other hand, it might be the ennobled but landless, and often penniless, sons of civil servants or army officers; for all Russian army officers were automatically enrolled on the lists of the hereditary nobility. By itself the term 'hereditary nobility' was of little significance; it merely meant that one's name was 'entered in the book', by which entry some rights and privileges were conferred but certainly no income or property. Nor did all officers in

5

the Russian service at this time necessarily have much education, for some could barely read or write, and generally it was the foreign element that was the more technically experienced and able, since it often had had years of campaigning in the Prussian or the Austrian service. There was of course an enormous difference of privilege between officers and men, particularly since the officers could, with permission, enter and leave the service at will; and in the case of many of them, those that had property and wide interests and ties with the government, bureaucracy and landed gentry, there was a social, educational and cultural difference as well.

The other ranks formed a race apart from the Russian people, for although by law the peasant serf conscripts should have been drawn by lot, in fact they were often nominated by the elders or owners as a punishment. When the conscripts left their native villages it was as outcasts and usually for ever, for their wives could divorce them, and thereafter they had little or no contact with the civil population.

The Russian Army during the eighteenth and nineteenth centuries was probably shaped more by the national characteristics of its conscripted rank and file than by the professional ability of its higher command and officers, and these national characteristics were a source of both strength and weakness. The conscript's character was a reflection of his origins, his history and his environment, in that nearly three centuries of Tatar yoke, serfdom, the cruelty of his owners, the absolute despotism of the tsars and ruling classes, the severity of the climate and the harsh living conditions inside Russia with constant poverty and toil, all had bred into the soldier passiveness, even meekness, unthinking obedience, an exaggerated respect for authority and rank, indolence and a lack of individuality and initiative; they had also given him stoicism and great physical endurance. Mental stamina was lacking, however, for the Russian soldier hated work that was routine or that demanded dogged application of his wits or strength; he was easily swayed by his emotions and by any rumour, however fantastic, and he was the prey of any clever agitator: the soldier was primitive, superstitious, suspicious, devious, volatile, subject to great extremes, heroic yet cowardly, generous and kindly and yet capable of unspeakable cruelty; even by the European standards of the time the Russian was barbaric. In battle he was unpredictable: for he might flee yesterday, fight with the greatest of bravery today, only to desert tomorrow. So it was that

6

when, on the morning of 12 August 1759, Frederick the Great's 50,000 troops, marching into battle under their black eagles, attacked a larger Russian force under Saltykov near Frankfurt on Oder, the Russians gave way and fled before the onslaught of the Prussians. Half the Russian guns were taken and Frederick sent a courier off to Berlin with news of a complete victory. By the afternoon, however, the Russian infantry had returned and entrenched themselves in the Jewish burial ground at Kunersdorf: the fighting then flared up again and this time the Prussians were driven off with fearful losses, and before nightfall Frederick and the few thousand of his men that remained with him were in full flight. This extraordinary unpredictability has remained a feature of the Russian armies right through to this century.

During the reign of the German-born empress Catherine the Great there came to the fore a Russian commander of great renown who, unlike most Russian officers of his age, devoted his whole life to soldiering and who owed his fame to his ability to use to the full the fighting characteristics of the Russian soldier born of serfdom; because of this, Alexander Vasilevich Suvorov, the son of a general in the Russian service, has become a legend both in tsarist and Soviet Russia. Suvorov's success lay in his understanding of the Russian infantry soldier, for he rid the soldiers' routine of all that was not essential and reduced training to a level that could be understood by the illiterate of the meanest intelligence, reinforcing his lessons by a host of pithy and easily remembered maxims that were well suited to the Russian mentality. Suvorov's methods were also revolutionary in that the relationships between himself and his subordinates and between his commanders and the troops were much less formal than those in Prussia and elsewhere in Central Europe at that time. Suvorov was, apparently, a great reader of military history and the foreign military press.[2]

The basis of Suvorov's creed was that boldness always paid, his usual tactic being to move quickly and to attack. He did much to improve the fighting efficiency and the morale of the Russian infantry, trying to instil into the rank and file a patriotic sense of purpose, himself sharing the soldiers' hardships and dangers. Suvorov probably owed little to the Prussian military school, for he himself was typically Russian with Russian weaknesses as well as strengths: flexibility was lacking in his character: he was entirely brutal and losses meant little to him, for he would rather waste lives than powder. During the reign of Catherine the Great, Suvorov had been promoted to field-marshal, but Catherine's successor, the emperor mad Paul, had strong opinions on military matters and these were at variance with those of Suvorov. Suvorov was retired and exiled to the country, and the Russian Army reverted to its former Prussianism.

In December 1805, the main Russian forces under the cautious commander-in-chief Kutuzov were retiring from the French into Moravia, when they were forced by the tsar Alexander I, against Kutuzov's wishes, to halt and fight at Austerlitz. The engagement lasted barely two hours, and the Russian troops fled, cursing their Austrian allies as they did so, for the Russian is very quick to cry treachery. Napoleon claimed that Austerlitz was the easiest of his many victories. Yet, seven years later, another Russian army under this same reluctant Kutuzov, consisting of both regular troops and the reserve (*opolchenie*), gave battle against equal numbers of the enemy at Borodino in front of Moscow, and stood their ground all day. The doubtful victory, at the cost of 30,000 French casualties in the single day's fighting, went to Napoleon, yet the Russians retired unbroken, and Murat and Ney were agreed that it was one of the toughest battles that the French had yet fought. In 1813 Russian troops distinguished themselves, together with their Austrian and Prussian allies, at Leipzig in the Battle of the Nations. After 1815, however, Russian arms suffered a steady decline, though the soldier remained what he had always been, tough, obstinate, and slow, usually inferior to the German, equal to the Turk and the Pole, and superior to most other troops in East and Central Europe.

One of the principal reasons for the military decline in the nineteenth century lay in the characters of Paul's two sons, the emperors Alexander I and Nicholas I, and of his grandson Alexander II, the despots and military autocrats who ruled over Russia for eighty years from 1801 to 1880. The unstable Paul had had the greatest of admiration for the Prussians and, like his father and great-grand-father, he had dearly loved to play the soldier. Paul passed on this passion for military matters and the continued Prussian bias to his decendants, none of whom had any real military ability.

The stern Nicholas commanded his empire as though it were a regiment; and he directed the Russian Army as its commander-in-chief, for he made all senior military appointments and controlled the size and shape of the army often down to the minutest detail. Everything was organized on the Prussian model. Baron Diebitsch, born in Prussia and educated in a Prussian cadet school, became the chief of the emperor's military staff, and a general staff academy was founded in 1834, together with a general staff corps, more or less on Prussian lines. Military organizations, methods and drill were copied from Prussia, and by 1840 a *Pickelhaube* type of spiked helmet and the Russianized form of military goose-step were general throughout the army: uniforms were mainly Prussian: the Russian army ranks (*Rotmistr*, *Vakhmistr*, *Ober-ofitser*, *Unter-ofitser* and *Erfreitor*) were entirely German in their origin. Officer cadet schools were introduced according to the German pattern, the *corps des pages* for the regiments of the guard, and military and cadet schools for the line, together with a *junker* entry through the ranks. Everywhere there was a veneration for Prussian militarism, for the Russian had always had an inbred respect for all things German. Part of the royal family and aristocracy were German by birth; numbers of Germans served in the Russian Army, though these German nationals were greatly outnumbered by Russians of German descent who set great store by their German names. And, according to the popular belief among Russian officers, a German name was a great aid to promotion. Yet these Germans, known as the *liebe Brüder*, were disliked in Russia, and their presence was unsettling to the officer corps.

The Russian had, however, neither German efficiency nor German integrity and honesty, and the St Petersburg copy of the Berlin military original laid undue emphasis on the showiness of the outward form, uniforms, drills and parades, while neglecting the true sinews of war, strategy, tactics, field manoeuvres and training, tactical organization, and, above all, modern armament and the means of producing it. When, in 1854, it came to the test of war in the Crimea against modern French and British arms, the much vaunted and million strong Russian Army, that had been the dread of Europe for half a century, was soundly defeated, for it never won a single engagement. Only when Alexander II came to the throne in 1855 were some attempts made at military reforms.

At the time of the Crimean War the officers of the guard came from the wealthy or landed aristocracy; officers of the line came from the hereditary nobility, but this covered, as before, the widest spectrum from the rich to the penniless, from the cultured and educated to the rough and illiterate. Others of these officers were from politically active circles that considered themselves to be liberal or reformist. The iron tyrant Nicholas I had, however, held all firmly in check. His son, Alexander II, the reformer and modernizer who ended serfdom, was a well-intentioned man without great strength of character, whose liberalizing measures earned him not gratitude, but widespread criticism and hostility, and an incessant clamour for total freedom. Revolutionary movements began to flourish in universities and schools, and, by 1861, the empire seemed to be drifting into chaos. Even the army was becoming affected, for a foreigner noted that 'from general to major all officers are reliable but of limited intelligence: from major to ensign all are unreliable: the common soldier is unpredictable and will follow the leader who has most influence over him.'[3] Alexander then reverted to the methods of his father: political trials began again and by 1866 police rule had been re-established throughout Russia.

★　　★　　★

From 1861 to the end of the century the whole Russian Army was turned about in that a new professional officer corps was built up, the like of which Russia had not seen before, a corps that, except in the guard, was almost monastic in its isolation from the people.

In the last decades of the century there was a complete falling-off in the numbers of hereditary nobility that entered the army as officers, and the principal reason lay in the army reforms that followed on the abolition of serfdom between 1861–5, reforms that permitted suitably qualified youths to be taken as officers into the line and technical arms, irrespective of wealth or social origin. In consequence a very different type of officer corps emerged in that, except in the guard, the junior and middle ranks came from very diverse origins: a few came from the landed aristocracy, and some, a small minority, from the lists of the bureaucratic nobility; numbers came from the *bourgeoisie*, but a large part were the educated poor, the *raznochintsy* without rank, class, or means, the so-called intelligentsia (originally a Russian expression); some were former serfs, and even more were the sons of serfs. Yet, according to General Denikin, himself the son of a former serf and major of the border guards, this new officer corps had been brought together by a common desire for soldiering and, irrespective of its origins, it became strongly unified by military training and tradition, even by an acquired spirit of conservatism, a corps that, unlike the one that it replaced, was completely loyal to the tsar. The intellectual standard of these officers was not high, although they were at least all literate, and, as a class, they were entirely separate from the court, the ruling circles of the government, and the political, intellectual and cultural movements of the day; most officers had little interest in the world outside of the mess, the barracks and the training grounds, for, except in the guard, the officer corps, particularly in the middle and lower ranks, had already become a people apart. Neither this, nor their social origins, necessarily detracted from their military efficiency; indeed it is probable that these line officers were more effective and more technically proficient than the officers of the guard, and had a much better understanding of their men than their predecessors of half a century before. There was, however, no improvement in the standard of the higher ranking, particularly the general, officers, since many of these owed their advancement to preferment in the guard.

With the other ranks of the Russian Army, on the other hand, the process was to be reversed. During the first seventy years of the nineteenth century the Russian conscript had served for twenty-five years, and sometimes longer, so that he formed a class alien from the populace. The Russian Army had imitated the Prussian in every particular except one – that of short-service conscription – for the Russian monarchs had resolutely declared themselves against this course. Nicholas I, in particular, had had a number of objections to following the Prussian lead. Since, by Russian law, no man could serve in the armed service and remain a serf, a short-service and general conscription army would have meant the end of serfdom. Nicholas believed that only life-time soldiers, long separated from their peasant origins, cut off from the people and forming a class in themselves, could be sufficiently disciplined and loyal to provide the mainstay against civil disorder and rebellion: for the long-term Russian soldier would fire on his countrymen with as little compunction as would have been shown by a Cossack. Although it was admitted that the long-service army suffered an obvious disadvantage in that it was unable to create and maintain large numbers of trained reservists (the shortage of which was to be felt during the Crimean War), Nicholas had countered this with the argument that the vast distances that would have to be covered by mobilized reservists, and the great difficulties in movement and transportation inside Russia, made it essential to rely on up-to-strength peace formations of long-service soldiers that were ready for war at short notice on Russia's frontiers.

The unexpected victory of the Prussian short-service armies over the French in 1870 caused a reversal in Russian military thinking; and, since serfdom had already been abolished by 1865, it was decided to dismantle the long-service army. The 1874 law set the active part of the conscript's service at six years, eventually to be reduced, by the turn of the century, to four years for the horse and three years for the foot. Whether or not these changes resulted in any great improvement in the Russian Army is perhaps open to doubt, since they raised new ills without curing many of the old. And as the Soviet Army is, in many respects, a reflection of the old imperial army, a number of these ills still exist today.

The officer corps had become long-term and professional in that most officers served for life; but there was of course no war reserve of trained officers. The corps of long-term sergeant-majors (known in the British Army as warrant officers) and senior non-commissioned officers, that had been the backbone of the old Russian Army, disappeared, for it proved very difficult to persuade suitable conscripts to extend their service voluntarily beyond the third year, even by inducements of promotion, additional pay and other privileges. Training and discipline suffered because of this lack of good senior non-commissioned officers, and a greater load of work was thrown on the junior officers.

In spite of these difficulties the regimental officers coped, for they were able to exercise adequate control over their men in peacetime conditions, as was shown during the suppression by the army of the 1905 civil disorders in the capital. But the officers were not equal to the task of dealing unaided with the recalled reservists during the Russo-Japanese War, since there was no additional reserve of trained officers that could be mobilized with the men, and the ratio of officers to men in the peacetime army was quite inadequate. In the first two years of the First World War it was this little corps of regular officers that suffered the main casualties, and they were losses that could not be replaced.

There was, however, much else that was wrong with the imperial army during the period from 1875 to 1914. Some measures had been taken towards the end of the century to provide it with modern artillery and small-arms; but the country was very backward, and its own heavy industry base was relatively poorly developed so that it relied heavily on foreign imports of armament and equipment. There was also a shortage of money. Russia was soon to be in a position where it could find men by the million but had neither the officers nor the equipment to provide for more than its peacetime establishment.[4] The loyalty of some of the rank and file, too, was suspect, in that many revolutionaries from the intelligentsia had been compelled to enter the army under the terms of the general conscription.[5]

The real fault lay with the political and military leadership, and the conditions that had been part of Russia since time immemorial; for the inefficiency, fraud, bribery and moral turpitude that had been so widespread at the time of the Crimean War still existed everywhere. In 1878 the British military attaché Wellesley, who spent eight years in Russia, could see nothing but rottenness and corruption in every department of the administration from top to bottom, a lack of initiative and a state of unpreparedness and chaos, with dishonesty from the highest to the lowest; nor did Wellesley believe that any reforms were possible in the military organization 'as long as the present [Alexander II's] effete patriarchal form of government should continue.' For the most influential and the more senior of the military posts were the perquisites of the royal family and the guard. General officers were incompetent and often dishonest, having grown rich at the expense of the soldier, their campaigning ability, according to Wellesley, being 'beneath contempt'. There was little understanding of the meaning of discipline or example, and this applied even to the emperor, who, in Wellesley's presence and in that of about 200 junior Russian officers, would dress down a senior aide-de-camp general in a manner, said Wellesley, 'which, fortunately, would be inconceivable in Britain'.[6] Officers' grievance meetings and deputations of complaint, somewhat reminiscent of the 1825 Decembrists, still occurred, usually in the guard but occasionally in the line and artillery, deputations that would have been regarded as mutinous in a western army. The striking of soldiers by officers, even general officers, was so common as to have been regarded as almost traditional; and the flogging of men, though it came to be forbidden, was still carried out in defiance of the law.[7]

Wellesley's accounts are borne out by Greene, a United States officer with the Russian Army at that time, and by some of the Russian generals themselves.[8] General Kuropatkin of the Turkestan rifles, who became both a commander-in-chief and a minister for war, said that the government of Alexander's later years, and the governments of his successors, were 'a blight on the civil population and on the military'; peculation and dishonesty were rampant 'and commanding officers thought it right and proper to augment their pay by dipping their hands into the forage fund, a practice winked at by those in authority.' The command of line regiments was given to the younger sons of the court nobility to enable them to exist, and the favouritism shown to guards officers was 'the curse of the service'. The dead-weight of bureaucracy was everywhere and any display of initiative by officers could be severely punished, for the generals were unwilling either to shoulder responsibility themselves or to delegate authority to their subordinates. The Turkish War of 1877–8 had proved the first test for the short-service army, but the mobilization and planning were unsatisfactory, there was disorder and inefficiency throughout, and, said Kuropatkin, 'up to a point it was the Crimean War all over again;' only the jealousies and incompetence of the Turkish leaders saved the Russians from defeat. Most of the Russian generals, in Kuropatkin's view, were incapable of commanding.[9]

Present-day Soviet historians have discovered hitherto unseen virtues in the old imperial army of that time, and would have their readers believe that the proven and world-accepted military philosophy of the twentieth century, if it did not actually have Soviet origins, can trace its roots back to the old Russian empire, particularly to the theorists Leer and Mikhnevich. Marshal Sokolovsky, a former Soviet chief of general staff, goes so far as to say that 'Russian military theory of the nineteenth and early twentieth centuries far surpassed that of other countries,' and Marshal Rotmistrov and others say much the same.[10] Yet all the contemporary evidence is entirely to the contrary.

Successive British, German and United States military observers, many of them fluent in Russian since they had been accredited to the imperial Russian forces for many years, had a low opinion of the imperial high command and of Russian generalship, and they reported accordingly to their governments. And this low opinion was shared by the Russian officers who administered or attended the imperial general staff academy at that time and who personally knew

Leer, Mikhnevich and the other professors that are praised so highly in today's Soviet military press. Kuropatkin, too, writing in 1909, had no illusions.[11] Another imperial general, Denikin, who was a general staff academy student under Leer, then about seventy years of age, said that Leer produced 'infallible dogma that had outlived its practical application'; for these professors taught the campaigns of the archaic past and rarely dared to venture into the world of the present.[12] When Shaposhnikov (like Kuropatkin, an officer of the Turkestan rifles) joined the staff academy as a student in 1907, Neznamov was the professor of strategy and 'he had relieved Mikhnevich unwillingly because he knew nothing of the subject but had been told by Palytsin to learn by reading the Germans;' in consequence his lectures were direct translations from Schlieffen, Bernhard, Balck, Alten, Falkenhausen and others.[13] And, added Shaposhnikov, himself an impeccable source who in due course was to become a Marshal of the Soviet Union and its chief of general staff, 'there was no Russian doctrine at that time – just complete disorder in tactics and strategy.'[14]

Because Russian tactical and strategic teachings were merely an echo of the Prussian, then it followed that the Russian field organization at the turn of the century was patterned on the German. An infantry line regiment, commanded by a colonel (sometimes by a major-general) was the basic unit, having a territorial or town name with a numbered seniority from 1 to 208: each regiment had four (occasionally three) battalions, usually commanded by lieutenant-colonels, each of four (sometimes three) companies under the command of captains. Battalions were numbered in Roman figures from I to IV, while companies took Arabic numbers in regular sequence throughout the regiment from 1 to 16 – this again being in the German fashion. In peacetime a company numbered 100 men and a regiment about 2,000, although at full war strength these figures were nearly doubled. Two infantry regiments formed a brigade, under a major-general, and two brigades made up an infantry division under a lieutenant-general. The infantry division, with a strength varying from 12,000 to 18,000 men, was the basic tactical formation and had its own artillery and technical and supply services, and for this reason it was reckoned to be capable of undertaking independent operations. A cavalry division was made up of two brigades, each of two regiments; in all it had no more than 6,000 men and very little artillery and technical support. Three infantry divisions usually formed a corps and two or three corps made up an army; several armies comprised an army group – known in Russian (and to the Soviet ground forces) as a front. The 1914 Russian field organization is still recognizable in much of the basic fighting layout of the Soviet ground forces today.

The general staff academy was also an imitation of the Prussian, its teaching being based principally on German material culled from the German military press. The selection, training and qualifying of its staff aspirants, and the organization of its general staff corps, were very much according to the Prussian model except that the chief of general staff was subordinate to the war minister and had no direct access to the emperor. Entry to, and promotion in, the general staff was generally admitted to be fair, provided that the general staff officer adhered to the exacting and somewhat incongruous rules; rank, social origin and connections appear to have been of little account.[15] Kuropatkin thought that the trained general staff officers were good, though the burden of too much clerical work tended to keep them out of touch with the troops.[16] Denikin, who was something of an individualist, said that the more highly regarded staff officer was too malleable, in the interest of his own advancement; this, however, applied to the officer corps in general, for both Kuropatkin and Denikin were agreed that 'officers of independence and strong character were persecuted rather than promoted.'[17]

Ethnic or minority origin was no bar to entry into the officer corps provided that the candidates had a thorough knowledge of the Russian language and did not air any views in favour of political separatism away from Russia; practising Jews, however, were never allowed to become officers. Inevitably, the majority of the officers were Great Russian, but there were numbers of Ukrainians, Belorussians, Russianized Germans, Poles, Finns, and nationals of the Baltic States, as well as some Armenians, Georgians, Tatars and other Turkics, Kalmyks and other Mongols; a few of the Caucasian and Asiatic minority were to be found as officers even in the guard. The Great Russian tended to have an advantage, although, in the main, according to Denikin, who had had a Polish education since his mother was a Pole, all officers within a regiment got on well enough irrespective of their national origin.[18] Although a tsarist formation or regiment might have a national or place title or designation, this, under the empire (and the latter-day Soviet) system, had little or no relevance to the ethnic origin of those making up the unit; in fact the officers and other ranks in the Finnish, the Turkestan, the Caucasian, Transcaspian and Siberian rifles were mostly Russian to a man.

The standard of the regimental regular officer was uneven. Too often the officers, as the American Greene reported, 'did not return with due courtesy and consideration the unfailing good-nature and respect shown to them by their men.' But in the main the regular regimental officers were paternalistic and were generally solicitous of their men's welfare, and there was often a feeling of good-fellowship between officers and men.[19] The officers were the daily spectators at the men's choirs and dances; athletic sports were rare in the army at that time, and to have joined in the men's sporting activities would, in any event, have been out of keeping with the officer's idea of his own dignity. The officer's attitude towards his men tended, as Wellesley said, 'to be of a curious nature, being at times over-familiar and at others most severe.'[20] The officer had a quaint, antiquated and touchy sense of honour, for duelling was only just passing out of fashion. Attacks or infringements on what the officer reckoned to be his reputation or on that of the regiment, or behaviour that might be considered to be unfitting for an officer, if they could not be dealt with by the disciplinary code, were submitted for trial by an 'officers' court of honour', an official body elected by the officers themselves; and this court had considerable power in that it might require an officer to leave the service.[21] And yet, side by side with such sensitivity, there existed another lawful and yet degrading practice – the arrest and confinement of officers. For an officer could be summarily sentenced by his superior to a term of arrest and close confinement with a sentry at the door, either in his quarters, the guardhouse or prison stockade, for almost insignificant misdemeanours – a practice even at that time regarded by General Meves, the commander of 20 Russian Corps, as 'a disgrace to our profession'.[22] Meves was almost alone in his condemnation, however, for these practices, the courts of honour and the summary arrest, both originally copied from a Prussian model, continued until 1917 and have been reintroduced into the Soviet Army of today.

Lenin's and Trotsky's descriptions of the 1914 tsarist officer class as coming from the nobility and landed gentry and being 'the depraved sons of the rich' are of course false.[23] For the officer's career was open to any youth who was physically fit and of good character and who had the necessary qualifications. The military schools gave a free education to the children of the poor, and the aspirant needed no private income to be commissioned in the infantry or technical corps or, as Shaposhnikov has made so clear, even in the line cavalry.[24] Since these officers came from such diverse origins and had been accepted into the service on their personal merits, it might be supposed that they would have formed a progressive and truly professional cadre, untrammelled by the deadweight of the past. But instead of this there was a fostering of what was thought to be tradition. Many line cavalry officers, in particular, however humble their origins and however empty their purses, tended to give themselves foppish airs and affected speech and mannerisms. For they aped the elegance and exaggerated graces of the guard cavalry where the old guard regiments professed to be unaware of the existence of those of the new, and where, according to General Ignatev's *50 Let v Stroiu*, officers of the first guards cavalry division did not deign to notice those of the second and all guards cavalry affected to despise the cavalry of the line. And, as Shaposhnikov and Knox have said, this was copied in the line cavalry divisions, so that the hussars ignored the lancers who themselves despised the dragoons, while all three showed their contempt for Cossacks and the foot.[25] Such affectation finds an accepted place among effete and rundown societies, and was apparently a part of nineteenth-century tsardom. The average tsarist officer was, too, keenly aware of rank, arm, and what he believed to be privilege; nor did this trait disappear in Russia with the coming of the revolution.

The regimental officers at the turn of the century have been portrayed by Kuprin, himself a former junior officer.[26] The young officers began their chosen careers with determination and ambition, and courage was rarely lacking; but they soon found that little was demanded of them beyond absolute obedience and the performance of routine duties according to regulation, and that the display of any initiative might get them into trouble. Little encouragement was given to them to learn their profession and too rarely were they interested in any sport.[27] Youthful enthusiasm was soon dulled, and in time the young officers became demoralized by the inefficient, selfish and corrupt command, by boredom, bad stations, cards and drink and debt, and by the restricting and suffocating atmosphere of the regiment and cantonment. The officer's pay was poor and differed little according to rank so that he could barely exist on it. From 1859 until the end of the century the salary had not been increased in spite of the steady rise in prices, so that by 1890 a junior captain (*shtabs-kapitan*) not in command of a company, who might have twelve years' commissioned service or more, had a salary of only forty-three rubles a month, compared with a factory foreman who might earn as much as sixty rubles.[28] This low pay was possibly part of the cause of the widespread dishonesty and corruption amongst officers and officials of all ranks, for really honest men seem to have been in a minority. Promotion was slow, and the prospects of command were poor unless the young officer had qualified at the general staff academy. Many of the better line officers despaired of their career and left the army, with the result that the peacetime officer strength was always many thousands below its proper establishment.[29] Amongst those that remained in the service the suicide rate was high, and battalions and companies were commanded by men who were over-age, no longer interested in their profession, but too poor to retire. Yet, despite this ill-usage, the regular regimental officer of the line was the emperor's faithful champion; without him tsardom would be unable to survive the coming revolution.[30]

Since there was no regular reserve to replace these officers, the solution arrived at by the military authorities of the time was to create a reserve of ensigns, potential second lieutenants known as *praporsh-chiki*, educated conscripts who, on passing an examination after only a year or eighteen months with the colours, were sent to the reserve as probationary officers. All sources are agreed that, for the most part, these men had no liking for the military profession, had little military training and had no authority whatever over the men, for most had opted to become ensigns merely to escape the full term of conscript service.[31] These ensigns, that in 1914 numbered 20,700, or nearly half the officer strength of the standing army, were to become officers on mobilization; a further 200,000 civilians became ensigns by 1917; some of these ensigns brought the revolution into the army; others, by their inertia, helped to make it possible; only a small minority proved to be good officers in the field. A few subsequently became Marshals of the Soviet Union.

★　　★　　★

The great mass of conscripts who served their three- or four-year term as privates or corporals probably differed little on entering the army from the old-time long-service soldier, being mostly of peasant origin and usually illiterate, for in 1897 only one in four could read and write and only one in a hundred had received any higher education.[32] Forbes saw them as 'flat-faced, small-eyed, pug-nosed, stalwart of frame, strong of odour, placid of demeanour, even when the vodka was in their noddles, which was very often.'[33] Greene thought that they 'reflected the dull sombre countryside, the cheerless climate, a superstitious religion and a monotonous life, for they were gentle and good-natured – even their drunken brawls being harmless, maudlin, foolish and noisy – and they were as incapable of taking care of themselves as children;' yet when drunk or in panic they could be like wild beasts.[34] Like their forebears they were unpredictable, or, as Denikin said, 'often incomprehensible to themselves, and an absolute enigma to foreigners.'[35] In Wellesley's opinion, 'the Turk and the Russian were excellent material for a soldier, since both were capable of the maximum of work on the minimum of food.'[36] Strong in the staying qualities but very weak in those requiring initiative or energy, the soldier, according to Greene, 'went into battle with grim solemnity, marching forward lustily singing the national hymn and thoughtless of his fate:' he instinctively looked for orders and obeyed them blindly without stopping to question their merit; left to his own resources, he was almost helpless. This lack of initiative that, said Greene, was no great disadvantage in an army if the leaders were equal to every emergency, was a terrible defect also among the officers themselves. Yet without the rigid control, for better or for worse, of the professional regimental regular officer, the soldier was lost. And when the officer fell, too often there was no experienced sergeant-major or sergeant who could take his place. Everywhere about him this American could see only backwardness and dense ignorance, with an incredible amount of time lost in religious holidays and ceremonial parades.[37]

The period that the new conscript spent with the colours was too short to instil into him true patriotism, a military spirit or a detachment from his origins, for he soon returned to his village and relapsed into his peasant ways. He was not a trained reservist in the German sense of the word, and the longer he remained in the reserve, the less use he was when eventually recalled to the colours for war service. At the time of the Russo-Japanese War, a war that was unpopular with nearly all classes in Russia, the peasant reservists came back to the army unwillingly and often in a mutinous frame of mind, for they were gullible and easily swayed and had not escaped the infection of revolutionary propaganda of the agitators who picketed the railway stations. When they arrived in the regiments the reservists even called themselves 'the peasants' to distinguish themselves from 'the soldiers'; and they so shirked their duties that feelings ran high, and it often came to fisticuffs between the serving conscripts and the peasant reservists. Kuropatkin saw these reservists deserting in droves both before and during action, and there were army and navy mutinies in Siberia and Russia.[38] These peasant soldiers were unlikely to prove to be the stalwart successors to the old-time long-service veterans in suppressing the disorders of their kith and kin. The industrial workers from the towns, very much the minority in the tsarist forces, were usually allotted to the sappers and miners or to the navy, where they were of even more doubtful quality than the peasants, for they were active in fermenting unrest.[39] According to Knox, the British military attaché at the time, the Russo-Japanese War had shown up, too, the many shortcomings, both educational and moral, of the officer class, a situation that led to the many more resignations of the better educated of the officers, since these no longer had any hope that standards would improve.

When general conscription was introduced it had been said that military service was the sacred duty of every citizen. But since the numbers reaching military age each year were far in excess of those required to man the military establishment, hardly fifty per cent of those eligible for service were taken into the active army or fleet, most of the remainder being posted to the *opolchenie* reserve without carrying out any full-time service at all.[40] In theory, those that had to serve were drawn by lot, but, in practice, there were numerous exceptions granted by recruiting officials and commissions; this was open to abuse and it was suspected that the more wealthy were buying their exemptions from service.[41] And the inhabitants of those areas that had proved, or might prove, recalcitrant to Russian rule, Finland, Turkestan, the Moslem Caucasus, and the fragmented polyglot aboriginal races of Siberia (who would have been difficult to train anyway), were not required to serve in the imperial army at all. Ukrainians, Belorussians, Poles, Latvians, Estonians, Lithuanians, Tatars, and others were conscripted; many had no knowledge of the

Russian language so that their presence in the ranks became what Denikin called 'a grave burden' to those that had to train and command them; in consequence there was a distinct tendency to discriminate against these minorities as well as against the Jews, for tsarist autocracy was bent on 'russifying' and restricting the use of the Polish, Finnish, Lithuanian and other languages.[42] These problems are not unknown in the Soviet Army of today.

The tsarist régime relied principally on the loyalty of the Great Russian national and there was an established rule in the new short-service army that not more than a quarter of the rank and file of any unit should be of non-Russian origin: and even the Great Russians in a regiment would be drawn from two or three widely separated recruiting regions, neither the Russians nor the minority subject races being allowed to serve in their home areas. At the time of the annual call-up, batches of conscripts would, in consequence, be shuttled from one end of the empire to the other, so that infantry regiments drew the majority of their recruits from regions quite different from that of their territorial designation.[43] This meant that Russian regiments, unlike those of the German empire, lacked common roots and homogeneity, and the *esprit de corps* that these give, and this is still the situation in the Soviet Army now.

The Russian emperors had striven to fashion their empires and armies in the Prussian image without taking account of the vast ethnic and social differences between the two countries. In Prussia patriotism had always been strong, not just in one section of the population but throughout the land from king to peasant; in the united Germany of 1871 patriotism and nationalism had been the binding force from emperor to cottager and from field-marshal to drummer-boy. And the nation was united by origin and speech. In the Franco-Prussian War the real victor had been the chauvinist German schoolteachers, since it was they who were constantly inculcating into the young a crude and aggressive sense of nationalism, and this was carried forward into German military conscript service so that the bearing of arms, a duty that was shared by all except the unfit and the criminal, was looked upon as a privilege. The Hohenzollern emperors, and this applied particularly to the last of the line, regarded themselves as the first soldiers of the empire, and their bellicose pronouncements met with popular approval throughout Germany, for such was the spirit of the times. Instead of having a national army, Germany had become a nation at arms. In Japan, too, very much the same conditions applied, where families considered it a personal disgrace if their sons should be rejected for military service, and where the army and navy were a source of great pride to the nation.

In Russia, on the other hand, there was what Kuropatkin called an absence of morale and of military spirit in the army and a lack of determination to push anything through to a finish.[44] Knox said, in 1917, that although the Russian soldier in action needed more leading than any other troops in the world, even that was not always enough: 'What was wanted was rather something behind [storm battalions] to drive the reluctant units forward.'[45] This, too, was a course that the Bolsheviks would adopt both in the Civil War and in the Second World War.

The emperor Nicholas II, who ascended the throne in 1894, was the *de facto* commander-in-chief, but was without military training, experience or ability. The higher command, in addition to having an unworkable administration with a large number of officers who had direct access to the sovereign, was as corrupt and inefficient as it had always been, for the war minister Sukhomlinov was, according to all accounts, without principle and was entirely incompetent.[46] There had been six chiefs of general staff in as many years.

Whereas the German and Japanese conscripts were willing and intelligent and all had had some schooling, it was fairly common among the better educated Russian classes to evade military service. The majority of Russian recruits continued to be illiterate and lacking a sense of patriotism and nationalism; substantial numbers were in no sense Russian, and many had a deeply inbred and acute resentment – indeed enmity – against the Great Russian predominance; for the Russian emperor had become too remote a figure, particularly to the peasants, whose feelings anyway, as General Danilov said, were unpredictable and prone to great change; and the slogan 'For faith, tsar and country' had become catchwords uttered as a kind of national and religious ritual, the mysticism of a backward people.[47] Even the Great Russian's loyalties were regional rather than nationalistic, and this could hardly have been otherwise since the majority of the peasants had not been to school, could not read a newspaper, and, when adults, were not given national or propagandist education of any sort. To give such an education would, in any event, continued Danilov, have proved very difficult because of the vast size of the country, local loyalties, the sparsity of the population and the poor communications; the revolutionary agitators, the populists, nihilists, socialist-revolutionaries and other subversive groups, had found this too, for they had had little success in winning over the population in the country areas; the peasant was notoriously secretive and had no interest in anything except his own business and the ownership of land.[48] The conscripts from the intelligentsia had no conception of duty, and those from the proletariat or peasantry that *had* received any sort of primary education had been taught by the urban or village schoolteachers, an underprivileged, underpaid and despised class of tsarist society that was not required to serve in the army, and that, far from teaching its pupils any sense of patriotism or civic pride, was republican, anti-militarist and often revolutionary in its convictions.[49] And how could one, Kuropatkin wrote in 1909, maintain discipline in the army, when the mass of the nation no longer had respect for authority and where the authorities actually feared those under them?[50]

It has been said that the last emperor Nicholas II was heir to revolution. He was certainly unfitted by character and disposition to have altered the course of events. Though Nicholas was a kindly man, simple, charming and devoted to his family, these attributes by themselves do not make a tsar. And Nicholas had neither the head nor the determination to be an autocrat and he was out of place as a monarch, for he was weak and had poor judgement of the political and social problems of his day and of the ability and character of those about him: he was both ill-informed and misinformed; he was lethargic and lacking in common sense; when forced to take action, too often the action was based on caprice and too rarely on the opinions of honest and competent advisers. When he should have been liberal, he was repressive; when firmness was required, he did nothing. In the opinion of some of those who knew him, the emperor was lacking in straightforwardness, in honesty and in moral courage, so that there was little trust or confidence in the man or in his actions. The conviction had taken root among the people that the emperor was unlucky. His government was characterized by inconsistency, absence of purpose, hesitancy and aimlessness, and this was to spread to the command and control of the forces.[51] Or, as Knox said, class divisions and a bureaucracy of the German model but without German honesty and efficiency, that had been imposed on a people without education and patriotism, had produced a state edifice too rotten to survive.

The tsarist autocracy relied for its self-preservation on the civil police and on its secret departments, and these, even under Nicholas II, were still efficient enough to scent out dissension and opposition to the régime. Their task was, however, to prosecute, not to find antidotes or remedies for the ills. The only antidote known to the government was execution, imprisonment or exile, and it could no longer apply even this effectively, for the check kept on the numerous exiles was so haphazard that they easily escaped and returned to Russia. In the event of large-scale disorders or rebellion, the tsarist police by itself was helpless, for it had no substantial paramilitary reserves of its own. Its first call was on the Cossacks, and these were later to prove of doubtful reliability: its second was on the army. If the Cossacks or the army were unable or unwilling to answer the call, then the police would be swept away, often to be hunted down and murdered. If part of the army should mutiny, and the guards, Cossacks or other troops be unfit or unready to put down the mutineers by force of arms, then except for the border guards, a force that was both small and remote, there was no other independent and loyal armed force ready to act in defence of the government. And tsardom must fall.

These were lessons that the Bolsheviks, when they came to power, did not forget: the indoctrination of the young in schools and party organizations; an incessant and ubiquitous party control and propaganda; the use of what eventually became general military conscription to educate youth according to the party programme; the maintenance of a very large officer cadre in peacetime; the binding of the army officer to communism by stimulation and reward; checks and counter-checks on all ranks within the armed forces; the formation and maintenance of a numerous and powerfully armed internal security force of proven loyalty to the régime, a force that was entirely separate from the armed forces and the police; and finally the founding of a gigantic armament industry that would make Russia independent of imported equipment and materials. All these were to form the bedrock of the communist state and remain so to this day.

CHAPTER TWO

The Birth of the Red Army

When imperial Russia went to war in 1914 the Pan-Slavic *bourgeoisie* was enthusiastic, so much so that the court and government circles believed that 'all party and national differences were forgotten and that even agrarian and urban unrest had died down.' On the other hand, others thought that the Russian peasant reservist served unwillingly right from the beginning, and Danilov, the deputy chief of general staff, afterwards said that most of the people – the peasants – hardly understood what they were going to war for, and that they reported for duty only because they did everything that the government ordered them.[1] Yet, all in all, it was probable that morale, both in the country and in the forces, was better than it had been at the time of the Russo-Japanese War in 1904, mainly because Germany was seen to be the aggressor.

The army mobilized and increased from its peace strength of seventy infantry divisions and nineteen brigades to the equivalent of 114 infantry divisions, and it began its movement westwards in order to help its western allies. The deficiencies, mainly in armament and in numbers of officers, soon became apparent. When matched against the multi-national troops of the Austro-Hungarian empire, troops that belonged to an army that was not in the first class since it suffered from many of the same problems that beset the Russian Army, the Russian forces were often victorious; even so, the Austrian-German element, while acknowledging the excellence of the Russian artillery, held Russian infantry in low esteem. The Russian forces made less impact when pitted against the German troops of the German empire, trained on the Prussian model, so that the British attaché Knox noted 'the German's contempt for Russian fighting power'; for, concluded Knox, the Russians were outclassed, except in the number of fighting men that they had and in their ability to recover after a severe defeat.[2] As the war progressed the exaggerated Russian respect for the German fighting men and for German methods became an obsession so that all ranks were convinced that 'the Germans could do anything.'[3]

During the war years Knox, a blunt and irascible Ulsterman, lived with the Russian Army at the front and had ample opportunity to judge its performance. The generals and staffs he believed to be lacking confidence and largely incompetent. Typical of them was General Antipov, whom Knox observed to be 'not flurried, only quietly incapable: second lieutenants offered their advice and he listened but did nothing.'[4] Among the more junior regimental officers, that is to say the company and squadron commanders in the line, there were many excellent leaders: these were the officers who would become the casualties in the first two years of the fighting. But, as for the rest, it was the same everywhere, discipline being far too slack, and there had been many panics, the men running off and throwing their rifles away, scenes that were to occur again in 1941 (except that then the offences did not remain unpunished).[5] The men and the new-style officers were lazy, happy-go-lucky, doing nothing thoroughly unless driven to it, and 'as the Russian had no very high ideal of efficiency to strive after, he was content with very little.'[6] They mistrusted all foreigners, including the allied officers that were attached to their headquarters, and they went to great lengths to keep information from them by misdirecting them and trying to waste their time by long drawn-out and futile entertainment.[7] A general suspicion was part of the national character. The Russians had no confidence in the foreign expert and thought that they themselves knew better; they also held any foreign new-fangled article that they could not understand to be of little account; they mistrusted their own government and the high command, for treachery at the top was a comfortable explanation for the many defeats; primitive ignorance abounded and there was certainly no strong patriotism as in Germany and Great Britain to weld all classes together.[8] And it was not in the character of the average Russian to persevere long in any uphill task, for he was a curious mixture of the serious, the mystic and the frivolous. In general a Russian lacks method.[9]

Yet it was surprising what the Russian Army, with all its defects and apparently poor material, did achieve, and the long periods of bitter fighting that it sustained. Knox thought that the army's strength lay in the Russian soldier's stamina and extraordinary power of recuperation; Odishelidze, a Georgian officer in the imperial army, thought much the same and considered that the morale of the Russian soldier did not suffer permanently even after a prolonged retreat, for the soldier was only 'a slightly superior sort of animal without nerves that soon forgot things'; General Novitsky, the Russian commander of 3 Infantry Division in 1915, thought that the soldier soon forgot his defeats but did not learn by them, for 'the Russian is an excellent fellow if all goes well, when he knows where his officers are and he hears his guns supporting him . . . but when the unexpected happens, as is generally the case in action against the Germans, then that is a different matter.'[10] By the second and third years of the war little artillery ammunition remained, and attacks were being made with scant or no artillery support so that the infantry advanced unwillingly. For the Russian command was expecting its troops to die rather than to conquer.

The attached British officers could see all the seeds of revolt even as early as September 1915, and were of the opinion that the St Petersburg government richly deserved the coming revolution.[11] Whether or not the army would hold together, said Knox, was entirely a matter of officers, for Russia was feeling the shortage of experienced officers and non-commissioned officers as well as of armament, so that the fighting value of divisions varied in direct ratio to the number of officers who had served before the war and in accordance with the number of guns remaining to it. The temporary officers (many of them the former conscript *praporshchiki*) were lacking in moral training and gave a poor example to their men, and they made no secret, even to Knox, that a revolution was coming, since, as one of them told him, 'the attitude of the army had completely changed following the deaths of so many of the old cut-and-dried reactionary type of pre-war officers.'[12]

The emperor Nicholas had assumed the post of commander-in-chief of the field army and, having abandoned the reins of government in Petrograd (the new name for St Petersburg) to the unpopular empress, sojourned at the *Stavka*, the imperial general headquarters at Mogilev, playing, so it is said, endless games of patience; the emperor's decision to take command had shaken his own council of ministers and was generally unpopular with the army since the generals were well aware of the tsar's military deficiencies; and due to the emperor's supineness of character, the authority and function of the *Stavka* were soon undermined.[13] The whole country, however, was completely demoralized, and could no longer offer the army support or encouragement; indeed it could only contaminate it with the spirit of defeatism.[14] Some of the new young army officers consciously or unconsciously fomented the coming break-up; as for the rest, lacking political awareness or training, they were unequipped to deal with the revolutionary social problems that suddenly confronted them.

⋆　　⋆　　⋆

The first outbreak of revolution occurred not at the front but in the rear, as was to happen with the German Army in 1918, the mutiny erupting in the reinforcement battalions of the foot-guards, among drafts who, for the most part, had never seen the front. Other than a few dragoons and Cossacks in the suburbs, the Petrograd garrison had at its disposal only the training and reinforcement battalions of the fourteen guard and two infantry regiments in the capital. In neither Petrograd nor Mogilev were there disciplined and loyal troops with any experience of war, even in the imperial guard, that could be relied upon to quell a serious army mutiny.

In February 1917 there was a series of mass demonstrations in Petrograd, sparked off by a shortage of bread, in protest against the war, the government and the police. Socialist-Revolutionaries, Mensheviks and anarchists (there were few Bolsheviks in the capital at that time) took advantage of the situation, and the police were singled out for attack. The demonstrations could easily have been dispersed except that the Cossacks, when detailed to break up the crowds, declined to interfere, or did so very half-heartedly, for the agitators had already been at work among them. A training detachment of the Pavlovsky guard fired on the crowd when ordered to do so; but they then mutinied the next day; and, on that Monday 27 February, a body of the Volynsky foot-guard killed its commander, and called on the men of the Preobrazhensky and Litovsky guards to join them. The Cossacks, when ordered to move against the mutineers, refused to do so on the pretext that they had insufficient infantry to support them; then the three Don Cossack regiments together with the *Konvoi*, a Cossack imperial household regiment, went over to the revolution.

The defection of this mere handful of troops led to the downfall and abdication of the emperor.

The period between the first February revolution and the Bolshevik October revolution saw the desertion or self-disbandment of much of the old imperial army. The reins of the administration had been taken up firstly by Lvov's and then by Kerensky's provisional governments, although in fact both governments were overshadowed by the self-appointed Petrograd soviet of workers' and soldiers' deputies (a collection of delegates of factory workers and soldier rank and file in the capital) that was led by radicals and revolutionaries, Mensheviks, Socialist-Revolutionaries, anarchists and later by Bolsheviks. In consequence there were in existence two opposing governing bodies in the capital competing for power. But the area controlled by the provisional government and the Petrograd soviet was very restricted, and many self-appointed and independent revolutionary bodies were springing up all over the country; these local soviets often disregarded any orders coming from the centre that were displeasing to them and tended to ignore all of those from the provisional government unless the Petrograd soviet was in agreement. So it came about that the armed forces, that had begun to elect soldier committees to supervise and sometimes replace the officer commanders, were being courted by both Kerensky and the Petrograd soviet.

Revolutionary Russia was still at war with the Central Powers and Kerensky's provisional government was in favour of continuing the fight, being supported in this even by part of the Petrograd soviet. The revolution had, as yet, been without many victims except in the armed forces where a number of officers had been murdered, for there the intoxicating spirit of liberalism had already given way to excesses. Military order No.1, published in *Izvestia*, the newspaper of the Petrograd soviet, and the 'declaration of the rights of soldiers' that followed it, had separated the armed forces from the provisional government, the parliamentary *duma* and the *Stavka*, for the control of military operations and warlike equipment had been handed over to the soldiers' elected committees. Officers were not to be allowed to carry arms and the troops were encouraged to refer complaints against officers to these committees. Saluting and standing to attention outside of duty hours were stopped, and the old and traditional modes of addressing officers, such as 'Your Excellency' and 'Your Honour', were forbidden. All officers were condemned as a reactionary and privileged class, and the removal of their authority over the troops could only lead to the rapid paralysis of the old army. A deep wedge had already been driven between officers and men, and Bolshevik and other radical agitators were urging, often in crude and violent terms, the replacement of officers by commanders elected from the ranks. Desertion became rife, the numbers running into millions.

The provisional government meanwhile dug its own grave by its ineptitude. Early on, Guchkov, the civilian minister of war, had dismissed all officers that he considered to be of a reactionary character, and these included about seventy divisional commanders; then Guchkov himself resigned 'because of the army disintegration' for which he was partly responsible.[15] Kerensky, a lawyer without stability or determination, wooed, with his foolish demagoguery, those elements that were to bring about his downfall.

The February revolution had caught the Bolsheviks by surprise since many of them were abroad or in Siberian exile. They soon, however, collected together in Petrograd and, after admitting the half-way Menshevik Trotsky into their ranks, began to make their presence felt within the Petrograd soviet. The Bolsheviks regarded Kerensky and the many parties represented in the Petrograd soviet with as little favour as they did the tsar and, as they were intent on seizing power, a power that they would share with no one, they were determined, as a first step, to bring down Kerensky and his provisional government, using the Petrograd soviet and the All-Russian Congress of Soviets (made up of delegates to the capital from the provincial soviets) and its standing executive committee (the *Vtsik*) as springboards. And since what remained of the imperial army was not at first under the control of the Bolsheviks and might therefore become a threat to themselves, they intended to bring about the total destruction of the old army, come what may. The Bolshevik slogans promised peace and land to the peasant and independence to the many minorities within Russia, of which minorities the Cossacks formed a significant part: these promises served to incite the peasant and minority soldier to desert. The Bolsheviks had singled out the officers as the class-enemy of the soldier and they did their utmost, through the Petrograd soviets and their own agitators in the field, to have them killed, arrested or expelled, and replaced by elected commanders responsible to the soldiers' councils, commanders that were no commanders at all. This was the death-knell of what was left of the old army, for it rapidly fell apart. In order to conceal from the Russian people of today that Lenin's Bolsheviks deliberately set out to destroy the imperial army by conspiracy and subversion, the present Moscow leadership has put the blame for the break-up on tsardom, the officers, war weariness and the selfishness of Russia's allies.

On 10 October the Central Committee of the Bolshevik party, in support of a motion of Lenin's, decided on armed insurrection against the provisional government, and two days later Trotsky assumed control of the Petrograd soviet revolutionary military committee, an unofficial body that had originally been formed at the suggestion of the Mensheviks to keep a close watch on, and counter the actions of, Kerensky's provisional government and so 'defend the revolution'. Trotsky used his position as president of the soviet and leader of its military committee to seize control of the government arsenals and clandestinely to distribute arms to the Petrograd factory workers sympathetic to the Bolshevik cause, these workers having been organized throughout the summer months into militia detachments that numbered thousands, if not the tens of thousands claimed by Trotsky, and these came to be called the Red Guard. Trotsky also used the committee to establish direct contacts of his own with the main military units remaining in the capital, and at the same time brought into the city sailors that were staunch in their support of the Bolsheviks.[16]

On 24 October Kerensky made a last half-hearted attempt to suppress the Bolshevik newspapers and bring troops into the capital, troops that he hoped would be loyal to himself, but his orders were not carried out. The Bolshevik insurrection began the next day. Although communist propaganda subsequently painted graphic descriptions of what became known as the storming of the Winter Palace, resistance was, in fact, very light, for Trotsky had done his work well and there was little or no fighting. By 26 October the members of the provisional government had either fled or been imprisoned and Lenin's mainly Bolshevik government had seized power, power that it was never to relinquish. And, in order to confuse the simple revolutionaries of all parties, it called itself the Soviet government.

The authority of the new Bolshevik government was not recognized throughout Russia and certainly not by the Cossacks, the Ukrainian nationalists and many of the minority peoples of the old empire, some of whom began to declare their independence. And since the Bolsheviks, who had long promised peace and land and independence, were now in power, what was left of the old army departed homewards without waiting for further orders. Many officers went into hiding or began to make their way south to the Ukraine or south-east to the territory of the Don Cossacks, the most powerful and the most conservative of the Cossack hosts. Many generals joined them on the road, adding to the throng of the aristocracy, the wealthy, the educated and the conservative, towards what they hoped would be the security of the established order. The Don in particular was to prove the Vendée of the Russian revolution, although the counter-revolution and Civil War were to come also from the Ukraine, Poland, the Baltic States and from Siberia.

*   *   *

The communist Bolshevik régime, from its inception, was unlike any form of government known to the free western world, in that it was eventually to provide itself with all the democratic machinery of government, a president, a prime minister, a cabinet of ministers and two houses of parliamentary representatives, but give them no voice or power. For the sole source of power in the Bolshevik state was, and still is, the party leader and his party deputies, and they alone decide all matters great and small.

With this end in view the first step taken by the 1917 Bolsheviks was to set up a so-called democratic government called the Council of People's Commissars (*Sovnarkom*) and, as they did not want it known that this was in reality responsible to their own party machinery, they claimed that the *Sovnarkom* got its mandate from the All-Russian Congress of Soviets and its executive the *Vtsik*.[17] In fact, this Congress, made up of worker or soldier representatives from the regional soviets, the majority of whom owed allegiance to radical or liberal parties other than the Bolsheviks, had already outlived its usefulness. And when the Bolsheviks had power firmly in their grasp, they began to dismantle the Petrograd soviet, themselves taking over the Soviet name and introducing (though with a somewhat different function) the Congress *Vtsik* into their own organization, under their own Bolshevik chairman Sverdlov. The Bolsheviks had used the appeal of pacificism and compromise and the promise of a popular mandate to further their own interests: once in power, however, they made it clear that force was their main instrument of policy and they dissolved the newly elected constituent assembly and sent it packing. Then they turned on the other revolutionary parties that had been their allies.

The power now lay entirely with Lenin and the political executive of the *party* Central Committee, later to become known as the Politburo, and the dictatorship that was exercised by this select and arbitrary *camarilla*: for it issued orders to the *Sovnarkom*. Theoretically this political executive could operate only in the name and with the authority of the party Central Committee. In fact the Politburo controlled the Central Committee, the party and all its political organs, and decided all party and government policy and matters of state; the enactment of these party decisions was then carried out by the separate *government* executive organs, the former ministries known in Bolshevik terminology as commissariats, under the Council of People's Commissars, the *Sovnarkom* body of ministers that in the west would be known as a government cabinet. Members of the Politburo or Central Committee sometimes wore two or more hats and were, in addition, commissars heading the government ministries, though this was not necessarily the case; a Politburo member might not have a commissariat and a minister might have no party function. All important government decisions rested, and continue to rest until this day, in the Politburo and not in the government council of commissars, where the prime minister and cabinet, by themselves, are entirely unimportant.

Lenin (Ulianov) had graduated in law, but he had not remained a practising lawyer for he was a professional revolutionary who, like most of his colleagues, had never had any gainful employment in his life: his father had been a government school inspector, originally from a poor family, who had risen by his own merit to the bureaucratic hereditary nobility. According to modern Soviet accounts, Lenin's forebears were Great Russian: on the other hand there is some evidence that his mother's parents were of Volga German stock while his father's mother and father were Astrakhan Kalmyks: certain it is that Lenin has Kalmyk-Mongol features, as can be seen by comparing his photograph with the face of the background Kalmyk Cossack in the celebrated early nineteenth-century painting of Count Platov by Orlovsky, for they look one and the same.[18] In the half-century since his death, communist literature has built Lenin up into a Bolshevik deity, a genius of boundless wisdom and understanding on all political, cultural, military and scientific matters, a fountain of inspiration and the source of all knowledge. In reality he was a man of great political acumen who stood intellectually head and shoulders above his colleagues, a political strategist rather than a tactician, though not necessarily a good judge of character, even of those in his immediate circle. He was hard, implacable, devious, entirely ruthless, impatient and intolerant, although very understanding in his day to day dealings with his Bolshevik associates. As for the others, mass killings and bloodshed did not deter him, and he was the prime advocate of government by terror; his own correspondence shows that he readily advised the shooting not of class-enemies of the state but of unsuccessful Bolsheviks, Bolshevik supporters or ordinary workers who, in his opinion, were responsible 'for a lack of productivity'.[19] Among Lenin's principal colleagues at this time were Bolsheviks who came from the minorities in the empire, particularly Jews, Georgians, Armenians, Poles and Latvians.

*　　*　　*

The Central Powers, taking advantage of Russia's weakness, began a steady movement eastwards against the imperial army remnants known as screens. Lenin's government was, in addition, threatened by the counter-revolutionary forces that were beginning to make their presence felt in the west, south and east. Red Guards were hastily mobilized and despatched to the distant fronts, but these untrained armed civilians were of little military value and certainly no substitute for a standing army. The Bolsheviks had, at first, no clear plan and certainly no military command organization, and in the first few months there appeared to be nothing but disorder. A Bolshevik committee for military and naval affairs had already been set up at the end of October, consisting of Antonov-Ovseenko, a former court-martialled ensign, Krylenko, another *praporshchik*, and Dubenko, a naval rating.[20] But this was ineffective and was only one of many Bolshevik revolutionary committees, headquarters and staffs that followed each other in quick succession during those days of near-anarchy and chaos, few of them with clear responsibilities or function, some members serving on several committees and holding many posts.

The first real military headquarters was set up in the Petrograd area under a Left Socialist-Revolutionary, a tsarist guard lieutenant-

35

colonel named Muravev, with Antonov-Ovseenko as his deputy, to command troops in the interior and in the area of the capital; later on, Muravev was killed fighting the Bolsheviks after they and the Left Socialist-Revolutionaries had come to blows.[21] General Dukhonin, the last chief of staff and *de facto* commander-in-chief at the old tsarist *Stavka*, declined to carry out Lenin's telegraphed orders and was lynched by *praporshchik* Krylenko's Bolshevik soldiery, Krylenko being appointed commander-in-chief in his place, with General Bonch-Bruevich, a former Litovsky foot-guards officer and brother of one of Lenin's close associates, as his chief of staff.[22] Krylenko was given the task of withdrawing the remnants of the old army and disbanding the *Stavka*. But since there were sporadic though widespread outbreaks of fighting even in the Petrograd and Moscow areas, another field headquarters was set up at Mogilev to direct the Bolshevik detachments in the internal war against the counter-revolutionaries, the new command being entrusted to another *praporshchik* Ter-Arutiuniants, working under Antonov-Ovseenko. Ter-Arutiuniants was more fortunate than most in that he had at his disposal a fairly reliable Latvian rifle regiment under a lieutenant-colonel by name of Vatsetis, a regiment that was committed to the revolution: in December Antonov-Ovseenko left his committee duties and was sent south to take command of operations against the Don Cossacks and the nationalist Ukrainian *rada*. These operations took the form of fighting for the main towns and railway stations, the troops moving along the railway tracks spearheaded by armoured trains, in what became known as 'echelon war'.[23]

The screens, the detachments left behind, mainly in the west and north-west, consisted of imperial army remnants, reinforced by Red Guards and local revolutionaries, and these at first served as the only defence against the Germans.[24] They seem to have been under the control of the Committee for Military and Naval Affairs, at least in the early days, but they were unreliable, and, according to what the Old Bolshevik Gusev said of them, they 'only had to see a German helmet on the horizon and they took to their heels.' The Central Powers were not to be won over easily by talk of peace and showed every intention of waging war, and in face of this danger the Bolsheviks were quick to realize the need for a standing army. Since the final breaking-up of the old army could not be halted, Lenin's government ordered on 3 January 1918 'as part of the Declaration of Rights of Workers and the

Exploited People' that a new force should be formed, to be known as 'the Red Army of Workers and Peasants'.[25] On 21 January a committee of five party members was appointed to form a collegium with the task of making recommendations on the raising of the new Red Army.

Very little, if anything, was transferred from the old army to the new in the way of formed units: according to the communist account there were some Latvian and Siberian rifles, and the imperial *eger* guard was supposed to have joined the Red Army 'as a formed regiment'.[26] But the Bolsheviks were never of one mind as to what sort of standing army they would need, and in December 1917 they had ordered the old tsarist general staff (that had remained at its desks in the war ministry) to work out a project for the formation of a citizens' territorial militia army. This project, however, had been overtaken by events and by new dangers, so that the first war minister Podvoisky came up with proposals that the framework of the army should consist of 300,000 men, to be raised principally from volunteers recruited, not only from the industrial workers, a class that was generally sympathetic to the Bolsheviks, but also from working peasants, the peasantry being regarded by the party with somewhat less enthusiasm.[27] The rate of pay was initially fifty rubles a man per month, increased the following June to 150 rubles for single men and 250 rubles for those that were married. At first the junior leaders were to be elected.[28] Less than 200,000 volunteers were actually taken in during the next three months and these included former soldiers (but very few officers), Red Guards and some volunteers from town and country who were without military experience. The 23 February 1918 (new style) was subsequently declared to be the birthday of the Red Army and was celebrated annually as the day on which 'the young Red Army brought the Central Powers to a halt'.[29] In fact, of course, this propaganda claim was entirely false as the infant Red Army was powerless in the face of such an enemy.

The Bolsheviks had to make peace before the Central Powers should destroy them and this forced the signing of the Treaty of Brest-Litovsk on 3 March 1918, by which agreement Russia had to give up extensive territories in the west, in particular the whole of the rich agricultural and industrial Ukraine. The peace treaty did, however, leave Lenin's government free to fight the White counter-revolutionaries and to transfer Trotsky from the post of Commissar for Foreign Affairs to that for War in place of Podvoisky.

★ ★ ★

Trotsky (Bronstein) was a Ukrainian Jew of a prosperous family who had left Odessa university, after only one year, to become a professional revolutionary. In his youth he had worked closely with Lenin abroad as Lenin's literary cudgel, but differences between them had soon arisen so that the cudgel attacked the leader who wielded it: Trotsky had then aligned himself against the Bolsheviks; he was not in fact a Menshevik since he preferred to be just Trotsky, and he did not join the Bolsheviks until August 1917, shortly before the October revolution. Like Lenin, Trotsky towered intellectually over his Bolshevik associates, but he was erratic and impetuous to the point of instability, and was too independent and perhaps too vain and petty to subordinate himself to the majority in committee. He was a brilliant writer, though the power of his oratory is disputed by some. He was a man who liked to shine but who attached more importance to the form than to the content, and was more concerned in how he spoke than in what he said – more of an actor than a statesman or politician, for politics were for him a stage.[30] He was energetic and mercurial, with a satirical and venomous tongue, brazen in his latter-day claims, for he was no more truthful or righteous than Lenin and his colleagues.

As soon as Trotsky took over the military, some order became apparent on the Bolshevik side. On 4 March 1918 a Higher Military Council (VVS) came into being, with the new war minister Trotsky as its chairman, taking control, firstly of the screens and fronts facing the German and Austrian line, and then of all military operations, whether these were external or internal.[31] All the members of the council were old Bolsheviks without military experience, except for the naval officers Altfater and Berens: General Bonch-Bruevich, who was a man of no great military ability, served with the council as Trotsky's mentor and adviser, filling the appointment of 'military director'. This council was also entrusted with the enlarging and strengthening of the new Red Army, and, on 15 March, the VVS chairman gave to Lenin Bonch-Bruevich's plan for the raising of an army that was to number about one and a half million men.[32] On 29 May 1918 Lenin used Sverdlov's *Vtsik* executive committee of the All-Russian Congress of Soviets to issue the first decree ordering compulsory military service, and this was followed by the calling-up of age groups from the class 1896 onwards in the Petrograd, Moscow, Volga, Ural and North Siberian districts.[33] The conscription to the armed services was in the first instance limited to workers and poor peasants, it being intended that the *bourgeoisie* and professional classes should be forced to serve in unarmed labour detachments.

The military command still remained very confused, however, for even as late as March a special operations department had been formed in Moscow by grafting the Mogilev field staff on to the Moscow military district headquarters, and this was supposed to be responsible for the control of all interior fronts. The position was only regularized when the Russian capital was moved from Petrograd to Moscow on 10 March and the Moscow staff was taken over by Trotsky's war ministry. Trotsky did much to rationalize the military direction by absorbing the many directorates, some newly created as part of the Red Army and some the remnants of the imperial army (many of them putting out orders at variance with each other) into an All-Russian Main Staff, what was in effect a central general staff, with the former general Stogov (who later deserted to the Whites) and the military commissars Egorov and Bessonov at its head.[34]

Whatever they might have told the world subsequently, Trotsky and his fellow Bolsheviks were helpless without the advice and support of the former generals and colonels that remained to them, and Trotsky soon came to appreciate the urgent need to re-employ tsarist officers in the Red Army at all levels, since there was neither time nor the means to train new revolutionary commanders. Some of the old regular officers in the ministries, the larger headquarters and the defensive screens in Western Russia had become part of the Bolshevik military organization without a break in their service. Others, already demobilized, Shaposhnikov among them, wrote in and volunteered.[35] Some, like Littauer, were courteously invited to join and were permitted to decline.[36] Those who entered the Red Army came from a wide variety of tsarist regiments, the general staff and foot-guards being well represented, but there were comparatively few from the guard cavalry or the cavalry of the line, and it was for this reason that the Red cavalry came to be commanded by former non-commissioned officers. The tsarist cadre officers' motives for joining the Red Army were probably varied and personal, for there are no apparent grounds to suggest that they were based on divisions of wealth or social origin.

The recruiting of former officers was soon put on to a compulsory basis and all were required to register. According to the White General Denikin, those who did so, if they did not later pass over to the Whites, were eventually exterminated or sucked down into the Bolshevik mire 'wherein human depravity and real tragedy found oblivion'.[37] Trotsky regarded the 'idealistic officer', that is to say the officer with a genuine belief in the Bolshevik cause, as being in an insignificant minority, 'the rest who remained with us being without principles or energy to go over to the Whites.' Lenin, although he later admitted that the Red Army could not have been created without the former officers, said that he was going to 'make use of the enemy – compel those who are opponents of communism to build it.'[38] Many may have joined through fear, for, on 29 July 1918, Trotsky ordered that any officers who refused to join should be sent to concentration camps, and, on 30 September, had the families of those who had deserted to the Whites arrested: Lenin elaborated this further by directing that reluctant officers should be shot 'for evasion of mobilization' and he ordered the taking of hostages from the families of officers and the *bourgeoisie* as a safeguard against desertion or treason.[39] Officers and their families were murdered by the Bolsheviks. Numbers of those who *did* register for service were immediately thrown into concentration camps or the cells of the Cheka secret police, from which they were brought out from time to time for examination or torture. Some died; some rotted away in forced labour camps; some passed via the Cheka into the Red Army. Yet, during 1918, according to Bolshevik figures, more than 22,000 former officers volunteered or were mobilized into the Red Army, and between 1918 and 1920 this figure rose to 48,000.[40]

Before they came to power the Bolshevik leaders had been vigorous protagonists of the principle that officers should be elected and that commanders should be supervised by soldier-elected committees, since this had been one of the principal means of subverting the old army: but there was never any intention that this should continue in *their* Red Army. For they intended to exercise the strictest of control through military commanders that were accountable only to their superiors and to the Bolshevik leadership, and through military commissars whose task it was to keep a check on the military commanders (these military commissars being quite different from the departmental commissars [ministers] in charge of the various government commissariats). The use of military commissars in the armed forces to supervise the commanders was not a Bolshevik innovation; Napoleon had had revolutionary commissars accredited to his army in Italy; Kerensky's provisional government had used them since the previous summer, and, immediately before the 1917 October *coup*, Trotsky had substituted his own military commissars for the non-Bolsheviks attached by the Petrograd soviet to military units in the capital. But the replacement in the army in the field of Kerensky's commissars by Bolsheviks and Left Socialist-Revolutionaries (who at this time were still temporarily allied to the Bolsheviks) appears to have been done in a haphazard manner, and it was not until Trotsky had been in office some time that regional soviets and local partisan organizations were brought under the control of the centre by the appointment of Bolshevik commanders and commissars everywhere. The purpose and function of the military commissar was to act as the Bolshevik party's eyes and ears, and to supervise the actions of the military commander, known as 'the military specialist' (since the use of the word 'officer' was forbidden), this commander being usually, but not always, a former officer or non-commissioned officer of the old army. The military commissar was intended as a safeguard against treachery, and he, in fact, shared with the commander a collective responsibility in event of failure, since failure was often associated, in the minds of the Bolshevik leadership, with treason. Military commissars were eventually appointed down to regiments. The main qualification for a commissar was that the man should be a trusted Bolshevik; relatively few had any military knowledge at all.

The election of commanders ceased in the first few months of the life of the Red Army, and the dictatorship of the proletariat was soon applied by the arrival of military commissars with an urgent sense of purpose; the soldiers' elected committees were dissolved and replaced in name, but not in substance, by Bolshevik revolutionary military councils formed at all higher (army and above) headquarters. Although the name of these councils was in harmony with the spirit of popular revolution, in fact they consisted of the commander, probably though not necessarily a former officer, and two or more political members of the council nominated from the capital and usually approved by the Politburo: at this level the political members of the military council were in fact high-grade and politically powerful military commissars. None of course was elected and all members of the council were jointly accountable for their actions to a superior headquarters and to the party.

★　★　★

Except for this collective command responsibility and for the fact that many of its military specialist commanders were forced to serve the Bolsheviks, in that their families were held hostage, the appearance and organization of the new Red Army was very close to the old imperial army that it replaced. The Red Army was also very similar to the White armies that opposed it, the only difference being in the way in which the men talked to their commanders (for the Whites still used 'Your Excellency' and 'Your Honour' when speaking to officers), and the wearing of a piece of white or red cloth to distinguish them from their enemies. In both armies the rank and file were forced into joining, and most served very unwillingly, but the Red leadership at the top was much superior to that of the White in that it was united in its aims, was most ruthless, and was determined to succeed at whatever the cost in the blood of others.

Armament and equipment in both armies were standard in that they were all imperial Russian. The basic Red field formation was the rifle division made up of two or three brigades each of two regiments, but it differed from that of tsarist days in that a cavalry regiment was sometimes included so that a division might number over 20,000 men.[41] But, in fact, even the organization of the basic rifle division varied considerably according to local conditions, and often according to local ideas. A standard cavalry division at that time had three brigades each of two regiments with some artillery, in all about 9,500 men.[42] Two cavalry divisions might make a cavalry corps, but generally the Bolsheviks made little use of the corps organization and preferred to group their divisions, whether rifle or cavalry, directly under an army headquarters, an army being made up of several divisions. The strength of a Bolshevik army was usually no more than that of a tsarist corps. Two or more armies formed a front, the equivalent in western terms of a small army group.

A phenomenon became apparent in Soviet literature from this time, in that every Bolshevik military move, and certainly every change, was described as a Bolshevik or Russian innovation, a discovery hitherto unknown to military science. The waging of war in the field, according to the Bolshevik view, was planned and executed at three distinctly separate levels, strategy, operations and tactics, this being a superior concept to that used elsewhere in the world where fighting was held to be the province of either strategy or tactics. And although the present-day communists are now willing to give the imperial Russian Army of 1914–1917 the credit for this innovation, in reality the tsarist military copied it from the Germans who had used it for some years before. Similarly the communists have laid claim to the discovery and mastery of the art of mobile warfare waged in the south and south-east, in the Ukraine and on the Don and the Central Asian steppe, where the frontages were wide and operations were carried out in great depth; in truth, of course, cavalry hosts have traversed the area since time immemorial. This Soviet claim is taken to such lengths that the communists have come to postulate that the creation of cavalry armies represented a zenith of military thought, even though these armies were tsarist cavalry corps under a different name, for they rarely consisted of more than two or three skeleton cavalry divisions, with a total army strength of less than 10,000 men.[43]

Most of these political revolutionary leaders, civilians all, had found themselves a military service cap and uniform of sorts, a parabellum pistol and sometimes even a sword, and, irrespective of the fact that their appointments were those of military commissars, they went out to act the general; and some of them afterwards took a hand at the writing of Soviet history and assumed the mantle that rightly belonged to others, and particularly to the unnamed and unknown military specialist. The notable exception was Lenin, though we know that he interested himself closely in military matters and that he did, on occasions, interfere, even to the extent of reinstating, without reference to Trotsky, a military specialist front commander whom the Commissar for War had just dismissed. Lenin's life was, however, short, and his fame as a military man has been written up for him by others, by communist historians and biographers, who, acting under orders, have described him as the ablest of strategists. Trotsky was his own publicist. Stalin used his minions to assign to him the reputation for military genius, establishing a Soviet pattern that was to be followed, though not quite so brazenly, by Khrushchev and Brezhnev.

Trotsky's place in the annals of fame is not easy to assess. Communist authorities after Lenin give him no recognition and, wherever possible, he is ignored as though he had never existed; this is so to this

43

day. Yet Trotsky needed no chronicler, because he has described the events of those times in great detail, giving himself the main credit for the raising of the Red Army and for the subsequent victory over the Whites, emphasizing at the same time his closeness to Lenin and his contempt for his adversary Stalin. Much of what he has said is probably true, particularly concerning his own energy and organizing power, energy without which the Red Army could not have been welded together in so short a time. On the other hand the real fighting value of the 1918–1920 Red Army was very low, little, if at all, superior to that of the Whites, for Denikin came very close to success in his final push. And when pitted in 1920 against the newly raised army of the small Polish Republic, the Red Army was defeated. But Trotsky has allowed his vanity and his detestation of Stalin to assume such proportions that little reliance can be placed on his uncorroborated word in his descriptions of the part played by himself and by others in the winning of the Civil War.

According to Trotsky it was his own military genius that enabled him to discern the correct strategic and tactical solutions, often in the face of obtuseness and obstruction from those about him, his solutions being those that brought about the final victories. Stalin, according to Trotsky, was a man of little military ability who occupied only minor military posts, apparently with inconspicuous success. Such Trotsky views have been accepted by some of his distinguished biographers in the west.

These Trotsky claims cannot, however, be substantiated: many indeed can be disproved by the official documents of the time, those brought out of Russia by Trotsky himself (and edited and published in the west), and the versions of the same documents since published in Moscow. Apart from the omission of a few items, both series are surprisingly exact and they show that the strategic decisions that brought the victory to the communists were not inspired by Trotsky or even by the direction of the Bolshevik party, but were the result of painstakingly written appreciations and recommendations of the military commander specialists and their staffs.

Trotsky, when in latter-day exile, was not a little irritated at the picture drawn within the Soviet Union of Stalin as a military genius and Lenin's closest supporter; but Trotsky's pen was guided by venom and not by reason or truth, so that it contradicted what was established fact and what was corroborated by his own collection of papers. For Stalin *did* hold a number of most important military posts in the areas of vital strategic importance, usually as the principal front military commissar, and, moreover, both Lenin *and Trotsky* did at that time hold Stalin's *supervisory* military abilities in high regard.

As far as Stalin's claim to military genius is concerned, there appears to be little that can be proved that might give him the major credit for raising the Red Army or for the winning of the Civil War.

Stalin (Djugashvili) was a Georgian from a very poor family whose only education had come from a few years at a religious seminary from which he had been expelled: for Stalin's mother had intended that he should be a priest of the Orthodox Church. Stalin, too, then became a professional revolutionary and, eventually, a close associate of Lenin's. Stalin was rude, crude, deceitful and untrustworthy, full of malice and intrigue, ambitious and with 'an aptitude for striking secretly by the hands of others while remaining in the background himself'; he lacked Trotsky's brilliance, but he had an outstanding memory and head for detail and, except when motivated by an insane suspicion, he was entirely practical with a great fund of common sense.[44] Political acumen he certainly had, but his chief value to the Bolshevik party at this time was in his organizing flair and in his ability as party watchman and supervisor. He was jealous of Trotsky and lost no opportunity to undermine his position behind his back, for neither Lenin nor Trotsky realized that Stalin was making use of his appointments at the fronts as a military commissar to try to control the course of military operations, in dictatorial fashion, unaided by military council or military specialist.

*   *   *

By the early summer of 1918 the military situation had developed very unfavourably for the Bolsheviks, since a Czecho-Slovak corps (of former prisoners of war taken by the tsarist army) had gained control of the Trans-Siberian railway and, together with the Ural and Orenburg Cossacks, had formed the nucleus of the White Siberian Front, that, moving westwards, advanced almost as far as the Volga. To the south the Don and Kuban Cossacks were already in arms, while the Austro-German occupation of the Ukraine had been enlarged when German troops moved into the Don borderlands of Rostov, Bataisk and the Donets basin.

The Soviet state was threatened with extinction and all measures were geared to the fight for survival. Lenin himself remained in the Moscow capital and sent members of the Politburo and Central Committee as party and personal representatives to the threatened areas. Trotsky boarded the train that was to become his headquarters for many months ahead, a train so heavy that it needed two locomotives to pull it, equipped with offices, library, printing press, radio and telegraph station, and carrying its own motor vehicles and an armed escort, dressed in black leather uniforms to make them look, Trotsky said, more imposing.

Stalin was originally sent to Tsaritsyn (later Stalingrad now Volgograd) on the lower Volga to assist, in a purely civil capacity, Ordzhonikidze, a fellow Georgian, who was Lenin's Commissar Extraordinary there.[45] But Stalin soon inserted himself into the Bolshevik military organization, eventually replacing the military specialist commander, a former general Snesarev, by Voroshilov, an Old Bolshevik, the leader of a partisan band that had been driven out of the Ukraine by the Germans. Voroshilov, though he was shortly to command a Red Army military formation, known rather grandiloquently as 10 Army, had no previous military experience, for since 1914 he had been in what was presumably a reserved occupation, the government ordnance factory at Tsaritsyn, where, according to the official Soviet history, 'he had cloaked his activities as a political agitator under the cover of leading the workers' choir.'[46] A 1917 photograph shows him as a diminutive and clerkly figure, dwarfed by eleven burly soldiers, the only civilian member of the Lugansk soviet.[47] That Voroshilov never acquired any military ability there seems no doubt, even though he was later to become a defence minister and a Marshal of the Soviet Union, for Voroshilov, cunning and unscrupulous, rose to fame at Stalin's coat-tails. The close association that was to exist between Stalin and Voroshilov over the next thirty years dated from this time, and it was to include other military figures that became famous under Stalin's dictatorship; these were known collectively as the Tsaritsyn group since they served either at Tsaritsyn or as part of the South Front, and they included Budenny and Timoshenko, and many others who later became well-known between the wars or during the Second World War. Most of them belonged to the cavalry but none was a former officer. Stalin and Voroshilov regarded the military specialists 'appointed and supported by Trotsky' as counter-revolutionary; and, in defiance of orders from the centre, they had them arrested and either shot or sent back to Moscow.[48]

Further Red Army troops were being sent south from the interior to form a new South Front, to be made up of no fewer than five armies, of which Voroshilov's 10 Army was one, and this front was to be commanded by a former general Sytin, Stalin being appointed by Moscow as the chairman of the military council of South Front and the senior military commissar there.[49] Trotsky ordered that the front headquarters should be sited in Kozlov. But as Stalin regarded himself as both the commander and the commissar, and since he declined to moved from Tsaritsyn (about 400 miles from Kozlov), a situation soon arose where there were two South Front headquarters, one at Kozlov with Sytin and a commissar, and another at Tsaritsyn under Stalin, both giving out their own orders.[50] This resulted in Stalin's removal by Lenin for insubordination.

Meanwhile Trotsky had built up a command organization headed by a Revolutionary Military Council of the Republic (RVSR) that replaced the former VVS higher military council.[51] The RVSR was chaired by Trotsky and was made up of six (later ten) Bolsheviks all without military experience, together with one military specialist, the former colonel Vatsetis of the Latvian rifles who had been so helpful to the Bolsheviks in the previous year.[52] Vatsetis was appointed as the first commander-in-chief of the Red Army.

Vatsetis was certainly not one of those military specialists sneered at by Stalin at that time as being 'strangers or guests' with the Red Army, for Vatsetis, a Latvian, identified himself with the revolution. The new commander-in-chief was irascible and impatient and certainly not lacking in confidence, for he sent out, often over his own name and without the necessary commissar's counter-signature, the most peremptory signals to the front military councils, although he might have been a little less self-assured if he had seen Lenin's draft of 30 August 1918 (afterwards amended) suggesting that an example should be made of Vatsetis, who should be shot *pour encourager les autres*.[53] Vatsetis's original sympathies were presumably those of a minority separatist, since he was not a Bolshevik and he was to remain outside the communist party until the day that he was liquidated in 1938, for the Vatsetis of 1918 was soon to come into conflict with the young Stalin. Vatsetis was probably a man of mediocre ability since, though he had completed the 1909 staff course, he had not been accepted for the general staff. He got on well with Trotsky, though Trotsky called him 'stubborn, cranky and capricious'.

Many of the Bolsheviks in the field were dissatisfied with Trotsky and with the newly emerging Red Army, and they used the Eighth Party Congress in March 1919 to criticize both the high command and the military specialists; many of the delegates were particularly irritated when it became known that Trotsky had pleaded his operational commitments as a reason for not attending and defending himself at the Congress. Trotsky's defence was, however, ably undertaken by the conciliator Lenin, in particular against the attacks of Voroshilov who, it was subsequently suspected, was acting as the spokesman for the silent Stalin; Voroshilov was the leader of the Tsaritsyn partisan group that wanted to be rid of all military specialists.[54] At the closed session, on 21 March 1919, Lenin refuted the charges made from the floor of the meeting about Trotsky's high-handedness and dictatorial attitude, of his 'adoration of the military specialists' and of his 'torrent of ill-considered telegrams sent over the heads of commanders and staffs, changing directives and causing endless confusion'. Nor would Lenin agree that 'a feudal army was being raised again, based on serfdom and a hierarchy of rank,' and he defended Trotsky against the accusation of not carrying out the policy of the Central Committee, Lenin pointing out that 'the Politburo decides all questions of strategy and the movement of reserves, discussing these questions almost daily.'[55] And this was in truth the accepted way in which the Bolsheviks waged war. Important military recommendations or papers might have been prepared by, even suggested by, the military specialist staff; but they had to be presented to Lenin or the Politburo for endorsement or veto. Yet the personal criticism levelled at Trotsky, in particular of his high-handedness, was not without foundation, as Lenin was to find out in the course of the next few weeks.

By the early summer of 1919 the Bolshevik fortunes had improved in that the Whites were being held on the Baltic sector while the Poles were quiescent in the west.[56] The First World War had come to an end and the Central Powers had withdrawn out of the Ukraine to their own frontiers; the Bolsheviks then renounced the Treaty of Brest-Litovsk and themselves went back in to the Ukraine to fight a barbaric war against Ukrainian nationalists and the Russian Whites.

It was in Siberia that the Bolsheviks won their first main victory when the East Front, under a military specialist, a former tsarist colonel of the Poltava regiment named S. S. Kamenev, began to force the Whites under Admiral Kolchak back into Asia. But this gave rise to a problem as to whether Kamenev should advance eastwards into Asia or give up troops to reinforce the Bolshevik fronts in the Ukraine and on the Don. Kamenev was, by reputation, easy to get on with, and his three military commissars on the front military council, one of whom was Gusev, spoke very well of him.[57] Trotsky and Vatsetis, however, disliked Kamenev and his military council. Vatsetis did not want Kamenev to pursue Kolchak beyond the Urals, though Kamenev was in favour of doing so. Trotsky supported his comman-der-in-chief and, on 5 May 1919, at Vatsetis's urging, he summarily dismissed Kamenev, without, one suspects, putting the details of the affair to Lenin or the Politburo. It was this incident that precipitated another rupture of confidence between Lenin and Trotsky.

Gusev and the other East Front military commissars protested by signal to Lenin against Kamenev's removal, and sent Kamenev to Moscow where, on 15 May, he was required by Lenin to give him a personal briefing on the Siberian situation, a briefing given on an old railway time-table map since no other was available. The leader then reinstated Kamenev in his old command.[58] Trotsky knew nothing of this – he was unaware of Kamenev's whereabouts – and he first heard of the re-appointment on 21 May.[59] Trotsky was losing influence with Lenin since his military judgement and political reliability were being called into question: Trotsky's fault would appear to have been a failure to consult Lenin and an over-reliance on Vatsetis, and Vatsetis's personality was such as to sharpen the conflict, for his correspondence shows him to have been an arrogant pedant. Lenin, having sided with Kamenev against Trotsky and Vatsetis, privately told Kamenev's military commissars to let him have, by ciphered telegram, details of any future disagreements with Trotsky and the RVSR.[60]

This incident marked out Vatsetis for removal, for he, and Trotsky, continued their stubborn ways; matters eventually came to a head when, on 3 July, the representatives of the Central Committee decided to replace Vatsetis as commander-in-chief by Kamenev, Kamenev being instructed to bring with him his own East Front chief of staff, Lebedev, a former general of the Moskovsky guard.[61] Trotsky stormed out of the meeting and threatened to resign his offices, an offer that was not accepted: smarting at his reverse, Trotsky declined to work with Kamenev and remained for the rest of the summer of 1919 with the South Front at Kozlov, his absence and estrangement from the R V S R in the capital, serving, in Kamenev's view, to bring the military organization closer under Lenin's personal control. In committee Stalin had supported his colleagues against Vatsetis; a few days later Stalin's crony, the Pole Dzerzhinsky, the head of the Cheka secret police, charged Vatsetis with treason.[62] Vatsetis was arrested, subsequently cleared and released, and then, since the Politburo felt itself to be in his debt, was given an academic post as an instructor. Of the two military specialists, Kamenev was the better qualified and the more able.

*　　*　　*

The last White offensives of the Civil War came from the Ukraine and the Don, where Denikin had taken over the command of all White forces in the south, forces that increased in strength between May and October 1919 from 64,000 to 160,000 men, following a forced conscription.[63] Denikin said that his main aim was to take Moscow, but in fact his formations weakened themselves by fanning out across the Ukraine and South Russia, apparently intent on recovering territory and material resources and on protecting the Ukraine from the Poles. However that may be, Denikin's advance was very rapid, taking Kharkov and Belgorod, and threatening Saratov and Orel, the momentum showing no signs of falling off as the Red Army formations that were trying to block the White advance broke one after the other. For, in the Russian forces of those days, mass desertions thinned the ranks of the losing side.

In Moscow there was a sense of grave crisis and all available reinforcements were hurried off to the South Front facing Denikin; Denikin's rapid success had caused another split in the views of the Bolshevik government and its military command, a conflict of ideas that continued to be ventilated in the world press, generations after the event. Expressed in simple terms, it was whether to counter-attack Denikin in the flank, on an axis running roughly from east to west, or whether to penetrate his centre by a thrust running from north to south. Subsequently, both Trotsky and Stalin claimed to be the sole author of the victorious plan, imputing to the other the unsuccessful course of action.[64] Published copies of the documents covering these operations are available for study, and the evidence appears conclusive that neither of the plans belonged to Trotsky or to Stalin since both of these solutions, the right one and the wrong one, were Kamenev's. Kamenev first tried the one way from east to west and was unsuccessful. Then he had second thoughts and, at some time between 21 and 26 September, he wrote an undated appreciation for Lenin's benefit, justifying his original choice of axis but saying that, in view of the changed conditions and Denikin's thrust northwards, it was too dangerous to continue operations on this line: he therefore recommended that all Red Army forces should be regrouped immediately to the south of Moscow ready to meet the enemy head-on.[65] Lenin and the co-opted members of the Central Committee, after considering this document, told Kamenev 'not to consider himself bound by his former recommendations or by any previous recommendations of the Central Committee', and they gave him 'full powers as a military specialist to take whatever measures he thought fit'. This instruction reveals the extent to which Lenin's government relied on Kamenev's judgement, and it supports Denikin's contemptuous dismissal of Trotsky's military ability and that of 'the other commissars' as being 'quite fictitious'.[66] The documents show moreover that Trotsky and Stalin were at this time away from the capital, where the main decisions were being taken.

Kamenev's counter-offensive, carried out by the former colonel Egorov's South Front (Stalin being the principal military commissar with Egorov) decisively repulsed Denikin's forces. A Red Army cavalry force of three cavalry divisions was then committed to the pursuit. This mobile force numbered in all no more than 9,000 men and twenty-six guns, and though it was called a cavalry army and 'a new phenomenon of the military art' its strength was no greater than that of a tsarist cavalry corps.[67] The cavalry army commander was a former extended-service sergeant of imperial cavalry named Budenny, a man of little education and no great military ability, Voroshilov and Shchadenko, a Ukrainian Old Bolshevik, being attached to him as his military commissars.[68] After a forty-day advance the Red cavalry reached the Sea of Azov, splitting the enemy between the Crimea and the Caucasus, Budenny and Voroshilov earning a name amongst the Whites, even in those barbarous times, for cruelty and atrocity. Denikin's forces and the Don and Kuban Cossacks had been mainly broken; many of them disappeared in a

flood of desertion. Except for Wrangel's last stand in Taman and the
Crimea, the White forces were never to recover.

★ ★ ★

The next test for the Red Army came in Poland. The new Polish
Republic had been trying to push its own frontiers eastwards at the
expense of the Bolsheviks, and its armies in Belorussia had continued
to edge towards Smolensk. Then, in April 1920, the Poles suddenly
attacked in the south and, by May, were in Kiev, the capital of the
Ukraine.

The Russo-Polish War of 1920 was fought in two theatres of war
nearly 300 miles apart, being separated by the great barrier of the
Pripet marshes. The Bolshevik counter-offensive against this Polish
invasion was based on a Kamenev plan whereby Egorov's South-West
Front (that had formerly been the South Front), with Budenny's
cavalry army under command, would first clear the Poles out of the
Ukraine; then Tukhachevsky's West Front in Belorussia north of the
Pripet would take up the offensive westwards on a general line
Bialystok-Warsaw. Initially this Kamenev plan went well in both
sectors, and, as soon as Red Army troops had entered on Polish soil, a
so-called 'provisional Polish government', in reality a Bolshevik
Russian government, was set up under the chairmanship of the head
of the Soviet Cheka, the Pole Dzerzhinsky.[69] By the first week in
August Tukhachevsky's four armies were lining the Polish Vistula
and stretched out over a hundred-mile front even to the north-west of
Warsaw.

Tukhachevsky was one of the most controversial military figures of
the period. Born of impoverished landed gentry from Dorogobuzh
near Smolensk, he had entered the Moscow cadet corps at the age of
eighteen and then, the next year (1912), had been admitted to the
Alexandrovsky military school.His preliminary military training, that
had begun so late, did not last very long, however, possibly due to the
approaching war, for in July 1914 Tukhachevsky, at the age of
twenty-one, was commissioned into the Semenovsky foot-guards. In
February 1915, still a second lieutenant, he was taken prisoner just
south of Warsaw: and, as he remained a prisoner until after the
Russian revolution, his military experience and knowledge amounted
to very little. On his return to Russia he must have volunteered for
military service with the Bolsheviks, for he is next heard of, in the

spring of 1918, as being on Sverdlov's staff in the military department of the *Vtsik* in the Kremlin, one of the links between the political centre and the military organization. There he gained the confidence of the leading revolutionaries, for Tukhachevsky's party membership dated from April 1918. For a short time he seems to have been a military commissar in the Moscow area, for it was not unknown at that time for 'reliable' military specialists (and Left Socialist-Revolutionaries) to be appointed to military commissar posts.[70]

The ambitious Tukhachevsky was then appointed to command an army in the area of Penza and Samara with the East Front; but he found little favour there with the more senior re-employed officers, for Muravev, the Left Socialist-Revolutionary and former lieutenant-colonel of the guard, had once had him arrested, and the military specialist commander of South Front, presumably the former colonel Gittis, had forced Tukhachevsky's removal. In 1919, before being chosen to command the West Front against the Poles, Tukhachevsky had commanded the Caucasus Front where he had impressed Ordzhonikidze, the principal military commissar, 'because he had read Clausewitz'; but while he was there Tukhachevsky had been so unwise as to try to discipline the errant Budenny and Voroshilov, who had secretly reported the events to their protector Stalin.[71] Although Tukhachevsky had had successes in fighting the Whites, his experience and knowledge of war at that time could not have been great.

Kamenev and his chief of staff Lebedev had sketched out the strategic plan of the Bolshevik offensive in Poland, and Tukhachevsky and Egorov, the two front commanders concerned, were generally in agreement with it. But a difficulty could arise in that, as the two fronts moved westwards and left the Pripet marshes behind them, a great void would appear between the two fronts, a vacuum not occupied by Red Army troops. As Tukhachevsky's West Front was due to outflank and partially encircle Warsaw from the north, this gap would have to be filled by formations of Egorov's South-West Front moving northwards and making ground to their right. Tukhachevsky urged on Kamenev that Egorov's formations earmarked for this task, together with Budenny's cavalry army and a further rifle army of Egorov's, should be transferred to Tukhachevsky's command as soon as they should enter into the gap around Lublin. This solution, and particularly the transfer of command, found little favour with Stalin, who was Egorov's principal military commissar, or with Budenny or Voroshilov, since these saw no reason why Tukhachevsky should gain all the laurels. Stalin's little band thought that they could collect some military renown by taking the Polish city of Lvov, away to the south-west and far removed from the Warsaw battle.[72]

The fighting that followed was a disaster for the Bolsheviks, a battle in which Poland crushed Tukhachevsky's forces. It is by no means certain that Tukhachevsky would have succeeded even if he had been given the timely support promised to him from Egorov's front, for the Polish troops were probably superior in leadership and in morale. But without Egorov's support, Tukhachevsky was doomed to failure.

A very large number of the documents, including the vital Baudôt and Hughes teleprinter messages between the Bolshevik political leadership and the commander-in-chief and the fronts, have since been published. An analysis of these shows that some responsibility for the defeat can be attached to Kamenev, and even to his staff and co-signatories Klim and Shaposhnikov, for not drafting terse, concise and clear orders, instead of the loosely worded directives that included such imprecise phrases as 'the timely breaking-off of the Lvov operation' and orders to send 'as large a force as possible towards Lublin'.[73] Tukhachevsky, too, can be blamed for moving, contrary to Kamenev's orders, too far to the north of Warsaw and so increasing the gap between himself and Egorov. But the principal responsibility for the defeat rested on Stalin, who was determined that the South-West Front would give up no troops until Lvov had been taken: and so he resorted to obstructionism and deceit, in which he was ably supported by his henchmen Budenny and Voroshilov. All sorts of delaying tactics were used; signals coming in from Kamenev were left undeciphered for days; Stalin refused to attach his military commissar signature to Egorov's order detailing the formations to move off northwards to Tukhachevsky.[74] Budenny, when he received a telegraphed order direct from Tukhachevsky, telling him to leave the area of Lvov immediately and move northwards, noted that it bore only Tukhachevsky's signature without that of a military commissar (the commissar's name had in fact been omitted due to a telegraphist's error). This convenient omission enabled Budenny to return the message for authentication.[75] Technically Budenny may have been justified in doing so, although he should at the same time have put in hand preparations to disengage and to move; in fact military orders not bearing a commissar's signature were not unusual, Vatsetis and Kamenev being common offenders, and in practice these orders were usually acted upon.

On 16 August Tukhachevsky's left flank was shattered by a Polish striking force that had moved into the vacuum of the Lublin gap, and the remainder of Tukhachevsky's armies began to be enveloped from the south-east. The war was already lost. Stalin had been recalled to Moscow on 17 August to explain himself, following his refusal to sign Egorov's order, Lenin remarking, according to Trotsky, 'Stalin again caught in the act'. Yet Budenny and Voroshilov obstinately disobeyed the orders from the West Front that they received between the 17 and 19 August, and the complaisant Egorov continued to side with Budenny, even as late as 21 August, when he asked the already defeated Tukhachevsky 'that the cavalry army should be allowed to remain to complete the capture of Lvov.'[76]

Lenin declined to allocate blame for what he called 'this military defeat' and was content to 'leave the analysis to future historians'. But Lenin's own political and military judgement had not been without fault, for he himself, on 12 August, had been opposed to the move of Budenny's cavalry and had said that Tukhachevsky (who had already, according to Tukhachevsky's own claim, taken in 50,000 local 'volunteers'), could well manage by himself with a little more self-help, simply by 'calling up all the adults in his area'.[77] Trotsky's subsequent account makes no mention of Lenin's interference, since Trotsky was determined to put all the blame on Stalin, but Trotsky himself was not as averse to the Polish adventure as he afterwards made out.[78] Current Soviet literature usually ignores the existence of Trotsky, attributing his blameworthy actions to Skliansky, his deputy.

At the Tenth Party Congress, in 1921, Stalin attempted to deflect the culpability for the defeat on to Tukhachevsky by blaming the staff of West Front (a view still ventilated by Budenny in 1965); as against this, Tukhachevsky during his 1923 lectures in Moscow touched, with some circumspection, upon the responsibility of the South-West Front and the cavalry army.[79] By 1929, Egorov was sufficiently bold half-heartedly to deny 'the legend of the disastrous role of his front'; for, from 1927 onwards, Stalin had become the unchallenged dictator of the Soviet Union, and in consequence Soviet literature of the thirties placed the responsibility for the defeat on Trotsky's treasonable activities. After Stalin's death history was again rewritten according to the Khrushchev pattern, to show that Stalin was mainly responsible for the defeat, only Lenin remaining unassailable.[80] Yet, amidst this maze of misrepresentations and labyrinth of lies, the mass of documents, a large number of which have been published within the Soviet Union, stands out as a coherent, logical and apparently reliable record of what actually took place.

The Red Army losses in prisoners and internees had been very heavy and the number of desertions was even greater. At the time, the Poles claimed to have taken 10,000 prisoners, and 4 Soviet Army, two divisions of 15 Army and 3 Red Cavalry Corps were disarmed by the Germans in East Prussia. Once the dream of a Bolshevik Poland had vanished, Moscow wanted an immediate peace so that it could be free to concentrate its forces against the last of the White remnants. The Soviet-Polish Peace Treaty of Riga of March 1921 gave to Poland regions with large Belorussian and Ukrainian populations and shut off Russia from direct contact with Lithuania and Germany, so establishing a frontier that was to remain until 1939.

CHAPTER THREE

The Years of Military Doubt and Indecision

Trotsky in his writings has told the world of his closeness to Lenin, and he and some western biographers have implied that the Bolshevik leader, shortly before his death in 1924, would have preferred that Trotsky succeed him rather than Stalin. On the other hand too much trust cannot be placed on what Lenin might or might not have said to Trotsky. For Lenin, like the party that he fashioned, allied himself, under the guise of friendship, with any elements that might secure him power, fully intending to destroy these friends of convenience as soon as they had served their purpose: and this was fully understood by the inner core of his Bolshevik movement.

In the very early days of the first revolution the Bolsheviks had arrived late on the scene and were very much in a minority, both in the Petrograd soviet and in the All-Russian Congress of Soviets. But they made a show of uniting with the revolutionary majority and, in particular, with the Left Socialist-Revolutionaries and the hated Mensheviks. Trotsky, too, had his uses, for he already had a following in the crowds. The Bolsheviks took over the revolutionary bodies of the others and converted them to their own use, still retaining a tight and centralized control in the secrecy of the Politburo, while offering the populace some semblance of the sharing of power. With the aid of the Left Socialist-Revolutionaries and their bomb-throwing assassins, the Bolsheviks began to neutralize all other revolutionary parties, eventually condemning their former allies as enemies of the people; they then fought it out with the Left Socialist-Revolutionaries whom they suppressed with the help of Vatsetis's army units that were loyal to the revolution. And then it was Trotsky's turn.

Trotsky has said that the growth of the anti-Trotskyite faction was Stalin's work from behind the scenes. As against this, there are old party members still alive today who can recall the first purges of the Trotskyites taking place in the provinces behind the closed doors of the party, as early as 1921, when Lenin was still fit and in undisputed control of the organization.[1] That Trotsky was ignorant of these early purges is doubtful: that Lenin did not know of them is most unlikely; and if he knew of them, it is virtually certain that he himself approved and instigated this cleansing of the organization, using Stalin as his tool. For as Bazhanov, the Politburo secretary at that time, has told us, Lenin, who was unwilling to share his power with anyone, could not have been unaware of the possible dangers of the new course that he had set himself, that of using the three party secretaries, Stalin, Molotov (Skriabin) and Mikhailov, to assume a plurality of functions and begin the inquisitorial overhaul of the whole party organization and membership. Bazhanov thought that Lenin knowingly took this risk, believing that the three secretaries were entirely loyal to him and that Stalin was the obvious choice for the many key posts since he was unlikely to be a rival on account of his poor education.[2] Trotsky was ill-fitted to protect himself against this intrigue, for he was arrogant and impetuous and, though not lacking in cunning and guile, was more likely to meet opposition head-on, in stormy meetings, denunciation and invective; and because he was independent and generally without friends he was less able than his Bolshevik associates to protect himself by conspiracy and secret aggression, aggression aimed at defending himself by bringing down his colleagues – who were in reality his enemies – plotting their political destruction or death, and getting his blow in first. For such is the way of the Bolsheviks, where all defence is based on attack.

Nor indeed had Trotsky many political allies or supporters at this time, even outside of the Politburo, for he scorned friendships and easily made enemies; he was an *arriviste* among the Old Bolsheviks with no political organization that he could call his own. Admittedly, he still remained a member of the Politburo, together with Lenin, Stalin, L. V. Kamenev and Bukharin, later to be increased to seven members by the addition of Zinovev and Tomsky. But, since the death of Sverdlov, it was Stalin and Lenin who had the control over the all-Bolshevik party organization: for Stalin was a controlling member of the *Orgburo*, that decided party organization, and of the Central Control Commission, that investigated and disciplined party members, and the commissar of *Rabkrin*, a body formed at Lenin's direction to inspect all branches of government administration; and, what was more important, Stalin was the Politburo member responsible for the secret police (the GPU after it had absorbed the Cheka in 1922). And, as if to emphasize his plurality of functions, Stalin was appointed in 1922, at Lenin's suggestion, to the new post of general secretary to the Central Committee that was to prove the most influential post of the party and, by extension, of the government.

When Lenin selected Stalin for these many posts, he was, in all probability, looking for a loyal organizer who would faithfully do his bidding, a sort of latter-day Stalin's Voroshilov, a toadying conspirator and shadow, a man incapable, and indeed fearful, of initiating any measure of his own. In this, Lenin had badly chosen his man for, when the Bolshevik leader was sick and enfeebled, Stalin was to make use of his party controls in a move to isolate and undermine Lenin, exactly as the young Lenin had himself treated his former chief Plekhanov many years before.[3] Lenin reaped what he himself had sown.

Trotsky and Trotsky's latter-day literary followers in the west have reflected on the change in direction that the party took after the premature death of Lenin, and they have stressed the terrible price that Russia paid under Stalin during the dispossessions and famines that followed the collectivization of agriculture, and during the fearful purges that took place in the late thirties. Yet Lenin, Trotsky and nearly all the leading Bolsheviks were men of the same stamp who were no less responsible for the terror that began with the revolution and continued unabated throughout the twenties and the thirties; mass arrests, beatings, torturings and killings were a part of Bolshevik life, and many of those who fell victim to Stalin's great purges, Bolsheviks like the Politburo member Zinovev, had themselves a grisly and bloody record of murder.

Bazhanov had been a young student at Kiev university who had entered the Bolshevik centre by way of being a secretary, firstly to Kaganovich and Molotov, and then to Stalin and the Politburo. He came to know Stalin well in the few years that he was in his service until, eventually, fearing for his own life, he fled the Soviet Union to Persia. According to Bazhanov, Stalin was a rough-mannered Caucasian with little understanding of politics, economics or finance, who read virtually nothing beyond a dozen official documents a year. Stalin's main characteristics were cunning, malevolence, political ambition and a pathological desire for power; he entrusted to no man his innermost thoughts and was strangely out of place in a country where everybody talked too much. When he spoke, he used words to conceal his opinions, for he was independent, obstinate and sly, the simple down-to-earth mentality of the peasant taking the place of intelligence. Stalin never generalized, he was not capable of it, for he had to have concrete facts.[4] In some respects the antithesis of Trotsky, when given a question, he had an eye only for the practical solution; when not motivated by ignorant prejudices or insane suspicions, he solved positive uncomplicated problems logically and with perspicacity, and he had the good sense to leave anything alone that was beyond his powers.[5] Stalin was vindictive, said Bazhanov, and the forgiveness of a slight was foreign to his nature, and if it was in his interest he would sell anyone. Yet he kept up a disarming pretence of *camaraderie* and, when it so suited him, was not above fawning flattery. Scornful of real friendship and displaying an unbelievable cynicism in his personal relationships, Stalin was entirely treacherous and credited others with his own dark motives. He respected only those who stood up to him, though this would not save them.

To Bazhanov is owed the well known description of Stalin who, after Lenin's death, lived in the servants' quarters of the old Kremlin eking out the existence of a state employee; in the presence of his family he was contemptuously silent and one of his wives was said to have shot herself. Stalin was not interested in money, possessions or women, and art, literature and music meant nothing to him. The legend of the decisive Stalin was untrue, said Bazhanov, for he had rarely seen so mistrustful and cautious a man.[6]

During these years Stalin was steadily bringing his own men forward: Molotov, Stalin's creature, a stutterer and slow thinker who never had an opinion of his own, 'but was an industrious and thorough worker withal'; and Voroshilov, 'who was quite a man, very full of himself' yet in reality only Stalin's pliant puppet; the Pole Dzerzhinsky, who was an emotional, excitable neuropath; and Budenny, coarse, ignorant and limited, a man without pretensions who, said Bazhanov, when asked by his subordinate for direction on an important military question said 'Do what you like! My speciality is to sabre them down!' Yet Budenny, like Voroshilov, was not without much cunning, and, like Voroshilov, he was entirely brutal.[7] According to the Moscow military rumour of the time Budenny had shot his own wife.[8]

It remained to get rid of Trotsky, a task that required some preparation and care, since it was easier to purge Trotsky's supporters behind party closed doors than to dispose of the great man himself, for Trotsky was a world-known figure and Stalin was not yet sufficiently confident of his own position to employ the executioner or hired assassin against him. So Stalin formed the conspiratorial Politburo *troika* using Kamenev and Zinovev to do his work; Stalin himself, unlike his two colleagues, maintained a pretence of cordial relations with Trotsky. At Politburo meetings, Stalin had already arranged what was to be said by others for him, so that he himself rarely spoke, but walked up and down with his waddling gait, his hands clasped behind his back, puffing at his pipe, making no comment until the discussion was finished. He would then summarize the majority view as if it came from himself, as it usually did. Later, when his ascendancy was assured, he disdained to do even this, but let Bukharin do the talking. Stalin rarely interrupted, but when he did so, his intervention was decisive and the other members hastened to agree with him.[9]

Stalin marshalled all his henchmen to attack and isolate Trotsky, removing him from his official posts one by one, a process that took several years. Crowds were rented to break up Trotsky's meetings and, in 1926, the former war minister was dismissed from the Politburo, to be deported three years later. But he could not be silenced and his opposition was more effective abroad than it had been in Russia, where the party membership at large knew little about the leadership dissensions, either before or after Lenin's death. Silence came only with Trotsky's murder in 1940.

*   *   *

The compulsory call-up had rapidly increased the size of the Red Army from 263,000 in May 1918 to 5,500,000 men in 1920 so that its field formations are said to have numbered about ninety infantry and twenty cavalry divisions.[10] By 1920 there were 48,000 former tsarist officers serving in the Red Army as specialists and, so it is said, a further 14,000 officers who had been compulsorily mobilized into the White armies, who had then deserted to, or had been absorbed into, the Red Army. In addition there were 214,000 former non-commissioned officers with the new army, mostly of peasant origin, and many

61

of these held military specialist command appointments. The commanders of the Voroshilov type, revolutionaries who had no former military experience, were very much in the minority, although some, like Frunze, were appointed to senior commands; and for the most part they were without education or special talent. The other source of military specialist recruiting was in the new Red Army schools, but here again the general standard of education was low and the graduates were less able and less effective than the pre-war non-commissioned officers.

The system of military commissars acting as the party's watchdog over the military specialists, irrespective of the specialists' military or social origin, had come to stay. The commissar was the party's representative with the army and was the immediate executive of the Bolshevik government: his position was unassailable by the military of any rank, and an insult to the commissar was a serious criminal offence. One of the commissar's most important responsibilities was that of safeguarding against conspiracy and counter-revolution, and 'to see that the army should not become a thing apart' from the party and state. In order to accomplish this the commissar was required 'to receive, jointly with the military commander specialist, all orders and correspondence and to countersign all orders', for according to the Bolshevik regulation only countersigned orders were valid. The military commissar was also responsible that all orders received from above were promptly executed by the military specialist.

In the early days, the interpretation of the military commissar's responsibilities varied widely. Vatsetis enjoyed Trotsky's confidence, and, being, like Trotsky, capricious and high-handed, he often acted independently without troubling himself about commissars' agreements and counter-signatures. His successor, S. S. Kamenev, had the backing of Lenin and seems to have been allowed a remarkable freedom from commissar interference, so that even Stalin (as the military commissar of the South-West Front in 1920) treated the military specialist commander-in-chief with outward deference, as the published teleprinter traffic clearly shows. On the other hand this situation did not necessarily apply elsewhere. At front level, S. S. Kamenev, as an earlier military specialist commander, had been supported to the full by his commissars, who had fought his battle against Trotsky for him; Ordzhonikidze had similarly supported Tukhachevsky; but Egorov, as commander, was not held to be of any great account at Stalin's headquarters, and Sytin had been ignored; some of the subordinate military specialists had actually been shot at Stalin's or Voroshilov's order. Generally speaking, and with some exceptions, the lower the level of headquarters, the greater the commissars' exercise of power, and this power was often used capriciously by the more ignorant of the commissars, some of them keeping their specialist commanders in a permanent state of terror. For the commissars had rights of arrest and summary punishment and were not responsible to any commander of any rank, but only to the commissar at the next senior headquarters. At the top level the Commissar Political Department of the RVSR was headed by a member of the Central Committee and was responsible directly to that Committee and the Politburo.

The military commissars' exact responsibility with regard to the conduct of operations was ambiguous and, in fact, remains so to this day. The commissar was entirely responsible for the reporting and suppression of counter-revolutionary activity, and for the revolutionary spirit (that is to say morale) of his unit. Theoretically, he was not supposed to interfere in operational work, or use his power of veto, unless he had reason to suppose that the military specialist intended treachery. In fact, however, military failure, even lack of complete success, could be regarded by his political masters as treason, and the consequences could be visited on the commissar as well as on the specialist commander. And although, according to the letter of the law, a commissar's counter-signature to an operational order did not make him jointly responsible for its military success since it signified only that the order contained nothing treasonable, it was in the commissar's interest to be careful what he did sign since he well understood that he might be called to account for it anyway. A plain veto, on the other hand, might be regarded as a wilful delay in the execution of orders. Some commissars, and Stalin was one of them, sought military glory, and did interfere with operations, usually claiming the credit that was by no means theirs. The worst type of commissar was the fanatic, and there were many, those who desired to make a name for themselves, those who feared denunciation and those who spied on their fellows. Others did their duty as they saw it, as best they might: but the result was usually the same in that the commissar completely overshadowed the commander; both tended to avoid responsibility and certainly all initiative, and, in case of doubt, referred all matters back to their superiors. Such a system of command, unique in the armies of the world at that time, made the new Red Army slow and unwieldy.

The other of the commissar's responsibilities was that of controlling and co-ordinating the Bolshevik party organization within the formations or units, and using party members to spread propaganda and to act the spy, reporting to the commissar events and attitudes within the units; this was done from the earliest times, the zeal of these other-rank communist cells being such that they would publicly criticize the military specialists, even divisional commanders being subject to their rebuke.[11] The commissar was also supposed to undertake political and educational work within his unit; this probably did not mean much during the time of the wars, but it came to be of prime importance in the days of peace that were to follow.

The use of military commissars, now a seventy-year old institution in the Soviet Army, had not always found favour with the early Bolshevik founding fathers, for Voroshilov's Tsaritsyn guerrilla school of war would not have employed the military specialists either. Trotsky was largely responsible for first employing the paired specialists and commissars. Lenin, too, was enthusiastic in support of commissars, insisting that all military commanders, whatever their origin and politics, should have politically reliable commissars to shadow them, and he was quick to point out any irregularities – formations that lacked strong commissars – to Trotsky. But as soon as the war was won and the danger over, the leading Bolsheviks were of varying opinions as to the necessity of retaining the commissars in the armed forces. Even as early as 1919 Smilga, himself an Old Bolshevik commissar and member of the RVSR, had recommended the abolition of commissars 'where the commander was of proven reliability', a view supported by Trotsky as 'being desirable'.[12] But Trotsky had not cared to tackle this thorny problem by being specific about who should or should not have a commissar accredited to him, nor would he support the opposite die-hard view that commissars should assume more operational responsibilities from the specialists. Trotsky was content for the moment to leave matters as they were. Svechin, an artillery general of the old army and a military academician who had been re-employed by the Bolsheviks, wanted to put the clock back to 1914 and restore the unity of command, whether this commander be called specialist, commissar or officer, and was not in favour of the continuance of revolutionary military councils at the higher levels of command.[13] Svechin's writings were attacked by Trotsky. And so matters were left where they were, since the Bolsheviks were fearful of any measure that might weaken their hold on the armed forces. A few years later, between 1925 and 1927, there was what was called a partial introduction of one-man command, but the measure was temporary and, in reality, it altered nothing, since it was the old commissar system under another name. Military commissars had come to stay.

★　　★　　★

But this was not the only doubt that troubled the Bolsheviks. Originally Lenin did not want a professionally organized standing army, and was at one time in favour of a proletarian militia.[14] The realities of the Civil War had, however, forced him to accept an army that was organized and recruited along modern lines, for without such an army the Bolsheviks could not possibly have hoped to have defeated the Whites. The new Red Army was, admittedly, a bad army, its organization, discipline and training being of a low standard, even inferior to that of the Whites: for the Bolshevik success had been due to the ruthless and disciplined organization and control of Lenin's government and the Lenin-Trotsky high command, for, unlike the Whites, they knew what they wanted and where they were going. But when the fighting was over and the mass army demobilized, the many party political theorists, Trotsky among them, began to air their second thoughts on military matters.

Trotsky had brilliance but lacked mental stability: and there were many sides to his character. During the Civil War the practical Trotsky was uppermost as, faced with dangerous reality, the threatening situation forced him to listen to his military specialist advisers and commanders. Much of what he learned stood him in good stead later on in verbal battle when he came under attack by the party politico-military philosophers after the war. Some of these strategists, that included Frunze, Gusev and Tukhachevsky, were men of talent, but none had any great knowledge or experience, and some had their heads in the clouds. Some of them were interested in the struggle for power that followed Lenin's death, power for themselves or for others, rather than in the rights or wrongs of the military measures under discussion: and any stick served to beat Trotsky. Yet many of them did in fact make some contribution to the military literature and to the propaganda that has become part of the writing of Soviet military history today.

The Frunze school of revolutionary military thought had been joined temporarily by Voroshilov, the guerrilla partisan chief. Frunze, Gusev and Voroshilov believed that they had discovered a new revolutionary doctrine of proletariat warfare that 'relegated to the scrap-heap the theories of the old army generals that had been based on the experience of world war and the study of military history.'[15] According to them, everything of value in the waging of war had been thought up by the Bolsheviks, learned as a result of the scattered skirmishes in the far-flung areas in the black-earth region, the steppe and the Siberian railway. Frunze and Voroshilov put their ideas to the Eleventh Party Congress in the form of a thesis, stressing the Bolshevik discovery of the value of the offensive in strategy, operations and tactics, of manoeuvre and mobility and of the use of the cavalry arm: guerrilla activity in the enemy rear was stressed in particular. And in this they were supported in some measure by Tukhachevsky, who had now taken on the mantle of the militant internationalist, for Tukhachevsky was one of those who wanted to export revolution, if necessary on the bayonets of the Red Army, and he advocated the setting up of an international general staff to plan such an undertaking.[16] And, unmindful of his own experience in ethnic Poland, he professed to believe that the invading armies could be reinforced by the proletariat of the nation being attacked. Some of these seemingly wild theories were to be transmitted into reality in years to come, when Poles would be forced, against their own interest, to fight for communism, and when subversion would be planned, exported and controlled from Moscow, if not by an international general staff then by the Comintern and the KGB and GRU.

Trotsky of course ridiculed his opponents, and often with good reason. He denied that the Bolsheviks had invented a new concept of waging war: a war of manoeuvre had been necessary, he said, because of the nature of the terrain, and any forces fighting over those vast areas would have fought in exactly the same way. Cavalry mobility over the steppes was no new thing. Red Army manoeuvre, said Trotsky, had been learned not from the Bolshevik self-styled innovators but from the Cossacks, for the White troops had been inferior to the Reds in numbers but superior in ability. War, he continued, was a practical art, a skill, a trade; and to learn it one did not have to be a Marxist, for the tsarist military specialists did it well enough. If the young school of Bolshevik militarists wanted to invent something better than the *tachanka* (a horsed carriage mounting a machine-gun), sneered Trotsky, then they had better take lessons from the *bourgeoisie*; for when strategy was developed by revolutionaries, then the result was chaos! Meanwhile he advised these inspired innovators to come down to earth and to confine themselves to the mundane but no less necessary task of teaching the soldier how to shoot, to clean his rifle and to grease his boots.[17] And, in his condemnation of functionarism in the Red Army, Trotsky said that according to Red Army history – as written by Trotsky's opponents – there were only heroes in the Bolshevik ranks, where every soldier burned with a desire to fight; in battle, according to this school of communist writing, the enemy was always superior in numbers whether the glorious Red Army was victorious or vanquished! What Trotsky said is still true of the greater part of Soviet military history today, in that it is written as propaganda for both home and abroad, a much distorted and one-sided political and military account based on truth, half-truth, misrepresentation and lies.

Trotsky's rejection of Frunze's thesis and his condemnation of the views of the Frunze school were based on good common sense. But when it came to deciding what form the Red Army should take in the time of peace, Trotsky's own ideas were somewhat bizarre.

Many of the Old Bolsheviks, like Lenin, were generally opposed to a professional standing army – what they called a 'cadre' army – as 'a force of reaction'; if they had to have an army at all, they would prefer a militia part-time territorial force made up of citizens who would be given short military courses of instruction and then returned to their homes, to be called up from time to time for refresher training. Some Bolsheviks, the few idealists, believed that in the best of worlds, a Bolshevik world, even a militia army would be unnecessary, as, when the need for them was removed, all armies 'would wither and die'. Meanwhile, however, the task facing the leadership was to decide on the type of army that would meet the Soviet Union's needs without overburdening the new state in its demands for men, equipment and money. Trotsky thought that the poor economic condition of the country was such that the state simply could not afford a regular standing army, and for this reason he supported the case for a militia.

But Trotsky's idea of a militia was a very odd affair, a part-time army that would be centred on the industrial areas from which it would get its commanders (that is to say the equivalent of officers and non-commissioned officers) and its technicians, the principal commanders coming not from the ranks of the regular army but from the management of trade unions and factories. The private soldiers for these units would be the peasants, the agricultural workers from the countryside surrounding the great towns.[18] This concept found no support from his own military specialists, most of whom, like Tukhachevsky and Svechin, did not favour any militia plan at all; but the Bolshevik party men, particularly those on the left, liked it, and proposed further to eliminate all commanders who were not of urban proletariat origin; this would have rid the army of all peasants who had risen to positions of authority.[19] But the post-war Kronstadt naval rebellion and the peasant risings in Tambov and in the Ukraine forced the Bolsheviks to see matters in a different light, for they could not afford to drive the peasant into the arms of the counter-revolutionaries. So they turned their backs on Trotsky and sided with what came to be a later Frunze compromise between the cadre and the militia: the army was to be made up of both elements – a number of cadre divisions that were to be fully manned, trained and equipped to meet emergency operations, and a larger number of militia territorial divisions, based on small cadre headquarters and frameworks, their personnel being found by part-time territorial soldier-reservists that could be embodied for training or war.[20]

Behind these seemingly theoretical discussions the desperate struggle for influence, position and power, continued, a struggle in which Trotsky, Stalin and Frunze all played a major role; the vociferous Voroshilov's part was that of the silent Stalin's placeman and spokesman.[21] There had been a number of changes in the Bolshevik hierarchy and Trotsky was being further isolated, in that his few allies and associates were being detached from him. Lenin and Sverdlov were dead. Skliansky, a deputy to Trotsky as Commissar for War, had been transferred to economic work in 1924 and died by drowning the following year, his place as deputy war minister being taken by Frunze. Antonov-Ovseenko, another collaborator of Trotsky's, was removed from the key post of chief military commissar and head of the Red Army political administration (PUR) in 1924, to be replaced by Bubnov, formerly a commissar with Budenny's cavalry army.

Muralov, the commander of Moscow military district, an Old Bolshevik but a supporter of Trotsky, was replaced by Voroshilov in this most important of military posts. In June 1923 the inquisitorial Central Control Commission set up an inquiry into the military organization, and its report, predictably, was an indictment of Trotsky.[22] In March 1924, as part of a far-reaching reorganization, S. S. Kamenev's post of commander-in-chief was abolished and his chief of staff Lebedev was replaced by Frunze, who became in fact, if not in name, the chief of staff of the Red Army, Tukhachevsky and Shaposhnikov remaining as the two deputy chiefs of staff.[23] The Red Army high command, though it still retained its tsarist pattern, was broken down into a central staff, an inspectorate (under S. S. Kamenev) and separate directorates for each of the armed forces, all subordinate to the Revolutionary Military Council (the RVS, formerly the RVSR). Finally, in January 1925, war minister Trotsky was replaced as Commissar for Military and Naval Affairs by Frunze. By the autumn of that year the establishment of the peacetime Red Army had been set at twenty-five regular cadre and thirty-six territorial militia divisions.[24]

Frunze was said to have been the son of a doctor, and a Bolshevik party member since 1904. Arrested for taking part in armed insurrection in 1907, he had been sentenced to hard labour in Siberia, from where he escaped in 1915. Like his other Bolshevik fellows he had no military experience or knowledge, but in 1918 he was appointed to a military commissar post from which he moved to become a military specialist commander of an army, and then a front in the east, appointments that he filled successfully in that he was victorious over the Whites and insurrectionists. Frunze was obviously talented and able, though the extent of his military knowledge and experience cannot have been very great, certainly not sufficient to have qualified him for the latter-day description of 'brilliant', used by writers both within and outside of the Soviet Union. It is said that some of his success in the Civil War was due to the presence of the former general Novitsky.[25] Frunze was another communist internationalist who saw the Red Army as the means 'to defend the interest of [the world's] workers everywhere' for 'between our [Soviet] proletarian state and the rest of the *bourgeois* world there can only be war to the death.' But his military writings, now published in the Soviet Union as a collection and given there all the reverence due to Clausewitz or to

Napoleon's maxims, show little military understanding or historical knowledge; his style is that of an uneducated man lacking clarity of thought, and much of his work is both pretentious and trite.

The reasons for Frunze's advancement and fall are unknown. Until Trotsky was ousted he was, or served as, a counter to Trotskyism, for he was antagonistic to Trotsky and, for that reason, may have found himself allied to Voroshilov and Stalin. But he was also on friendly terms with Zinovev; and Zinovev, after Trotsky's removal, came out in opposition to Stalin, until he himself was removed from the Politburo and the party. Bazhanov, who was present at the seat of power at the time, believed that Stalin suspected that Frunze was trying to bind the army to himself by personal loyalty, for he was active on behalf of the army's welfare, particularly that of the command personnel. In 1925 the Politburo decided that Frunze should have a surgical operation for an ailment, said by some to be an ulcer or by others a gall-stone, an operation that Frunze was unwilling to undergo; according to Wollenberg, Stalin's hand could be traced in the affair. Frunze died under the operation.[26] His death may have been accidental, except that Frunze's wife was said to have shot herself immediately afterwards; a number of these Old Bolsheviks' wives knew too much and sometimes paid the penalty. The timing was very convenient for Stalin. Zinovev proposed that Lashevich should replace Frunze; Stalin wanted his man Voroshilov to have the job of war minister; and so Voroshilov was appointed Commissar for Military and Naval Affairs, a post that he was to hold until 1940. Voroshilov was later to be given the rank of marshal although he was in fact no soldier and had little understanding of military matters: yet his lack of qualification probably was no greater than that of his predecessors, Frunze and Trotsky. Voroshilov needed neither knowledge nor experience, for he was there as Stalin's tool and trusty; by 1926, when Trotsky and Zinovev had been removed from the Politburo, the Red Army already belonged to Stalin. According to what the military defector Barmine has said, Voroshilov was afraid to make any move on his own and consulted Stalin on the smallest detail.[27]

Stalin, as the new dictator, sometimes posed as an eminently reasonable man, particularly to foreign statesmen and diplomats and to the foreign press; he said that his own conciliatory and moderate methods were continually opposed by the hard-line members of the Politburo, intimating that these nameless and faceless beings had to be placated in their demands, as otherwise he, Stalin, might be voted out of office! This is an age-old communist sophism, trickery that still deludes some Kremlin-watchers of the western world. In reality Stalin had the whole of the Politburo and the party organization in his power, and he was, as Radek, the Trotskyite Central Committee member, said, hard, cautious and distrustful and endowed with the greatest of willpower.[28] Stalin spoke for the whole of the Politburo, and if any member of the Politburo or government expressed an opinion in public on any matter of importance, it was Stalin's voice that spoke. Stalin's own writings or pronouncements give little information as to his military philosophy at this time since he said little and wrote less: he preferred to rule through others, concealing the nature and extent of his power not only from the outside world but also from the population of the Soviet Union; unlike Lenin, he was never the chairman of his own committees and he held no government position, being content to let others occupy the sinecure posts of state president and prime minister. It is to Voroshilov that one must turn to know Stalin's military policies at this time.

The army under Voroshilov did not alter radically from the army under Frunze and the changes and developments already under way (that had, in any event, been approved by the party), continued under Voroshilov: this in itself supports the view that if Frunze was deliberately removed from his office it was for personal motives and because he was distrusted by Stalin.

*　　*　　*

The other ranks who were called up for full-time conscript service were originally taken from the working peasants and those who had an urban proletarian or semi-proletarian background, this latter element of the population being regarded as that most sympathetic to the Bolshevik cause. In the infantry the colour service was for two years, and in the technical corps, including the artillery, this was extended to three. Whether or not the conscripts were to be taken into the standing regular cadre army or were to go to the militia depended on the man, his place of work and on his medical category; service in the militia lasted for five years, two months in camp on joining and then a six-week training period every year, so that the conscript underwent, in all, about eight months' service with his unit.[29] No arms or uniform were kept at home. The territorial militia officers were found mostly from demobilized commanders who had been retained on the reserve lists.

In the new army, as in the Bolshevik army of the Civil War, there were, at least officially, neither officers nor non-commissioned officers, and the rank structure of commanders was designated according to the commands that they held, section, platoon, company, battalion commander and so on. Newly designed badges of rank were worn, originally on a common plain-pattern uniform, but these badges were usually put on only when on duty. The pay for the conscript, thirty-eight kopeks a month in 1924 and a ruble thirty in 1925, was sufficient only to keep him in small necessaries, and was no more than that in the former tsarist army; the pay of the commanders, particularly of those who had formerly been classed as officers, was much below even the tsarist rate, since a corps commander in 1924 had a salary of only 150 rubles a month, that was the equivalent of that earned by a well paid metal worker.[30] The ration scale was the same for all and there were no officers' messes, the commanders eating in common with the rank and file, this being considered necessary to keep the military community closely-knit and in touch with each other. The married cadre commanders were allotted accommodation of sorts, but even Frunze had remonstrated against the shabby way in which they were treated, for some families had no more than part of a room. Yet, notwithstanding these poor conditions for the command personnel, there was no difficulty in recruiting sufficient numbers; for the truth was that Russians everywhere were living in conditions of great hardship.

Frunze said that the training of the 1925 Red Army was below that of the tsarist army, and that about one-tenth of the commanders were without any basic education.[31] At that time over half the senior commanders in the Red Army were still the former military specialists and officers from the tsarist army, and the larger part of the junior commanders from the company to the regimental level were former peasants. The relationship between the commander and the soldier was not particularly good, and for this there were a number of reasons.[32]

The military commissar, of course, was very active, and he remained, by and large, the most important man in the unit. In addition to his military duties he organized the communist cell or cells within his unit, so that there was in fact a unit within a unit, the party organization being the inner kernel where all military matters and personalities were discussed. In party work there was no distinction between senior commanders and privates, only between members and candidate members of the party or young communist league (Komsomol) on the one side and non-communists on the other; officers, whether inside or outside of the party, could be severely censured by the soldier of the meanest rank, for the commissar alone stood supreme.[33] These communist cells were invaluable to the commissar, not only to disseminate propaganda, but also to maintaining his own control and keep himself informed as to what was going on at every level in the unit; in the early days these cells were believed, in addition, to be a guarantee of the class nature of the army and some security against the development of an exclusive officer class. Any soldier, whether a party member or not, could send private complaints by letter to the office of the military prosecutor, even though these charges were against his unit commander; the men themselves did not escape attention, for all mail addressed to soldiers was read by the censor, or political or command personnel, before being delivered to the man: all ranks were closely watched for signs of disaffection.[34]

The military commissar's duties were repeatedly listed in regulation and in the military press, but this did not necessarily mean very much as the functions were so loosely described as to admit of widely different interpretations.[35] In 1926 it was said that the commissar was 'to assist the commander to maintain discipline, to educate the unit both generally and politically, *even though this education should border on military training*, and to accept complaints from the personnel.' In addition the commissar was supposed to interest himself in welfare work and supervise the libraries, the Lenin corner and the propaganda wagon. Since the commissar was not under the control of the military leader, being responsible only to the commissar in the next higher headquarters (to whom he made his own confidential reports evaluating the political reliability and military worth of the commander), the official description of the commissar's duties was so imprecise as to permit him to interfere in anything he might choose: and many did so. At the lower levels the political control over the army had been strengthened in that a political director had been appointed as far down as the company, this *politruk* being part of the battalion commissar's organization and being independent of the company commander even to the extent that the *politruk* was under no obligation to consult or work in concert with the company leader. The institute of commissars was in fact a two-man system of command.

The morale of the military commanders was, presumably, at a low level, so much so that Voroshilov continued what had been begun by Frunze, in that he made a show of upholding the commander and restricting the commissar's powers, introducing what he called unity of command. From 1925 those commanders that were judged to be 'sufficiently politically mature' were designated as 'one-man commanders' and were theoretically freed from political controls, such commanders becoming responsible both for the command and for the political education of their own units.[36] But, in reality, the situation had hardly changed, in that the former commissar remained in place but was simply renamed as the deputy political commander (*zampolit*): the commander's measures for political education had to be done through the former commissar, who retained his own control over the formation or unit political organization of party members and young communists, as well as his own confidential commissar channels of communication to the next higher authority. The commander's control over the former commissar and the political network within his command or unit was therefore purely formal, almost fictional, except that the commissar was not supposed to sign any orders other than those of a political nature. But the shadow was still there, even with commanders that were judged to have the party's confidence, and the shadow could, and did, report on the military commanders. Without the approval of these representatives of the party, whether they be called commissar or *zampolit*, a commander could not hope to prosper.

From 1926 onwards the social and rank structure of the Red Army began to change. There had already been some small increases in the conscripts' pay, but these were insignificant compared with the improvements made to the salaries and the living conditions of those commanders of the ranks that were equivalent to those of officers elsewhere in the world. Red Army Houses became officers' clubs and a form of officers' mess was introduced: over the next few years, to use the words of Wollenberg (who was a Red Army commander at this time), 'the international spirit and socialistic basis of discipline in the Red Army were swept away, everything being focused on a new Soviet patriotism and nationalistic arrogance.'[37] The natural and easy relationship between officers and men, he said, also went by the board, so that, by the 1930s, the Red Army commanders' standards (except in that of accommodation) were probably not so very different from those of armies elsewhere in the world; the standards of the conscript soldier and the Russian people were, however, immeasurably lower than those in the west. 'A privileged class and a special type of non-political commander had been created, and their champion was Voroshilov.' Many of the more senior of these commanders were Old Bolsheviks who began to divorce their urban proletarian or peasant wives and remarry with younger women, actresses, ballet dancers, or survivors of the old aristocracy or *bourgeoisie*, this being, according to Wollenberg, 'a mass phenomenon'.

The Soviet conscription laws, in their pattern and their application, were not very much different from those of the tsarist empire, except that the Soviet laws were not so sympathetic to exemptions on family grounds. Theoretically the law applied to all nationalities but, as in tsarist times, it proved impracticable to recruit and train many of the tiny splinter minorities, particularly those that were primitive or entirely hostile to the Bolsheviks. Non-Russian speaking peoples were not exempt, however. The burden fell most heavily on the Great Russians, Ukrainians and Belorussians (these making up sixty-four per cent, twenty-two per cent and four per cent of the whole in 1925), but, as in tsarist times, virtually all units were formed of mixed nationalities. In 1924 and 1925 there was talk, in deference to the susceptibilities of the regions and minority nationalities, of forming national formations and units, and, according to Soviet sources, a few national formations were in fact brought into being.[38] Whether or not this really was so is of little significance since they were reportedly disbanded a few years later. Certain arms, particularly the air force (that formed a component part of the Red Army), the artillery, the technical services and what was eventually to be a nucleus of an armoured corps, were obliged to take a high quota of conscripts of industrial worker origin.[39] The conscription law was not, however, universal, in that certain social classes, the aristocracy and *bourgeoisie*, former professional men such as lawyers, writers and artists, and all Cossacks, were either not recruited or were confined to service in unarmed labour units, and thereby the Red Army lost what might have been an important source of better-educated recruits.

The Red Army did what it could, however, with the material available and made determined efforts to improve the military and general education of its command personnel. Between 1928 and 1931 discipline was tightened everywhere. It had had its own general staff academy since 1918 and this, renamed as the Frunze in 1925, continued to turn out middle-ranking staff officers; it was the successor to the tsarist Nikolaevsky staff academy before the war. There were in addition a large number of military schools of various types for commanders of all ranks, and potential candidates for promotion to battalion or regimental commander had to qualify on a one-year training course before being promoted, this eventually becoming an accepted part of the system of all higher training in the Soviet Army, where senior officers were continually being retrained and requalified.[40] Budenny himself had had to attend such a course and had had great difficulty in qualifying on account of his poor education. According to Soloviev, the military correspondent of *Izvestia*, who at that time was detailed to lecture on military history to a generals' course, a course that included in its students Eremenko and Apanasenko, the education and mentality of most of these Red Army commanders was such as one would expect from 'corporals in generals' uniforms'; among these courses the chief instructor, a former tsarist general Evseev, was sadly at a loss.[41] In most other schools, too, the main difficulty was to find suitably qualified instructors who could surmount not only the ignorance and prejudice of the Soviet hierarchy but also the very low standard of general education of the student officers of all ranks. Great Russians, because of their knowledge of Russian, were generally in a favoured position among the students, but minority nationalities were accepted for all courses as were Jews, although anti-Semitism remained a feature of Soviet rule, much as it had been in imperial Russia, though for different reasons. Women were admitted to the military schools for the first time in 1929, but their numbers were, and remained, very small.

The determination to improve the standard of commander was such, however, that these difficulties did not deter the high command; considering that this Bolshevik command was both corrupt and very inefficient it is remarkable what progress it did make. Command personnel were encouraged by cash awards and by additional qualification pay to attend courses and pass examinations, and attention was concentrated on the use of records of service and education to select men for appointment or promotion; promotion was to be by merit rather than merely by seniority, and, with the continued insistence on further schooling and refresher training, it became the custom to award a promotion at the end of the course, and this was to remain a feature of the Soviet Army of today. The officer category, in particular, was to be rewarded for its efforts, in pay, promotion and in accommodation: this was the intention: *in practice*, however, the granting of ranks and appointments was often done arbitrarily and capriciously.

Yet the distinction remained between the commissar and commander, and between commanders who were party members and those who were not, with the commissars and party members getting preferential treatment. Political reliability and devotion to the party were more important than patriotism and loyalty to the state, for the army was not only meant to defend the Soviet Union, but had to ensure the keeping in power, in perpetuity, of the minority communist group ruling it. Whatever Voroshilov might have said about the unity of command and however much he repeated his assurances to the non-party commanders, the 1928 internal service regulations entrusted the commissar 'on an even footing with the commander' with the supervising of normal training, so that the commissar's influence was felt where one would expect the commander to be solely responsible. The party political organization permeated the whole army and strangled its leadership, so that people saw, or imagined they saw, in everyone around them, on the one side traitors or spies against the state, and on the other informers and *agents-provocateurs* against themselves. The Red Army commander was urged on not only by inducement and favour and an incessant stream of propaganda, but also by force and fear.[42] For the disappearances, the night arrests, the imprisonments and the shootings, continued as a regular feature of communist daily life.

*   *   *

The military thought, tactics, equipment and organization of the Red Army, during the twenties and the beginning of the thirties, had remained very much the same as they had been in the tsarist period. And although today's Soviet military literature brazenly postulates that the new Red Army was at this time developing a doctrine of modern warfare, based in small part on that bequeathed to it by the imperial army, a doctrine that in any event was much in advance of any military philosophy elsewhere in the world, this is quite false, for

Soviet military thought at that time was in ignorance and doubt. That the Red Army had inherited something from the tsarist empire was true, but this amounted to little more than some armament and equipment, a reserve of trained or partially trained officers and non-commissioned officers, and half-digested German military theory. For the tsarist army had, even at its best, never been more than an indifferent copy of the Prussian Army; and a military doctrine or philosophy of its own had been entirely lacking, for the main weakness of the imperial army had been in its higher direction, that is to say in its generals. Yet the Soviet Union has given some of these former tsarist officers that it attracted or forced into its service what might be called the Admiral Ushakov treatment, and has endowed them with outstanding abilities that are contradicted by the men's records, their writings and the descriptions of those who knew them. The Soviet Union's evaluation of these officers and the claims that it makes concerning the predominance of Soviet military thought at this time, have, by dint of constant repetition, gained some acceptance by a new generation of western military writers.

Bonch-Bruevich was of little account. Vatsetis's writings show Vatsetis to have been unexceptional and lacking in clarity of expression and thought. S. S. Kamenev was probably an able commander, manfully carrying the *impedimenta* loaded on him by the Bolsheviks while he fought their battles; but, except for his memoirs, he has left nothing lasting behind him. Lebedev and Samoilo were well known to the British in tsarist days and were reckoned to be able men by tsarist standards, though not outstanding.[43] The writings of Svechin, now lauded in the Soviet Union as a military thinker of a high order, show him to be a verbose and somewhat muddled pedagogue of no great merit. About the genius of Shaposhnikov, Soviet literature makes fewer claims, and this partly because Shaposhnikov, being only a captain in 1914, could not be counted as one of the tsarist sages; and partly, too, because originality was never Shaposhnikov's forte. Shaposhnikov, also, was known to the British in tsarist times and he stood out, in their opinion, as an excellent staff officer, and this is amply supported by the clarity and pertinence of his military writings that are of an excellence rarely found in Soviet literature; and this early British assessment was confirmed also by those allied officers who attended conferences with him in the Second World War, for he was conspicuous amongst his fellows as a first-class military brain.[44]

But he was too cautious and too fearful of his communist masters to propound anything original on his own account.

Among the communist politico-military theorists, writers and leaders at that time, there are very few of really outstanding merit. There is no evidence that Lenin, Trotsky, Stalin or Frunze made any lasting contribution, though Lenin, Trotsky and Stalin certainly learned something of military matters, and Stalin was yet to learn much more. Voroshilov apparently absorbed little during his many years in the Commissariat for Military and Naval Affairs; yet he was a shrewd and cunning man. The same can be said of Budenny, who never learned anything, because of his poor education and because he was unintelligent. Newer commanders were admittedly coming to the fore, many of them former tsarist cavalry sergeants or corporals, some eventually to show outstanding ability in the field; but they had little or no influence on the course of Soviet military thought or on the development of the Red Army between the wars. One only, Timoshenko, rose to high appointment at this time, and by the contemporary Russian standards he was reckoned to have some ability as a strategist and a tactician. But he had neither education nor experience, for he was what he had always been, a Bessarabian Little Russian cavalry non-commissioned officer, no disliker of drink, who talked in a loud tone that brooked no contradiction, who never discussed questions but just made definitive pronouncements; he was, according to one who knew him then, a man of limited horizons who was quick to adopt the mantle of the prophet so that the simplest of truths sounded like the ten commandments. It was Timoshenko who discovered what he called 'the wall of fire' that he demonstrated on the manoeuvres in Central Asia: in reality he had understood a moving barrage for the first time. Timoshenko was disliked by his fellows.[45]

There remains Tukhachevsky. Tukhachevsky was certainly not a tsarist sage, but he later acquired belated recognition in the Soviet Union and sometimes fulsome praise on the pages of western histories. Tukhachevsky had espoused the revolution and burned to be at the forefront of the cause; at times he was more revolutionary than the revolutionaries. Some of his ideas, like those of Trotsky, were grotesque. His military experience and knowledge in 1918 were slender, but he was clever and could impress those around him. In the Polish War, as the commander of the West Front, a post that would normally have been held by a full general, Tukhachevsky had been disastrously defeated, though the defeat had not been entirely his fault. He had then regained his reputation, in part, by his speedy suppression of the Kronstadt rebels; and that was the extent of his active military experience, experience during which he had incurred the enmity of Stalin, Voroshilov and Budenny. The Pole, Pilsudsky, who defeated him, believed Tukhachevsky to be energetic and purposeful, even obstinate, with no self-doubts, and thought that the Russian had handled his troops well in the advance on Warsaw; but Pilsudsky also considered him somewhat blinkered and unable to see the broad picture.[46] Trotsky said much the same, 'that Tukhachevsky was extraordinarily talented, but lacked the ability to see and judge a military situation from every point of view:' and Trotsky added that there was always an element of adventurism in Tukhachevsky's thought and that he tried to create 'a new doctrine of war' from hastily digested Marxist formulas. Trotsky concluded that he himself did not know whether or not Tukhachevsky might have become a great general: only another war could have proved it, one way or the other. Trotsky's summing up of the man's ability and character was probably an accurate one.

Tukhachevsky had been a deputy chief of staff, together with Shaposhnikov, under Trotsky and Frunze, then chief of staff from 1925 under Voroshilov until 1928, when he left to command in Leningrad. He had also been charged with the production of field service regulations, a publication that, when it appeared, bore a striking resemblance to the French regulations of the period. Yet Wollenberg believed that it was the Soviet intention at that time to keep Tukhachevsky in the public eye by boosting his reputation since he might be called upon in war to fill the appointment of commander-in-chief. But the young Tukhachevsky was full of vitality, blunt, impetuous, even violent in his speech, and, a remarkable figure during those days, appeared to speak his mind somewhat freely, according to hear-say rejecting Voroshilov's 'foolish chatter' that victories could be won by enthusiasm; Tukhachevsky urged instead that the Soviet Union should win its wars by developing superior technology and armament.[47] Tukhachevsky advocated the development of the battle in the enemy's rear; and the idea of parachuted infantry originated with him, although he believed that the principal purpose of the parachutists would be to help the capitalist proletariat rise against their governments. Tukhachevsky's writings show that he could commit his thoughts to paper clearly and logically; even in this he was an exception among his fellows. He was a firm supporter of mechanization, though he was unable to encompass its operative and tactical possibilities, for his military papers show that he had very little understanding of the characteristics and the tactical uses of tanks, or any inkling of the revolutionary pattern of armoured war of the future.

*   *   *

It was at this time, in 1928, that Stalin had begun the first of his two five-year plans aimed at the creation of a powerful heavy industry that would form the basis of a massive armament production complex intended to make the Soviet Union independent of foreign arms and equipment and of most imported raw materials.[48] To do this within the ten-year time scale, it was, according to the plans of Stalin and his advisers, necessary to cut back on most light industry and on manufactured goods for consumption at home. From this time onwards the remaining private traders within the Soviet Union were largely eliminated; Lenin's New Economic Policy, that had permitted certain private enterprise and peasant farming production, was abolished, and there began a period of particularly heavy repressions and, in 1929, the immediate collectivization of forty per cent of the land. The peasants resisted and the Red Army was ordered to assist the security forces in suppressing disorders and herding the peasants off, under guard, to labour and concentration camps. This, apparently, caused large scale desertions among the peasant conscripts in the army. The new collective state agriculturists were, at first, entirely inefficient, and by 1931 there was famine, starvation, sickness and deaths that were estimated to run into millions. The worst of the crisis was not over until 1933.

This was the price that the Soviet Union paid in Russian, Ukrainian and Turkic blood in exchange for the creation of a heavy industry and an armament production that had a capacity and potential below that of the United States but roughly equal to that of Germany or of Britain at that time. But the Soviet Union differed from the United States and Britain in that it not only had an armament potential but it actually entered into full-scale production of arms and equipment, manufacturing tanks and artillery pieces by the tens of thousands and small-arms by the million, together with large stocks of ammunition: such an undertaking normally involves the probability that this most costly equipment will become obsolescent soon after manufacture and obsolete after a few years of peace, a probability that deters the democracies from laying up great stockpiles of armament. But though the Soviet Union had become a weapon storehouse, it had no clear-cut plan of re-equipment.

Contrary to what is now asserted in the Soviet military press, there was at that time no independent military philosophy or doctrine, and Russia did what it has always done, that is to say it followed the German lead. Except for one or two military experiments that were tried out and then dropped during the Civil War, the Red Army fell back on to the Prussian-pattern tsarist army organization and tactics.[49] In 1922, when it had become clear that von Seeckt's *Reichsheer* had abandoned the use of the infantry brigade headquarters within the infantry division, the Red Army did the same.[50] Red Army infantry and cavalry tactical organization and equipment remained a close copy of the German. Only on the question of air, armoured and chemical warfare weapons (weapons that von Seeckt was not allowed to possess) could there be some difficulty; but the German was still regarded as the world's foremost soldier, and, as he had had enormous experience of air and chemical weapons in the First World War and had been one of the main users of tanks, his help was requested in these and in other matters.[51]

The details of the Russo-German military collaboration that began round about 1921 and ended in 1933 are by now well known from German, Polish and French sources; the Soviet Union of course is silent on the matter since it is unwilling to admit that it collaborated with German militarists and had to resort to their help. But the importance and extent of this collaboration that, outside of some technological, industrial and financial measures, consisted of little more than an interchange of a limited number of observers and students, and the use of three German testing grounds *by Germans* on Russian soil (all in contravention of the Versailles Treaty), has become greatly magnified and distorted in the western press. It is erroneously asserted by some that the German Army could not have rearmed with such speed between the years of 1933 and 1939 if it had not been for the use of the Russian training grounds. Other westerners appear to believe what can be read in some sections of the present-day Russian press, that the Soviet concept of mobile and armoured operations at this time was so in advance of any held by western nations, that the Red Army served as mentors to the Germans.[52] Nothing could be further from the truth.

The 100,000–man *Reichsheer* at its inception included about 180 German flying officers of the First World War, and von Seeckt, who had always shown a keen interest in the retention of a secret air force within the new German Army, had set up a small air force staff under a Colonel von Thomsen within the general staff *Truppenamt*. In 1923 about 100 first-class Fokker D XIII fighters were secretly purchased from Holland, and, about two years later, these were crated and sent to the leased German fighter school that had been set up at Lipetsk in Russia. The first courses to be trained there consisted of German former war fighter pilots undergoing refresher training, and these were followed by officers and potential officers who had already gained a civil pilot's licence but had no military flying experience, the serving officers being sent to Russia in civilian clothing and with passports made out in false names. In all, 130 fighter pilots and eighty air observers were trained at Lipetsk between 1925 and 1933, together with a few navy fliers.

The German-leased flying base at Lipetsk was paid for by the *Reichswehr*, and its direction and management were entirely in German hands. The actual flying was done mainly in the summer months and, at the most, about fifty German students qualified each year; the German flying and ground staff numbered something less than 200 officers and men in summer and about sixty in winter. The Russians took no part in the instruction at all but merely serviced and guarded the camp. The Germans did, however, run courses for the Red Army, particularly in the winter months, but these were restricted to the technical training of ground staff, particularly mechanics and riggers. The flying school at Lipetsk helped the Germans make a quicker start when they began to create an independent *Luftwaffe* in the thirties, in that they had more trained aircrew than they would otherwise have had, but the numbers were small and they pale into insignificance beside the gigantic training programmes undertaken in Germany from 1934 onwards.[53]

The siting of a German armoured school on the Kama near Kazan on the Volga was first discussed in 1925 but it did not open until after 1928, the year of the first Soviet five-year plan. The accommodation was constructed and leased, but there were no tanks to be had, for the Soviet Union at that time had no tank production of its own and was unwilling to loan or sell the Germans such models as it did possess. The Germans therefore manufactured their own, six heavies weighing 23 tons, each powered by a 300 h.p. BMW aircraft engine and mounting a 75mm gun, and three mediums of 12 tons each mounting a 37mm gun. These tanks were sent to Kama in 1928 and formed the basic training equipment, later supplemented by a few light British-built Carden-Lloyd tankettes that were obtained from the Russians in exchange for some German ancillary tank equipment. And the Soviets refused to provide anything else.[54]

The nucleus of the *Reichsheer* panzer force at that time was the very small motor transport corps, in reality a service corps or *train*, and it was to this corps that Guderian, Paulus, Harpe, von Thoma and others yet to become distinguished in armoured warfare, belonged: that they succeeded in developing and controlling the panzer arm was due to an accident of history, firstly that the very strong German horsed cavalry arm, that consisted of no fewer than eighteen regiments, was not interested in mechanization, and secondly that Guderian and his enthusiasts were able to interest Hitler in their ideas. What was to develop as German armoured doctrine was originally based not on the writings of de Gaulle, Liddell-Hart and others, and certainly on nothing that appeared in the Russian military press, but on the official provisional British armoured handbook of 1927. That this was so was affirmed by Guderian himself, in 1943, when he was writing for a National Socialist readership and not for the foreign press after the war. This early British bias was of course modified according to German needs, experience and study, but it owed nothing to the Russians at that time. The reverse was in fact the case.

The tank school on the Kama was under a German lieutenant-colonel and the instructors and instruction were German: in all, the permanent staff was no more than about fifteen, and the school took in courses of only a dozen or so students at a time, mainly captains and lieutenants from the German motor transport corps, and the whole course covered two summers in Russia and one winter in Berlin where the theoretical training was carried out. In addition the Russians were allotted five vacancies on the course and they also attended the theoretical instruction inside Germany. The German motor transport officers detailed for courses on the Kama were retired from the

Reichsheer and travelled by rail through Poland as civilians, using passports in their own names; on finally returning to the Reich they were reinstated in the German Army. Their names and those used by their Russian fellow students were noted by the Polish authorities and passed on to the *deuxième bureau* in Paris; and, as German army lists were at that time public property, the French intelligence service had no difficulty in knowing what was going on.

The Kama tank training and testing ground was undoubtedly of use to Germany, particularly to the motor transport corps, since these enthusiasts became the only element in the *Reichsheer* that had any theoretical knowledge and practical experience in handling even a handful of armoured vehicles; before Kama, Guderian had never seen a tank. But, as was the case with the Lipetsk *Luftwaffe* air school, Kama itself had little direct bearing on the development of the panzer arm relative to the enormous expansion that took place inside Germany from 1934 onwards.

High-ranking Red Army officers, including Tukhachevsky, visited Germany and attended German manoeuvres, and certain facilities were given to *Reichsheer* officers to return these visits during the period before Hitler came to power in 1933. A number of Soviet officers were admitted to attend *certain parts* of army courses in Germany, and even then, because of their inquisitiveness and tendency to regard themselves as Bolshevik propagandists, it soon became necessary to restrict their participation and activities. But to suggest, as has been said in some western studies of this subject, that Tukhachevsky, a chief of general staff and then the commander of Leningrad military district, attended the whole German *Truppenamt* equivalent of the staff college course at this time (a course for senior lieutenants and junior captains spread over two or three years), and that this was one of the reasons for the similarity of the strategic and tactical concepts of the Red Army and the *Reichsheer*, is wrong. Among the items of Tukhachevsky's business, when he visited Germany, was *the request* that Red Army officers should be attached to German schools. Uborevich was the only Red Army officer of note who attended certain parts of German army courses. Some German officers did go to the Soviet Union, but, as far as is known, the purpose was mainly liaison, technical, or for language training.[55]

Who were the winners and who the losers from the collaboration during this period is fairly easy to determine, as viewed from the

German side at least. The technical and industrial enterprises were of little lasting benefit to Germany except in the consignment from the USSR of half a million shells. Everything obtained from the Soviet Union had to be paid for in hard cash. The air and tank schools were of some benefit to Germany but their significance overall was certainly not great. The Soviet contribution to German military thought was nothing – because the German officers believed, and not without good cause, that the Red Army at that time had little worth-while to offer; as a parallel one can understand that British naval officers of the twenties and early thirties might have been equally sceptical that there was anything to be learned from the Red Navy's strategical and tactical thought.[56] One of the principal benefits to Berlin of this Russo-German liaison was not military but political, in that it created in Polish minds a threat against Poland; this was one of the reasons that the co-operation was continued, even though the military advantages to Germany were doubtful, particularly in view of the heavy cash payments made to the USSR.

What the Red Army got out of this collaboration can only be a matter of surmise. It intended, as von Manstein, who visited the Soviet military staffs twice during this period, has said, to get as much as it could while itself giving very little, although Voroshilov gave them fair words, praise and promises enough.[57] Up to a point the Red high command courted the German ambassador and the military attaché, assuring them that they regarded the liaison as being of the greatest importance, adding, with what could only have been with their tongues in their cheeks, that 'orders had been given that nothing should be concealed from their German guests.' The Soviet Union's relationship with the other world powers was poor and so it made the most of this temporary friendship.

The Red Army still kept a large number of cavalry divisions side by side with the growing nucleus of the new mechanized forces; but then so did the Germans, for their ratio of horsed cavalry was very high indeed. But whereas the German panzer arm at first existed only in Guderian's head, on paper or in the form of mock-up or experimental models, Russian-built tanks were already becoming available in numbers by the end of the first of the five-year plans in 1933 – probably about 2,000 – for, although Soviet literature claims 5,000, this greater target was not reached until 1935. By October 1934, however, the founding and fast expansion of the German panzer arm was already under way.

Present-day Soviet literature, in an effort to predate the German panzer field organizations, claims that the Red Army formed a mechanized corps as early as 1932, 'the first mechanized corps in the world', a corps that numbered, it says, 500 tanks.[58] In reality this mechanized corps did not make its appearance until 1934, and this so-called corps was in reality the equivalent of an armoured or panzer division, made up of two mechanized brigades (in reality regiments) each of three battalions of thirty-two tanks, together with a support rifle and machine-gun brigade; knowledge of the Red Army tactical establishments of that time tells us that this vaunted armoured formation could not have had a strength of more than 200–250 tanks. The Soviet mechanized corps was in fact the equivalent of the Guderian panzer division that commenced forming in 1934, and its organization was in fact very similar.

Guderian had been chief of staff to Lutz, the inspector of motor transport troops, from 1931 onwards, and his views would presumably have been taught to the handful of Russian officers at the little tank school on the Kama. Guderian's recommendations had been accepted, in Berlin, *faute de mieux*, when the first panzer divisions were put together. And Guderian and his little band of supporters were telling the world, (for in those days the unclassified military journals were freely used to provoke thought and to promote support), that the proper use of tanks was *en masse* as an operative (that is to say semi-tactical semi-strategic) and independent main arm, with artillery, motorized infantry and *Luftwaffe* ground-attack aircraft serving as supporting arms *to assist the tanks* forward to their objectives deep in the enemy rear. The large operative tank forces, said Guderian, were designed to carry out single and double envelopments and so destroy the slow moving infantry armies of yester-year. These teachings were read in the Soviet Union as elsewhere.

The second five-year plan was to increase the Soviet armoured strength by *a further* 10,000 vehicles, according to what the Soviets themselves say: foreign military intelligence estimates of 1939/1940, that, in hindsight, have shown themselves to be remarkably accurate, put the *total* Soviet strength as at least 10,000 tanks. Whatever the real strength might have been, the Soviet military leadership was rapidly arriving at a situation in which it had more than a sufficiency of tanks but was not at all clear as to how it should use them. For even the

German lead gave them no clear guidance. Guderian was saying one thing, but the opposing school of thought, led by Beck, the chief of the army general staff, and made up of most of the prominent German infantry generals, said another: and these German infantrymen, as Guderian himself said, did not attach much importance to the tactical opinions and training of the officers of the *Reichsheer* trucking corps and the drivers of supply vehicles. When Guderian was replaced in the motor transport inspectorate by Paulus, both Lutz and Paulus were forced by the general staff *Truppenamt* to raise a number of independent panzer brigades and regiments (at the expense of further panzer divisions), designed *to support* dismounted line infantry divisions. To the outsider it appeared that neither the one nor the other school was predominant in Germany. Nor were the French or British ideas at the time any clearer. So the Russians decided to hedge their bets, and they had a sufficiency of tanks to do so; by 1936 they were raising mechanized brigades consisting of tanks and motorized infantry designed for mobile operations, and tank brigades of tanks only that were intended to support infantry formations moving on their feet.

From 1938 onwards, Hitler began to take a close interest in military matters and he supported Guderian against all others; in consequence the independent panzer brigades and regiments, called into being by the general staff to support infantry, were converted and used to form more panzer divisions. It was in 1938 that three German motorized (later known as panzer) corps first made their appearance, and these really *were* corps, and not the Soviet type divisions that were *called* corps; for the German corps were made up of standard divisions. But Beck was still dissatisfied with what he believed to be Guderian's over-reliance on the tank, for the chief of the army general staff appreciated that the tank could win ground but could not easily hold it, and that the tank was, at that time, inhibited by difficulties of visibility and terrain; so Beck contrived to have his view accepted that Guderian's panzer corps of two panzer divisions should have a standard infantry division added to it, this infantry division being fully motorized. This proved to be the happiest of decisions since it established a very suitable balance between tanks and infantry that was to last for many decades, an organization that was, some years afterwards, to be copied in its entirety by the Soviet Army and still retained, in a modified form, to the present day.

In 1938 and 1939, however, this shift in Guderian's favour would not have been revealed to the Soviet Union. When its full impact became known, in 1940, it was already too late to save the Red Army from the colossal defeats of 1941 and 1942.

CHAPTER FOUR

The Race Against Time

Between 1928 and 1932 the chief of the German army general staff (then known as the *Truppenamt*) visited the Soviet Union each year for military talks and to attend the annual Red Army manoeuvres; and, of course, he took with him a German military and specialist staff. The Germans were aware that the Russians used the visitors for what they could get out of them, in cleverly rehearsed and orchestrated meetings, saying anything that would achieve their object. Yet the German opinions of the Red Army officers whom they met, and these opinions were often based on the impressions of an acquaintanceship of only a few days, proved to be fairly accurate.

The Germans were surprised at the wide diversity in origin, education and ability of the Red Army senior officers. These usually fell into one of three classes: the 'politicals' without much military background; the imperial tsarist; and the new generation that had been trained in the Red Army schools. A very few in each category were noted to be officers of real talent – Shaposhnikov, Uborevich, Blyukher (or Blücher – his true name was Medvedev), and Tukhachevsky 'that lively and shrewd questioner'.[1]

The visitors concluded that the Red Army men wanted to keep clear of all political matters, though Voroshilov and Uborevich did broach the possibility of a Russo-German attack on Poland, a subject that they had presumably raised with the visitors on Stalin's orders. All Red Army men, with the possible exception of Voroshilov and Budenny, feared to say a word without the approval of their shadowing commissars.[2] Voroshilov was reckoned to be more of a political than a soldier, but, even so, the Germans noted, he was able to keep a firm grip on what was going on around him (much the same description as that used about him by Trotsky many years before). Budenny, that child of nature, was 'a coarse and ignorant swashbuckler', while the Red Army chief of staff Egorov, the former colonel of the Bendersky regiment and a man of only moderate ability, made no particularly strong impression on the German visitors.[3]

Von Blomberg, at that time the chief of the *Truppenamt*, had reported that the Red Army command staffs were 'in relation to the visiting German officers as pupils are to masters, and their sole desire was to absorb as much German teaching as possible.'[4] The efficiency shown on the Russian manoeuvres was poor and the Germans thought that the Red Army was still untrained and unfit for large-scale operations of the European type: the tactical training of the officers, they thought, was low, a description that was to be repeated by others over the next few years. A Colonel Kühlenthal, head of German military intelligence (although his official designation did not admit this), spent six weeks in Russia in 1929 observing exercises: what particularly impressed him, and this time favourably, was the Russian conscript, who still had the primitive toughness of the generations of his forefathers, uncomplainingly cheerful in the face of severe weather and of appalling conditions.[5] Von Manstein said exactly the same of the Russian rank and file that he saw in the Caucasus in 1932, the only soldierly beings that stood out against a background of command and staff inefficiency and confusion.[6] The Russian soldier, thought von Manstein, was still what he had always been and he deserved better than was done for him by staffs and officers who lacked ability, training, confidence, initiative, and, above all, the willingness to accept any responsibility.

Another interesting source of information at this period was the German military attaché, a Colonel (and later Major-General) Köstring. Köstring was born and educated in Russia, of German merchant parents, and had attended the Moscow *Realschule* at the St Mikhail church: in 1895, at the age of nineteen, he had gone to Prussia to do his conscript service in an uhlan regiment. Finding German military life to his liking he eventually became a regular officer in an imperial Kaiser cuirassier regiment in which he served in the First World War: he later passed into the *Reichsheer* 100,000–man force, eventually commanding *Reiter-Regiment 10* as a lieutenant-colonel in 1927.[7] Notwithstanding his long and distinguished service, his record and experience were by no means outstanding, for he did not belong to the general staff and he had not held any key appointments: because of his background and his knowledge of Russian he became the German military attaché in Moscow in 1931, a post that he was to hold, except for a break from 1933 to 1934, until 1941. He was an able and observant officer with a very wide knowledge and understanding of Russian life and history.

According to Köstring's evaluation, Red Army military thought was based on the German, and he could see German ideas everywhere running through the whole pattern 'like a continuous red thread'.[8] The Red Army leaders, thought Köstring, were pupils of the Germans with much yet to learn, for he considered that the Red Army standards of military efficiency were low compared with those of the German Army at the time. The Red Army was a curious mixture of the revolutionary new, the German Army present, and the imperial tsarist army past: and he reported a lecture that he had attended at Moscow university, a lecture on the Red Army given by the former tsarist general Count Ignatev, an earlier court page to the tsaritsa, during which Ignatev said that it was 'the intention of the Red Army to take over and preserve all that was good and useful in the tsarist army'.[9] Köstring, though a reliable witness, suffered from the same difficulties experienced by other foreign military attachés in that he was not allowed access or freedom of movement and he saw only what the Red Army leadership intended that he should see: moreover his knowledge of the Red Army, like that of the other embassy staff, was not profound since it was based largely on chance observation and on hearsay in the artificial little diplomatic community in the Russian capital. And although, after the Second World War, Köstring said that he had warned Berlin of the extent of Soviet military might, the written record does not support this claim – in fact he had made light of the Red Army strength.[10]

After Hitler had been voted to power in January 1933, the Russo-German military collaboration abruptly ceased. Voroshilov and his men, presumably at Stalin's order, then focused their attention on the French, the British and, later, on the Americans. In 1936 British and French military observers were invited to attend the Soviet manoeuvres, and the British team was made up of the Russian-speaking General Wavell, an air force representative, and the armoured specialist Martel, who had been an early proponent of the tank and was a writer of note on mobile warfare. Martel had, in addition, an excellent knowledge of French, that was well understood by the old tsarist officers, and, in particular, was used by Tukhachevsky, who was himself very fluent in that language. Tukhachevsky, so it seemed to Martel, was 'by far the ablest officer with whom we came into contact', and was particularly interested and well-informed on the equipment side. Uborevich, the commander of Belorussia military district, possibly because he was German- rather than French-speaking, made less of an impact on Martel. None of the British team was impressed with the extent of Voroshilov's military knowledge and, according to Martel, Budenny's 'sole idea of a war was the cavalry charge'. And Martel saw Egorov as 'a figure-head', adequate enough if he had a good staff but unlikely to have the drive or ability to initiate much on his own. All of Martel's evaluations of these personalities were shrewd and well founded.[11]

Martel was particularly struck by the Russian commanders' desire to learn, and by their eagerness to impress their visitors with their new equipment and new ideas; and he was gratified when his own military books, in Russian translation, were produced for his inspection everywhere he went. Martel recorded and reproduced in detail the Soviet armoured organization as it was used on the manoeuvres: there were no less than five mechanized brigades and a tank brigade on one side, and four mechanized brigades on the other, all operating independently under rifle corps that had a number of rifle and cavalry divisions under command as well – there was no mention by the Soviet leaders of the existence of any armoured formation higher than that of a Soviet brigade (that is to say a western regiment). The armoured battle that resulted from such a diverse order of battle was spectacular but highly confused, with little skill being shown in the handling of armoured forces, 'among which horsed cavalry charged to and fro': in all, concluded Martel, 'an impossible situation'. No effort was made by the Russians to umpire the exercises or assess the effect of fire; and the whole business, said Martel, was obviously designed to impress the spectators – a demonstration to exhibit the might of the Red Army, 'more like a tattoo than manoeuvres'. But even with this little spectacle, the directing staff and commanders proved incapable of controlling and co-ordinating the troops taking part.[12]

Martel noted that the Red Army regimental officers seemed young and keen and that there were distinct signs that they had already become a class quite apart from the rank and file. The relationship between officers and conscripts appeared good. But Martel was sure, from the British team's questioning of the officers themselves, that the tactical training was very inadequate and that the officers suffered from a lack of confidence in their own ability to command, and this failing became immediately obvious as soon as they were given tactical questions. In all, said Martel, 'we saw nothing original in their tactical doctrine and it was obvious that the Red Army was content to follow the normal standardized teaching of the other continental armies.' Moreover, he continued, 'they were in fact going to have some difficulty in catching up, due to the poor training of their officers and non-commissioned officers: Russian ideas on tanks and armoured warfare had nothing new and they obviously had not made up their minds as to which way they were going.'

Once again, however, the Russian conscripts, the junior rank and file, did not fail to make an outstanding impression, this time on Martel. For these conscripts, he said, were excellent from a physical point of view and they carried more on their backs than was done elsewhere in western Europe: two meals a day seemed to suffice, and they appeared to be quite impervious to the cold. These descriptions were similar to those of the Germans Kühlenthal and von Manstein, some three years before, and echoed the accounts of the British officers of a generation earlier, Knox, Ironside and Williamson, or those of Wellesley and the American officer Greene in 1878, the British General Wilson of 1812, the French marshals of Borodino or the Prussians at Kunersdorf in 1759. Martel was to be in Russia again, in the war years. The rank and file of the Second World War were still very much the same: it was, he said, the 1943 officers and senior non-commissioned officers that had improved so immeasurably.[13]

In 1936 the foreign observers were treated to the sight of a mass descent of a parachute brigade, a display that did impress the somewhat sceptical visitors: for most of the men were carried lying face-down on the wings of giant bomber aircraft, holding on to a rope to prevent themselves from being blown off. At a given signal they slid off the wings and pulled the rip-cords of their parachutes.

The British team's overall impression of the manoeuvres was of tanks that were apparently reliable, for very few breakdowns were seen, but of an absence of direction and control, with little radio communication and little or no reconnaissance and preparation. The demonstration, by any standards, was badly done. The main summing up was that, apart from a truly formidable array of tanks and aeroplanes, the Russian Army had not changed greatly and still exhibited its former virtues and faults, great hardiness, great endurance but considerable tactical clumsiness that would result in very severe losses in war.

★   ★   ★

At the beginning of the thirties the concept of 'the battle in depth' had become popular in Russia, this being applied to both offensive and defensive operations, in the strategic as well as in the operative field. In 1931 Voroshilov had repeated many of Tukhachevsky's ideas when he said that future war should be waged deep in the rear of an attacking enemy. And there was the usual Russian mania that things should be bigger if not better, and in 1934 Stalin seized on the slogan that the Red Army should be the greatest army, in that it should be stronger than any possible combination against it; and he drove the point home in his address to the Red Army academy when he stressed 'the sacrifices that had been necessary to enable this to be done'. Consumer goods had had to be cut, he said, and reserves and currency husbanded in order to meet the needs of heavy industry and rearmament.[14]

In 1927 the highest control body for military affairs had been the committee of defence, also called the defence commission, headed by Stalin's man Molotov, and this was supposed to decide matters of important policy: Stalin, when he attended the meetings, might or might not take the chair at Molotov's insistence, but he was always the *de facto* chairman even if he chose to attend only as a listener. The implementation of the commission's policies was in the hands of a second and subordinate council, the RVS revolutionary military committee under its chairman, Stalin's other obedient voice, Voroshilov, using the People's Commissariat for Military and Naval Affairs as its executive. The chief of the military air force, that was an integral part of the Red Army and wore army uniform, came directly under Voroshilov, but the air force administrative control was separate from the ground forces of the Red Army; the air force had no general or, at this time, air staff of its own, since this was embodied in the general staff of the ground forces of the Red Army. The Red Fleet was of course an armed service in its own right and wore naval uniform; but its chief, too, came directly under Voroshilov, and it had, as yet, no independent general or naval staff since this, like the air staff, formed part of the Red Army general staff. The chiefs of the military air force and the navy were styled 'the air and navy commanders-in-chief' even though they had no independent operational commands. The ground forces had no equivalent appointed head and it was assumed by foreign observers, and probably correctly, that Voroshilov would, in the event of war, be both the commander-in-chief of all the armed services and the commander of the ground forces. As in tsarist times, the air force and the navy were in a totally subordinate position to the army ground forces.

In 1934, however, certain changes were brought about. Voroshilov's commissariat had been renamed the Commissariat for Defence (NKO). There was, as yet, no fear of immediate war, and there had been some slight relaxation in the commissar control of the Red Army, in that the collegiate (military council) principle of command had been done away with at military district and independent army level. Since it was believed that Molotov's and Voroshilov's committees duplicated each other and since it was intended that Voroshilov, too, should have the semblance of the powers of a commander-in-chief with his own unity of command, without being jointly responsible with a council, Voroshilov's RVS committee was done away with in June of that year.

There were other changes, too, that were made during 1934 and 1935. The tsarist officers' ranks of colonel, major, captain and lieutenant were reintroduced, except that the word 'officer' was still in disrepute and its use was not permitted: nor could the communists bring themselves to use the word 'general', except as a printed term of abuse. So the ranks that were the equivalent to those of general in the old army remained as army commander (*komandarm*) 1st or 2nd class, corps commander (*komkor*) and so on, even though the term was used to distinguish a rank and not a function. And a new rank, that of Marshal of the Soviet Union, was introduced, this rank being given in the first instance to Voroshilov, Tukhachevsky, Egorov, Blyukher and Budenny. The marshal's insignia of rank was a large gold star, that of an army commander of first rank a smaller gold star and rhomboids, while those of other general and officer grades remained what they had been before, mainly red rhomboids, rectangles or squares mounted on a piped backing. In September 1935 the chief of staff of the Red Army (*Shtab RKKA*), still headed by Egorov, became the chief of general staff of the Red Army.

1 (*above left*) A NCO of the imperial Preobrazhensky foot-guard in
field service order

2 (*above right*) A soldier of the imperial Moskovsky grenadiers in winter field
service order

3 (*below*) Members of the imperial corps of pages (officer aspirants from the
aristocracy) in a variety of uniforms

4 Armed civilians forming a Red
Guard street patrol in St
Petersburg, 1917

5 Stalin when commissar of the
South Front (1918)

6 A January 1927 meeting of the Revolutionary Military Council (RVS),
Voroshilov with his back to the camera. Most of those present, including
Egorov, Tukhachevsky, Gamarnik, Blyukher and many others easily
identifiable in this photograph, died in the purges

7 The five 1935 Marshals of the Soviet Union (from the left): Tukhachevsky,
Voroshilov, Egorov, (rear) Budenny and Blyukher. Only Voroshilov and
Budenny survived the purges

8 Red Army cavalry with a Maxim machine-gun mounted on an open carriage (the *tachanka*)

9 A column of 1937 Vickers-based T 26 with machine-guns mounted in twin turrets

In April 1937, the defence commission was renamed as the commit-tee for defence, Molotov remaining as its chairman, and it included among its members Voroshilov as well as Stalin. In December 1937 a separate Commissariat for the Navy, with its own supreme naval staff, was established, theoretically independent of Voroshilov's renamed Commissariat for Defence.

On paper at least, 1934 appeared to herald a period of partial political relaxation in the USSR. Some consumer goods had been permitted under the second of the five-year plans, or so the newspapers said, and there had been an introduction of incentives and payment; no longer 'to each in accordance with his needs', but 'to each in accordance with his responsibility and his ability'. From a produc-tion and morale point of view this had obvious advantages, but it also had the effect of perpetuating new and well-defined communist privileged classes. Stalin had constantly assured the people that a better day was dawning, and some of Lenin's agricultural concessions, that had been forcibly removed a few years before, were returned, so that a peasant was to be allowed to keep a cow, sheep and pigs: even the collective farms were to be allowed to sell, on the open market, surplus produce over their quotas, the proceeds being divided among the members. And the professional commanders of the armed forces were to have their share in incentives and privileges.

Meanwhile, however, other factors were at work. At the end of June 1934, in the night of the long knives, Hitler effectively disposed of opposition within his own party by murdering Röhm and a hundred or so of Röhm's brown-shirted SA stalwarts. These murders made a deep impression on Stalin, since he now knew that Hitler was master in his own house, and Stalin came to understand the type of man with whom he had to deal. It was from this time that it became apparent that Germany was set on a programme of an enormous and rapid rearmament, with Hitler openly flouting the French and British by announcing, in 1935, the return of Germany to general conscrip-tion and the raising of the *Luftwaffe*. Hitler's treatment of the German communists, who, in 1933, had been a numerous and powerful force, had been immediate, horrific and effective: Hitler had been legally voted into office by a large popular vote; but then, on the death of the president Hindenburg, he seized dictatorial powers for all time and successfully destroyed all forms of opposition. The German dictator had never made any secret of his enmity to Soviet Russia. In the Far

East a nationalist and militarist Japan had already set out on its path of expansion, and this was a new and dangerous threat to the USSR.

In view of the resurgence and rearmament of a National-Socialist Germany, Stalin and his associates were forced to reassess the Soviet Union's foreign relations and defence policies. The Red Army in 1934 stood, in reality, at about eighty-two infantry divisions, twenty cavalry divisions and one mechanized division, irrespective of what is said in today's Soviet literature; and nearly three-quarters of the infantry divisions were not regular standing divisions but were made up of part-time territorial militia. The decision was made to revert rapidly, though by stages, to a regular army, by converting the territorial divisions to standing formations, partly by ordering militiamen on to full-time service and partly by drafting in conscripts to serve a two-year term: air force, armoured, artillery and technical units were already for the most part on full-time service. The plan intended that seventy-one of the existing 103 divisions should be regular by January 1938 and that most of the remaining territorial formations should be converted during the following two years. According to the Soviet account this change involved the increase of the 1933 standing army of 885,000 to a figure of one and a half million by 1938, and the 1936 conscription law was amended to include all Soviet citizens irrespective of race, creed or social origin.[15] Even former Cossacks were to be conscripted. In March 1938 the old RVS was revived as the Main Military Council of the Red Army, with Voroshilov as chairman, and Stalin as one of its members. The navy also had its own council, but Stalin did not attend its meetings regularly.

Concurrently with this frantic scramble to reorganize the military forces of the Soviet Union to bring them on something approaching a war footing, there occurred the massive and widespread purges that shook the whole of the Soviet Union, and the Red Army, to their very foundations. There had always been purges and so-called repressions, a Soviet euphemism that covered anything from individual arrests, beatings and torture, disappearance or execution, to mass deportations, imprisonments and shootings: this had been going on all the time from 1918 onwards, and the Soviet population in both urban and rural areas, together with the now trapped foreign communists that had flocked to this Bolshevik paradise, lived in perpetual fear of the secret police and the NKVD successors to the GPU. Any connections with abroad or with foreigners made the Soviet citizen doubly suspect. This had always been a feature of life under the communists.

In 1934, following the murder of Kirov, one of the old guard Bolsheviks in Leningrad, there began a mass investigation in a search for what were called spies, traitors and opponents of the régime. In August 1936, Zinovev, L. V. Kamenev and five other old party leaders, formerly close associates of Stalin who had either, at one time, opposed him or had otherwise incurred his hostility or suspicion, were put on trial and executed. Five months later there was another major show trial of men who had once been prominent among the Bolsheviks. Meanwhile investigations and arrests were occurring everywhere in every walk of Soviet life, those arrested disappearing without even the formality of a trial. Then came the turn of the armed forces with the arrest, trial and shooting (or in some cases the disappearance), of Tukhachevsky, Blyukher, Uborevich and Egorov, and many of those other tsarist military men who had thrown in their lot with the early Bolsheviks, these including Vatsetis, Svechin, Sytin and hundreds of others. This massive purge, during the next two years, cost the Red Army three of its five marshals, only Stalin's cronies Voroshilov and Budenny escaping, all the heads of the military districts and the deputy commissars for defence, the chief of the political directorate (the PUR) and tens of thousands of its commanders. In 1937 the military commissars were restored to their former position of pre-eminence and the military councils came into being once more.

There appears to have been no clear design or motive for the arrests, arrests that covered the whole spectrum of Soviet life, for it is certain that most of those who were purged were guiltless of the charges brought against them. And it is impossible to establish even a general pattern within the armed forces. When, in 1936, Tukhachevsky had visited Paris, at the French invitation, he had appeared quite sure of himself: but he had caused the greatest surprise to his listeners when he publicly attacked any attempt to align the Soviet Union with collective security, telling a journalist *that the Germans were already invincible*. These views were undoubtedly Stalin's, although whether the volatile Tukhachevsky had been instructed to give them an airing in this particular fashion is another matter. According to German intelligence sources, Tukhachevsky tried to contact the emigré Russian general Miller, Miller himself being shadowed by another emigré

Skoblin, subsequently thought to have been in touch with the NKVD or the Gestapo security service or both. Hitler and Heydrich are said to have taken a hand in the feeding back of false information on Tukhachevsky, through President Benes of Czecho-Slovakia, to Stalin, causing the Soviet dictator to have the marshal arrested for treason. But this is all surmise. Stalin needed no evidence other than that of his insane suspicion; and he suspected everyone. The great purges were already under way before Tukhachevsky visited Paris.

Nor can one calculate the effect of these great purges (that swept away most of the command structure of the Red armed forces) on the efficiency of the Red Army and on its ability to withstand the German invasion in 1941. Many western writers believe that Stalin did near-irreparable damage to the military, damage that resulted in the terrible defeats suffered by the Red Army in 1941 and early 1942, the majority of these writers basing their case on the assertion that Stalin had done to death military leaders of the highest quality, whose presence on the 1941 battlefields would have turned the scales of war: Tukhachevsky and Uborevich are sometimes elevated to rank among the great captains of war. And these same writers tend to portray the pre-1936 Red Army as being one of the first-ranking, if not the foremost, army of the time, in its military thought and leadership, its equipment and its organization and efficiency. Such a belief is indeed encouraged by the post-Stalin Soviet military press, particularly that of the Khrushchev era, when nothing good could be said about Stalin.

But the truth about the pre-1936 Red Army was very different. There is no evidence that Tukhachevsky or Uborevich were military geniuses, whatever their undoubted talents, and there were few, if any, other outstanding Soviet military men who were prominent at that time. And all these Red Army commanders, including Tukhachevsky and Uborevich, were fearful of their military commissars and would not initiate even an opinion that might be construed, or misconstrued, as being contrary to the party line. Military thought in the Soviet Union was very uncertain, and the training standards of the Red Army were still very low. Tukhachevsky's only contribution was in demonstrating the possible uses of air-dropped forces: even so, the Soviet Union had not the practical or tactical ability to develop even this idea further, and it was left to the Germans to do it. The Soviet Union's sole achievement during this period was to remedy the besetting sin of the late Romanov tsars who went to war without first establishing an armament industry: for, by 1940, the USSR had produced an enormous amount of military equipment that included very good-quality artillery and tanks that, in the words of a 1940 foreign military intelligence chronicler, 'were truly astonishing both in quantity and in design'.

There is another school of thought among both political and historical commentators that takes an opposite view, though these commentators are much in the minority, the view that Stalin rid himself either of military traitors or military deadwood, so putting the Red Army on a better footing and enabling it to withstand the storms of war that broke over it a few years later. One such political commentator, Hitler, after the unsuccessful 1944 attempt on his life by members of his own high command, actually applauded Stalin's actions, and regretted that he, Hitler, had himself not eliminated the German general staff 'as a treasonable organization'. Hitler knew little about Soviet politico-military matters, but, in the few months of life that he had remaining to him, the German dictator tried to make up for lost time by killing off the military that were suspected of treason or disloyalty, or were simply unsuccessful in battle. But the views of such political and historical commentators are based only on conjecture, and there is no evidence to suggest that there was any improvement in Red Army efficiency when the former 1936 commanders were removed: youth, and inexperience, were certainly given their chance, when colonels were replaced by lieutenants; but these, too, were under the repressive hand of the commissar system, the secret police special department in the Red Army, and the party and Komsomol organization within the ranks. And the end result was much the same. For the purges saw the end of any pretence of one-man command, and the military councils and the military commissars had been restored, if anything, with increased powers.

If the 1936 Red Army had been in existence in 1941 it would probably have fared no better or no worse than the army that was called upon to withstand the German invasion, and Tukhachevsky and his fellows would *then* have paid the ultimate price for their failure in the cellars of the Lubianka.

★   ★   ★

One of the many reasons for the Soviet victory in 1941–45 was the heavy industry and the armaments complex that came into being during the two five-year plans, and that continued to turn out equipment during the whole of the Second World War. Much of the enormous tank force that was in existence in 1941 was destroyed or fell into German hands, but even so it exacted some price, relatively small though this might have been, in the form of German losses. The responsibility for the setting up of this great Soviet armaments base appears to rest, and perhaps to rest solely, with Stalin. The success of Stalin's intervention in military matters during the thirties and the forties has, however, been a subject of much dispute, both in the Soviet and in the western press.

During the Civil War Stalin had been used by Lenin as one of the party's eyes and ears, a high-grade and powerful military commissar and trouble-shooter who acted as one of Lenin's representatives in threatened areas. Stalin's employment at this time had been no different from that of others in the Politburo and Central Committee, though it is probable that he may have been more effective, because of his arbitrariness and the weight of his fist, than all others except Trotsky. Stalin afterwards set himself up as a military brain of the highest order, because of what he called his defence of Tsaritsyn (that he later named Stalingrad in his own honour), of Perm and of Petrograd; and he used Voroshilov and his biographer to bring the Soviet public round to this view. But whereas much of Trotsky's military genius rested, in reality, on the promptings and advice of the military specialists, Stalin by his own volition would have nothing to do with them, preferring to consort with Voroshilov, Budenny, Dzerzhinsky and Shchadenko. And he wantonly interfered with military matters about which he knew little. The Red Army would probably have been unsuccessful in front of Warsaw in 1920 anyway, but it was largely due to Stalin's meddling that the Red Army was vanquished. In consequence it may be said that Stalin had occupied the most important of the commissar posts in the field but had shown evidence of no outstanding ability: he certainly had achieved little by his own design.

Even in the early twenties Stalin knew the importance of the army both to himself and to the Soviet Union and he continued to take a keen interest in the development and organization of the military; and, as the emerging dictator in 1925, he had successfully bound the armed forces to himself by replacing Frunze by his own man Voroshilov. Principally through Voroshilov and partly through

Molotov, Stalin had continued to exert the closest of control, through the direct military command as well as by political and police supervision, over the growth of the Red Army during the next sixteen years. His military experience was scanty and his knowledge may have been defective, but he thrust himself into the centre of military affairs and, in particular, of armament matters. Without Stalin's agreement, no army, air or naval armament decision of any importance could be settled.

When in the late thirties the admiral Kuznetsov was first appointed as People's Commissar for the Navy, in place of the purged Smirnov, he said that 'in his ignorance' he took all the important naval questions to Molotov, the defence committee chairman and chairman of the Council of People's Commissars (the prime minister). Molotov, however, merely waved him away and advised him to go to Stalin. Stalin, according to Kuznetsov, devoted much time to naval affairs and no one dared to act without his approval.[16] Kuznetsov's account is entirely supported by Hilger, who was part of the staff of the German embassy, for, in the renewed and brief Russo-German honeymoon in late 1939 and 1940, the Soviet leadership had regular meetings with the Germans seeking German naval assistance, meetings that the Russian-speaking Hilger (whose background was much like that of Köstring) had to attend. Hilger considered that Molotov had no creative mind or personal initiative, for he kept strictly to the rules laid down for him by Stalin. At meetings, Stalin, who held no government post, would ask Molotov to take the chair, and it was one of the rules of the game when important issues were at stake, said Hilger, that Molotov would decline. Stalin's manner was simple and unpretentious, but the paternal friendliness used to disarm the Germans that were present would turn into icy coldness when he rapped out short orders to People's Commissars (ministers), these standing to attention and making rapid written notes. Hilger had, in particular, noted the submissive attitude of Shaposhnikov, the successor to the purged Egorov as chief of general staff, when Stalin was in conversation with him.[17] Hilger was, however, surprised by the assurance with which Stalin made decisions on a wide variety of subjects, and by the extent of his technical knowledge when he chaired a joint meeting of Soviet and German naval experts, discussing the ordnance specifications of the turrets for a cruiser that Germany was to deliver to the Soviet Union. Without Stalin's express permission, said Hilger, it was impossible to obtain any Soviet agreement.[18]

Voroshilov's main military council appears to have been conducted in much the same way. Voroshilov had no head for detail or expert military knowledge and he preferred to act the extrovert and deal with people rather than with intricate problems; but, in any case, the onus of decision did not rest with him. Meretskov, the latter-day marshal, who was at that time the secretary of the council, has described how the council met two or three times a week; Stalin often attended the council meetings, but, whether he did or not, the minutes of the meeting were forwarded to his office to confirm or veto as he thought fit. Stalin was, according to Meretskov, well informed about the military commanders and army life in general, and he would frequently have supper with the council and the military district commanders and their senior staffs, and continue his talks far into the night.[19]

Military equipment seems to have been a near-obsession with Stalin. The Soviet designer Grabin said that Stalin wanted to know everything about artillery development and attended the artillery proving trials in 1935, together with Molotov and Voroshilov, and questioned the staff on the characteristics and performances of the guns on trial. He would pit the designers against each other, encouraging them to criticize each other's work, and bring them to the Kremlin so that the arguments could be continued in his presence.[20] Sometimes Stalin would get an idea into his head about a piece of equipment, and it would be difficult, even dangerous, to try and talk him out of it. Voronov, the head of artillery, had, in 1937, held to his own views, against Stalin's criticism, as to the acceptability of the 1936-pattern 76mm gun, Voronov's attitude being described, even in the 1969 Soviet press, as 'courageous'. Eventually Stalin had agreed with him, but matters did not always turn out that way.[21]

Soviet writers, whether favourable or unfavourable to the dictator, are unanimous that Stalin took a personal and the directing role in the development of army equipment.[22] According to Zhukov, the 1941 chief of general staff, no single pattern of armament could be adopted or discarded without Stalin's personal approval, 'a measure that certainly cramped the initiative of the Commissar for Defence [Voroshilov]'.[23] Stalin's direction, in the main, was of a practical nature and was usually based on common sense, and it is perhaps surprising what first-rate military equipment was produced at this time. The small-arms were still mainly of tsarist design, except for some new automatics and machine-guns, and these were all good: the artillery had been partly developed from tsarist originals and some of the newest designs were excellent. In so far as tanks were concerned, the Soviet leadership was still not sure of the armoured war that it was likely to fight or of the use to which it would put its own tanks; in consequence a large number of tank types began to appear, heavy and light, slow and fast, some being based on British or American originals. Inevitably the Soviets paid the price for overproduction in peace, and the tanks, untried in war, rapidly became obsolescent or obsolete. Even so, the standard of tank design was generally good and the tanks were much superior to the light-weight Mark I and II, the early German models that formed the first stopgap provision of the larger part of the German Army. In radio and in optical equipment, however, the Red Army was very poorly looked after, and its military aircraft were, at this stage, distinctly inferior to those being introduced into the *Luftwaffe*. But then Hitler had the advantage that he knew when he was going to start *his* war, and it would be before his newly manufactured equipment got out of date.

Stalin's overall direction was essentially practical and yet his knowledge was uneven, as was to be expected in one who had had no military experience or scientific training, and who would not necessarily be guided by those who had. Vannikov, the Commissar for Armament at that time, has told how Stalin wanted to equip the future generation of tanks (T 34s and K Vs) not with the 85mm anti-aircraft gun that Vannikov proposed but with the 107mm field gun, 'for Stalin knew the 107mm gun from the Civil War.'[24] The 1910–pattern 107mm gun with the 1930 recoil modification was, admittedly, still in service, and it had an excellent anti-tank capability; but to have used a gun of this type would have meant producing a new tank.[25] In another incident a year or so later, Stalin was said to have told Hopkins, Roosevelt's representative, who was not always a reliable source on military technicalities, that he needed a million or more American rifles, but not the ammunition since, 'if the calibre was the same as that used by the Red Army he had plenty'.[26]

Vannikov complained that a sudden idea or casual comment often settled a very weighty issue, and Kuznetsov said that it was easier to talk to Stalin alone than in committee or in company, where a decision often rashly given by the dictator was final, for he would not alter it. Emelianov, a metallurgist, confirmed this when he described a 1939 meeting in Stalin's office in the early hours of the morning to discuss a paper by one Nikolaev on double-skinned tank armour, a proposal that had already been judged as valueless by Emelianov. Nikolaev had described his armour as 'active instead of passive, because instead of being destroyed it protects'. These catchwords had fascinated Stalin and appeared to convince him. Stalin asked Nikolaev what had been the reactions of 'the representatives of industry': and when Nikolaev replied, using Emelianov's own words of rejection 'that there are no miracles in this world', the dictator had become angry and wanted to know *who* had said this. Nikolaev, trying to protect Emelianov, mumbled that he could not remember: 'Such people should be remembered,' Stalin had replied. Emelianov, who described himself as sick with fear, sat silent, though he knew that the experiment must fail.

In 1940, Emelianov attended another meeting to discuss the use of cast instead of pressed and welded turrets for the T 34 tank. Stalin wanted to know the tactical and user effects of such a turret as opposed to the technical production advantages. When Emelianov asked permission to speak, Stalin rounded on him, with 'What are you, a military man?' Undeterred, Emelianov provided the required answer, but since he unwittingly addressed the dictator as 'Josef Vissario-novich', using his forename and patronymic, instead of 'Comrade Stalin', he earned in thanks a scowl. Stalin turned back to the designer and the generals. 'How would the centre of gravity be changed by the new turret?' and 'What was the difference in load on the front axle?' The designer's reply of 'slight' was probably adequate at that stage, but the reply angered Stalin, for 'slight', he said, was not an engineering term. Emelianov again knew the answer, but his upraised arm was ignored. The proposal was rejected as inadequately prepared and Stalin ordered a new commission to handle it, the members to be the armoured general Fedorenko and 'him', Stalin pointed to Akopov, and 'him' with a jerk of the thumb towards Emelianov.[27] The cast turret was eventually introduced.

Air Marshal Vershinin said in 1948, when Stalin was still alive, that the dictator alone made the final decisions in aircraft development; this is supported by the air designer Iakovlev's account, written in 1966.[28] In 1940 Iakovlev was sent to Germany to inspect and purchase military aircraft, for the technical heads of Soviet industry were the great copiers and sometimes improvers of western designs; and Iakovlev had to cable his recommendations for purchasing direct to Stalin. Yet Stalin also sought opinions from outside of his immediate circle of official advisers, and would not necessarily be impressed by the success of a foreign pattern; and sometimes, according to Iakovlev, he sought opinions from the ignorant and inexperienced, accepting impractical plans sent direct and unsolicited by junior designers, simply because they caught his fancy.[29]

Though Stalin had no justifiable claim to military genius, there can be no doubt that he had great ability and flair. His associates and his foes are agreed that his was the controlling, and repressive, hand, with many weaknesses and many strengths, that armed the Soviet Union at this time, giving it, in terms of numbers, the greatest army in the world. There was in fact some similarity between the character and methods of this primitive Georgian, the self-made heir to the Romanov's, and those of the rough and untutored Austrian dictator who had set himself up as the successor to the Hohenzollerns.

*　　*　　*

In July 1938 fighting had broken out against the Japanese in the area of Lake Khasan, and, in the following May, there began a series of actions near Khalkin Gol. Soviet histories have, of course, built up their descriptions of what cannot have been more than scattered border fighting, into campaigns, almost a war, from which the Red Army emerged as totally victorious; these uncorroborated stories need to be read with reserve. But, in any event, they are unimportant in the story of the development of the Red Army.

The other foreign adventure made at this time was in Spain and, according to the Soviet account, it was as a result of the lessons learned there that the Soviet high command began to revise its earlier theories and armoured organizations that, so it now says, were based on Soviet-formulated doctrine of the use of massed tank forces as an operative arm. From the Soviet narrative it is not at all clear what were the factors in Spain that persuaded them so convincingly that they were on the wrong track, so leading them, they say, to break down their large mechanized corps into smaller brigade formations meant to support their dismounted infantry divisions. The Red Army men sent to Spain were few in number; on the enemy side, the German armour with Franco's forces was merely a small tank detachment under von Thoma. Pavlov, the Red Army general of tank forces in Spain, was subsequently blamed for the decision to break up the large armoured groupings, although this in itself means nothing.

The actual Soviet tank strength in the Soviet Union, contrary to what the Soviet military literature now says, was probably about 4,000 tanks in 1935 and 10,000 tanks in 1939, and its mechanized corps, each the equivalent of a panzer or western armoured division, stood at one only in 1934, increasing to two by 1936 and three by 1937. There is good evidence that by 1939 the total stood only at five; and there was no armoured formation above that of divisional size. However this may be, in November 1939, according to the Soviet account, the Red Army mechanized corps was phased out in favour of numerous independent brigades (in reality regiments) each with a fighting strength of about ninety tanks.

Soviet literature makes much ado about this as though the course of the 1941 battles were to depend on it. In fact it had little significance. Five or six mechanized corps, each of no more than 300 tanks or probably a good deal less, account for a very small proportion of the 10,000 tanks known to have been with the Red Army at that time: most of the remainder were presumably dispersed as independent units or as part of infantry field formations. All of this supports the view that there was no predominant school of Red Army thought that advocated the use of tanks in operative concentrations, and that the real change took place only after the victory of the massed panzer corps in France.

Guderian's theories were, however, impracticable without tactical air superiority, and here the Red Army was to be found wanting. But as the pattern of the new *Luftwaffe* emerged, the Soviets copied it, in that the Soviet heavy four-engined bomber force was relegated mainly to troop transport and air supply missions; and Soviet industry, like the German, began to concentrate on the production of fighters, ground-attack aircraft and light twin-engined bombers suitable for the support of ground operations. The Red Army aviator was of course a soldier whose main task, together with the artillery, was to provide fire support for the ground forces: he wore army uniform and could only be distinguished from an artilleryman or infantryman by the light blue colour of his service gorget patch. Neither he, nor his senior commanders, was interested in the destruction of the enemy economy or in strategic bombing in depth.

The air arm of the Red Army was made up of air brigades each of three squadrons, totalling about 100 aircraft, although this depended on the type of squadron; three brigades made an air corps.[30] From about 1940 the air brigades were replaced by air regiments, air divisions and air armies. Generally speaking, the air formations were not centralized at a high level, most air formations being put under the command of the military districts or the independent field armies to which they had been allocated. Nor, except in unusual circumstances or in the case of special air formations, did the chief of the military air forces exercise any personal control over the air battle, since the role of the air force was that of a support arm to the ground troops, like that of artillery, and the ground commander decided on the form this support should take. Operative or tactical orders came from the commander-in-chief (Voroshilov), through the army general staff, to the districts in peace and the fronts (army groups) or independent armies in war. From 1935 an independent air defence/anti-aircraft arm had been set up within the defence ministry and this was the nucleus of what was to become the homeland *PVO (Strany)* air defence command.

By 1939 the Red air force was large in numbers, having a total of about 5,000 military aircraft in service, but, of these, about eighty per cent were obsolescent or obsolete, and were, by German standards, often of crude design and poor performance. The speeds credited to the planes by the Soviet press are usually much exaggerated, for the standard fighters were the I 15 and I 153 biplane and the I 16 monoplane known as the *Rata*, planes that at maximum air speeds could be outpaced by some of the 1939 German medium bombers. Soviet aircraft auxiliary equipment was either of poor quality or entirely lacking, and radar and direction and locating aids were non-existent. Because the Soviet radio industry could not meet the needs of the armed services, there was little radio equipment available and planes could not communicate with each other, with the base airfield or with the troops on the ground, pilots being obliged to use flares or flight manoeuvre signals. This same shortage of radio equipment was to paralyse the Soviet armoured forces.

The Soviet forces were in fact, what the tsarist army had always been, numerous, cumbersome and unwieldy, with a command system that was largely inefficient, partly due to the inexperience and lack of training of the commanders of all ranks, and partly due to its poor system of control, particularly the lack of radio links at all levels. And superimposed on this outdated and inefficient command was the dual-control of the military commissars and the still fresh memories of the great purges. The Red Army commander at this time was much less ready to accept responsibility than the tsarist officer whom he replaced.

From May 1937 to August 1940 the commissar's powers had been fully restored so that he had a veto over the military commander in all matters, and his control and propaganda network of party members and Komsomols ensured that he was the best informed man in the formation or unit.[31] The most junior commissar ranks were those of political and senior political instructor (*politruk*), then battalion and senior battalion commissar, followed by regimental and brigade commissar, and so on, up the scale, the description being that of a rank and not of a function, so that a battalion commissar would be found with a regiment or a division, while a brigade commissar would be appointed to an army or front. In 1940, after the Finnish War had shown that the commissar's interference could be near disastrous, the principle of one-man command was re-established, only to be cancelled again in July 1941 in a vain effort to stem the German invasion. And it was not until October 1942 that the theoretical one-man command came back again and the word commissar fell into disuse, the former commissar becoming the political deputy (*zampolit*) and being given an army officer's rank. In reality the change was only one of name.

At this time there still remained some interchangeability between commanders and commissars, not only to fill immediate gaps caused by casualties but also in the structuring of their careers. A combatant commander could be transferred to and remain at commissar duties, and commissars could rise to high rank as commanders, Marshal Konev being such an example. But such exchanges were exceptional. The exact relationship between the commander and his commissar depended in part on their personalities and on the success that the formation or unit was enjoying at the time. Sometimes the relationship was good. It was not unknown later in the Second World War, when everything was going well, for a senior commander to have a trouble-making commissar removed – after a direct appeal to Stalin. But much depended on the political climate at the time. In times of repressions or purges, or if a purge were believed to be imminent, no man could trust his neighbour, and, at such times, the commissars, in self-preservation, would work hand in glove with the feared special department or sections of the NKVD secret police, and would themselves become objects of hatred. This was generally the situation between 1937 and 1942.

A secret police organization independent of commissar or *zampolit* remained then, as today, an integral part of the armed forces. In addition to the counter-intelligence NKVD special sections, who of course wore the normal Red Army uniform of the regiment to which they were accredited, there remained the border guards and internal security troops wearing army khaki uniform with their own distinctive badges, organized into divisions with tanks and artillery. These had their own generals who were in no way part of the Red Army, though these NKVD generals might, on occasions, be found in high military appointments and even commanding Red Army fronts or armies in the field. In emergency, NKVD field formations could be put under Red Army command, though it was only rarely that this happened, as their main purpose was to hold vital centres and to act as a backing and counter to the Red Army and prevent it from breaking under the stress of battle. In some respects the NKVD had similarities with the German *Waffen SS*: its members were mostly volunteers for that arm and were of proved political reliability; many of them, even by the Red Army standards at the time, were particularly brutalized.

* * *

The Second World War became inevitable when, on 23 August 1939, the Soviet Union signed the secret treaty with Hitler's Third Reich, a treaty of friendship by which the Soviet Union guaranteed the delivery of important raw materials and promised to undertake a war against Poland, jointly with Germany, in exchange for the half of Poland with ethnic Belorussian or Ukrainian (Ruthenian) populations and for the recognition by Berlin of certain Soviet interests in the Baltic and the Balkans. That the Soviet Union knew that this would bring about a general European war, there appears to be little doubt.[32]

Germany attacked Poland on 1 September and, that same day, the Soviet government lowered the conscription age for its own male population from twenty-one to nineteen; the two additional age groups were called up during October and November, this increasing the size of the armed forces to over 4,200,000 men, not including the quarter of a million men in the Internal Security Troops and Frontier Guards. The conscription term still stood at two years, except for technical arms and the air force and navy, but the service of army conscript non-commissioned officers had already been compulsorily extended from two to three years. No action was taken by Stalin to order war against Poland, notwithstanding the urging of the German Foreign Minister, von Ribbentrop, until a truce to the border fighting had been signed, on 16 September, with Japan. The fighting in Poland was by then almost over. Four armies of Kovalev's Belorussian military district and three armies of Timoshenko's Kiev military district crossed the frontier in what was little more than an advance to meet the German troops. This was followed by the mass murder or mass deportation of those parts of the Polish population that were considered to be inimical to the Soviet Union – the nobility, clergy, professional classes and intelligentsia: meanwhile, on the other side of the new Russo-German frontier, the Gestapo's heavy hand fell on the Polish Jews, the nobility, clergy and intelligentsia, with more murders and mass arrests.

Stalin intended to make good the gains that had been promised him by the secret protocol of the Russo-German Pact of the previous August. Already, as early as June 1939, he had instructed Meretskov, the commander of Leningrad military district, to draw up plans 'for a counter-offensive blow against Finland', a war that had to be won in the space of three weeks. Meanwhile the dictator set other planning staffs to work on the same project, independently and unknown to each other, and he accepted Meretskov's plan in preference to that of Shaposhnikov, the chief of general staff, because Shaposhnikov, in the dictator's view, exaggerated the difficulties and the likely resistance of the Finns.[33]

About twenty Red Army divisions were deployed against fifteen divisions of the Finns. The Red Army preparations had, however, been poorly planned and executed, and the command and control system soon broke down; this, and the exceptionally bitter weather, led to repeated Soviet failures and defeats.[34] Stalin was particularly agitated about the delays since he feared French, British and Swedish intervention, and he was very sensitive about the foreign press that was full of unfavourable, even derisive, comment on the quality of the

Red Army. In January Timoshenko took over the operational command from Meretskov, and Mekhlis, the head of the PUR political administration and chief military commissar, was sent to the area 'to recommend the shooting' of divisional commanders.[35] The final offensive began in February and lasted for four weeks, and among the commanders who were said to have distinguished themselves were the cavalryman Timoshenko, the artilleryman Voronov, the tankman Pavlov and the infantrymen Meretskov and Kirponos. Finland had been defeated but not overrun, and it remained an independent nation.

The experience of the Finnish War had had a sobering effect on Stalin and, in April and May of 1940, he was reported to have said that 'the cult of the revolutionary war and the experience of the Civil War were proving to be obstacles to progress in bringing the Red Army up to date.'[36] The first casualty was Voroshilov, who was replaced by Timoshenko as Commissar for Defence. An attempt was made to sweep away some of the political jargon and shibboleths of the revolutionary army, and to equate the Red Army with the armies on the European model. The ranks of general and admiral were restored (instead of *komandarm*, *komkor* and *komdiv*) and the contemporary Soviet military press actually began to praise the military discipline *of the German troops* of the First World War.[37] In August 1940, the principle of single command was reintroduced, the military commissar again becoming theoretically subordinate to the commander. Discipline had broken down during the Finnish War where some commanders 'had been unwilling or unable to control their men;' by the new 1940 disciplinary code, commanders became liable to be court-martialled if, in cases of necessity, they did not use their personal arms to shoot any who disobeyed an order.[38]

Between November 1939 and May 1940 the mechanized corps (that is to say the armoured divisional) headquarters had disappeared, leaving, according to the Soviet account, thirty-five medium and four heavy tank brigades (the equivalent of regiments) and ninety-eight tank battalions with the rifle and cavalry divisions, in all, the Soviets claim, 13,000 armoured fighting vehicles (of which probably not more than 10,000 were tanks of all types and ages).[39] Then, following on the defeat of the French Army, the Red Army armour was hurriedly reorganized on the German pattern, the new mechanized corps being this time real corps and not understrength divisions like the old: these were in fact copies of the German motorized corps and each consisted of two tank divisions and one motorized infantry division, each mechanized corps consisting, they claim, of over 1,000 tanks – in reality probably nearer 700 tanks – of which some were said to be the new KV 1 heavies and T 34 mediums.[40] The Red Army was still floundering, however, and there remained a wide difference of opinion as to the proper role of armour and how to use these new formations. Even Timoshenko, the new minister of defence, and Meretskov, as director of training, were unable to find common ground.

With the benefit of hindsight one can now say that the Red Army might have been better advised to have kept its old 1940 small tank formations in that the 1941 invasion was to find it with a new and untried field organization: in any event the Red Army did not have the military education and skill, the mental agility or flexibility, the radio communications or the air power that were all vital to the conduct of mobile armoured operations on the massive scale. And when the Germans had almost wiped out the Russian tank force in the course of the first year of the war, the Soviet military command was forced, for the next two years, to be satisfied with smaller armoured formations, generally not exceeding 100 tanks, as this was the greatest number that could be controlled and maintained and that could operate as an entity under an unfavourable air situation.

In the short period left before the German invasion of the Soviet Union there was a hurried reorganization of the Soviet high command and of the Red Army field forces. Zhukov, a former tsarist cavalry non-commissioned officer, was recalled from the Far East, to take command of Kiev military district: the Belorussian military district went to Pavlov, the tank man with experience in Spain; Kirponos was given the Leningrad military district while Voronov returned to the main artillery directorate.[41] And Stalin continued his late-night *dacha* consultations that were attended by his military chiefs and also by Voroshilov, Budenny and Mekhlis, for none of the old guard seems to have fallen out of favour, together with Beria the head of the NKVD and secret police. Shaposhnikov had been unwell and had not escaped some censure for the Finnish débâcle: he went to military fortifications and was replaced by Meretskov as chief of general staff: the latter, proving unsatisfactory because his education was not sufficient for the appointment, was replaced at Timoshenko's request by

Zhukov, another who was to prove unsuited for the staff either by education or temperament.[42] Zhukov's command at the Kiev military district went to Kirponos who was himself replaced in Leningrad by F. I. Kuznetsov.

By February 1941 the principal actors had already taken their places for the opening stages of the Russo-German War. The Soviet Union had collected a great mass of intelligence information that pointed towards the imminence of invasion, but Stalin did not choose to believe it and threatened dire consequences to any adviser who expressed a view to the contrary.[43] Nevertheless there had been a secret partial mobilization in the early part of 1941, and the 150 Soviet divisions in the west, that were, in fact, slightly more numerous than the whole of the German invasion force, had been brought up to a war footing. The total Russian tank strength was numerically three times the size of the German, while the air force was nearly twice as strong as the attacking *Luftwaffe*. The total Red Army field establishment, including skeleton divisions not yet embodied and the two independent armies in the Far East, stood at a little over 300 divisions, that is to say it was, in numbers of field formations, one and a half times as strong as the 208 divisions of the whole of the German Army.[44] But numbers by themselves mean little without taking into account training, battle experience, morale, leadership and equipment. Except in equipment, the Red Army was a poor second to the *Wehrmacht*, and this was well known to Stalin.[45]

For a man so able, it is surprising what extraordinary notions Stalin had and how very wide of the mark was his evaluation of the worth of those around him. Like the other dictator he required implicit obedience; loyalty he got through fear, together with praise and flattery, of which, apparently, he could never have enough. Self-willed, he secured his own achievements and made his own mistakes, for his advisers feared to advise him, although they knew that he would hold *them* responsible for *his* mistakes. Some of the senior 'politicos' and generals in his circle were of limited worth, yet he retained them in high and responsible positions: there was Voroshilov, who was shortly to be given a group of forces; Budenny, the first deputy to Timoshenko; Kulik, the head of the main artillery directorate responsible not only for the provision of all artillery but for much of the ammunition of all types and the guns and common-user equipment for the whole of the Red Army, a man who was known to be of little use: Mekhlis, the Commissar for State Control, the chief military commissar and head of the PUR, and Shchadenko who headed the main Red Army directorate for personnel, both of them dangerous, ill-natured men of a destructive turn of mind. All of these had been part of the 1918 Tsaritsyn group. Many, if not all, were Stalin's spies who were ready to inform on and denounce those about them. And they were also ready, as were even the more talented of Stalin's military men, to subordinate their own wills and characters according to the Stalin mould, and they could always be relied upon to do Stalin's bidding at any cost to themselves or to others.

CHAPTER FIVE

The Second World War

In the first few months of the German invasion of the Soviet Union the Red Army suffered a series of staggering defeats, the extent of which is still hidden by the Soviet government and historians, for the German panzer forces, closely supported by fighters, dive-bombers and other ground-attack aircraft, made deep inroads into Russia. By August Pavlov's West Front in Belorussia had been encircled and destroyed with a loss of 309,000 prisoners, 3,000 guns taken and 3,200 tanks out of action or captured.[1] But when they had reached Smolensk and were close to Moscow, the Germans unaccountably changed direction; instead of resuming the march eastwards on the capital, that was virtually undefended, on Hitler's orders they regrouped and struck due southwards, encircling and destroying Kirponos's South-West Front in the Ukraine, taking, by 26 September, a further 665,000 prisoners, another 3,000 guns but only 800 tanks.[2] It appeared as if there were no Russian forces left to defend the oil-bearing Caucasus. Once again, however, Hitler changed the axis of his main strategic offensive and decided to resume the march from Smolensk in the centre on to Moscow.[3] These changes of strategic plan, stretching over fronts a thousand or more miles in extent and involving the movement of a million troops, first to the south and then back to the north, could not be carried out without delay for concentration and preparation, and it was October before the reinforced German Army Group Centre, that had been idle since late July, was ready to resume the advance on Moscow. By then the onset of winter was hardly two weeks away. Nevertheless, the immediate German successes were colossal, with the capture in fourteen days of 558,000 prisoners, 4,000 guns and 1,000 tanks, from the force that the Soviet military command had built up anew to defend Moscow.[4] Once again the road to the capital seemed to be open.

The reasons for the disastrous failure of the Red Army are not hard to find. The Germans did not catch the Soviet Union by surprise, for the *Wehrmacht* build-up before June 1941 was known not only in Moscow but also to the Red Army field command: more could and should have been done to put the border military districts on a war footing, but, even so, the Red Army was, in numbers and equipment, as strong as the German forces that attacked it.[5] In general it was quality that was lacking in the Red Army, in leadership, training, morale, and, above all, in battle-experience. The showing of the Soviet high command was very poor because Stalin and his immediate circle, ignorant of war, tried to direct all operations, from strategic counter-strokes to tactical engagements, from their map tables in the Moscow Kremlin, allowing no initiative or latitude to the men in the field. Stalin ordered his hard-pressed demoralized formations to launch great counter-offensives; he forbade any withdrawals, and so delivered them to the German POW camps.[6] And the dictator put his two incompetent aides, Voroshilov and Budenny, and later Timoshenko, as theatre commanders in the west, these men being given the command of groups of fronts.[7] But, in any event, beyond his stand-still order, Stalin and his immediate subordinates had little effect on the battles at any levels, since there had been a breakdown in the Soviet communication system everywhere. The field commanders themselves did not know what was going on and were helpless to influence events since they lacked the means, the competence and the initiative to rectify the situation, and fatalistically regarded their own freedom or lives as forfeit as soon as the Moscow command should re-establish itself and Stalin should learn of the true extent of their defeat.

The reaction of the foremost units in those early days was varied and unpredictable. Some fought stubbornly and well. Others took to their heels: many threw away their arms and uniforms and donned looted peasant clothing, much as their fathers had done a generation before.[8] Many took to the forests in great bands, not with the purpose of harassing the Germans (that was to come later), but solely to escape the enemy: and from these hide-aways they pillaged and terrorized the countryside as the earlier tsarist army deserters had done in the First World War. But, in general, the well-documented count of prisoners and warlike equipment falling into German hands tells its own story.

The Soviet Union has made much of the heroic resistance put up by its troops during this first six months of the war and it has compared its showing, to its own advantage, with that of the French Army during 1940. That some of its troops did display outstanding heroism in the field there can be no doubt, but that is generally true of some of the troops of all nations in war. But, in the main, the Soviet account is grossly exaggerated and much of it is quite false. In Soviet fashion, certain incidents and certain sectors were selected for propaganda treatment, to bolster morale at home and present the Red Army in a better light to the world; these press releases were repeated in the British news media, for no foreign correspondent was allowed near the front; and, as time went on, the descriptions were further embellished and were given a permanent place in the Soviet history books. The Soviet defence of the frontier town of Brest-Litovsk is such an example, where an obstinate defence of a few days has been extended to an epic saga of six weeks, with the usual communist descriptions (that Trotsky had once sneered at) that made everyone a hero, always fighting 'to the last man and the last round', dying with curses to the enemy and with the praises of the Soviet Fatherland on their lips.[9] Much of it reads like a boys' paper.

Another such propaganda exercise was that which centred on the heroic Soviet defence of the Smolensk sector in August and September 1941 where the Red Army is supposed to have brought the *Wehrmacht* to a standstill before Moscow (the halt that was in reality brought about by Hitler's orders and the change of direction to the Ukraine in the south).[10] It was later portrayed as a defeat of the German forces moving on Moscow, and the Soviet units that took part were given the title of guards, a piece of propaganda that may have been of some benefit at the time if it improved the morale of the Soviet people: but the fiction has now been widely accepted as truth inside, and sometimes outside, of the USSR.[11] The propaganda use in wartime of isolated incidents, real or fictitious, and their magnification and dressing up to sweeten the bitterness of defeat, is not new; the chroniclers of ancient Rome tried to conceal the extent of their military disasters in the same way. The Germans were relatively free from it at this time because they were winning and did not need to resort to such trickery, but when the fortune of war changed after Stalingrad, they indulged in it frequently enough.

However this may be, guards titles became a feature of the Red

Army from this time onwards for the rest of the war, the titles being given to formations or to units of the air and ground forces, even to warships. With the award went guards badges and special rates of pay for officers and men. The word 'guards' can still be found today in the designations of some higher headquarters, but it is now merely an honorific traditional title of historic interest only.

Soviet military and political historians, in comparing the performance of the Red Army with those of the western nations and, in particular, with the French Army, have claimed, somewhat inconsequentially, that no state in the world could have lost so much territory to the enemy and still have remained in the war. As against this, of course, it can be argued that no other country had as much to lose. If the territories of the Soviet Union had been no more extensive than those of France with a frontier and a hinterland of 600 miles with an ocean behind, then nothing could have saved the Soviet Union or the Red Army, in the condition in which they stood in 1941, from complete and utter defeat at the hands of Hitler's *Wehrmacht*, notwithstanding the determination of its communist leaders and the resistance and stamina of its rank and file. This defeat would have been complete within three months, for there would have been no place to which to withdraw or to flee.

The 1940 German military intelligence handbook on the Red Army was poor; its British equivalent, on the other hand, was very well informed.[12] Yet the British (and United States) military observers in Moscow had apparently shared Köstring's view that the Red Army was, at the best, a second-class force; for it is said that the British military appreciations made in London in that late summer of 1941 considered that Soviet resistance could not last much longer.[13] Based on a purely military assessment of the capabilities of the inexperienced Red Army with its poor showing and appalling losses on the one hand, and the known prowess of the battle-experienced *Wehrmacht* on the other, it is easy to see how these opinions were arrived at. But the conclusions proved to be entirely wrong, for they took too little account of the nature of communism and the Soviet leadership: nor did the British at that time have any real understanding of the revolutionary changes that had taken place since 1938 in the German politico-military leadership; nor did they know the extent of the crisis in the German Army equipment situation, for the German Army was already over-extended. But the all-important factor that was presumably not appreciated by the British staff spokesmen, the factor that outweighed all others, was the climatic and geographical conditions within Russia and their effect on movement, supply and on the waging of war. For the effect of space and of the *rasputitsa* (the breaking up of the Russian roads and tracks due to frosts and thaw, that might occur several times in a winter), to say nothing of the cold and snow, to use Köstring's words, 'had to be experienced to be believed.'[14]

The mid-October frosts, interspersed with continual heavy rain and cold that was to herald the snow, brought an immediate stop to German movement and a sudden falling off in the violence of the *Wehrmacht* attacks. For many weeks after that there was little activity in front of Moscow, and this gave the Soviet leadership sufficient respite to allow new armies to be brought up to replace those lost. In November the ground froze and hardened, so permitting some movement, but then came the snow. The German panzer formations, that had numbered no more than 3,300 tanks all told at the beginning of the war, were a shell of their former selves, largely due to track mileage, wear and tear and the inability of the tank repair and resupply organization to replace tank casualties quickly: personnel casualties had not been made good and the fuel and parts supply was precarious, for the wide Russian railway track had not been converted to Central European gauge and the *Reichsbahn* locomotive and rolling stock were inadequate in numbers and unsuitable for cold weather.[15] The larger part of the German Army was not motorized but relied on the draught-horse to move artillery, equipment and supplies. German tank mobility over ice and in deep snow was not good owing to the narrow design of the tank tracks. In any case, German operative armoured mobility was already a thing of the past, and the lack of numbers precluded any use of tanks *en masse*: German air support had been much reduced, partly because of the weather and partly due to the enforced transfer of a *Luftflotte* to Sicily. When the German advance was resumed it was made by the plodding riflemen of the understrength infantry formations, tired and battle-worn, frozen and ill-equipped for winter, for no winter clothing was to be had.[16] The war had already entered an entirely different phase.

What was left of the Red Army in the west was made up of formations from the far north or the far south flanks, divisions that had not yet been engaged or had managed to escape in front of the advancing enemy forces, together with some troops from the interior, including some withdrawn from Siberia and the Far East; there were, too, new divisions that had been hastily thrown together. Comparatively few tanks were left and these were grouped into small supporting units, rarely above a regiment in strength and never above a brigade, and these tank units were thinly spread over the whole front. The artillery losses had been so heavy that the artillery regiments within infantry divisions were often re-equipped with a variety of mortars, light smooth-bore weapons that were either portable or towed on a light wheeled axle; though these lacked range and accuracy, they were very mobile and rapid-firing, and, if the mortar bomb supply allowed, could bring down a very heavy weight of fire. The Red Army still seemed to have plenty of small-arms, rifles and machine-guns, and this gives some indication of the large stockpiles that the Soviet Union must have amassed during the two five-year plans. There was very little motor transport available, and the bulk of the Red Army depended (as did the German infantry divisions) on the horse and the soldiers' feet for movement, though a few ski battalions were used for deep reconnaissance.[17]

The Red air force had been completely outclassed by the *Luftwaffe* in skill and training and in the speed, range, manoeuvrability and rate of climb of its aircraft, and it had suffered enormous casualties. Yet at no time, even in the earliest and darkest days, had it been completely overwhelmed. In some sectors it had been obliterated, but in others it was active in small numbers, and for this it had to thank the vast extent of the fronts and hinterland and the fact that the *Luftwaffe* was not large enough to control the whole theatre of war. For a large part of the German air force had already been withdrawn after the first few months of the war to cover the western defence of the Reich and the new war in the Mediterranean.[18]

Another reason for the survival of the Red air force lay in the large numbers of aircraft that it had kept in service, using them for purposes for which they had not been designed. Come what may, the Russians always seemed to have something in the air in the most adverse weather conditions, for, in spite of the relatively low standard of their training, aviators and ground crews had great endurance and hardiness, being particularly clever at improvisation, and it was the Soviet practice to keep on operations even obsolete aircraft of very doubtful value. Yet, though the Red air force came into its own again during that first winter, in that it could occasionally be seen and heard, its numbers were too small and its use too scattered for it to have had any important effect on the course of operations, where low cloud and poor weather conditions blanketed off the men on the ground.

The German soldier of early 1941 and his officer were at that time probably the most competent in the world: and the German Army appeared to be provided with a lavish supply of brand-new equipment. Yet in truth the German Army would not have defeated the French in so short a time – might not have defeated the French Army at all – had it not been for its dynamic leadership and the revolutionary use of tank and air power. If the German Army had invaded France counting, as it had in 1914, on the strength of its foot-marching infantry divisions, the advancing tide might eventually have been held by the French. And the situation in Russia would have been similar. If the German Army of 1941 had invaded the Soviet Union relying for success on its 110 dismounted infantry divisions rather than on its thirty panzer and motorized formations spearheaded by *Luftwaffe* fighters and dive-bombers, then – taking into account the resources available to both sides and the frontages, depths, terrain and endless hinterland, together with the harshness of the climate – it is probable that the Red Army would have brought the German advance to a halt much earlier. This would have been likely within three months of the start of the war and on a line not more than 250 miles within the Russian frontier. For, saved from the conditions of blitzkrieg war, the Russian would have had time to gain battle experience, and time and opportunity to dig himself in. A Russian, once dug in, becomes a formidable opponent.

It was not until late November 1941 that the Red Army remnant was finally able to come to grips with Hitler's invading forces on rather better than equal terms, for the German Army had, for the moment, shot its bolt and lay dispersed and exhausted over a vast territory that measured 2,000 by nearly 1,000 miles: the *Wehrmacht* was, in addition, holding down an occupied and enemy Europe, stretching from the Arctic circle to North Africa and the Atlantic to Rostov near the gateway to the Caucasus. For the moment its massed panzer forces were no more, being immobile or temporarily abandoned. What was to have been another brilliant *summer campaign*, this time to destroy the Soviet Union, had misfired, leaving Germany with the prospect of a long and costly two-fronted war. In the December of that year, Hitler, without taking advice from anyone, declared war on the USA.

The German dictator then began his search for scapegoats for the failure of his blitzkrieg in Russia, purging his high command of its more eminent generals, including Guderian and other armoured specialists; for Hitler had himself taken over the post of commander-in-chief of the German Army in addition to that that he already held of commander-in-chief of the *Wehrmacht*.[19] From this time onward, and for the rest of the Second World War, Hitler became obsessed with the holding of ground: any withdrawal, however minor, was forbidden: all that was needed, he said, was to keep one's nerve at the front.[20] In doing this Hitler repeated the error already made by Stalin during the summer of 1941. But Hitler could not stop the turn of the tide, and his insistence on trying to do so by holding ground merely exposed his ill-clad and unsheltered men to the bitter weather and encirclement by the Russian infantry who were operating from bases close to their rear. The German Army was forced back, in the centre nearly 200 miles, and its casualties, particularly in sick and in abandoned equipment, were very high. For the first time in the war there had arisen a feeling of acute anxiety among the generals in the German high command, and uncertainty within the ranks of the German troops on the eastern front, fearful doubts that would be lifted, and then only temporarily, by the coming of spring.[21]

★   ★   ★

Stalin's initial reaction to the June 1941 invasion had been one of shock, and a withdrawal to his own quarters in a state of mental depression. Then followed a search for scapegoats, spies and traitors.

Very shortly before the German invasion, Stalin had replaced Molotov as prime minister, an appointment that had been made public in the Soviet and world press, presumably to give Berlin notice that Moscow knew of the critical, threatening situation. Immediately after the invasion, fourteen annual classes were mobilized and Stalin began to reform the high command defence organization, taking as his precept Lenin's committees during the Civil War. A defence committee (GKO) was formed with Stalin as its chairman, its character being mainly political and industrial. Timoshenko the minister of defence was appointed as the nominal commander-in-chief of the armed forces until, a week or so later, Stalin himself took over the post (though this was concealed from the outside world). To assist him as commander-in-chief Stalin formed what he called a *Stavka*, an organization that had nothing in common with the tsarist general headquarters (that had consisted of about 200 officers), but was a small military committee of advisers, most of them generals.[22] And, just as Lenin had done before him, Stalin sent out Politburo members and trusted communists to replace the professional military commissars at the principal fronts: at first these had no ranks or else took commissar ranks, but after 1942 they all took generals' ranks. Timoshenko was sent into Belorussia, with Bulganin as his commissar, to form a West Theatre and try to save the only front at first under his command, Pavlov's West Front, from destruction. Voroshilov, with Zhdanov as his commissar, went to Leningrad, while Budenny and commissar Khrushchev set out for the Ukraine. Pavlov was replaced by Eremenko, and 'on Eremenko's recommendation', so said the Stalin-edited order, Pavlov and those around him were shot.[23] Numerous arrests followed, and there were fears among Red Army officers of a new purge of 1937 proportions. The command personnel were those who suffered, the military commissars usually saving themselves by denunciations, and this led to a reversal of the previous restoration of one-man command, the party-watchdog commissar having his original veto restored to him so that he openly became what he had secretly always been – the commander's commander.

Stalin's mania was such that he put down all failure, even his own inadequacies, to the treachery of others: Hitler was to behave in very much the same fashion between 1943 and 1945. Stalin's immediate reaction to defeat was the restoration of the powers of the military councils and the military commissars: in 1944 Hitler, too, introduced his commissars.[24] Whether or not Stalin's new repressions proved any safeguard of the armed forces' loyalty is more than doubtful, and certain it is that they did nothing to improve efficiency. The general staff and the command in the field became unnerved, for the military commissars were not slow to take advantage of their new position, 'making wild accusations of treachery, exaggeration and panic-spreading'. The Germans reported that the Red Army officer was generally liked by the rank and file, but only too rarely did the 1941 commissar enjoy their trust: on being captured, commissars hastily rid themselves of the hammer and sickle insignia stitched on the sleeve; but this did not save them from detection, for they were often denounced to their German captors by the Soviet other ranks. The Pavlov *affaire* shook the confidence of the troops and the civil population in its Red Army commanders, doing much more harm than good, and for this reason it was a pattern that was not repeated.[25] The shootings continued, of course, but the disappearance and subsequent fate of unlucky or unsuccessful commanders remained a state secret, unknown to the public inside of the Soviet Union.

During the summer and autumn of 1941, disaster followed disaster. Zhukov was replaced as the chief of general staff by Shaposhnikov who returned to his old job once more; Zhukov said that he himself was sacked by Stalin because 'he advised the withdrawal of Kirponos's South-West Front before it should be destroyed.' Budenny, apparently, took the same view as Zhukov, but as Stalin regarded any hint of withdrawal as treason or panic, Budenny, too, lost his post to Timoshenko, who was sufficiently inflexible in his mental attitude to find some temporary favour with the dictator.[26] These many changes of command and the frequent interferences from the Kremlin-based Stalin, who was haranguing and threatening his front commanders over the Baudôt line teleprinter (in the periods when this was working), speeded the already rapid collapse. Eremenko's Bryansk Front was defeated and Kirponos's South-West Front was destroyed: the fate of Kirponos and the other three members of his military council, one of them the Soviet military attaché in Berlin until the outbreak of war, has never been satisfactorily explained.

The same chain of events followed when the Germans resumed their early October offensive, in what was to have been the march on Moscow. After Timoshenko had been moved to the south, the West Theatre no longer existed and the two new fronts that were being formed there, Konev's West Front, and Budenny's Reserve Front, together with Eremenko's Bryansk Front, were directly under Stalin's command, their orders being received through the general staff – for the general staff was Stalin's personal executive. The final German armoured offensive of 1941 had opened like a whirlwind between 28 September and 2 October, and had had lightning success in what was left of the fine weather. The Bryansk Front fell apart and Konev's and Budenny's Fronts were mostly encircled and destroyed in the area of Vyazma in a space of ten days with a loss of forty-five divisions, von Bock's Army Group Centre war diarist noting that 'the enemy has been surprised and put up little resistance.'[27] On the Soviet side there was the usual inadequacy of command and lack of control, followed by a general paralysis once battle was joined, very much as had happened to the French Army in 1940, for this was the effect on the victim of the panzer onslaught. Rokossovsky, one of Konev's army commanders, said that he did not know what was going on from first to last, since he received few orders and no information.[28] Konev subsequently blamed the *Stavka*, that is to say Stalin.[29]

A cogent reason why information and intelligence was not passed back to the *Stavka*, even when the communication system to Moscow was still working, was that commanders feared to report reverses; for if they should be held in any way responsible for the defeat they might be punished as traitors, and if they were merely reporting the failure of others they could be arrested as panic-spreaders. At this time the head of Moscow military district air force was threatened by the NKVD with arrest when he produced air photographs showing German tanks at Yukhnov, well in the Soviet rear.[30] And when, on the night of 7 October, Zhukov was sent from Moscow by Stalin to the West Front headquarters to report what was afoot, he found the West Front military council, consisting of Konev, Sokolovsky and Bulganin, 'in session'. According to Zhukov, the West Front council did, at this time, understand the full extent of the defeat and encirclement, but they had not told Stalin, and they left this unpleasant duty to Zhukov.[31]

A day or two later came the very heavy rains and the onset of winter that brought all German movement to a halt. In Civil War fashion, Stalin set up a number of political, NKVD and military investigating commissions bent on arrest and shooting, the most senior of these being a GKO commission made up of Voroshilov, Molotov, and Malenkov, with Vasilevsky from the general staff in attendance. The stuttering civilian Molotov, according to Konev, dictated 'with the greatest of persistence' how the troops should be redeployed.[32] Konev lost his post to Zhukov but eventually reappeared with a newly forming Kalinin Front in the same sector.

On 7 October *Pravda* had reported the giving up of the city of Vyazma 'after a glorious and heroic struggle'. There had been no struggle in Vyazma and the extent of the disaster could not be concealed from the Muscovites. There was panic and looting in the capital, and the foreign embassies and some departments of goverment were speedily evacuated eastwards to Kuibyshev.[33] A new

GKO decree, dictated by Stalin, provided for 'the strengthening of controls, the setting up of military tribunals and the shooting on the spot' of real or imaginary offenders.[34] Much of the Soviet armament industry that was in Western Russia at the outbreak of the war had already been moved to the Ural armament complex founded in the thirties.

The early winter respite was apparently used to good advantage in that more replacement armaments began to arrive in the war theatre, 2,000 guns, but only 300 tanks, arriving at the West Front during early November.[35] According to the Soviet account, nine new armies were concentrated in depth roughly on a north-south line from Onega to Astrakhan, the forming and concentration of these armies being, in Vasilevsky's opinion, one of the most important factors in deciding the outcome of the winter war. With the break-up of the roads the Red Army became largely reliant for movement, and wholly reliant for supply, on the railways: this was an advantage denied to the Germans. In order to ensure that these nine Soviet armies could be moved westwards as soon as they were needed, the Moscow railway network and the main east-west lines were put under the control of the military.[36] About fifteen regular divisions were brought from the Far East and Siberia at about this time, and more were to follow after the Japanese attack on Pearl Harbour.[37]

In 1940 the general staff in Frunze Street had been part of the NKO and was entirely subordinate to the Commissar for Defence. From July 1941, after Stalin had become the commander-in-chief and ground forces commander, the general staff no longer had any direct responsibility to the NKO since it had become Stalin's personal instrument and reported to him in the Kremlin: no one else could give it orders or demand information from it, not even the most senior members of the GKO or *Stavka*. That summer Stalin removed from the general staff a number of supplementary and technical responsibilities such as signals and supply and rear services planning, transferring them to the NKO, since he wanted the general staff to concentrate entirely on the immediate war strategic and operative battle plans. The lot of the general staff was not, however, an enviable one, for Stalin held it in low regard during the first months of the war and he constantly vented his anger on it. It was rarely consulted and military decisions were usually taken above its head by Stalin, following discussion with Politburo or GKO members or those whom Stalin

10 A 45 mm anti-tank gun in action in the streets of Rostov on Don in 1942

11 Red Army artillery moving through Kiev at the end of 1943; the gun is
a 76 mm 1939-pattern field piece

12 Cavalry of 3 Ukrainian Front in March 1944 taking artillery ammunition
forward

13 Red Army infantry supported by open-topped armoured SU 76
tank-destroyers (on T 70 chassis) in East Prussia in April 1945

14 Crews of 76 mm guns M 42
in Hungary, March 1945

15 Red Army sappers and
pioneers building a bridge over
the Oder in 1945

16 T 34 tanks on the Pacific coast, August 1945

17 From left to right: (*front*) Konev, Vasilevsky, Zhukov, Rokossovsky, Meretskov; (*rear*) Tolbukhin, Malinovsky and Govorov (all eight Marshals of the Soviet Union), and army generals Eremenko and Bagramian

judged to be informed on the subject. In the early days the general staff was used merely to transmit Stalin's orders.[38]

Vasilevsky, later a Marshal of the Soviet Union, had once been a tsarist *praporshchik* and *shtabs-kapitan* of the Novokhopersky regiment; he was a man of ability and great lucidity of thought and expression. According to Vasilevsky's 1974 memoirs (and Vasilevsky, firstly as deputy and then as chief of general staff, came to know Stalin very well indeed), Stalin covered the widest range of subjects and demanded exhaustive information about any matter under discussion, occasionally asking the chief of general staff for comment, but, more often than not, deciding himself: and, said Vasilevsky, the dictator gave out his orders without using a single superfluous word — certainly a departure from the general staff direction of the tsars. Stalin, continued Vasilevsky, spared neither himself nor others: he was an excellent organizer and his organizing ability was eventually to play the main role in bringing strategic and operative plans to fruition. He alone found and allocated reinforcements and *matériel*. All this, however, was to come at a later stage of the war, for early on, particularly in 1941 and 1942, as Vasilevsky has said, 'Stalin made miscalculations, some of them grievous, for he was unjustifiably self-confident and presumptuous [*samonadeian*] and overrated his knowledge and ability in the military field.' He often changed commanders without good reason and his interference brought about what Vasilevsky euphemistically called 'unsatisfactory results'. Stalin demanded that others should not be enslaved by old ideas and should learn by modern methods, but in the beginning he could not do this himself. His leadership, said Vasilevsky, was personal and arbitrary. Vasilevsky's judgement is borne out by what was reported by western participants at such joint meetings that did take place in Moscow at this time.[39]

There was in fact some similarity in Stalin's and Hitler's characters, in their methods of waging war and in their relationship with their generals and military staffs, with one most important exception. Before 1941 Hitler worked fairly amicably, at least on the surface, with his generals, though there were a few whom he did not like, notably Fritsch and Beck: most of the German generals were in fact supporters, often enthusiastic disciples, of the *Führer*, and the German dictator's relationship with his high command was generally good. Hitler learned much from his generals and in turn benefited them by his unconventional approach to warfare and by his support of new and revolutionary ideas. But this honeymoon lasted only until December 1941, when the generals realized at last that the *Führer* had overreached himself; they then saw him for what he was, a glib, quick-thinking and convincing adventurer with a military flair that had, however, no basis in a foundation of experience or study. They paid for their disenchantment with dismissal, and the political *Führer* became the military *supremo*, personally controlling the German war machine on the eastern front, as elsewhere. Indeed, until the end of his life, he did little else, and the war in Russia developed into a mania, so that, as the German failures and the defeats began to mount, he directed his rising fury against his military subordinates. From this time onwards German generals were allowed no initiative or latitude: they simply had to obey the dictator's orders and hold on to every inch of Russian ground under threat of punishment. His unlucky com-manders, many of whom had done nothing more than obey his orders to the letter and thereby invite encirclement, were removed to the reserve: later, as the war situation worsened, they were, at Hitler's order, stripped of rank and pension, or court-martialled and sen-tenced to death: then, at the final stage of the war, were to come the Gestapo arrests, the torture chambers and the hangings. From 1942 onwards Hitler waged his own personal war, sacrificing the German people and Germany's allies: and he did this entirely arbitrarily and without seeking political or military advice, for he could not abide any who would not agree with him.

With Stalin, on the other hand, the situation was largely reversed. Stalin's military direction during 1941 and 1942 had much in common with that of Hitler from 1943 to 1945. But Stalin's working relation-ship with his own general staff and high command was to improve in some degree, as the war progressed and as the Red Army slowly became an effective fighting force; and this improvement dated from the 1941–42 winter campaign. As soon as the final German thrust had been brought to a halt in the northern outskirts of Moscow in the first few days of December, and the exhausted and near-frozen Germans had begun to give ground not only near Moscow, but in the north and south at Tikhvin and Rostov, there was for the first time in the war a rise in Soviet morale both in the Kremlin and with the Red Army troops in the field. Stalin, by degrees, became more knowledgeable in the ways of the general staff and came to know the personalities of its members. For he dealt daily by phone and nightly by Kremlin meeting, not only with the chief of general staff and his immediate subordinates but with the heads of staff departments and sections, since he preferred to deal directly with the specialist on points of detail.

Yet Stalin had some strange ideas on the working of the general staff, and, as soon as he had got used to a face and trusted it, he began to think that the man was wasted scribbling in Moscow. In consequence he would use the general staff as a reserve pool of trusted commanders, posting out key general staff men as formation commanders or as senior staff officers with front or army headquarters. In this way the general staff was being continually drained of its principal and experienced members. In addition, the dictator began to use the senior general staff officers in the same fashion that he had used Zhukov during that autumn, as his military, as opposed to his political, ears and eyes, sending them out to the fronts for short periods to investigate and report back to him; then, the following year, they actually took over field commands in key sectors for short periods. These temporary commanders of groups of fronts, that included in particular Zhukov, Vasilevsky and Voronov, might or might not be members of the *Stavka*; but the *Stavka* membership itself meant little, for in the wartime USSR, rather on mad Paul's Pavlovian principle, a man was important only while Stalin was talking to him, and his official position and recognized channels or responsibilities mattered little.[40] For Stalin was continually convening investigating committees to look into this or that, and he personally agreed or vetoed their findings. That Stalin learned from his generals and military staffs there can be no doubt, for he lived almost day and night in the company of military men.

Yet it would be entirely wrong to suppose that the nature of the man, or the communist system under him, changed in any degree, for we know from western observers that Zhukov and the other senior generals and admirals remained, until the very end of the war, in mortal dread of Stalin and retained a great fear of the commissars and NKVD men that were attached to them in one guise or another.[41] Arrests, imprisonments, beatings and shootings remained an integral part of Russian communism, and they continued throughout the war. And Stalin went on making his own military miscalculations, though these appear to have become more rare as time went by.

★ ★ ★

Stalin, reliving 1812, had begun to believe, in a moment of euphoria, that he was going to defeat Germany utterly during the 1941–42 winter war, and he favoured any offensive action of any type. Timoshenko, still commanding the South-West Theatre in the south, had worked out a plan for a great spring offensive to clear the enemy from the Ukraine. Stalin was enamoured by it and asked his chief of general staff Shaposhnikov's views. Shaposhnikov was against it, since he believed the Red Army to be so weak that it needed to husband its resources; but he was immediately silenced by Stalin. Vasilevsky thought that Shaposhnikov was right; but, as Vasilevsky so disarmingly admits, none of them dared to speak out when Stalin had made up his mind: and the result was another crippling disaster for the Red Army.[42] For the coming of the fine weather had dried and hardened the ground and the German troops were in better heart and were mobile once more.

Timoshenko, although he had been warned by Shaposhnikov of the dangers of doing so, attacked out of the Izyum salient, surrounded on three sides by the enemy. After some bitter fighting a German army succeeded in holding Timoshenko's offensive to its front, while a panzer group counter-attacked the salient in its flank and completed Timoshenko's destruction by encircling the attacking Russian armies. Against German casualties of 20,000 men, quite a considerable number in view of the short battle, Timoshenko lost 214,000 men in prisoners alone, 2,000 guns and 1,200 tanks; in fact Timoshenko had had more tanks in the salient than the Germans numbered in their attacking panzer corps.[43]

The fighting fronts in the north (near Leningrad) and centre (before Moscow) remained fairly static during 1942: in the south, however, the annihilation of the new South-West Front that was the greater part of Timoshenko's South-West Theatre, opened the sluice-gates to a rapid German overrunning of the East Ukraine and an advance eastwards to the line of the Upper Don, that was defended by another Soviet front under Golikov. Golikov had entered the party and the Red Army in 1918 through the Red Guard as a military commissar, and by 1941 was a lieutenant-general in control of the main military intelligence administration, the GRU, from where he had been sent for a short time to London and Washington to head the Soviet military mission. Golikov was unusual in that his career was divided between military and political appointments, for he was obviously a party 'trusty' (in the late fifties he was made chief commissar and head of the PUR political administration). Back in 1942, however, he had been given command of the front near Voronezh, a front remarkable in that the wartime Soviet tank production had been such that it had allowed the raising and equipping of what was called a tank army of 400 tanks, and this was under Golikov's command. In addition to this tank army, Golikov was said to have had a further 600 tanks in smaller groupings, and of this total of 1,000, nearly 800 were of modern T 34 and KV type.[44] Once again the Red Army outnumbered the attacking Germans in the sector and had enough tanks to have beaten them off; but it did not have control of the skies.

When, in July, the Germans attacked across the Don at Voronezh and down the Don valley, there was very fierce fighting in Voronezh itself where the Germans allowed themselves to be pinned; but then the Soviet defence again fell apart. The German motorized troops emerged on to the open steppe country, reaching the Volga at Stalingrad and penetrating deep into Caucasia. Except where it was bottled up and captured, as in the Crimea, the Red Army appears to have taken to its heels once more, for the Soviet resistance was light in the south and the prisoners taken by the Germans during the late summer were few.[45]

Golikov blamed his defeat 'on the *Stavka* representative Vasilevsky', by then chief of general staff in succession to the sick Shaposhnikov; for Vasilevsky had been sent by Stalin to supervise the defence of the middle Don. Golikov complained to Stalin afterwards, when he was removed from his command, that Vasilevsky 'had got in his way and interfered and, in general, had overridden the front commander.' To which Stalin had replied that Golikov should have complained before and not after the battle and that 'the party and government had entrusted the front to *you* and not to the *Stavka* representative.' Soviet military organizations and functions were usually what Stalin happened to say that they were at the time. Rokossovsky, who replaced Golikov and was present at this Stalin interview, said in his memoirs that it was a lesson that he never forgot – that, in case of difficulty, it was better to brave the dictator's wrath and tell him the truth by phoning him directly.[46]

By August 1942 the *Wehrmacht* had reached the furthest point to the east that it was ever to reach, the high-water mark of German territorial expansion. Hitler had seized far more ground than he could ever hope to hold. Unless the Germans were going to cross the lower reaches of the wide Volga and advance into Asia, the time for offensive mobile operations was passed; German tank production was still limited since the full industrial potential of the Reich had not yet been developed, and Hitler was already faced with the prospect of withdrawing formations to Western Europe in preparation for the Second Front invasion that, according to the German dictator's own intelligence forecasts, might be expected in the late summer of 1943.

The brunt of the fighting was taken over by the German infantry formations that were concentrated on the easternmost corner (in the Volga basin): but there were not enough Germans to cover the 400 mile distance between Voronezh and Stalingrad, so Hitler provided his own solution and, doing what earlier in the war he had promised his generals that he would never do, he handed over these vast flanking frontages on what he believed to be quiet sectors, to his Rumanian, Hungarian and Italian allies, even though he himself had a poor opinion of the fighting qualities of their troops.[47] The few remaining German formations that had been holding these exposed flanks, mainly infantry but including some much understrength panzer divisions that were no longer grouped in operative mass, moved to the distant eastern and south-eastern battle areas on the Volga and trans-Don where there was an inferno of fierce fighting against Red Army infantry. For the beaten and demoralized Russian troops, many of whom must have withdrawn or fled nearly 200 miles, had been reformed and got back into the battle in the built-up and factory areas of Stalingrad and the steep hills of the Caucasus. In these conditions where the soldier was tied to the ground, requiring little more than the will to fight from a weapon pit or a ruined house, Russian infantry, with its remarkable powers of recuperation and stamina, proved an obstinate foe, for everything was in its favour: and the longer the Russian infantry fought the more confident it became.[48] The fighting raged for months throughout the autumn with no ground being given. In close-quarter battles of this type with little or no movement, the German casualties rose rapidly and the German infantry divisions, that were no longer being reinforced and kept up to strength, began to burn themselves out, so that they became mere shells with hardly the strength or effectiveness of a regiment.

In late November 1942 came the first successful Soviet counter-offensive that was to prove the turning point of the war on the Russo-German front. For the great Axis salient protruding in the south-east was cut roughly from north to south by a concentration of Soviet tanks, motorized troops, cavalry and infantry that struck the Rumanian divisions holding the quiet sectors to the west of the German spearheads in Stalingrad and the Caucasus. The encirclement, planned, it seems, by Zhukov and Vasilevsky and their general staff colleagues under Stalin's overall direction, was completed in four days, for the Rumanians gave way, almost without a fight.[49] Twenty German divisions were surrounded inside the Stalingrad pocket. These divisions could probably have fought their way out westwards if they had been allowed to do so, but Hitler was determined that they should remain where they were, and his decision was their death knell. For Hitler had no armoured reserves to deal the Russians a counter blow, and the *Luftwaffe* strength in the sector was insufficient to help remedy the situation. Such were the German straits that Hitler had to order a single panzer division to move from Brittany to the Don, and it was around this division that the relief force was to be built. Yet it was known to the German commanders in the field, if not to the *Führer*, that to be sure of ejecting the Russian he must be counter-attacked immediately: the longer that Russian infantry were allowed to dig in, the more difficult it was to get them out. Hitler took over the direction of the relief attempt, for his subordinate von Manstein was allowed little latitude, and the attempt failed.

The Red Army had had, admittedly, some success during the bitter weather of the 1941–42 winter war, but the operations planned and executed by the Soviet high command during the summer of 1942 had been a wretched failure. Then suddenly had come a series of brilliant winter victories, for the original Stalingrad offensive of late November 1942 was followed by further counter-strokes made from behind the middle and upper Don, during January and February, again singling out the sectors held by the weaker Axis allies, the Rumanians, Hungarians and Italians, and avoiding the areas occupied by German troops. Each of these counter-strokes was an envelopment made on a north-south axis, each in sequence and each further west and behind the other, like the teeth of a comb, successive wedges that forced the Germans further back from the Volga.[50] Each offensive was carried out by a large Red Army tank force supported by numerous cavalry and marching infantry divisions: the Axis allies put up no great resistance. Paulus's 6 German Army in Stalingrad, by then isolated and beyond any hope of relief, finally surrendered in February 1943 with a loss of 94,000 German prisoners; the German relief forces had to withdraw and the Caucasus was evacuated, the German line falling back westwards to the area of Kursk in the Ukraine. German casualties in the south during that winter, apart from those of the Axis allies, were probably over 300,000 men.[51]

The reasons for the outstanding Red Army victories were many. Germany was already beginning to weaken, since it had undertaken to fight most of the world with too little resources. In December 1941, though it had added Japan to its Axis allies, this had been of no benefit to Germany since Japan had not declared war on the Soviet Union. Indeed Japan's involvement in China and its attack on the USA and the British Commonwealth, a war that Hitler had encouraged, had in fact improved the Soviet Union's chances of survival, since Stalin knew that he need no longer fear a Japanese attack on the Soviet Far East, this allowing him to withdraw many of the Red Army divisions there. In December 1941, Hitler, bogged down in Russia, had, on his own initiative, declared war on the USA. By the end of 1942 the USA and the British Commonwealth, rapidly arming, were soon to take control of the Mediterranean, and the air war over the Reich and the growing threat of a renewal of hostilities in Western Europe were to cause a redeployment of German forces out of Russia.

From 1941 Hitler's war direction was eventually to prove of inestimable value to his enemies. Instead of isolating the Soviet Union both politically and militarily, he had actually found powerful allies for the USSR by going to war with the Americas. And, though Hitler's egotism was such that he was incapable of learning by his own mistakes and he certainly was not to be guided by the advice of others, he, who knew little of generalship, had personally taken the military command over the whole of the eastern front, a command he was to hold until the day of his death. Under such direction the German Army began its steady decline. The Red Army, on the other hand, once it had got over the initial shock of war, began to make a remarkable, indeed surprising, recovery, the characteristic associated particularly with Russian troops. At first the improvement was not very marked, though Red Army troops had shown in the winters of late 1941 and 1942 that *in cold weather* they might be a match for

German soldiery and, except in Finland, were much superior to Germany's field allies.

Substantial material aid was reaching the USSR from its allies, mainly from the USA, by way of Vladivostok in United States-built freighters, crewed by Soviet seamen, and by British convoys to Murmansk. And although the Soviet Union has subsequently denigrated or ignored this help, Stalin himself at the time protested vehemently when convoys were delayed, for the aid included essential technical equipment and materials that the USSR could not find for itself. Among the goods delivered were 427,000 motor trucks (the whole of the Red Army motor vehicle holdings at the end of the war were only 665,000 vehicles of which two-thirds must have been American), 13,000 armoured vehicles including 10,000 tanks, 19,000 good quality aircraft, 1,900 railway locomotives, 11,000 railway trucks (flats), ninety freight ships, 105 submarine chasers and 197 torpedo boats, 2.6 million tons of petroleum products, mainly blending agents and high octane fuels not obtainable in Russia, 4.5 million tons of concentrated foodstuffs and large quantities of other materials. The enormous numbers of high-quality trucks, including the ubiquitous 6x6 Studebaker, and the stocks of radio sets made over to Russia at this time, must have had considerable bearing on the improvement in the performance of the Red Army, since the rapid and lengthy advances westwards that the Soviet troops were to make from this time onwards would hardly have been possible without the use of allied radio equipment and transport.[52]

The coming of the spring in April of 1943 saw the Red Army back roughly on the line Leningrad-Velikie Luki-Kursk-Rostov, for in the centre and north the fighting line remained much as it had been in March 1942. Kursk was not far from Izyum, and surrounding Kursk there was a great Soviet salient very much like the Izyum salient of the previous year, surrounded on three sides by the German positions. Hitler had become convinced that the Soviet successes of the previous two winters were due to the superior mobility of the Red Army during the periods of the *rasputitsa* and the intense cold, for the Soviet railway system continued to run throughout the winter and Soviet arms and equipment and Russian quilted and felt-lined clothing were winter-effective; the fact that the Red Army was closer to its home supply base was also a very great advantage. The *Führer* imagined that the return of the fine weather and the hardening of the ground would give him the opportunity, not this time to destroy the Red Army or topple the Soviet leadership, but to deal the enemy fronts in the south a devastating blow as had been done in 1942, a blow so shattering that it would prevent the Red Army from going over to any offensive for a year or more. Hitler would then withdraw the bulk of the German forces out of Russia to France and the Low Countries to await the Anglo-American landings, for the *Führer* said he was confident that he could destroy the invading forces on the beaches, dealing *them* such a crippling defeat that would allow Germany perhaps two years respite before the western allies would be in a position to make a second attempt. Hitler would then use this interval, he said, 'to finish off Russia'.[53] Such at least was his plan.

Guderian had been restored to favour and re-employed as the new inspector-general of panzer troops, and an attempt was to be made to use German panzer formations in operative mass under a strong *Luftwaffe* air umbrella in the fashion of 1940 and 1941; the object of the new German offensive, that had the code name *Citadel*, was to envelop and destroy the very powerful Red Army forces that were being assembled in the Kursk salient, ready, so Hitler believed, for a Soviet offensive later in the year. About 2,500 German tanks and armoured tracked tank-destroyers were allotted to the battle, and numbers of these were of first-class quality, heavy Mark VI Tigers, Mark V Panthers and Mark IV mediums, the Mark VI being the most powerful tank in the world at that time and the Mark V a match, or even more than a match, for the Russian K V and T 34.[54] The concentration of *Luftwaffe* in the Kursk area was such as to promise air superiority.

The Soviet order of battle in the sector was no less formidable, Rokossovsky's Central Front and Vatutin's Voronezh Front with Konev's Steppe Front in reserve, certainly with 1,500 tanks and probably a good deal more, for Soviet accounts put the figure at more than 3,000. The Red air force allotted to the area was also very strong. The Soviet high command knew well that a major German offensive was imminent and could foretell exactly where it would fall, and, since the German preparations were spread over the space of several months, the defending Red Army forces had ample time to dig themselves in and fortify and mine the area. Stalin had detached both Zhukov and Vasilevsky to the salient, and both had much difficulty in counselling patience on the irritable and anxious Stalin, who, tired of waiting for the German offensive, wanted to repeat the error of Izyum and have the Red Army be the first to attack out of the salient.[55]

When the Germans began their offensive it soon proved to be an act of folly, for the attacks were made into wire and minefields and dug-in positions, many miles deep, and the Soviet enemy was well prepared. Torrential rains washed away roads and tracks and the low cloud hampered the *Luftwaffe* air operations: some progress was made in crumbling away the ground defences, but at a heavy cost in casualties; eventually the *Luftwaffe* was unable to sustain the gigantic air effort demanded of it. Within a week the German high command knew that the battle was not going well, and in two weeks that the offensive had failed. The *Luftwaffe* then lost air superiority to the Red air force, and the Soviet fronts began, without any delay, gigantic counter-offensives from the Kursk salient and the adjoining sectors, offensives against a repulsed and disorganized German enemy that were to take the Red Army in a succession of victories across the Ukraine and to Belorussia.

Before the battle of Kursk the Red Army had been able to match the Germans only in winter weather. After Kursk the Red Army did not meet with a defeat in summer or winter. Before Kursk the Germans usually succeeded tactically but failed strategically: at Kursk they failed strategically because they were unsuccessful tactically. The whole concept of *Citadel* reflected the bankruptcy of Hitler and his high command, for after *Citadel* the Axis lost all initiative on the eastern front and was never to regain it. For Hitler reverted to his own strategic and tactical doctrine of 'not one step back' and formations were to dig in and remain immobile where they were. This made the task of Stalin and his generals so much the lighter since they selected one German sector after another for obliteration, moving, at will, a Red Army reserve force of about sixty divisions up and down the front, hammering a great hole here and another hole there, letting loose into the German rear a great flood of tanks, cavalry and trucked and marching infantry.[56] It was from this time onwards, when Germany appeared to be fast losing the war and Germany's allies were faltering, that partisans began to make their presence felt in occupied Europe and the German rear areas.

★　　★　　★

There was much that was confusing and contradictory about the Red

Army at this time, particularly as it was seen by the Germans and by the few western observers in Russia. The British generals Martel and Burrows, on the rare occasions when they were permitted to see the army in the field, wondered that any results could be achieved out of what appeared to be administrative chaos, with many of the commanders apparently uninformed as to the overall situation, with little march order or discipline, masses of motor vehicles and horses, horse-drawn carts and marching men, all mixed up with no indication of design or control, moving along roads and tracks in an endless flood. But this was always the Russian way, for foreign military observers in the days of the tsars had commented on the same scenes with the same astonishment. Little seemed to be uniform, the men's equipment, dress, or their field organization. Supply appeared primitive and haphazard, and the same could be said of the technical maintenance and repair system.[57]

Stalin's arbitrary system of personal military leadership, based largely on the dictator's own interpretation of political situations and military values, could not have been a particularly efficient one. On the other hand it had the decided advantage that it was a copy of the Leninist example, in that Stalin knew exactly what he wanted and where he was going, and he pursued his communist political and military goals with brutal and ruthless force: his relationship with his western allies caused him no undue concern for he simply used them; for the most part he was indifferent; when he required something of his allies, he became momentarily genial; always he treated them with duplicity and guile.

Unlike the last tsarist commander-in-chief, the emperor Nicholas II, Stalin really did know what was going on in his army, for he had numerous tight controls and counter-checks on his military commanders through the commissar organization and the NKVD/NKGB secret police detachments within the Red Army. And, in addition, he exercised a most rigorous command over his front commanders and staffs, through the general staff (for the general staff had its own liaison officers permanently detached to the main formations, their duty being solely to keep Moscow informed of what was going on in the field), and through Kremlin conferences and order groups attended by the front commanders, who were frequently called back to Moscow.[58] The command relationship between Stalin and his front commanders was personal because he talked daily and nightly with them all over the Baudôt line teleprint and the so-called high frequency (*V Ch*) telephone (later radio) link that was secure against interception by ear: Antonov, the deputy chief of staff who did most of Vasilevsky's work during his chief's long absences in the war zones, was merely Stalin's mouthpiece. In addition, Stalin sent out his own commander representatives, usually Zhukov, Vasilevsky and Voronov, though others were used, even Timoshenko and Voroshilov on the less important assignments. And although much was made in the post-war foreign press, mainly on the basis of speculation, of the growing commander (as opposed to the commissar) power, Zhukov having been singled out for this doubtful honour, the evidence is much to the contrary. For Zhukov, the hectoring and blustering bully who acted as Stalin's strong-arm man among the military, was entirely dependent on, and subservient to, the dictator.

At the end of 1942, however, there had been another of the so-called relaxations of political controls and a restoration of one-man command. Early the next year the word 'officer' was officially brought back to favour, though of course it had been in day-to-day use from about 1940, particularly in the general staff.[59] One of the most significant changes at this time, introduced personally by Stalin, had been the introduction of imperial army-type badges of rank for officers and soldiers, together with the old tsarist shoulder-boards and the gold lace for the generals. Only the epaulettes were lacking. And to these tsarist insignia was added a profusion of medals and orders, no longer based on the party, the workers, the proletariat, revolution and Lenin, but going back into the imperial tsarist past, settling on tsarist admirals and generals, almost at random, for some of the new orders bore the names of men of questionable fame. For Stalin was fascinated and mesmerized by the imperial echoes of the old army.[60]

In the field itself there were comparatively few changes of note except that the Red Army was being provided with new battleworthy equipment of modern design both Soviet and foreign, that was becoming available in ever increasing quantities: this applied particularly to aircraft, and was to change the whole air situation over the battle front so that, from early 1944 onwards, the Red air force was able to fight for, and keep, tactical air superiority in all key theatres. On the ground the basic fighting formation remained the rifle division, usually of much reduced strength and rarely more than 9,000 men, still on the standard German pattern and not differing much from that used elsewhere, except that, German fashion, it continued to concentrate on the artillery group within the infantry regiment, with short-barrelled close-range 76mm guns that were usually used in a direct-fire role, together with heavy or medium mortars, a system that still remains today. This artillery, manned by infantrymen, gave the infantry regimental commander his own quick-fire support on which he could always rely, since it was never taken from him to be allocated elsewhere.

The Red Army had also copied from the Germans the production of 'assault-artillery', a turretless and heavily armoured tracked tank chassis carrying a limited-traverse medium- or high-velocity gun mounted in the hull of an open-topped fighting vehicle that could be used both as a tank-destroyer or to give artillery fire support to tanks or infantry. Soviet military literature has predated the 'Soviet invention' of this fighting vehicle, known as the S U, to before the war; but in fact it appeared in 1943 three years after the German model was in the field; the S U tank-destroyer was to become a feature of the post-war Soviet Army for the next forty years.[61]

Surface-to-surface free-flight rockets with a range of about 8,000 yards, that were fired in salvoes from truck-mounted launchers, known colloquially as 'Little Kate', or 'the Stalin organ', had been in use since 1941 and were to remain in the Soviet Army. Based on the Congreve rocket, they were not new, however, nor a Soviet invention, for they were used by the Germans, the German version being fired from a tracked carrier, a two-wheeled trailer mount, or simply from a frame-crate placed on the ground. Free-flight rockets had of course been standard army equipment in Europe throughout the nineteenth century.

Like Hitler, Stalin had a mania for impressive orders of battle. Both dictators tried to keep in being on the Russo-German front an enormous number of infantry divisions, so that each had a grossly inflated order of battle that had little relevance to its real strength and effectiveness. Many of these divisions on both sides were mere shells, a divisional headquarters, some supporting arms and perhaps two or three skeleton regiments barely capable of putting the equivalent of a battalion in the line.[62] The probability is that this was done by both to deceive the other's intelligence: and since the Germans did not do this with their divisions in the west in that they kept them at full strength, it is a factor that needs to be borne in mind when comparing the relative strength that the Germans deployed in the east and in the west, and in calculating the real strength of the wartime Red Army. For much of the war nearly all the Red Army divisions were grouped directly under armies, the infantry corps organization having fallen into disuse between 1941 and 1943.

For the first two years of the war the Red Army had returned to its pre-war use of tank brigades (in reality regiments) each of three battalions, in all about ninety tanks, partly because of the shortage of tanks during these years and partly because the field commanders lacked the expertise and the radio equipment to control large tank formations in the German fashion of 1941. These independent tank brigades, that eventually accounted for the greater part of the Soviet tank strength, existed as the main armoured grouping throughout the war. By the end of 1942, however, some experimental tank corps were being put together, and these usually consisted of two tank brigades and a lorried motor rifle brigade: these corps had a strength of about 180 tanks and 8,000 men, and were patterned on the German 1942 panzer divisions. In addition, there was introduced, in 1943, a new pattern mechanized corps that differed from the tank corps in that, although it was a mixed tank and infantry grouping, the preponderance of the strength lay in the infantry rather than the tanks.[63] It usually had three mechanized brigades each of a tank battalion and three motor rifle battalions, and totalled about 17,000 men and over 100 tanks; this mechanized corps was a copy of a German *SS Panzergrenadierdivision*. At a later stage in the war, as more radio and tanks became available, tank corps and mechanized corps were sometimes grouped together as tank armies, the equivalent of the 1941 German panzer corps. Red Army cavalry divisions still existed in large numbers but without an armoured element.

In 1943 Martel was back once more in the Soviet Union where he suffered the same Russian obstructionism and secrecy that had been commented upon, very much in the same terms, by von Manstein, Knox and Williamson earlier this century and by Wellesley in the last, the long bouts of drinking and the time-wasting entertainment and tours of no military value, deliberately thought up to keep visitors from seeing what was afoot. According to his own account, Martel countered obstructionism and rebuff with anger and insult, the only behaviour that, so he said, a Russian could understand, and this brought him some return in the way of information and access to the troops. Martel judged the regimental wartime officers that he met to be far superior to those he had talked with in 1936, being both competent and confident, for most of them had learned their jobs in action.[64]

The opinions of the western attachés and visitors, Eden, Brooke, Ismay, Deane, Miles, Tedder, Burrows, Birse and others, confirmed what had been known before about the Soviet high command and its senior commanders. Stalin was in complete control and, irrespective of his military merits or failings, appeared to have an extraordinary knowledge of what was going on. Shaposhnikov and Antonov, the deputy chief of general staff (a former tsarist *praporshchik* of the tsarist *eger* guard regiment), were highly intelligent and had good military brains, but were both entirely in Stalin's shadow. Zhukov, the deputy commander-in-chief, was less well known, yet it was noted that he too stood in fear of the dictator. The chief of general staff Vasilevsky and the artilleryman Voronov were outside the circle met by visitors and attachés. Voroshilov and Budenny were familiar figures and were not highly regarded, nor did Timoshenko much impress the western military men. All of them, except Voroshilov and Budenny, still took second place to their shadowing commissars, and this included Golovko, then the admiral commanding the North Fleet, and Gorshkov, the latter-day commander-in-chief of the Soviet Navy. All this the westerners understood though they were told little and had to work on impressions; and very accurate these impressions were to prove. Yet it was difficult for those stationed inside the USSR to make any overall assessment as to the general pattern of the war and know what was going on, and those outside were often better informed on current Red Army activity through captured German material and the interception of German military radio traffic. All in all, the western observers and military staffs were able, by pooling and collating their knowledge, to arrive at a more accurate estimate of the Red Army's characteristics, of its strengths and weaknesses, than has been done by many of the post-war writers of forty years since, who have relied overmuch on subsequent Soviet literature that portrays the Red Army at that time as Moscow would have wished the world to see it.

★   ★   ★

The year 1944 saw the Red Army moving steadily forward, launching offensive after offensive, towards the 1939 Soviet frontier. Then, in midsummer 1944, came the series of grand operations, timed to coincide with the Anglo-American invasion of France, offensives that fell in sequence from north to south throughout June until the end of August, from Finland and the area of the Baltic States down to Bessarabia and Rumania.[65] Italy had already been forced out of the war in the west and Finland and Rumania were shortly to ask for peace terms.

In the Belorussian campaign, against the German forces of Army Group Centre, something like twenty-eight German divisions were encircled and smashed, so that the total German casualties in Belorussia, in a campaign that had lasted for little more than three weeks, were put at 300,000 men by the German OKW war diarist at the time.[66] The Germans also suffered very heavy losses to the south in Galicia and the West Ukraine. Towards the end of August, Rumania had been invaded, the two Rumanian armies there letting the Russians through since Rumania had already sought an armistice. This resulted in the encirclement and destruction of a new 6 German Army of twenty infantry divisions, a force that had practically no tanks and very little air support; in consequence this German army was cut to pieces in the space of about two weeks by Soviet air power and the new tank armies recently brought into being: in all, 200,000 Germans in Rumania simply disappeared, leaving the gate open to Hungary and to the Balkans.[67] The wheel of fate had turned full circle in that Germany no longer had massed air and panzer groups to smite the enemy or counter his armoured thrusts, and German infantry by itself was almost defenceless. The Germans even lacked artillery, and they had to rely on mortars or captured Russian or Yugoslav guns with meagre stocks of ammunition. The German infantry itself was no longer of the 1941 standard, though it still did not lack determination or leadership: the result, however, was a foregone conclusion, for no infantry could withstand an overwhelming enemy superiority of air, artillery and tank power.[68]

France and the greater part of Italy had been occupied in the west, and part of the German army general staff had unsuccessfully tried to assassinate Hitler. The end in Germany could not be far off, and it is astonishing, in retrospect, that the German Army managed to hold out until the following May of 1945. Hitler relied on the Gestapo and terror rule to keep himself in power and Germany in the war, while he bombarded South-East England, France and Belgium with his long-range V weapons, including the V2 rocket that was to form the prototype for today's Soviet (as well as for the American) strategic rocket forces.

Meanwhile the Red Army moved into the Balkans, Hungary and Poland, finally crossing the German frontier, using very much the same operative tactics that it, and the armies of the western allies, had learned from the Germans. Infantry formations, helped forward by artillery reserve groups, by ground-attack aircraft and by tanks in support, broke through the enemy-defended localities: tank formations were then poured through the gaps deep into the enemy rear, usually two or more separate tank thrusts meeting a hundred or more miles away to form a double envelopment or encirclement operation, these penetrations being every bit as deep, bold and imaginative as those made by the Germans in the halcyon days of 1940 and 1941. The key to success was air power and tank and mechanized movement; and the forces that carried out these Soviet operations, a minority in terms of numbers, came to figure as an *élite*. The remainder of the field formations, the horse-drawn artillery and the foot marching infantry, with little apparent cohesion and, seen through western eyes, little discipline, had been heavily diluted by the forced recruitment of civilians of any nationality, by prisoners of war, even the inmates of gaols; anyone in fact who could carry a rifle was immediately pressed into service with little preparation or training. This great and terrifying horde moved into Central Europe and Germany in the wake of the armoured forces, leaving behind a trail of destruction, murder and outrage.

★　　★　　★

The war against Germany ended at the beginning of May 1945 and the Soviet Union began its preparations for the waging of a new war in the Far East against Japan.[69] As the Red Army strength in the Far East had sunk to about thirty divisions, it was necessary to move four armies from the west to build up the Soviet forces to a figure said to have been about one and a half million men, over 5,000 tanks and 4,000 combat aircraft. The Transbaikal Front under Malinovsky, a former tsarist infantry non-commissioned officer, had the main role since this was to involve the rapid movement of large armoured forces over a great distance from Transbaikal and Outer Mongolia to the

Pacific coast; Meretskov's 1 Far East Front would have to penetrate the static defences built up long before the war on the old Russo-Japanese frontier. A subsidiary 2 Far East Front under Purkaev, another former tsarist *praporshchik*, had to cross the Amur. Vasilevsky was appointed as commander-in-chief of the Far East theatre, and this was unusual since it had been Stalin's normal practice to control the fronts himself directly from Moscow; in this particular campaign, however, he was obliged to delegate authority to Vasilevsky in view of the great distances that separated the capital from the Far East maritime provinces.[70]

The Soviet Union was still at peace with Japan even though it had, in April 1945, abrogated its non-aggression pact with that country. Then on 6 August the first atomic bomb was dropped on Hiroshima, with a second, on Nagasaki, three days later. Japan had wanted to get out of the war with the United States and for some time past had been putting out peace feelers. With the dropping of the first bomb, Japan was ready for terms. The Soviet Union was, however, determined to get into the war quickly before the signing of any American-Japanese armistice, so it hurriedly declared war in the early hours of 9 August, when the war was in fact over.[71] The Soviet fronts then advanced rapidly into the territory held by the Japanese Kwantung Army. Although Soviet historians now describe this exercise in movement as the victorious campaign that put Japan out of the war, it was in reality irrelevant to a victory that was already won and that belonged almost wholly to the United States.

On 11 August Molotov had proposed to the United States that Vasilevsky might be the allied supreme commander in the Far East or, in the event of the Americans maintaining their right to nominate MacArthur, 'there might be two Supreme Commanders, MacArthur and Vasilevsky.' Harriman, the United States Ambassador in Moscow, did not think so and the conversation became heated, for 'the United States had carried the main burden of the war against Japan and for four years had kept the Japanese off Russia's back.' The Soviet Union had been in the war only two days.

CHAPTER SIX

The Pre-Nuclear Army

Soviet historians writing in the days of the Khrushchev ascendancy, when little good could be said about Stalin, have blamed the Stalin personality cult for the slowness of the Soviet armed forces to adapt, between 1946 and 1953, to the likely conditions of rocket and nuclear warfare.[1] For Stalin's reaction to the United States supremacy in atomic weapons – the Soviet Union having none at all in 1946 – was to keep alive the threat of an invasion of Western Europe by the Soviet Army using the type of ground forces that had been so successful in 1945. For Stalin said 'that the artificially sustained hullabaloo about the danger of a third world war was meant to frighten people with weak nerves,' and he made sure that everyone knew that he was not one of these by his readiness to bring the world to the brink of war and his refusal, as he expressed it, to be frightened 'by their [United States] atomic blackmail'.[2] Yet he wasted neither time nor opportunity in beginning an extensive atomic and intercontinental, strategic and tactical rocket research programme, at first based almost solely on captured German equipment and on German scientists who were taken to the USSR to continue their work under Soviet supervision. When, after a few years in the USSR, the German scientists were released and repatriated to East Germany, it was clear that the USSR had no further use for them since Soviet rocket engineers had by then overtaken the Germans in knowledge and expertise.

Although present-day Soviet rocketry owes its early post-war existence to the teaching of German V-weapon specialists, Stalin's military leadership had long been aware of the possibilities of rocketry; as early as midsummer 1944 Vasilevsky had been asking Burrows that the British should send to the Soviet Union V-weapon information or 'German missiles that had failed to explode'.[3]

The development of the Soviet ground forces, that changed their name in 1946 from the Red Army to the Soviet Army, continued along the same lines as it had done since 1943, that is to say on the German Guderian pattern of tank and mechanized forces used in operative mass under strong air cover. These armoured and highly mobile formations were to be used boldly in all phases of warfare, the object being to break through into enemy rear areas and, with the support of airborne forces and, where they could be recruited, partisans or other foreign sympathizers, make great penetrations in depth without regard to the situation to the flanks or in their own rear. These great arrow-headed penetrations, perhaps a hundred or two hundred miles deep, would outflank and envelop the slower moving enemy, joining up with other parallel Soviet thrusts, and, turning into pincer movements, encircle the enemy. It was envisaged that the enemy morale would by that time have been shattered and that his command and control organization and his supply would have broken down. The final destruction of the trapped enemy would then become the easy task of the follow-up Soviet armies, made up of foot-marching rifle divisions and towed artillery.

There was nothing new in this concept of warfare since it was modelled on the German battle plans in the Low Countries and France in 1940 and in the Soviet Union in 1941 and the summer of 1942, where the German armoured columns had hurried on to their distant objectives assisted forward by every shock and terror tactic that the Germans could devise: a largely indiscriminate bombing that set the civil population afoot, blocking all the roadways to the rear of the enemy; siren-carrying dive-bombers; airborne troops seizing bridges and defiles in depth and destroying enemy headquarters and communication centres. Other German disruptive measures had included the use of deep penetration groups in enemy uniforms or in ambulance convoys, and the recruiting and arming of foreigners or dissidents believed to be friendly to the Axis: then there were the deliberate atrocities, carried out by special groups, incendiarism and the shootings of civilians or prisoners, all intended to create panic and flight. This the Germans did with signal success because at that time Germany's enemies had no understanding of such a pattern of warfare or of the means of countering it.

Stalin and his marshals further developed this theme of ground warfare, what western countries had earlier called the blitzkrieg, an expression that was not used, however, in Germany or in Russia.[4] There was of course no question that Moscow would admit that the pattern had been learned from the Germans, and Soviet literature even goes so far as to condemn such German methods as bankrupt 'military adventurism': yet the fact remains that the Soviet Union continued, for the time being, to follow the German lead. And although Stalin came to be criticized by the Khrushchev commentators for having failed to bring the ground forces into the nuclear age, Stalin, probably by good fortune rather than by design, lost nothing by leaving his ground forces equipped and trained in the fashion of the great armoured battles of 1945, aiming only to increase their mobility, armour and firepower.

In 1946 the two separate ministries, one for defence (the army and air force) and one for the navy, were amalgamated and replaced by a single ministry of the armed forces (MVS), while all supply and administrative responsibilities that were common to the three fighting services were placed under a unified organization known as the Rear Services.[5] Stalin remained minister of the armed forces until 1947 when he appointed the 'politico' Bulganin to the post; Bulganin, though he came to wear a marshal's uniform, was less of a soldier than Voroshilov. The minister had five deputy ministers, all soldiers or admirals, these being Vasilevsky, the new chief of general staff (who returned to the appointment in place of Antonov), Konev, the chief of the ground forces, Vershinin, the head of the air forces, Khrulev for the rear services, and Yumashev for the fleet: a sixth deputy, Govorov, was later added as inspector-general. The heads of the arms directorates for artillery, tanks, engineers, airborne troops and so on, came directly under the armed forces minister and not under Vasilevsky, since the chief of general staff acted only as the minister's executive; nor did they come under Konev, the ground forces commander-in-chief; similarly the new command for home air defence (PVO), that was responsible for the command and general administration of the PVO districts controlling the joint fighter and anti-aircraft gun defence of the Soviet Union, came directly under the minister. The chief political directorate (PUR), nominally responsible to Bulganin, was, however, as before, an extension of the Central Committee political organization.[6]

Contradictory though it sounds, the actual control of the ground forces had nothing to do with the commander-in-chief of the ground forces, for the commander-in-chief's duties were restricted to policy matters of a general nature and to administration, organization, equipment and training, though these latter responsibilities had to be shared and co-ordinated with the inspector-general and the arms directors. The title of ground forces commander-in-chief was therefore much grander than the post. The chief of general staff, as the minister's executive, was the staff and policy co-ordinator within the ministry. For the armed forces minister alone, when he happened to be Stalin, commanded all the ground troops, the PVO districts and other armed forces; when the armed forces minister was Bulganin, then he also had the same responsibilities and powers, except that he exercised them as directed by Stalin. Stalin remained the supreme political and military leader until the day of his death.

The ground troops within the Soviet Union were under the command of the twenty-one military districts, territorial based organizations of the type common to the tsarist, German and most other European powers. These Soviet military districts varied much in size and importance according to their population, location and strategic position, and they were usually commanded by marshals or by generals of various ranks. Although the district was responsible directly to the minister for the armed forces, the district commander's own responsibility was shared collectively with a district military council of up to five members, usually a deputy, possibly also the chief of staff and certain arms directors, one or two military commissars – one, appointed by the Central Committee through the PUR being known as 'the member (*chlen*)', and the other usually being the head of the district political directorate; in addition, the local civilian secretary of the regional communist party organization was often co-opted as a member. Orders of any importance had to be issued in the name of the council, signed by the commander and countersigned, usually by the *chlen*.

Although the military districts were capable of providing, or raising on mobilization, divisions, corps, and even armies and fronts, a military district was not in fact an operational theatre or formation, for its main tasks were to train and to administer. It called up the conscripts for all the services, including the navy, and did their preliminary equipping; it also administered the reservists who had completed their colour service, and raised new formations in peace and in war.[7] The military district controlled all military transport and supply resources, including the listing of those of the civil economy earmarked for war purposes; it commanded all military formations within its territory and supervised all military schools: it was also responsible for liaison with the PVO air defence districts within its area, and with the republic governments on matters of common interest, particularly the working of *Osoaviakhim*, the military training organization for the civil population and for the youth who had not yet been called up for military service.

The ground forces that were outside of the Soviet Union, mainly in occupied Germany and Central Europe, were organized not into territorial military districts but into mobile groups of Soviet forces, the largest of these being in East Germany. There the group (that came to be known in the west as GSFG) took the form of an enlarged front (army group) made up of a number of armies, these being kept on a near-war footing. The basis of the groups of forces was the rifle army: some of these armies, known since 1942 as 'shock armies', had been specially reinforced with additional artillery formations so that they could blast their way through enemy defended areas sited in great depth; the name 'shock' like that of 'guards' continues to be used today, even though the title is now merely historic and honorific. A rifle, a shock, or a guards army, and they were in fact much the same thing, usually consisted of three rifle corps, for the corps organization, dropped after 1941, had been gradually reintroduced since 1943. Each rifle corps had two or three rifle or infantry divisions, since, in Russian, rifle and infantry mean one and the same. The 1946 rifle armies, because they had a corps organization, had many more divisions than had been usual during the war. At first all infantry formations relied on horse-drawn first-line transport, although very rapid progress was made in the next few years to replace all horses by motor vehicles.

In 1946 a newly created mechanized army took the place of the various higher headquarters for mobile troops that had been used during the war; for the old pattern tank armies and their subordinate tank corps and mechanized corps (these corps having a strength of the equivalent of a German division) all disappeared. The new mechanized army structure had no corps headquarters under it but directly controlled a number of tank and mechanized divisions, usually two tank and one or two mechanized divisions, these divisions being of western standard divisional size.

Both the rifle and the mechanized armies had artillery formations allotted to them, a number of anti-tank brigades and anti-aircraft divisions (each of four heavy or light regiments) and sometimes a breakthrough artillery division made up of medium or heavy howitzers or specialized artillery such as rocket-launcher or heavy-mortar brigades; the strength of these breakthrough artillery divisions was considerable, possibly over a hundred howitzers and a hundred mortars to each. The army commander usually allocated these artillery formations or regiments to support his subordinate corps, according to his plan. The rifle corps commander had in addition his own corps artillery of medium guns and howitzers, at least equal in strength to the artillery of his line divisions, and he would use these, together with any artillery allocated to him by the army commander, to give additional support to his line divisions where he thought it would be needed. By German Second World War standards, standards where field branch artillery had not been given a prominent role, Soviet artillery was a most powerful supporting arm. Yet the Soviet Army followed the German precedent in that basic organic artillery tended to be regarded as the property of the divisional or regimental commander: he was not asked to give it up to his neighbours or support them by flanking fire, and in this respect Soviet artillery organization might be regarded as inflexible and wasteful.

The 1946 Soviet rifle division was considerably larger than its wartime equivalent, being about 12,000 men strong and having eventually, when the horse-drawn vehicles were replaced, about 1,300 motor trucks including gun-towers. It could not, however, carry all its men on wheels and most of its infantry had to march on foot. Its organization was of the standard German pattern, three infantry regiments each of three battalions each of three rifle companies and a medium machine-gun company: the rifle company (of about 120 men) had three rifle platoons and a medium machine-gun platoon. Organic artillery and mortar firepower were provided at every level of command, the divisional artillery being made up of a gun regiment and a howitzer regiment together with a battery of heavy mortars: in German fashion the Soviet rifle regiment had its own artillery battery of anti-aircraft heavy machine-guns, and a number of direct- or indirect-fire short-range 76mm guns, a mortar troop and six self-propelled tracked and armoured assault-guns (SU 76) with a long 76mm gun. This new rifle division, although of a lower category than the new Soviet mechanized division, certainly had a modern and formidable look in so far as its equipment was concerned, since it had about 100 tanks and SUs, some reconnaissance armoured cars, a flight of light intercommunication planes, about sixty field guns and howitzers, thirty heavy mortars, fifty anti-tank guns and about seventy dual-role anti-aircraft guns and heavy machine-guns. The division had some of the organizational characteristics of the late-war German motorized division except that its infantry were not fully motorized.

The new tank division was made up of five elements: three medium tank regiments, a motor rifle regiment, and a heavy tank/SU regiment. Each of the three medium tank regiments had two medium tank battalions each of thirty-two tanks (increased to three tank battalions in the nineteen-fifties) and a motor rifle battalion. The motor rifle regiment was simply three truck-borne rifle battalions, without tanks but with its own small artillery and mortar group; the motor rifle regiment could detach one or more battalions to support the medium tank regiments, or alternatively it was capable of fighting independently as a single infantry regiment. The heavy tank/SU regiment consisted of two heavy tank battalions equipped mainly with the new heavy Stalin (JS) tank and a heavy SU battalion, the heavy differing from the medium tank battalion in that it had only twenty heavy tanks or SUs and not thirty-two tanks to the battalion. An infantry battalion, or sometimes a company, of riflemen equipped with sub machine-carbines (SMCs) was included in the regiment to give the heavy tanks protection from enemy infantry close-range weapons.

The main fighting element of the tank division was made up of the 180 T 34 tanks of the three medium tank regiments: the heavy tank regiment gave the medium tanks some fire support against enemy tanks or fortifications, or, on occasion, spearheaded an attack: the motor rifle regiment worked in partnership with the tank regiments particularly in broken or close country and at night, for whereas a tankman in a closed-down tank is largely blind and deaf to what is going on around him, no man can see or hear better than a rifleman in the open; infantry are needed, too, to assist tank formations to hold ground against counter-attack, for even a handful of infantry can do this successfully for short periods of time. A tank division was made up of about 11,000 men, 180 medium and sixty heavy fighting tanks

(other than command and reconnaissance tanks) and about six battalions of riflemen, a rifle battalion not numbering much more than
400 men; the divisional artillery was of towed field guns, howitzers
and mortars, and a truck-mounted rocket-launcher battery. In all,
this pattern tank division was a well organized and well balanced
formation based on groupings tested by both German and Russian in
the closing stages of the war, and was easily commanded and
controlled.

The other type of 1946 Soviet mobile division was the mechanized
division, and this was the counterpart of, and the immediate supporting formation to, the tank division, the two working, as it were, hand
in hand. The mechanized division was the modern Soviet descendant
of the German motorized division of 1938, thought up by Beck to give
stability and substance to the headlong dash of Guderian's panzer
divisions. There was, however, an outstanding departure in that the
Soviet mechanized division was both a motorized infantry *and* an
armoured division. For while the 1946 Soviet tank division was, in the
approved German fashion, strong in tanks but comparatively light in
infantry – nine tank battalions to three motor rifle battalions – the
Soviet mechanized division had ten battalions of truck-mounted
riflemen – as many in fact as a dismounted rifle division – but had in
addition eight battalions of tanks. For the mechanized division had
one medium tank regiment similar to that of the tank division, and
three mechanized regiments: but since each of the three mechanized
regiments of three motor rifle battalions had its own organic tank
battalion, this made a divisional total of five medium tank battalions in
all. Added to this there was a heavy tank/S U regiment, as in the tank
division, so that the mechanized division totalled about 220 medium
and heavy fighting tanks and S Us, nearly as many as the tank division.
The mechanized division had a full complement of supporting arms
similar to that found in the tank division and it had a strength of more
than 15,000 men. By German standards the tank strength for this type
of division, that was originally intended to support the tank division,
was large, for the wartime SS panzer grenadier division normally had
about 100 tanks and assault-guns and the army panzer grenadier
divisions a good deal less than that; and yet one can still find a German
precedent for the Soviet 1946 mechanized division in that some SS
panzer grenadier divisions (and even the army panzer grenadier
division *Grossdeutschland*) from the time of Kursk onwards did in fact

number up to 200 tanks each.

To judge by its tactical organization and equipment the mechanized division might be held to be capable of supporting the tank divisions, enabling them to operate in difficult hilly or close country and even to hold ground, for, when dismounted, the mechanized division could fight as a standard infantry division: yet the mechanized division's own strength was sufficient to undertake independent mobile roles or, unaided, to engaged enemy armoured formations. It might be doubted that one man, the mechanized divisional commander, could effectively train, and control in battle, such a large heterogeneous force. But with the improvement in radio equipment this does not seem to have caused any difficulties, and divisions of a fifty-fifty mix of tanks and riflemen have remained in the Soviet Army until this day.

The Soviet Army of the immediate post-war years continued to be an amalgam of the new and the old. The horses were disappearing, yet some cavalry divisions lingered on. Air armies, equipped with really modern fighter, ground-attack and light bomber planes, remained as part of the Soviet Army but not of the ground forces, these air armies being, as before, under the commander of the groups of forces or the military districts. The airborne forces, part of the ground forces but wearing the light-blue air force gorget patches, had been much reduced in size, partly because they had had little success in the war; these, as specialist troops, came directly under the ministry for the armed services.

The once vaunted T 34/85 (the T 34 with the high-velocity 85 mm gun) remained the standard medium tank and it was to have a first-line life of about fifteen years until about 1956, before being completely replaced by the T 54 and its successors, by which time the T 34 had come to be regarded as a somewhat primitive and second-rate tank. The K V/85 continued in use as the heavy tank, though it was in fact hardly much more than a medium, but numbers of J S 1, J S 2 and J S 3 heavy tanks with a 122mm high-velocity gun came into service and the J S 3 was, from 1944 onwards, eventually to replace the K V/85.

About twenty per cent of the post-war Soviet armoured strength was to be made up of S Us, the turretless tank copied from the Germans that carried the main high-velocity gun in the hull. These A F Vs, though they were at a disadvantage in that the gun had a very limited traverse and in consequence could fire only to the front, had the distinct merit that the lack of the turret-weight meant that the frontal armour could be strengthened beyond the thickness of that of the normal tank and that the vehicle could mount a much more powerful gun than could have been carried by a turretted tank of the same size and weight. The SU usually had a lower silhouette than the tank. The chassis were sometimes those of obsolescent or obsolete tanks, and a wide variety of powerful guns and howitzers were used for the main armament, from the long 76mm field gun to the 152mm gun/howitzer. The box-like armoured crew compartment of the early SU – like those of the original German design – had no overhead cover, and this could have detracted from its suitability for use in nuclear warfare in that it gave little protection to the crew: it did, on the other hand, have the decided combat advantage that the crews could hear and see what was going on around them and were better able to orient themselves than tank men. Later models, however, had top decking. Soviet SUs, like the German assault-gun vehicle equivalent, were originally manned by artillerymen until they eventually also became part of the equipment of Soviet tank regiments. Although SUs were capable of long-range and indirect fire, using high-explosive shell in the manner of normal towed artillery, they were primarily intended for line of sight direct-fire at targets within a range of about 2,000 yards, usually much closer, firing stationary from hull-down positions, and their main targets were anti-tank guns and tanks, for they were excellent tank-destroyers. They had no equivalent outside of the wartime German Army (for the major western powers never took them into use), and they remained a pivotal force in the Soviet tank arm from 1943 for more than forty years, and even now it is not certain that they have been phased out. They are not to be confused with the armoured track-mounted self-propelled artillery that came to be used in the German Army and elsewhere both during and after the war, artillery that was designed only for indirect supporting fire from a self-propelled mobile platform. For the SU was essentially a heavily armoured *fighting* vehicle, used in the forefront of battle and capable of outfighting tanks, something that western self-propelled artillery on the lightly armoured chassis could never do.

Soviet tank equipment was simple, robust and effective, the strength of its armour design resting on the good sloping surfaces that it presented to enemy anti-tank weapons, for the greater the angle of slope the more impenetrable becomes the armour, partly because of the induced ricochet effect but, more particularly, because of the increased thickness of armour in the intended path of the anti-tank projectile. The main Soviet tanks were of low silhouette, had good wide tracks with better tactical mobility than those of German war-time models, and, from 1941 onwards, never suffered from that most serious defect of western tanks, that of being under-gunned: for the Soviet medium and heavy tanks all mounted a long high-velocity large-bore gun designed to fire various types of anti-tank projectile in addition to solid shot and high-explosive and smoke shell. The engines were usually V 12 diesels with the greater road range and fire security that diesel fuel gives, the T 34 and the KV engines being interchangeable. But in order to meet the opposing demands of armour and protection, low silhouette, tactical agility given by lighter weight and a good power/weight ratio, and as heavy and powerful a gun as could be mounted on a given turret ring, certain disadvantages had to be accepted: and these included the inability to depress the gun to below − 3 degrees (so forcing the tank to expose itself on forward slopes), and impaired crew safety and efficiency due to the cramped design of the interior. Mechanically the tanks were crude but very reliable. The main drawback to their battle-worthiness was in the layout of the turret fighting-compartment, in their indifferent optical, sighting and ranging equipment and, most of all, in their lack of sub-unit and inter-communication radio. During the war years many sub-units used flag signals for inter-communication between tanks.

Soviet towed artillery continued to be based on battle-tried models. The short-barrelled infantry regiment gun was now the M 43 76mm (M 43 being the year of introduction) that fired a 13lb. shell to a range of about 4,000 yards, this having an alternate anti-tank role with the western-invented chemical-energy round. The original 37mm (2 pounder) anti-tank gun had given way to the M 42 45mm and then the M 43 (9 pounder) 57mm gun. The artillery 76mm field gun M 42 was an improvement on the earlier gun that had been in use for decades, for it fired a 15lb. shell to a range of 14,000 yards and had such an excellent anti-tank performance that captured stocks were taken into use by the Germans as anti-tank guns. The 85mm M 45 and the 100mm M 44, both produced during the war, were among the best guns of their type in the world, while reliance was still placed on the pre-war vintage of howitzers that had served the army well, the M 38

122mm found in all divisional artillery and the M 37 152mm gun/ howitzer with the corps or army artillery. The Soviet heavy mortars, the 120mm, 160mm and the 240mm, were also of an excellent design and performance, so much so that the Germans had actually produced copies of them for their own use. Soviet free-flight rockets, fired in salvoes of from four to sixteen missiles, dependent on type, from tube, rail or frame launchers mounted on trucks, remained in service, as they do till this day: they were of short to medium range and, since they were not very accurate, were particularly suited to area targets, and they had great demoralizing effect on an enemy caught in the open: because the launchers were so mobile, they were difficult to detect and destroy by counter-battery fire.

In 1946 the Soviet Union had not, as yet, developed its new generation of small arms. The soldier's rifle remained the 5–round bolt-action 7.62mm Mossin-Nagant 91/30 firing a rimmed round, a Russo-Belgian designed rifle that had taken Russia through two world wars; for the 1940 Tokarev rifle had not proved a success. Much more successful had been the sub machine-guns, the M 41 PPSh and the M 43 PPS firing a shortened 7.62 mm rimless round, machine-carbines that had been manufactured in very large numbers; these assault carbines gave a great volume of fire at close range. The platoon and company light machine-gun, mounted on bipod legs and with a drum magazine, was the 7.62mm Degtyarev DP and DPM firing the 1908 rimmed rifle ammunition, the equivalent of the British Bren gun of that period with much the same characteristics, a slow rate of fire, but sturdy and reliable except for a tendency to jam-feed; it was used up to ranges of 800 yards, firing short bursts: the battalion medium machine-gun was the tripod Sokolov wheeled trailer-mounted Maxim M 1910, an old but reliably designed belt-fed water-cooled weapon that could be fired in very long bursts at targets more than 2,000 yards away, and this formed the basis of the long-range sustained small-arms fire, together with the M 38 12.7mm DShK heavy machine-gun. A post-war generation of infantry weapons was already in production or in preparation, but generally the wartime small arms were to continue in use for at least another ten years until after 1955.

Standardization was already a Soviet virtue and, having learned the lesson of the difficulty of maintaining the great number of types of tanks that had been developed between the two world wars, the tendency in the post-war years was to concentrate on a few well tested equipments, these equipments, with modifications, remaining in service for decades. When tanks or guns became obsolescent, sometimes even obsolete, they were used as training equipment or put into central storage to equip reserve formations or Soviet allies, or were converted to other uses, for the Soviet Union rarely scraps anything. Obsolescent tank chassis became the mountings for new and more formidable S Us. In similar fashion the artillery gun-carriage and mounting for the ubiquitous M 38 122mm howitzer also served for the M 43 152mm howitzer: the M 31/37 122mm gun had the same carriage as the M 37 152mm gun/howitzer: the two anti-aircraft guns, the M 38 76mm and the M 39 85mm, had the same carriage, and the same tracked carriage was used for the M 35 152mm gun, the M 31 203mm howitzer and the M 39 280mm howitzer. Soviet arms designers were clever, adaptable and practical and rarely strove for the purely desirable. But, as was the case before the war, the Soviet Union was not deterred by considerations of cost or by the inevitability of the need for continual replacement of armament that was already dated as soon as it entered service, armament that would, in all probability, never see a battlefield.

⋆　　⋆　　⋆

The strength of the immediate post-war Soviet Army was put at about two and a half million men. More than fifty per cent of its peacetime field organization, that probably stood at about 100 fully manned divisions, was of rifle divisions, about twenty or thirty divisions were tank or mechanized, the remainder being cavalry or artillery divisions. On full mobilization this number of line divisions could be raised, presumably, to something near the pre-war strength of 300 divisions, but most of these would have been the old-fashioned wartime infantry divisions on reduced scales of equipment, without tanks and with comparatively little motor transport. From this time onwards every effort was made to motorize all reserve divisions and convert all peacetime rifle divisions to mechanized divisions, at the same time increasing the overall tank strength of the Soviet Army in peace and in war.

The army remained basically a conscript force, the conscripts originally serving for two years, though this was shortly increased to three. Most of the Soviet male youth should have had some preliminary training in drill and small-arms instruction in *Osoaviakhim* or, from 1948 onwards, in the all-Union voluntary societies that replaced *Osoaviakhim*, DOSAV, DOSFLOT or DOSARM (for the army), eventually to be known collectively as DOSAAF. Conscripts selected for service were registered early in the year and were then called up in the autumn and sent to their units each December, most of their training being carried out in the unit to which they had been posted. The winter months were used for individual and sub-unit instruction, outdoor exercises starting in April and the large manoeuvres at the end of September. In the following December the new annual intake of recruits arrived and, as soon as they had taken their places in the units, the time-expired men were allowed to depart.

The non-commissioned officers were selected from the conscripts and were promoted to sergeants' or junior sergeants' ranks (for there are no corporals in the Soviet Army), some of them having attended the training courses run by their units. Once again the problem of a lack of a corps of experienced long-service non-commissioned and warrant officers, so well known in tsarist times, came to the fore, and every effort was made to induce conscript non-commissioned officers to extend their service voluntarily in the category of extended-service men, by the grant of a good rate of pay (that they did not enjoy as conscript non-commissioned officers), better rations and messing and the granting of coupons to buy extra luxury goods at officers' shops; they were also given the same leave as officers, thirty days a year exclusive of travelling time, together with compassionate leave should their circumstances justify it.

The officers formed the only permanent cadre of the Soviet Army and they served from the time of first appointment as junior lieutenants until they were transferred to the reserve for reason of age or infirmity. Theoretically the age for retirement was thirty-five years for a lieutenant, forty for a captain and fifty for a lieutenant-colonel, but at this time the officers were allowed to serve long after they had reached these limits. Retirement was possible on request, except that deductions were made from the officer's pension should he want to retire before having twenty-five years' service. In the troubled years immediately after the war, when Stalin began what was in effect a war mobilization that was to increase the armed forces from 2.8 million in 1948 to nearly six million at the time of his death in 1953, very few officers were permitted to retire voluntarily.[8]

The Soviet Army rank and pay structure was very close in its pattern to that of the tsarist army, both officers and other ranks getting a basic rate of pay according to rank, to which were added increments for years of service and for the appointment actually held at the time, so that an unemployed or sick officer would get less pay than one who was at duty.[9] A major-general at the 1948 rates might get between 3,000 – 4,000 rubles a month (the equivalent at that time of up to £360 or 1,440 US dollars): the rank differential among officers and extended-service men was not particularly great, in that a lieutenant might have a monthly salary of as much as £110 (or 440 US dollars), and a sergeant on extended service over £50 (or 200 US dollars). The conscript, on the other hand, was almost as poorly off as his tsarist equivalent, his pay being about £2 (or 8 dollars) a month. Marriage allowance was not paid to officers or soldiers, but there were no deductions for income tax. The amenities and accommodation for officers and extended-service men were, by Soviet standards, generally good, particularly abroad: those for the conscripts were sparse and Spartan, though the food and medical attention were said to be adequate. The conscripts had no home leave during their years of service, and abroad in occupied territories troops were forbidden to have any contact with the civil population. As in the days of their fathers and forefathers, theft, absence without leave and drunkenness were their besetting sins, sins not necessarily confined to conscripts since they were very common also among extended-service men and were not unknown among the officers. In occupied territories immediately after the war some Soviet families, usually those of officers, were permitted to join the units but, as the world political situation continued to deteriorate, this privilege was later withdrawn and the families were sent back to the USSR. In the Soviet Union there was a shortage of married accommodation for all but the senior officers.

From the late war period there had been a very significant improvement in the status of officers, in their privileges, education and dress. Count Ignatev, last heard of lecturing at Moscow university just before the war, had been made responsible in 1945 in some general way 'for the instruction of Soviet officers in etiquette', little though this must have meant.[10] Tsarist badges of rank were in use and there was an improvement in the style and the number of officers' uniforms. The grey-blue trousers with the red *lampa* stripe, reminiscent of the old régime, were already back: the traditional tsarist bluish-grey officers' greatcoat was making its appearance and was often red-embroidered for general officers; (the other-rank wartime khaki woollen greatcoat, often from British materials, was also giving way again to the tsarist-coloured brownish-grey). The newly styled Suvorov cadet schools had been founded to take in boys from the age of ten, sometimes even younger, usually the sons of officers or army orphans: these schools were patterned on the tsarist institutions and their pupils passed on to officer candidate schools of the arm of service to which they had been allocated.

In so far as the political control of the army was concerned, nothing had in fact changed in the post-war army. The NKVD special sections, that became part of the NKGB during the war, were still to be found at all levels down to that of regiment, these sections being headed by one or two officers who wore normal army uniform and the arms insignia of the unit; their true identity could not, however, be concealed from the other officers or, with great hope of success, from the rank and file, for they appeared to have no function or purpose in the normal day-to-day life of the regiment. What they did took place behind closed doors and their activity was cloaked in secrecy: they were feared and avoided. The task of these KGB officers was to watch, listen and report on anyone, the commander and military commissar included, regardless of rank, and to do this they established a secret network of spies and informers of any rank, down to the meanest private soldier, recruiting and controlling this network partly by payment but mainly by threats and blackmail. They had their own secret police. This system remains part of the Soviet Army today, for in all major units can be found the unobtrusive lieutenant 'to whom even the regimental colonel makes so polite a bow'.[11] Sometimes the KGB spy in the officer's house is his own wife.

In addition to the KGB spy network there remained the usual political controls that had existed in the Red Army since its inception, the military councils at the higher levels and the former military commissar, now known as the deputy commander for political affairs (*zampolit*), who, having lost the distinctive red star and hammer and sickle emblem on his sleeve, could no longer be distinguished in his dress from any other officer in the formation or unit. The *zampolit* was to be found at all levels of command, from the corps down to the battalion and at times to the company: he, too, retained his own private communication network independent of the commander, and part of his job was to make confidential reports on the commander's attitudes, efficiency and effectiveness, his political reliability and the morale of his unit. The primary task of the *zampolit*, as the representative of the party, remained the political control of the army and its political education, particularly the political education of the many conscripts that went through the ranks and returned to civil life after their military service. For the Soviet Army, like the German Army of Hitler's Reich, was, and remains, one of the principal political educators of the country's youth. The *zampolit* trained his subordinate agitators and activists, party and Komsomol members, to influence the man in the ranks by their example and, above all, by their talk: they were also expected to report political doubters, free thinkers or dissenters, and this was an important part of their responsibilities. The political deputy had, of course, other tasks, military, educational and even, up to a point, welfare, but his primary functions were those of political control, political education and propaganda, and on these was he judged by his superiors.

The border guards and the internal security troops continued their independent existence quite apart from the Soviet Army, at a combined strength of several hundred thousand men, all recruited from politically reliable conscripts who chose, or were selected, to do their national service with these armed security troops. One of their main roles was to keep the communist régime in power by the suppression of internal disorders and armed insurrection by the Soviet Army. The original Bolshevik *Cheka* that had become the OGPU in 1923 and had been renamed the NKVD in 1934, was successively under Yagoda, Yezhov and Beria. But since Stalin did not place complete trust in a unified NKVD the dictator had divided it, in early 1941, into the NKVD under Beria and the NKGB under Merkulov, and in 1946 this distinction remained, except that the two became known as ministries instead of people's commissariats and so were redesignated as the MVD and MGB. However, in 1946, the MVD, as the equivalent of the interior ministry, still had the control of most of the armed forces of the security police but had been separated from the MGB functions of world-wide political intelligence and counter-intelligence; but then, between 1946 and 1950, all border guards, railway troops and special-purpose troops, and part of the civil police, that is known in Russia as the militia, were transferred from the MVD to the MGB, leaving MVD with the internal security troops only. This Stalinist principle of divided control over the armed security police remained a feature of the Soviet government organization after his death in 1953, notwithstanding Beria's brief and unsuccessful attempt to bring all police troops under his personal MVD control: and the twin controlling organization continued, in apposition, in opposition, sometimes even at enmity, known respectively as the MVD (successively under Kruglov, Dudorov and Shchelekov) and the KGB (under Serov, Shelepin, Semichastny and Andropov). All of these security chiefs had long memories and Andropov settled his score with Shchelekov after he came to supreme power.

The border guard and internal security armed forces were made up of divisions, regiments and battalions equipped with tanks and artillery, their formations being well equipped and heavily motorized to a standard superior to that of the Soviet Army, and all ranks enjoyed status and privileges of a favoured class. Their fighting efficiency cannot be judged for, during the Second World War, they were held in depth behind the Red Army troops, partly as a reserve and partly to ensure that the army did not retreat or desert. On rare occasions, as at Voronezh in 1942, NKVD internal security troops were drawn into the main battle against the Germans, but such use was exceptional, as the régime could not afford to allow the weakening of one of its main security organs through casualties. Although there were many points of similarity between the Soviet border and internal security troops and Hitler's *Waffen SS*, fighting in the forefront of battle, as the SS had to do from 1942 onwards, was not one of them.

*   *   *

In the years between 1946 and 1953 the purges of the thirties were still fresh in the memories of all, particularly in the minds of Stalin's associates and the generals of the Soviet Army. Repressions, arrests, beatings, torture and killings continued throughout and after the war as a part of communist life: there were disappearances and shootings, too, in Stalin's circle, and it was merely the scale that had been reduced and the publicity that was lacking. And there could be no surety, certainly not as long as Stalin lived, that the colossal purges of the thirties might not be repeated, and those who were closest to Stalin were those who were in the greatest danger.

The cult of Stalin's personality had already become marked by the beginning of the thirties so that the men about him had become lackeys rather than colleagues. But as the years aged him, the obligatory adulation of the dictator, whom Djilas has called 'the greatest criminal in history', became grotesque.[12] For Stalin resented that fame or credit should be given to others.[13] At a 1946 meeting of the supreme military council (VVS), presided over by Stalin, all present, according to Shtemenko, 'had to listen to a long harangue directed against one of our most important soldiers [Zhukov] on the subject of immodesty, conceit and megalomania.'[14] This led to the removal of Zhukov to obscurity, and his main fault was that Stalin saw him as a rival not for power − as was commonly believed in the west at the time − but for fame.

Stalin's infallible pronouncements assumed the style of oracles even though they were often based on the work and ideas of others. In 1942 Stalin had published what he called his own principles of war, certainly very different from anything produced in the west, for they leaned heavily on the factual and the tangible. Stalin's principles were founded on what the dictator called permanently operating, transitory, or fortuitous, factors.[15] Three of the constantly operating factors, quantity and quality of divisions, equipment, and the organizing ability of commanders, being based on substance rather than theory, certainly reflected Stalin's cast of mind: but they were factors and not military principles. In Stalin's terminology 'morale' became 'morale of the army', and the fifth factor 'stability of the rear' was adopted directly from Lenin.[16] By 1949 Stalin had become, according to Voroshilov, 'the greatest man on our planet', and Soviet military science (that embraced not only the purely military elements of the military art, that is to say strategy, operations, tactics and the organization and training of troops, but also social-political, economic and home morale factors) became known as 'Stalin military science'.[17]

Stalin left his indelible impression on the development of the post-war Soviet Army and he had an influence much greater than that so fictitiously attributed to Lenin and the earlier socialist thinkers of the last century: his principle was 'control, control and once again control!'[18] In the summer of 1949 Stalin was lecturing the Politburo that the German failure was due to Berlin's lack of understanding that 'war is won in the factories.'[19] For Stalin said that the outcome of war depended on a firm home economic industrial base, safeguarded by the party and security troops; it was also important to disrupt the enemy's rear and homeland through propaganda among his workers and through partisan activity elsewhere, every effort being made to destroy the government of the enemy and the security of his lines of communication, the whole disruptive operation being controlled by a Moscow-housed central staff. But the corner-stone to Soviet success both in the Second World War and in the future remained, in Stalin's view, Soviet economic resources and the development of the Soviet industrial and armament base, under a very highly centralized control. And this remains the credo of the Soviet state today.

Most of Stalin's senior generals continued to hold high appointments, some for a decade or more after the dictator's death in 1953. There were, however, some changes. Vasilevsky was one of the ablest and best educated of the marshals, belonging, like Shaposhnikov, to a bygone age: his writings show that he stood head and shoulders above Zhukov in clarity of thought and expression. Vasilevsky replaced Antonov as chief of general staff in November 1948 and then, four months later, became minister for the armed forces in place of Bulganin. In 1950 Vasilevsky's ministry was renamed as the ministry for war; and the navy was removed and became a separate ministry, remaining independent until Stalin's death when it returned to the single ministry redesignated as the ministry of defence. In 1953 Bulganin came back as minister. Zhukov, removed from his post as deputy commander-in-chief in 1946, disappeared, at least from public notice, for several years, it is said to obscure and unimportant posts; but he was yet to return in 1952 as the inspector-general: he was largely a self-educated man, like his fellows completely in Stalin's shadow, though hard and decisive with considerable operative genius.[20] Nor had Zhukov been the only casualty. Colonel-General Gordov, a wartime front commander, was arrested when in command of the Volga military district and was done to death, as was the Politburo member Voznesensky. The air marshal Novikov and the admiral Kuznetsov were soon under a cloud, and Stalin suddenly took a dislike to Antonov with whom he had worked so closely during the war years, it is said because the dictator had decided that Antonov was a Jew, and he exiled him to the Caucasus.[21] When Montgomery visited Moscow in 1948, he noted that the ministers and generals 'stood in the greatest awe of Stalin' and 'shut up like an oyster in his presence'.[22]

Konev held a special position among the Soviet marshals because he was favoured by Stalin as a counter-weight to Zhukov, a man who had originally been thrust into the public eye by Stalin himself. Konev was a Russian who had begun his military career as a commissar, and he was a strong brutal character of great energy but limited education, unable to express himself well on paper: he realized his own limitations and sorted out operative and tactical problems on the spot, leaving all other matters to his staff. Konev was commander-in-chief of the ground forces from 1946 to 1950 when he became inspector-general, succeeding Govorov; the appointment of commander-in-chief of ground forces was to remain vacant until 1956 when it was assumed by Malinovsky, though the administrative structure remained alive in the interim as 'the ground forces headquarters'. Govorov, a Russian, a former officer of the Civil War White forces, was gloomy and taciturn, persistent and demanding, an excellent organizer who could use his staff well. Rokossovsky, said to be of mixed Russian-Polish parentage, was another tsarist cavalry non-commissioned officer who, after a period of brutal treatment in the NKVD cells at the time of the great purges, had risen to the top: he, too, had the secret of using and relying on his staffs, staffs with whom he always got on well, though he was subsequently to be less popular in Poland after he had been appointed as the Soviet commander-in-chief there, and was then imposed on that country as the Polish minister for defence. Meretskov, a Russian, was distinguished for cunning and circumspection, even by Russian communist standards, but was a thorough organizer: Meretskov had been appointed to an internal military district, as had Malinovsky and Tolbukhin, Russians both. Malinovsky was another hard and brutal character, from the ranks of the tsarist infantry, surly, dull and uneducated, but capable and practical; Tolbukhin was a former tsarist wartime officer, a man of surprisingly mild disposition.[23] Among the senior Soviet marshals and generals there were very few who were not Great Russian. The now *passé* Timoshenko, who was a Bessarabian Little Russian, Purkaev, who was a Mordvin, an ethnic group allied to the Finns, and Bagramian, an Armenian, were among the few exceptions.

Stalin had used his marshals in accordance with their capabilities but owed no great debt to any one of them. The higher their rank and the more popular their fame, the less they enjoyed his trust, so that the command of by far the largest and most battle-experienced front – the Soviet forces in Germany – went to Chuikov, a general of no great importance who had commanded only an army throughout most of the war and who was not on close terms with any of his illustrious fellows.

During Stalin's dictatorship it had been obligatory for the Soviet press to denigrate all capitalist states, the tsars, the old Russian empire and the old army, and it preached the equality of the many nationalities that went to make up the USSR. Whether Stalin really believed in his own propaganda is doubtful, for he was a strange revolutionary with complexes of inferiority unexpected in such a man. Stalin the Georgian had great respect for the Great Russian and for the old tsarist army, an army in which he himself had never served for he had no military experience whatever, and he admired the tsarist army's centuries of tradition and its imposing imperial names.[24] Yet, like the Russian, he stood in awe of German efficiency and of French military *élan*. During and after the Second World War there was an increasing emphasis on things Russian and the reintroduction of tsarist military methods and terms, an emphasis that continued after Stalin's death until this day. And since tsardom, unlike Trotskyism, no longer represented any form of threat to Soviet communism, tsarist military history has come to be rewritten in the present-day Soviet Union stressing Great Russian nationalism and patriotism, finding military genius and virtues in the imperial army not known before. Even the Russian Orthodox Church, an organ of the communist state, has been allowed to continue in existence, although its support is mainly from the elderly.

Later in life Stalin became a glutton, but his mind was never confused by strong drink although he encouraged that failing in others; for his own drinking was a pretence, and the special carafe of colourless vodka from which he drank his many toasts was in fact water.[25] Stalin was always sober. Yet once, during a 1944 supper, the dictator got up, hitched up his trousers as though he were about to wrestle or box, and cried out: 'The war will soon be over. We shall recover in fifteen or twenty years and then we shall have another go at it.'[26] This revealed the frightening mentality of the man. By 1948 his intellect was already declining, although his control over the affairs of state was as tight as ever. He became ever more suspicious and quicker to take offence. A foreigner, Djilas, could discern tension between the dictator and Molotov: Stalin had, some time before, had Molotov's wife put in prison.[27] According to Khrushchev, Stalin had decided 'to finish off' both Molotov and Mikoyan. In this murky twilight world,

Voroshilov, too, was in danger, for Stalin, toying with the idea that Voroshilov was 'an English spy', had for several years past forbidden him to attend Politburo meetings or to receive documents.[28] As a result of what became known as the Leningrad affair, Stalin had begun to purge his old Bolshevik associate Zhdanov's protégés. A new terror gathered momentum at home, while abroad the former western allies were provoked by the Berlin blockade. The world was probably nearer war than was realized at the time, and it may have been for this reason that Zhukov had been made inspector-general and Kuznetsov had been restored to the post as minister for the navy, while Sokolovsky replaced Shtemenko as chief of general staff.[29]

Then, according to Khrushchev, Stalin with maniacal cunning put together what came to be known as the doctors' plot, an alleged conspiracy of eminent Soviet medical specialists to murder prominent leaders loyal to the dictator. Vasilevsky, Konev, Govorov and Shtemenko were named by Stalin as among the proposed murder victims: it was those who were not so named who had most to fear. The doctors' plot, according to Khrushchev, was a fabrication from beginning to end, the whole having been set up by Stalin, 'who did not, however, have the time to bring the matter to the end that he had mapped out'.[30] Stalin's sudden death, under obscure circumstances, was very providential for many of his courtiers and henchmen, and perhaps a reprieve also for the populations of the USSR and the rest of the world.

★   ★   ★

In the late forties the organization and equipment of the Soviet Army was such that the Moscow high command could have been criticized for an obsession with the armoured battle and for what appeared to be a determination to fight the next war in the fashion of the last, and certainly in non-nuclear conditions.[31] Admittedly the transport horses had already gone and the cavalry divisions were to follow them into disbandment, but only the smaller part of the army was fully mechanized, the remainder not having as yet progressed much beyond the 1945 level of equipment and capabilities.

It was originally thought, by those western observers who considered that the Soviet Army was being trained on the lines of the lessons learned from the Red Army victories and the great advances from the Volga to the Elbe between 1943 and 1945, that Moscow would be content to have an *élite* minority of tank and mechanized divisions and tactical air forces, and that this *élite* would fight the future war in operative mass and make the spectacular advances, in 1941 German fashion, while the slower moving rifle divisions followed up behind 'like a great steamroller'. How such a strategy could be fitted into the context of a nuclear war was generally beyond the comprehension of this school of observers. The Soviet military literature of the period was reticent and cautious.

Equipment and field organizations are, however, very firm indicators of trends, and an experienced military observer should be able to foretell intentions, even a whole military philosophy, by analysing the general pattern of equipment and organization, since these permit him to know the characteristics, capabilities and intentions of a foreign army. This process is generally much more reliable than the reading of any number of articles in the Soviet military press – for these, useful though they certainly are, may signify only ideas. Under Stalin no military writer said anything of any real significance in the unclassified press, where difficult or controversial issues were avoided by editors. On Stalin's death it became customary to reprint, without editorial comment, articles on nuclear warfare culled from western publications. Under Khrushchev, a perceptible relaxation became discernible, somewhat reminiscent of that which occurred in the military press a century earlier on the accession of Alexander II. The partial and temporary slackening of controls that took place under Khrushchev in the unclassified military periodicals led to the appearance of a range of press releases and contributions, some of them random and some ill-considered, some possibly to provoke thought and counter-argument. Too much cannot be read into them. In due course the military press settled down into what appeared to be a fairly uniform party line, still cautious but not so reticent, and its teachings, as to be expected, were borne out by military groupings and equipment policies.

The indications were in fact already there that the Soviet Union intended, stage by stage, to convert *all* its forces into armoured, highly mobile formations, built up largely of tank troops but with infantry and supporting arms having a motorized battlefield mobility, all of them sheltered by strong air cover and helped on to victory by the massive firepower of artillery of all types.

By the early fifties the Soviet Army began to undergo an enormous and impressive change, not so much in its organizations, because these in fact changed remarkably little, but in the improvement of the pattern and the scale of its warlike equipment, and in the *matériel* that was suddenly becoming available to the divisions in the field. One of the most significant indicators was in the production, for the first time in its history, of a great mass of armoured personnel carriers (APCs), primarily designed for the carrying of its infantry, and this mass-equipping was far in advance of anything done by the NATO powers at that time. The first generation of APCs were open-topped wheeled vehicles, proof against small-arms and shell or grenade splinters, built on full-wheeled drive 6x6 or 4x4 truck chassis: these, the BTR 152 and BTR 40, had excellent road and track mobility, even in mud and snow, and a fair cross-country ability. Tracked amphibious APCs were to follow. These APCs replaced the unarmoured trucks used to carry infantry in the mechanized and tank divisions, and also served as command and reconnaissance vehicles: numbers of them went to the supporting arms. The mechanized divisions, after they were APC-equipped, were renamed 'motorized rifle divisions'. Then the many dismounted rifle divisions that existed in peace were progressively, and fairly rapidly, converted to fully motorized divisions, each of three motorized regiments and a medium tank regiment, the three motorized regiments each consisting of three APC-borne motorized battalions and a medium tank battalion of thirty fighting tanks. It thus became clear that the Soviet intention was to mount the whole of its ground forces on tracked or wheeled motorized vehicles and to fight its battles at tank speed, without any of the halts that would otherwise have been necessary to close up the masses of marching infantry in the rear.

A tendency became obvious, too, even as early as the fifties, for reliance to be placed on the medium tank as the main battle tank, and the heavy tank and heavy SU equipments were withdrawn from the field divisions, for the moment to be put in reserve as front units. A new range of tanks had appeared: the T 54 medium, equipped with a flattish mushroom-shaped turret and a powerful 100mm gun, being the formidable successor to the T 34; and, late in the fifties, a T 10 replacement appeared for the JS 3, like the JS 3 mounting a 122mm high-velocity gun, that has become known as the last of the heavies, though in fact it weighed hardly 50 tons. The Soviet Union was well abreast of new inventions and trends in anti-tank projectile design, and this showed itself not only in the types of ammunition provided for its high-velocity tank and anti-tank gun armament, but in the wide variety of light anti-tank weapons using rocket or recoilless ammunition and armed with a chemical-action rather than a kinetic-energy warhead: this meant that a tank could be killed not by the impact of solid shot fired from a high-velocity gun, but by the penetrating explosive effect of the missile, irrespective of the velocity at which the missile was launched or struck the target.

From the equipment and the training of the fifties it became certain that every effort was being made by Moscow to increase the mobility of the field army by giving it a rapid river-crossing capability, for no longer would it be possible to await the construction or repair of bridges across the many wide rivers that run from south to north across the north European plain. Soviet amphibious vehicles began to appear in numbers, amphibious light tanks, more types of amphibious APCs (the BTR 50 series), and light and heavy wheeled load-carriers that were capable of swimming and were power-driven in the water. The standard medium tanks were equipped, and their crews were trained, to cross large rivers of up to about sixteen feet in depth by underwater fording, a technique that had been developed and improved from the German experiments of 1941. And since the bulk of the wheeled non-amphibious APCs and load-carriers must still rely on bridging, a new class of truck-mounted pontoon bridging had been developed that could be slid into the water direct from its truck platform and then power-driven through the water, being made up as a powered ferry or raft or forming part of a pontoon bridge capable of taking tanks or trucks. The pontoon troops responsible for the building of such ferries and bridges, because of the excellent design of the equipment, were capable of bridge construction and dismantling in remarkably short times. Engineer equipment of an advanced design was appearing with field units, not only for bridging and rafting, but also for the crossing of dry gaps and all types of obstacles: these included vehicle- and track-mounted assault-bridges and mine-clearers. Mechanical road-layers and trench-diggers were also coming into general use.

Yet more significant was the mass production of military radios and other signal equipment for dismounted or vehicle-mounted use, for Soviet vehicles began to display a forest of radio antennas. All of this indicated a resolution of the age-old difficulty of flexible tactical control, at least in so far as the *means* of control were concerned; and that the Soviet Army should have an excellent reconnaissance and early warning capability, for radar equipment, too, began to appear in profusion.

New artillery had been brought into use, much of it tractor-towed and all of an excellent performance, capable of good range and a high intensity of fire: the quality and scale of issue was in fact generally superior to that found in many western armies. The artillery was, moreover, very varied in its type, and was made up of improved heavy, medium and field guns, howitzers, mortars, and the usual free-flight rocket salvo batteries mounted on trucks. After the mid fifties, single heavy rockets came into service, free-flight (that were fired from an elevating rail-launcher on a tracked armoured chassis), and guided (that were moved on a transporter and were elevated to a perpendicular position before firing from a ground pad). And it was commonly believed that these single heavy rockets, that belonged to the Soviet field formation artillery and had a tactical range of perhaps twenty to sixty miles, had a nuclear capability in that, like some of the Soviet heavier calibre artillery, they could be provided with nuclear in addition to high-explosive warheads. For by the nineteen-fifties the Soviet Union had demonstrated not only that it already possessed nuclear missiles but that it had also successfully developed rocketry up to the intercontinental range.

At about this time there appeared a new generation of infantry weapons to replace those that had taken the Red Army through the war. The old bolt-action Mossin-Nagant remained in service only as a sniper's rifle, for its place had been taken by the Simonov (SKS) carbine and the Kalashnikov (AK) machine-carbine, both gas-operated and firing the new rimless 7.62mm ammunition: the RPD light machine-gun was still in use, but the M 46 that could be either drum- or belt-fed was supplementing it. The use of rimless ammunition eliminated stoppages through double-feed jamming. New hollow-charge anti-tank projectiles launched by a rocket tube were provided for close anti-tank defence. Soviet infantry had taken on a really modern look.

★   ★   ★

In 1946 the Soviet ground forces, though greatly superior in size to all western forces in Europe, were, except in the tank arm, generally inferior in equipment, technology and in expertise, to the armies of the western powers. By 1956 the Soviet ground forces had been developed into a fully armoured and highly motorized force with a potential for strategic and tactical mobility the like of which had not been seen anywhere in the world. The Soviet Army was generally supposed to have about 170 divisions, although all of these would not necessarily be fully posted in personnel, or equipped with the most up-to-date weapons.

Some critics believed at the time that the Soviet ground forces had, however, some very serious weaknesses, and of these the most obvious were the dual command and political controls that were seen to inhibit the leadership, together with the inherent fear of responsibility and lack of initiative that dogged all levels of command. Other critics doubted the ability of the communist régime to change old Russia, with its easy-going ways, into anything like German efficiency or American enterprise, particularly when the communist government and communist society, purposeful and highly dynamic though it certainly was, was known to be as corrupt and possibly as inefficient as the tsarist society before it. Many foreigners who had disbelieved that the Soviets had the industrial and technical capacity to produce advanced military equipment, now doubted the Soviet ability to operate and maintain it. Others were inclined to the view that the impressive equipment demonstrated annually, sometimes twice annually, on Moscow's Red Square and lavished upon the groups of forces abroad, particularly the group in East Germany that could be seen by foreign missions, was window-dressing designed to impress or to frighten, and that the bulk of the Soviet ground forces in the military districts at home had to make do with the inferior and the obsolete. And the reservations of all these doubters were not entirely without foundation. There were also the politico-military critics in the west who regarded all ground forces as outmoded and the whole concept of nuclear war, particularly the waging of ground war with the use of nuclear weapons, as so revolutionary, because of the enormous destructive power of the missiles, as to put it beyond the limits of reason and practicality: these views, too, have a basis of common sense. But these particular critics rarely thought their objections through to the obvious and contrary conclusions: some, sheltering under the American nuclear umbrella, placed their hopes in nuclear deterrence, unmindful that the Soviet Union would no longer be deterred from expansion or aggression, an old-fashioned aggression of infiltration or armed conflict, when it had nuclear missiles of its own: others in the west used the umbrella and the deterrent as a convenient reason to dismantle their own ground forces, to reduce conscripted service or to do away with it completely, justifying their actions with the argument that large ground forces were unnecessary in peace and would never be needed for non-nuclear general war against the Soviet Union since this type of war had been outmoded – even ruled out of order – by the nuclear deterrent. Those that did ponder on the unthinkable, the fighting of a nuclear war where strategic and tactical nuclear missiles might be used in numbers, generally belonged to one of two western schools of thought, the one, usually political, that regarded ground warfare in these conditions as an impossibility, and the other, usually military, that doggedly held on to a counsel near despair, that tactical nuclear missiles, in some way known to themselves, would compensate for the lack of ground troops when facing forces as numerous as the Soviet Army could put in the field. This latter school, too, took little or no reckoning of the fact that by 1957 the Soviet Army was already in advance of the NATO powers in the development and production of tactical rocketry with a nuclear missile potential.

During the fifties some western theorists were apt to regard with more than a little scepticism the structuring of Soviet ground formations, since these had not really altered from 1946 and were apparently based on German ideas of 1938; these sceptics believed that such a gigantic ground force had no place in modern war. They pointed to obvious weaknesses that showed that the Soviet ground forces were not yet ready for nuclear war, in particular to the vulnerable open-topped APCs, and the very large numbers of towed guns that made up most of the Soviet artillery; and there was some basis for this criticism. On the other hand these detractors looked at only one side of the coin and closed their ears to other most powerful counter-arguments, namely that the new Soviet Army was capable of launching a general war in non-nuclear conditions, with little or no warning, aimed at the rapid occupation of Western Europe and other periphery areas, a type of war for which NATO, at the time, was ill-prepared. It remained conceivable that the Soviet Union, given the ground forces already at its disposal, might in fact completely nullify any theoretical NATO reliance on tactical nuclear weapons, merely by the suddenness and shock of its armoured attack, by deep and rapid penetrations, again in the pattern of the 1941 German invasion of Belorussia and the Ukraine but with greater mobility and much increased range; in the air swarms of ground-attack fighters would be screaming overhead at little more than tree-top height. The result might be much the same, in that the NATO command and control system would be in danger of collapse. Leaving aside the question of any political delays in authorizing the firing of western nuclear missiles, one can well imagine that in such a continually moving and changing battlefield, in which everything was fluid, with no lines and no fixed positions, it would be difficult, if not impossible, for the NATO powers to identify friend from foe and to target their missiles. In such circumstances it is possible that the Soviet high command might expect that their newly equipped forces, grouped in the old and tested tactical formations, would defeat NATO forces either in non-nuclear or in nuclear conditions. For even if the Soviet ground forces did not use their own tactical nuclear missiles, they might escape the effects of NATO fire by the tactics of 'hugging the enemy' and making deep and rapid penetrations into the NATO rear.

When it finally became clear that the Soviet Union, with its recently acquired arsenal of intercontinental rocketry and nuclear missiles could already deter the deterrent, and, with its new range of tactical nuclear weapons, could nullify any earlier western advantage in battlefield firepower, some NATO spokesmen began, somewhat belatedly, to change their ground. Gone were the days of the threat of the massive initial strike, in response to any act of war, and it became fashionable to talk of 'limited nuclear war' in which the use of tactical nuclear weapons would be restricted to the actual battle areas; to this was to be added 'the graduated nuclear response', as though one were about to enter a new age of chivalry with an agreed code and rules of warfare drawn up between Washington and Moscow. It is very doubtful that Moscow would be so accommodating.

CHAPTER SEVEN

The Rocket Age

Immediately following Stalin's death the power in the Soviet Union passed to a collective headed by Malenkov, who held the offices of Politburo chairman, party secretary and prime minister; for Malenkov appeared to have the support of Molotov, Kaganovich and Beria. But then Beria came under the suspicion of preparing his own *coup* to eliminate his fellows, and he was himself liquidated a few months afterwards, a removal and shooting in which, according to report, Zhukov, Konev and the Soviet Army formations near the capital, all played some part.[1] This was the first time in which the army could be said to have had any role in the political power struggle since the Bolshevik revolution, but its aid was essential to Malenkov and the other Politburo survivors as a counter to Beria's security police and armed forces.

Beria's demise advanced Khrushchev along the road to power, for there are grounds for supposing that Khrushchev, in self-defence, co-operated with Malenkov in killing off Beria. It may have been that Malenkov felt sure of Khrushchev's support, for the new leader resigned his party secretarial post leaving the field there clear for Khrushchev, who became first secretary in September 1953 and the sole boss of the party machine, seated in the chair that had been so long occupied by Stalin.

Malenkov, who had started his political life as a Red Army commissar and who was said to have had an unwholesome reputation for his part in the Stalin repressions both before and during the war, declared his intention to raise Soviet living standards by reviving light industry and the manufacture of consumer goods for the USSR market.[2] Since this could only be done at the expense of heavy industry and the production of armaments, it represented an abrupt departure from the Stalinist policies of the previous forty years.[3] Khrushchev opposed Malenkov, probably secretly at first, and he was eventually to make Malenkov's liberalizing plan the pretext, the lever, for easing him out of power. For Stalin's insistence on the pre-eminence of Soviet heavy industry and armament production over all other economic demands had stood the party and the country well during the Second World War and was popular with the leaders of the Soviet Army. And in view of what was said to have happened at the time of Beria's shooting it was not unlikely that Khrushchev might yet require the support of the marshals.[4]

Khrushchev used Stalin's tactics of the twenties and removed Malenkov's supporters from the key positions and substituted his own men. In February 1955 came the inevitable show-down within the Politburo when, in an unprecedented move, Malenkov's leadership was challenged by Khrushchev's thesis that was given the support of the Central Committee, that heavy industry should be given priority over the consumer production demanded by Malenkov. The Central Committee had already been reinforced with Khrushchev's followers: Bulganin, the defence minister, was in favour of Khrushchev, and Zhukov, since Stalin's death a first deputy minister of defence and a member of the Central Committee in place of Beria, was known to be dissatisfied with Malenkov's ideas. In January 1955 Malenkov resigned, his place as prime minister being taken by Bulganin. Yet the army's part in Malenkov's overthrow had been little more than the moral support given to Khrushchev and the votes of the military men in the Central Committee.[5]

For the moment all appeared well and the military were rewarded. Bulganin was premier and Zhukov replaced him in 1955 as minister for defence: twelve marshals and generals were promoted, most of them former associates of Zhukov or military men who had been staunch in their support of Khrushchev. In February 1956 Zhukov became a candidate member of the Politburo, the first professional soldier to have ever done so, while the Central Committee had six full and twelve candidate members from the ranks of the marshals and generals.

The raising of Zhukov, a man who was very popular with the masses, to military pre-eminence, was, for the moment, convenient to Khrushchev. But Khrushchev did not neglect to safeguard his own position. Artemev, for many years the commander of the all-important Moscow military district, a man who had had some links with Beria and who may himself have once come from the NKVD, was removed at the time of Beria's arrest and was replaced by Moskalenko, one of Khrushchev's wartime associates in the Ukraine.[6] And Khrushchev did what Stalin had done in his time, promoted and advanced the military men that he had once served with in the south, men who were either tied to himself or in whom he had some confidence, men who were not beholden to Zhukov. Among these were Bagramian, Chuikov, Biriuzov, Eremenko and Grechko. And, like Stalin, knowing that there was little love between Zhukov and Konev, Khrushchev kept Konev in the public eye as a counter to the new minister of defence.

In June 1957 the rump of the Old Bolsheviks, Molotov, Kaganovich and Malenkov (who had remained a member of the Politburo), attempted to remove Khrushchev from the first secretary-ship of the party, and the Politburo vote went against him. Khrushchev refused to accept the decision and, apparently supported by both Zhukov and the KGB general Serov, went back again to the Central Committee. Before Khrushchev's time this had been virtually unknown since the real power had always rested in the person of the party leader, and the Politburo had guided the Central Committee. Zhukov, who addressed the Central Committee plenum, presumed to speak in the name of the Soviet Army in favour of Khrushchev.[7] Khrushchev won his battle and survived as leader and contrived the disgrace of the 'anti-party group': but the lesson was not lost on him that the Cromwell who had this time supported him might next time turn against him, and this was probably the real reason that Zhukov was finally removed a few months later, in October 1957, from his post as minister of defence and from his seats on the Central Committee and Politburo (where he had since become a full member).[8] Zhukov was finally consigned to obscurity.

After Zhukov had gone, numbers of improbable charges were made against him, in addition to that of Bonapartism. It was said that he wanted to concentrate all direction and responsibilities under his own ministry and that he had opposed Khrushchev's measures for the decentralization of industrial administration. Zhukov had required, so it was *hinted*, that the main political administration (PUR) should be made directly responsible to himself and not to the Central Committee, so that the commissars would, in effect, be brought under military control at the highest level.[9] Whatever the truth of the matter, the years 1953 to 1957 are unusual in the history of the Soviet Army in that, for the first time, they show the military as a potentially political force. With the removal of Zhukov, the army lapsed back into its earlier apolitical and neutral position, subordinate to the party and the KGB controls; and Khrushchev, for the time being, was unassailable within the Politburo.[10]

Zhukov's ministry of defence went not to Konev, who remained as a first deputy minister and the commander-in-chief of the Warsaw Pact forces, but to Malinovsky, the commander-in-chief of the ground forces since 1956, a dull, uneducated sort of man who seemed to be without personal or political pretensions.[11] Malinovsky held the post of defence minister for ten years until his death in 1967: his senior deputies were Grechko, commander-in-chief of the ground forces from 1957 to 1960 and then commander-in-chief of the Warsaw Pact forces in succession to Konev, Zakharov, the chief of general staff that was shortly to become known as *the general staff of the armed forces*, and Chuikov, the commander-in-chief of the ground forces from 1960 to 1964.[12]

*　　*　　*

After Stalin's death the Soviet Navy had been taken back into the ministry of defence, but there were no further major changes in the Soviet high command structure until the end of 1959 when the new strategic rocket forces were established as a separate branch of the armed forces, its first commanders-in-chief being army artillerymen.[13] The strategic rocket forces, although entirely independent of the ground forces, over which in fact they were to take military precedence, were like the air forces and the PVO home air defence command in that they remained part of the Soviet Army; they wore Soviet Army uniform with the same gorget and arms patches that varied according to the soldier's technical unit and employment, so that it was in fact impossible to distinguish the soldier serving with the strategic rocket forces command from those elsewhere. The strategic rocket forces man the launching sites of the intercontinental long-range rockets and those of medium range that could cover all targets in Western Europe, while the tactical short-range rocketry with a register possibly up to 500 miles remains with the army artillery of the ground forces.

From 1960 onwards, the separate commands, or rather branches of the high command all responsible to the minister of defence, were the strategic rocket forces, the ground forces, the air forces, the PVO home air defence that included anti-aircraft guns and guided weapons and an air force fighter component, and the navy with the naval air force. In addition certain specialized parts of the air force are usually made directly responsible to the defence minister, and these include the long range air force, the military air transport force and the airborne forces. The operational control over the groups of forces and military districts remains, as before, vested in the defence minister using the general staff as his executive.

The early nineteen-sixties saw a reduction in the peacetime strength of the armed forces from the 1955 total of about 5,750,000 to 3,700,000 in the year 1960.[14] There was then a further cut of over a million so that the 1965 armed forces strength stood at 2,600,000, of which the Soviet ground forces numbered just under two million; the 400,000 frontier and internal security troops are not counted as being in the Soviet armed forces. By 1964 the Soviet ground forces were believed to be about 145 line divisions, of which forty divisions were probably tank divisions, the remainder being motor rifle divisions on varying scales of armament. Generally, only those abroad (that is to say in the groups of forces in the west) or on the Chinese border, were kept at near full strength. In the interest of economy much of the fighting equipment, including tanks and vehicles, even in the groups of forces in the west, was kept in light preservation and in reserve, that part that was in use for training being rotated and, at regular intervals, returned to store.

During the sixties and the seventies there was no change of any importance in the field organization and, except for the steadily improving armament, there was no change in the fighting characteristics and capabilities of the Soviet ground forces, the continued emphasis being on armour, mobility, fire power, shock action and deep manoeuvre.[15] Those armies that were not tank armies – the mechanized, shock and rifle armies – had been renamed as 'combined arms' armies, and they consisted of motor rifle divisions, perhaps three or four to each, with a possible addition of one or more tank divisions.[16] The tank army remained, as before, made up predominantly of tank divisions. Neither type of army had a subordinate corps headquarters, for in the mid fifties most corps headquarters had been disbanded, so that the armies were themselves, in effect, enlarged corps.

There had been some minor changes in the organization and equipment tables of the line divisions, but the difference between the two types of formations, whether they were combined arms or tank armies, or motorized rifle or tank divisions, remained, as before, only a difference in the proportion of APC borne infantry and tanks in each, for the 1965 tank division had ten tank battalions (300 tanks) but only three battalions (1,200 bayonets) of infantry, while the motorized division had six tank battalions (180 tanks) and nine infantry battalions (3,600 bayonets). A tank army might therefore have 1,200 tanks but only twelve rifle battalions, while a combined arms army might number 700 tanks and the equivalent of four infantry divisions, that is to say twelve infantry regiments or thirty-six rifle battalions. Tank divisions were faster, more flexible and easier to command and handle, this making them ideal for fluid conditions of the advance, the encounter battle when opposing armies meet, and the pursuit, particularly in open country; but they lacked the staying power of the motorized rifle divisions and were not so versatile in the number of roles that they could undertake. A tank division, by itself, because of its lack of infantry, could rarely overcome strongly defended localities, nor could it operate unaided in close or difficult country, particularly forests, marshes and in cities or built-up areas, and it could not hold ground for long periods. The motorized rifle division, when dismounted, has the characteristics and fighting power of an infantry division with its own tank brigade support; when mounted it becomes the equivalent of a western armoured division.

A third type of division, the airborne division, appeared in the autumn manoeuvres in the sixties, such divisions being temporarily allocated by the high command to carry out certain specialist operations, usually the securing of objectives way out ahead on the intended axis of advance, features of tactical even strategic importance, such as enemy airfields, enemy nuclear missile equipment, and river bridges, causeways and defiles. Airborne troops also had the task of disrupting the enemy's defence by destroying his main headquarters and radio and line communication centres, stopping up his main supply routes and generally disorganizing the enemy rear. Airborne divisions, that are usually parachute-landed, had the usual three-regiment and nine-battalion organization and, except for an anti-tank unit of small self-propelled tracked armoured SUs that were parachute-dropped on a wooden pallet platform, had no tank regiment.[17] These parachutists could be reinforced during battle by infantry from the motorized rifle divisions transported by the giant helicopters that often formed part of the air armies under front command; no specialized training was needed for this movement.

During the early sixties there were other significant changes in the Soviet forces, mainly in the field of equipment. Large single rockets were taken into use to augment the artillery, even down to divisional level, and these, of both solid- and liquid-propellant design, could carry a very large missile to a great range, the missile being armed with either a high-explosive or a nuclear warhead. At front and army level these rockets were liquid-fuelled, since a liquid propellant at that time gave greater range, and the rockets were guided on to their targets by an inboard inertial guidance system in the case of the front and army *Scud* missiles, which were believed to have a range of up to 200 miles. The line divisions were equipped with an unguided free-flight solid-propellant *Frog* rocket that was thought to have a range from twenty to forty miles. The *Scud* missile was transported on an armoured tracked carrier but fired erect from a pad (in the fashion of the German V2); the *Frog* was launched from an elevating rail mounted on the platform of a self-propelled tracked and armoured chassis.

The anti-aircraft gun, too, was giving way to the guided rocket. Anti-aircraft artillery forming part of the ground forces under front or army control, gave up their heavy 100mm and 85mm guns and had them replaced by surface-to-air (SA-2 *Guideline*) guided missiles, and surface-to-air missile regiments were to be found with all combined arms and tank armies. The SA-2 was a two-stage solid-fuel rocket with a command-guidance system and proximity fuse with an effective ceiling of 70,000 feet, and was the most commonly used equipment throughout the ground forces and the PVO: the weapon was moved on a wheeled trailer but fired from a mobile launching rail. Anti-aircraft guns of 57mm calibre and below were still kept by the ground forces as the main weapon for low level anti-aircraft defence, and these guns were often mounted in pairs or in fours on self-propelled armoured mountings together with associated radar fire-control equipment.[18]

Just as the heavier anti-aircraft gun was giving way to the anti-aircraft rocket, so were anti-tank guided rocket missiles supplementing or replacing some of the anti-tank gun artillery. The anti-tank rocket of those days consisted of a chemical-energy high-explosive anti-tank (HEAT) warhead propelled through the air towards its target by a normal solid-fuel rocket, two to three feet in length, fitted with wings or fins that acted as stabilisers and directed the flight path: the early model was fired from a light rail, frame or tube, and then, after it had travelled through the air for a few hundred yards, it was brought under control by the firer and then guided on to the target by electric signals sent through a trailing wire paid out behind the rocket, these signals acting on the flight fins. These guided missiles had the advantage that they were very light, being easily carried by a two- or three-man dismounted crew or by a small amphibious reconnaissance vehicle, and they fired a particularly lethal warhead that was effective on impact irrespective of the range at which it was fired; for the missile exploded against the armour and, by what was known as the Monroe jet effect, burned a hole through the metal, sending fragments, hot gases and incendiary particles into the tank. These advantages of mobility, lethality and simplicity had to be weighed against the inability of the weapon to engage a target *within* a distance of about 500 yards, together with its vulnerability to counter-fire and a lack of accuracy that could result from battlefield stress, since the soldier who had fired and was controlling the missile was entirely exposed to enemy fire and had to keep both the tank and his own missile in view during the relatively slow flight of the anti-tank projectile. Unlike the anti-tank gun, where firing and impact are almost instantaneous, the guided missile had actually to be steered on to the enemy tank throughout the flight: during this time the tank could move out of view; and a moving tank could be difficult to hit. Eventually, better guidance systems came into use, but even so, the guided anti-tank weapon can only supplement, not replace, the gun.

During the Second World War vehicle movement and fighting had been much affected by darkness: artillery and medium machine-guns could of course continue to fire at night on known targets, particularly if they were registered, but night operations in really dark conditions (and these operations could be of only a limited nature) were usually left to dismounted infantry, the only arm that had some close vision in the dark and knew where it was and what it was about. Some relief to this general night blindness, from which all armies suffered, could be had on clear moonlit nights or by the use of 'artificial light', searchlight rays reflected down from a low or medium cloud base, or by illuminating flare or shell. If the enemy were in full flight, then tank and vehicle searchlights and headlights might be used. Usually, however, fluid or fast moving operations and, in particular, tank fighting, stopped after dusk when conditions were bad. Before the end of the Second World War the Germans had already made some progress in experiments with night-vision equipment and this was taken up and rapidly developed by Soviet inventors. The results of their efforts became apparent in the early sixties when Soviet tanks and APCs began to appear fitted with night-driving and night-firing aids, usually of the infra-red type, that gave the driver a field of vision of from forty to 100 yards and the tank gunner a night sight that might reach 800 yards or more. This infra-red illumination is very similar to white light in that it is projected by searchlight or headlamps; though visible to the operating crew, it cannot of course be seen by the opposing troops unless they are themselves equipped with infra-red night-viewing devices. This night-vision equipment, provided on a large scale, gave promise that the Soviet armoured and motorized troops could continue the day-time tempo of fighting and movement without any apparent slackening at nightfall.

Once again the process of incessant re-equipping and the marked improvement in each new generation of tanks, APCs, guns and electronic material that was being provided in lavish quantities, indicated quite clearly the direction in which the Soviet ground forces were heading and the ultimate goal that they had been set. The medium tanks in service could cross most rivers up to about sixteen feet in depth simply by fitting a rigid breathing-tube or snorkel that was carried on the tank deck as part of its ancillary equipment. This tube, when put into place and erected in the vertical position, enabled the tank to take in air during the underwater crossing, air that was needed by the crew and by the engine. The accompanying infantry could not at first cross rivers in this style, for the standard APC, the 6x6 wheeled BTR 152, was not amphibious and could not deep-wade since it was open-topped. And so the next series of APCs that appeared in the early sixties, was amphibious: the BTR 50 armoured tracked amphibian, that was becoming standard in the tank divisions, and the BTR 60 8x8 wheeled armoured amphibious vehicle that eventually replaced all BTR 152s in motor rifle divisions and elsewhere. The BTR 50 was propelled through the water by twin turbine water-jets, up to a speed of about 40 mph: the BTR 60 has a single jet and a water speed of 6 mph.

Yet another most important change happened at about this time that concerned not merely the tactical handling of APCs but reflected the whole battle concept of the Soviet ground forces. In the Soviet Army, as with most other armies, the APC had been regarded as an armoured personnel carrier, as is signified by its name, intended to ferry troops, and in particular infantry, to the battlefield and, if necessary, into battle; and there was never any doubt that the infantry were meant to dismount from their vehicles as close to their objectives as was practicable, then form up, if possible in a covered or concealed area, and make their final assault on foot in support of the tanks. But a dismounted infantry assault is time-consuming and, inevitably, it slows up the rate of movement in the mobile battle. For, if the dismounted infantry assault is successful and the tanks then break out into open country, further time is wasted in waiting for the APCs to be brought up unless the infantry are able to ride forward on the decks of the second wave of tanks. The T 54 tank turret had been provided with a handrail for infantry to be carried in this way, but the practice was unsatisfactory, even during the last war, for the infantry were very exposed and could suffer numerous casualties from small-arms or shell-fire: in nuclear war conditions such a method would be impossible because of the massive blast, burning and radiation effects of a nuclear strike.

It is obviously desirable that motorized riflemen should stay in their APCs as long as possible. So the Soviet Army harked back to the days of 1944 and 1945 when a small proportion of German panzer grenadiers, known as armoured (*gepanzerte*) infantry (to distinguish them from the truck-borne motorized panzer grenadiers), were carried forward *right on to the objective* in armoured half-tracks, from which they actually used their infantry weapons, firing over the sides of the armoured vehicles. These armoured half-tracks had good tactical mobility and could keep up with the German tanks.

All Soviet motorized infantry in the line divisions began to use this tactic as a recognized and general practice, and firing ports for rifles, carbines and light machine-guns were made in the hulls of the new-pattern APCs, so that the Soviet infantry could fire on the enemy as the vehicles moved across the battlefield in the wake of the tanks. The new range of BTR 50 and 60 APCs had a much improved tactical agility than that of the 6x6 wheeled BTR 152, and were hardly less mobile than the tanks. But even the obsolescent BTR 152 vehicles were similarly modified and fitted with small-arms firing ports.

The overall insistence was on rapidity of movement and getting forward without delay or check, and from this innovation of motoring the infantry on to or through the objective was born the manoeuvre of *the assault from the line of march*, an indispensable tactic if the Soviet Army was to fight a ground battle in nuclear conditions. For if any body of troops was to delay while it closed up, concentrated and halted during the final preparation for the attack, it would risk annihilation, when it was most vulnerable, by an enemy defensive nuclear strike. To overcome this problem, Soviet attacks were to be launched suddenly and swiftly from dispersed positions a long way off, the attacking troops motoring forward in mixed tank, infantry and supporting arms groups, possibly in darkness, deploying without stop or check from their road columns into their extended order of motorized assault.

In this particular concept the Soviet military men were much in advance of their western counterparts. The APC in its new role of fighting-companion to the tank had become what many of its western users had long forbidden, an *armoured fighting or combat vehicle*. The design of the Soviet APC was changed in that it was given offensive armament, heavy machine-guns that often had good penetrative effect against enemy APCs, turret-mounted machine-guns and small-calibre rifled high-velocity guns, or larger calibre smooth-bore guns firing hollow-charge HEAT anti-tank projectiles, and even anti-tank guided weapons. A gunner was added as a permanent vehicle-crew member. The additional APC armament served not merely to defend the vehicle against enemy tanks and infantry anti-tank weapons, but was developed so that the APC gunner could actually give covering fire support to Soviet dismounted infantry, including the APC's own men who had debussed to make an assault across obstacles. The APC had become a combat vehicle.

The Soviet military literature of the fifties had been hesitant, perhaps uncertain, concerning the group tactics that it was proposing to use in nuclear war, preferring to keep to general principles rather than translate these theories into tactical doctrine and methods; by the nineteen-sixties, however, a clear and unmistakable pattern had emerged. Soviet journals had already come firmly down in their insistence that major war, that is to say European or world war against the west, would necessarily be fought with nuclear weapons as part of the ground battle, and they generally assumed that gas and other chemical agents would be used in addition. They did not subscribe to the view, then prevalent in the west, that the waging of nuclear war required a reduction in the number of ground troops, for the reverse, they said, was the case.[19] The Soviet high command professed to believe that ground operations were feasible in nuclear war, and that these operations should be based on nuclear strikes, probably in great depth, and the offensive action of armoured and highly mobile ground forces making deep and bold penetrations far into the enemy rear; these, together with the nuclear strikes, would paralyse the enemy's will and capability to offer organized resistance. It portrayed in fact something in the nature of a massive, speeded-up and awesome blitzkrieg, that would probably aim at a rapid occupation of Western Europe, an operation thought of in terms of days rather than in weeks. The theory of a controlled use of small-yield nuclear missiles, escalation and the graduated response as propounded within NATO, was treated with derision.[20]

Although Soviet military literature has been reluctant to discuss such a possibility, the Soviet ground forces are, in addition, admirably suited to fast-moving warfare without nuclear weapons, even a non-nuclear general or world war. And this could be undertaken with no change in equipment, organization or training methods. Flexibility is the hallmark of Soviet military philosophy with a consistent rejection of any doctrine that is based on a complete reliance on any one system, be it nuclear, rocketry, air, ground or sea.[21] If a time for war should come it will use those systems best suited to itself.

*   *   *

Although this military philosophy has remained the bedrock of the Soviet armed forces, it does not appear to have been unchallenged. Indeed during Khrushchev's nine years of power between 1955 and 1964 there were some indicators that the Soviet military concepts and doctrine might be about to undergo a cataclysmic change that would result in the ground forces being reshaped as a subsidiary to the nuclear weapon, designed merely to exploit its enormous firepower: this, if it happened, would have been an abrupt departure from the earlier attempt to adapt the use of the tactical nuclear missiles to the support of the existing ground forces, as if nuclear weapons represented no more than a particularly powerful branch of artillery.[22] There was some evidence, too, that those who were occupied in designing nuclear missiles and in the production and manning of rocketry of all types, thought that theirs was the ultimate arm that had largely superseded ground and air forces. Discussion and argument continued along these lines at the highest military level – behind closed doors – for the space of three or four years.[23]

The ebullient and erratic Khrushchev used these dissensions to suit his own political purposes, and his own personal position. In a change from what had been said by many of his predecessors since Lenin, Khrushchev told the Soviet people that armed conflict with the capitalists (the USA) was not necessarily inevitable in order that communism should be world victorious; but he still openly made crude threats to the United States public 'that we will bury you'. Like Stalin, he was intent on undermining and destroying the free world by proxy, and being confident, so he said, in Soviet nuclear and rocket power, he soon developed into a capricious loud-mouthed *provocateur* whose casual displays of war-brinkmanship became so alarming that they are said to have caused concern to his fellow Politburo members and to the military leadership.[24]

During Stalin's lifetime, as in the days of the tsars, the ground forces were the main, indeed the all-important, component of the armed forces, the navy and the air arm being of subordinate significance. During Khrushchev's ascendancy, however, there was a stated change in defence policy in that the first secretary had apparently become convinced that the possibility of nuclear war, and, in particular, the growing Soviet arsenal of rocketry and nuclear missiles, 'had relegated the bomber to the scrap heap' and forced the ground forces into a position of secondary importance after the strategic rocket arm.[25] Allowance must, of course, be made for Khrushchev's emotional and sometimes ill-considered outbursts that he was later forced to modify in the more rational surroundings of the military councils. The long-range bomber was not phased out, and the statement, made to British visitors, was not repeated in the Soviet press: but the strategic rocket forces that came into being at the beginning of 1960 were indeed set up as a command independent of the ground troops and ranking above them in importance.

Khrushchev had come to a view that was contrary to that of his military advisers in that he believed that nuclear parity, or superiority, would enable him to make substantial reductions in the strength of the peacetime standing army.[26] In the years 1955 and 1956 the leader announced reductions in the Soviet Army that would total 1,800,000 men, announcements that were treated with some scepticism in the west. But, in fact, it appears that about a million may have been returned to civilian life, of which number 250,000 were generals and officers. Khrushchev used this as an opportunity not merely to remove all unwanted deadwood, but to retire prematurely all generals who were displeasing to him. It is said that many good officers were removed in this purge. Khrushchev's treatment of the army following the departure of Zhukov is believed to have been particularly shabby; many of the officers who had been forced out before completing twenty-five years' service and thus qualifying for pension were given very small pensions or no pensions at all. Khrushchev began, too, an economy drive, cutting army pay, pensions and privileges (these affecting mainly officers), and Khrushchev restored certain *zampolit* political controls allegedly eased by Zhukov.[27] All this apparently caused a very significant drop in the general morale of the officer corps.[28]

In 1960 the demobilizations, such as they were, were stopped and some attempts were made to reverse the process whereby a number of manned divisions had been reduced to skeleton reserve formations.[29] Then followed the Berlin and Cuban crises and, in 1964, the removal of Khrushchev from power in the third – and this time successful – Politburo mutiny. Brezhnev became the new Politburo and party leader.

Khrushchev's stewardship was too short to have had any lasting effect on the ground forces. When Brezhnev came to power, the unsettling ideas and influences of the Khrushchev era, some of which may have been little more than inspired leaks into the unclassified military press, abruptly ceased, and the steady evolutionary improvements, particularly in the quantity and quality of replacement equipment, continued – evolutionary improvement that had not been checked significantly even in Khrushchev's time. And, what is more, the improvements continued without fluctuation or deviation towards the same goal, of armour, mobility and firepower, that they had been striving to attain since 1946.

Under the new leadership, Malinovsky remained the minister of defence until his death in 1967 when the ministry was given to Grechko, who in due course became a member of the Politburo, and it was left to Malinovsky and Grechko to try to repair some of the damage done to the officer structure and officer morale by improving pay, conditions, and career and civil employment prospects. The officer's career remained, however, an unpopular one in the USSR.[30] Marshal of the Soviet Union Chuikov gave up his appointment as the commander-in-chief of the ground forces in 1964, and the post remained unoccupied until 1967 when it was filled, no longer by a marshal but by a general of the army (Pavlovsky).[31]

★   ★   ★

The 1967 conscription laws reduced the period of conscript service in the land forces from three to two years, the navy and certain specialist corps in the border troops being set at three years. Part of the reason for this reduction may have been the need for economy and part of it was probably due to the drop in the number of men becoming available for military service owing to the falling birth-rate during and immediately after the world war. The manpower demands of Soviet industry, too, were on the increase. A further reason lay in the fact that conscription had been, or was shortly to be, either abolished or much shortened in the forces of the NATO powers. China was a threat to the USSR, but the Politburo was presumably confident that a two-year period of conscription would meet the requirements of most of its armed forces.

The ground forces did not suffer significantly from the reduction in the intake, for throughout the nineteen-seventies they appear to have been maintained at a strength above 1,800,000 men. During these years there was an actual increase in the number of nominal divisions maintained in peace, from 140 to a 1979 total of about 170, these being made up of fifty tank divisions, 120 motorized rifle divisions and seven or eight airborne divisions. More than thirty divisions were located in the four groups abroad: within GSFG, in East Germany, there were twenty divisions, of which a half were tank divisions; there were two divisions in Poland in the Northern Group; five divisions in Czecho-Slovakia in the Central Group; and four divisions in Hungary in the Southern Group. Inside the Soviet Union the majority of the divisions were concentrated in three general areas: sixty divisions were in West Russia and the Ukraine; forty divisions were grouped against the

18 Reconnaissance amphibians
(6 × 6 Zil-485 [BAV]) swimming a
river in 1956

19 Manoeuvres (about 1958):
assault infantry carried on a T 54
tank with APCs (6 × 6 BTR 152) in
the background

20 A 240 mm M 53 heavy mortar
in firing position (1965)

21 Artillery 'donkey's ears'
observation and ranging optical
equipment

22 One of the first strategic rockets on its testing stand

23 A *Scud* intermediate-range tactical guided rocket missile on a self-propelled tracked transporter

24 Parachutists making a descent by statichute from the rear-exit, probably from a four-engined transport (AN-12 *Cub*)

25 An Mi-4 *Hound* helicopter co-operating with a T 54 tank detachment (1965)

Chinese frontier; while thirty divisions stood in the troubled areas of the Caucasus and the Turkish frontier, in Turkestan and against Afghanistan. The overall tank strength of the armed forces, not including that of the Warsaw Pact allies and satellites, is generally reckoned to exceed 40,000 tanks of all types.[32]

When the Soviet ground forces entered the eighties there had been no real changes in military philosophy or in strategic or tactical doctrine for decades. The proportion of tanks to infantry had reached the highest level ever known anywhere in the world: everything continued to be staked on surprise and on the offensive (for the defensive is regarded as a temporary and unwelcome expedient), on movement and manoeuvre, on close, deep and double envelopment, and on air- and fire-power of all types. Since the time of the Cuban missile crisis the Soviet politico-military capability and strategy has both increased and widened with a very significant change towards great flexibility, a flexibility of offence and response that is becoming global in its application, where ground forces can be rapidly moved by road or air, even by sea, to undertake the most varied duties in all types of climate and terrain from the Polar regions to the Indian Ocean, from the Pacific to the Mediterranean and Atlantic. In addition the USSR retains the ability that it has always had, to commit something like sixty per cent of its land forces against Western Europe.

The same standard formations exist unaltered, the fronts, the combined arms and tank armies, the tank, motorized rifle and the artillery divisions; to these must be added the airborne troops. Officially the dismounted infantry that once formed the bulk of the Red Army in the last war, and was in fact the main basic arm, no longer exists as an element of the ground forces, although it is possible that it might come into being again in the event of a long war involving a heavy call-up of all military age groups. The basis of command and tactics remains the division, the regiment and the battalion, generally on the time-honoured triangle system, three platoons to the company, three companies to the battalion and so on, the fourth element, such as the machine-gun company or the mortar battery in the rifle battalion, or the tank battalion in the motor rifle regiment, being designed to support the other three elements of the triangular organization: this triangular concept has the obvious advantage of a fairly ready-made order of attack of 'two up and one in reserve', though variations are possible.[33]

193

Another Soviet, indeed Russian, military characteristic that has proved to be unchangeable, is the insistence on the inviolability of standard basic organizations, and in particular that of the regiment. As in tsarist days it is usually the regiment, particularly the infantry regiment, that is the basic self-accounting unit capable of an independent existence: the soldier's address and home is that of his regiment, the battalions and companies being sub-units and numbered, in sequence and in German fashion, throughout the regiment. The rifle regiment forms a complete tactical unit that is designed to fight as an entity, and the Soviet military have not followed a pattern recently popular in the west, that of fragmenting regiments, sometimes even battalions, in the interests of flexibility, so that they fight under commands and commanders that are not their own.[34] Up to a point this Soviet practice of regimental unity applies, too, to the tank regiments, particularly those of tank divisions, although much depends on which is the predominant arm in the formation for a particular operation, since the tank regiment within the motorized rifle division and certainly the tank battalion within the motorized rifle regiment can have sub-units detached in support of the rifle regiments, if the terrain and the phase of battle should demand it.

The only significant change in the field force of the late seventies and eighties from that of the late sixties has been in the arrival of yet more modern equipment. A *Scaleboard* ground-to-ground tactical guided missile is now additional to, or replacing, the *Scud* at front and army levels. New surface-to-air missiles, such as the S A-8 *Gecko* and the S A-9 *Gaskin*, both mounted on amphibious wheeled launcher-vehicles, have become available to replace or augment the earlier S A-2 *Guideline*, that was a somewhat cumbersome equipment. Another of the latest weapons is the S A-7 *Grail*, a man-portable weapon, fired from the soldier's shoulder and discharging a missile with an infra-red device that homes on to the exhausts of aircraft, probably a copy of the United States *Redeye*. Twin- and quadruple-mounted light anti-aircraft guns on self-propelled tracked chassis are still in service, mainly for the low-level air defence of forward areas and to augment the guided weapons. There has also been a new range of anti-tank guided weapons, some wire- and some radio-guided, and some that have largely overcome the inherent problem of the blind spot, the minimum range at which the earlier guided weapons had been ineffective.[35]

In tank design and production the Soviet Union has made another impressive step forward and has now equipped itself with tanks that are probably second to none. The medium T 54, that first appeared in 1947, and the improved T 55, weighed about 36 tons and had a 100mm high-velocity naval gun as their main armament: these were reckoned to be as superior to the American M 47 as the T 34 had been superior to the Sherman. Then, after nearly two decades of good service, these gave way to the T 62, a much superior and updated T 54, a radical difference being that it mounted a smooth-bore 115mm gun that fired a fin-stabilized round in a variety of missiles including HEAT and high-velocity discarding Sabot, the last having extra-ordinarily good penetration at shorter ranges: like the latter-day T 54, the T 62 was fitted with infra-red night vision equipment, the main gun of the T 62 being fully stabilized in traverse and in elevation, this allowing the gun to be locked, naval fashion, on to its setting irrespective of the movement of the tank. The T 62 had a gun that was probably superior to the NATO 105mm tank gun in use at that time, particularly at closer ranges, but the tank still suffered from the inherent defects of Soviet design, little room and ventilation for the crew (this of course affecting their fighting efficiency), bad loading arrangements for gunner and loader, and a gun that could not be depressed much beyond the horizontal plane. Moreover the commander, gunner and loader were cramped on the left side of the tank where a single penetration could hit them all. The T 62 was, however, like all the new range of armoured vehicles, fitted with some form of nuclear, biological and chemical weapon protection, having an interior that could be hermetically sealed from the outside.

The T 62 tank soon gave way, however, to two replacements, the T 64 and the T 72, that entered field service from about 1975, the first weighing 38 tons and the second just over 40 tons. Both had a particularly strong 'combined' armour, the *armour basis* (that is to say the real thickness plus the increase due to slope) at the strongest points being from 200 to 220mm, a frontal armour that is generally reckoned to be impenetrable by the US *Tow* and *Dragon* anti-tank guided missiles since it is apparently based on spaced armour and a new metallurgical technique: both tanks have a smooth-bore 125mm gun with automatic loading and a power rammer, and this gun can fire a variety of missiles including a high-velocity projectile the impact of which is reportedly increased by a rocket booster in addition to the conventional charge that speeds it on its way. The turrets of both tanks are small, but there is a great improvement in the fighting arrangements for the crew, and their fire-control optics appear to be based on a laser range-finder and a computer that converts range finder inputs and other data into range and elevation. These tanks have many other features that one would not normally associate with Soviet design, design that was formerly based on what was essential rather than on what was desirable, and these features include hinged skirting plates, power-assisted controls throughout, a 'live' track that tends to pick itself off the ground when not under weight or tension, a powered bull-dozer blade fitted close under the front of the hull that enables the tank to dig itself in by bellying down crab-fashion, and, so it is said, a lead-based foam interior lining protection against nuclear shock-waves and radiation. The T 64, and, in particular, the T 72 ended, at least for the time being, the United States qualitative lead in tank design, in that these Soviet tanks with their laser range-finders and auto-loaders can now equal or surpass N A T O battle-tanks in gun accuracy and range and in rate of fire. An improved level of technological sophistication has been introduced, a sophistication that the older generation of tanks lacked.[36] Yet even this older generation of tanks, despite their ruggedness, were among the best in the world.

Another Soviet battle-tank, known to the west as the T 80, is now entering service after its fourth year in production. This reportedly has the 125mm smooth-bore gun with a digital fire-control computer: it also incorporates, so it is said, hydro-pneumatic lifting suspension that enables it to increase or decrease its ground clearance, this serving both to clear obstacles such as tree stumps or concrete cones, and to lower its silhouette when in a stationary firing position: this design of suspension has already been used in the Swedish S tank and the Soviet SAU 122. The new T 80 tank is expected to have particularly formidable protection based on Soviet 'combined' armour and British-type Chobham armour. Such compound armour, according to Isby, can defeat all but the most powerful H E A T warheads and also gives good protection against most kinetic-energy solid shot, even that of the discarding Sabot type, where the specially hardened tungsten-carbide penetrating core retains its initial high-velocity by throwing off the outer casing in flight as soon as it has left the muzzle of the gun, this overcoming the air resistance that bears on larger calibre shot.

The S U tank-destroyers that have served as an important part of the tank forces since 1943 have now disappeared from GSFG, although it is said that new SUs on T 54 and T 62 hulls, mounting 122mm and 130mm guns, are to be seen in the USSR.[37] The airborne ASU 57 and ASU 85 certainly remain in service; the airborne SU 57 can be airdropped on a parachuted platform, but the airborne SU 85 is normally airlanded from transport aircraft.

A very great departure from normal Soviet practice has been the production, over the last few years, of a self-propelled artillery piece, mounted in a fully-rotating crew-compartment on a tracked chassis, and in this the Soviet Union has followed western ideas. These new equipments have a formidable tank-like appearance with what appears to be a massive gun; in reality they are self-propelled artillery, known as such in Russian by the name of SAU, and are not armoured fighting vehicles since they are only lightly armoured against small-arms and shell-splinters. The gun is a 122mm or 152mm howitzer intended, like the towed gun, to support tanks or infantry by normal artillery indirect fire, though it can be used for direct fire, particularly against emplacements or buildings. The reason that this type of self-propelled support artillery has at last appeared with the Soviet ground forces is that towed guns lack the necessary mobility to afford quick fire support to tank divisions, since they have first to be unlimbered and set up on their firing platforms: and towed artillery crews in the open are highly vulnerable to the effects of a nuclear strike. In mobile warfare there will be no time to build dug-in artillery positions with overhead cover.

During the fifties and early sixties, Soviet armoured vehicles, other than tanks and some SUs, lacked the armoured top-cover necessary to shelter the crew against nuclear attack. In the last two decades, however, nearly all of the newest Soviet armoured vehicles, the SU and ASU tank destroyers and the SAU self-propelled artillery, the APCs and the tractors, have been provided with armoured top-decking to give some protection to the occupants from nuclear burns, shock-blast and radiation, and so have a compartment that can be sealed against toxic nuclear dust and biological and chemical weapons; these compartments are being equipped with protective linings and air filters. Other anti-chemical and anti-gas protective equipment is already provided on what appears to be a realistic scale, and troops are trained in its use.

In the case of most of the APCs, or to give the APC its more recent and more accurate designation of 'combat vehicle', the steel armoured top-decking is now usually surmounted by a frontal squat fully rotating armoured turret that houses one of a variety of weapons. The airborne tracked amphibious combat vehicle, the BMD, has a 73mm smooth-bore gun, primarily meant as anti-tank armament, that fires fin-stabilized armour-piercing rounds up to 800 yards; other projectiles are effective up to 1,300 yards: an anti-tank guided missile is often carried in addition on a launcher above the gun, and this is effective up to 3,000 yards. Other infantry combat vehicles mount heavy or medium machine-guns in their turrets, the heavy machine-gun having a good penetrative effect against other APCs, and these turret-mounted machine-guns are meant for offensive action and to give fire-support to other combat vehicles or to dismounted infantry.

The BTR 50 tracked amphibian carrier combat vehicle, based on the chassis of the earlier PT 76 amphibious tank, has long been the standard vehicle for the motorized rifle regiment in the tank divisions, and it has a tactical agility and speed that is probably superior to that of many medium tanks. The eight-wheeled amphibious BTR 60, with variations in superstructure, turret and armament, is the workhorse in the motorized infantry regiments and makes up the greatest number of carrier combat vehicles in service in the motorized rifle divisions. Although the tactical mobility of the wheeled BTR 60 is inferior to that of the tracked BTR 50, it can keep up with tanks over all but the most rugged of broken country; and it has a number of important advantages in that, being wheeled, it has greater speed and has double the cruising range (300 miles) of the BTR 50.

Both the BTR 50 and BTR 60 are crewed by two, the driver and the turret gunner, the first vehicle carrying twelve passengers and the second fourteen, or nearly the same number of troops as was carried by the old wheeled BTR 152. But this passenger capacity is not really suitable for the infantry sub-unit since the infantry dismounted section numbers about eight men. The newest armoured carrier combat vehicle, that has been designed specifically for the infantry so that each section can be carried self-contained in one vehicle, is known as the armoured infantry vehicle BMP (*Bronevaia Mashina Pekhota*), and it transports eight infantrymen together with a crew of three. This tracked amphibious carrier has been designed basically as a fighting vehicle, and the interior is arranged so that the eight men sit back to back on a long bench that runs the length of the chemical- and nuclear- proof interior of the vehicle, this enabling all of them to see out of the periscope vision-blocks provided for each man, and allowing all of the eight to use their weapons, usually two light machine-guns and six carbines firing out of gas-proof ports at the sides and back of the hull. Exit and entry hatches are in the top deck and at the back of the carrier. The turret armament, like that of the smaller airborne BMD combat vehicle that it closely resembles, is the automatic loading 73mm smooth-bore gun, together with a coaxial machine-gun, and either a wire-guided *Sagger* anti-tank missile or a new type of guided weapon with semi-automatic guidance. This BMP class of combat vehicle is replacing all other types as an *infantry carrier* in the tank divisions and in one of the motorized rifle regiments of each motor rifle division, although eventually it will be provided everywhere: it has night-vision aids and is proofed to give some protection against chemical agents and against some of the effects of nuclear explosion, but, like all Soviet amphibians, it has a low freeboard and, notwithstanding the usual splash-plate trim-vane in front to give it floating stability, is not suitable for use in rough water. Its water propulsion is by tracks and its water speed is a relatively slow 3–4 mph.

All in all, the Soviet tank and armoured infantry forces are by far the largest and are the best equipped in the world.

*   *   *

To the outward eye, the Soviet artillery has not been favoured with the same priority of re-equipment as has been given to the tank and armoured infantry forces: according to photographs, many obsolescent, though very serviceable, guns are still part of the field force; the M 1938 122mm howitzer, the M 1931–37 122mm field gun and the M 1937 152mm gun/howitzer appear to be in regular use, the M number indicating the year that the gun design entered service. On the other hand, too much significance cannot be attached to photographs, even in today's press, since they are undated and are sometimes used just to catch the eye, and the Soviet Army tends to use obsolescent equipment for basic or early training in order to save wear and tear on the new models. Towed equipment could, admittedly, be at a serious disadvantage, even unusable, in nuclear war, because of its vulnerability, but it certainly could still be used with excellent effect in any ground operations that excluded the use of nuclear weapons.

The introduction of computerized fire-control equipment must have much improved the capabilities of the artillery. In the eighties the indicators point to a Soviet intention to replace most, if not all, of the towed guns in the groups of forces abroad by self-propelled indirect-fire artillery, each gun in a fully-rotating crew-compartment mounted on the lightly armoured tracked chassis, with nuclear and chemical protection. Of the artillery so converted, the SAU 122 howitzer is on an amphibious chassis that can be lowered or raised hydraulically; the SAU 152, however, is not believed to be amphibious or to have the deep-wading capability of the medium tank. Even so, both have good agility, with maximum gun ranges of 15,000 and 25,000 yards respectively, that can, apparently, be increased by a *further* fifty per cent by the use of a rocket-assisted projectile. As has already been explained, these two equipments are not tank-destroyers or tanks, but, when necessary, they can be used, in the usual Soviet fashion, in a short-range direct-fire role, particularly against bunkers, houses and strong-points; for the direct-fire projectile sometimes has better destructive effect than could be achieved by indirect fire, where the heavy howitzer shell tends to bury itself in the ground before exploding, so that the destructive force is fountained harmlessly upwards.

The standard towed divisional gun is the D 30 122mm gun/howitzer introduced in 1970 as a replacement for earlier obsolescent equipment, and this general-service weapon has a number of novel features, including a semi-automatic vertical sliding wedge breech-block that allows a high rate of fire, and a three-trailed firing platform lowered from the wheels that gives the weapon an all-round traverse and a low silhouette, this latter feature having been copied from German 1943 Skoda and Krupp models. The gun has a rifled bore of the usual pattern but can fire a non-rotating HEAT chemical-action anti-tank projectile (presumably by the use of a slip-band), a non-rotating or slow rotating round having better penetrative effect than one that is spin-stabilized at a high velocity. This D 30 towed artillery equipment is now more numerous than any other. But there remain in the Soviet Army considerable stocks of medium, heavy and super-heavy guns, from the M 46 130mm field gun and the S 23 180mm gun/howitzer to the new pattern 203mm gun/howitzer on a self-propelled tracked chassis.

Soviet small-arms and infantry weapons have not altered much in the last ten years except that a new small-calibre (5.45mm) carbine known as an AKS or AK 74 was introduced in 1981 for the first category divisions and for airborne troops, and this will probably become a general issue in due course. The AK 47 (Kalashnikov) assault rifle, first seen in 1949 as an adaptation of a German weapon, is still in use in the modified AKM form, with a chrome plated breech-mechanism, capable of being fitted with a night-sight and a knife-bayonet that is said to incorporate a wire-cutter. The light machine-guns are: the section RPK that is a modified AKM and fires the intermediate (shortened) 7.62mm cartridge from a bipod; the platoon PK that uses the full cartridge and is mounted on a bipod or tripod (when it is known as the PKS); and the older SGM Goryunov used on a bipod or on a vehicle mount. There is also a RPK 74 light machine-gun that uses the same 5.45mm small-calibre round as the AK 74.

A machine-gun type weapon of a new design (possibly a copy of an American weapon) that has become available in the eighties is the AGS 17 automatic grenade launcher, mounted on a tripod, that can fire 30mm high-explosive grenades from a belt or drum – and this is believed to have the same effective range as a light machine-gun, that is to say 600–800 yards. It lacks a machine-gun's accuracy since it is an area weapon; its fire and morale effect in the target area is, however, considerable, since each of the anti-personnel grenade missiles bursts on impact. These grenade launchers are to be found with each rifle company.

There has been a move away from the comparatively heavy towed and rifled anti-tank gun in favour of guided weapons and the many generations of lighter smooth-bore, wheeled, tripod-mounted or shoulder-fired launchers that project a rocket-assisted missile, usually fin-stabilized with a chemical warhead: those at present in use vary in size from the anti-tank artillery smooth-bore 100mm T 12 towed wheeled anti-tank gun with shield, that is very much like the older pattern rifled gun in appearance, to the 73mm recoilless tripod-mounted SPG 9 and the shoulder-fired RPG 7 85mm grenade launcher to be found in the rifle battalion and rifle platoon. In addition all indirect-fire artillery units equipped with gun or howitzer, irrespective of calibre, are provided with anti-tank ammunition for direct-fire use.

Much of this formidable array of equipment has been copied from foreign, principally German and United States, ideas or patterns: much of it, however, appears to be of Soviet invention or evolution; most of it is of very good quality and high performance and much is ingenious in its design.

CHAPTER EIGHT

Plus ça Change

Nearly two and a half million men reach the age of seventeen, the military registration age, each year, and, since the size and structure of the Soviet armed forces is known with some degree of accuracy, it is clear that more conscripts are available than are needed by the Soviet armed forces and that a fairly large proportion of the fit men are being excused their two years' compulsory service with the colours.[1] This situation is similar to that which existed under the late tsars. Officially, total exemption is granted only to the permanently unfit, all other exemptions being given as deferments of call-up; these deferments are allowed, according to the law, mainly on the basis of family hardship or the need to continue education. Deferments are subject to review, in that, if the man's circumstances should change, he would become liable for late call-up. After the age of twenty-seven, however, all deferments become total exemptions, and the names of those not drafted are immediately entered into a category of the armed reserves, this category having to undertake only part-time military training but being liable for full-time service in the event of an emergency. Many avoid the draft by becoming perpetual students, by family or party nepotism, some even by bribery, much the same as was done in the time of the tsars.[2]

In theory, however, all Soviet males are liable for service irrespective of social or former class origin, of nationality or of religious belief. The population of the Soviet Union, the same peoples that made up the tsarist empire, comprises only fifty-five per cent Russians, with the Ukrainians and Belorussians (who are not of Great Russian stock and speak languages that, although akin to Russian, are not readily understandable by a Russian) providing a further eighteen per cent; the rest of the Soviet population, peoples that are non-Slavic in origin, account for about twenty-seven per cent of the total and come from a hundred different nationalities and ethnic splinter groups, with a large variety of tongues and cultures. And, in spite of the communists' policy of discouraging or repressing all forms of religion, various faiths are practised outside of the state-controlled Orthodox Church, one still firmly holding on being that of Islam in Central Asia. Russian, that is to say Great Russian, is the *lingua franca* in the USSR and it is used extensively throughout the Soviet Union in all party, government and public affairs; without a fluency in Russian no man can be successful, except in the pettiest local politics.

These diverse racial origins are of course reflected in the call-up: even today, in an age of radio, television and a national press, not all Ukrainians and Belorussians are necessarily fluent in Russian: among the Asian minorities the proportion of conscripts whose Russian is poor, sometimes non-existent, is naturally much higher. And as there are no national groupings of troops in the Soviet Army, Caucasian, Asiatic or other foreign-speaking conscripts are separated from their fellows and distributed throughout units and sub-units; there they have to sink or swim as best they may. As was the case in the tsarist army, the presence of non-Russian illiterates is a burden to the officers and non-commissioned officers responsible for them, and life is difficult for the conscripts themselves.[3] Strict practising Moslems, too, can prove a problem in that atheist world where a Great Russian is more equal than others and where there is still more than a relic of tsarist prejudice against Moslems and Jews.

The 1967 law on military service reduced the conscription to two years but introduced the biannual draft in place of the annual call-up. In the February in which the young man reaches his seventeenth year he reports to one of the many military commissariats throughout the sixteen military districts of the Soviet Union, for physical examination, interview, and documentation, after which he receives a booklet as proof of registration. The draft commission that interviews the man recommends call-up, exemption or deferment.[4] Twice each year, in May or in November, those male youths that have reached their eighteenth birthday and been selected for service are called up to the commissariats, the call-up being stage-managed into a near festive occasion with patriotic speeches and band-playing to impress on the recruits the importance of the occasion and to speed them on their way. Many are already in a drunken state: all are in their oldest clothes and carry no valuables in case they should be robbed.[5] They are then railed off under armed guard, the rowdy and drunken columns differing little from those of a century or more ago.

At the basic training units, that are usually improvised detachments within formations, the recruit has his first month's elementary training: he then takes the military oath, an oath still not very different in form from that used during Trotsky's time. This oath, although still repeated at a ceremony, is, however, no longer merely read to the recruits and affirmed verbally or collectively, but the soldier has to sign the oath in printed form and this is kept with his records.[6] The conscript then joins his sub-unit where he will serve for the next two years, and the *ad hoc* training detachments are broken up for another six months until the next intake arrives.

Conscripts are not allowed to marry during their service and will not be given home leave except for very urgent compassionate reasons. The family of the conscript who is already married is not allowed to visit him or live near the unit, but it does receive a monthly marriage allowance. The basic army pay for conscripts is very small, about five or six pounds (seven to nine US dollars) a month at the most, and, as far as is known, even the conscript non-commissioned officer earns the same rate, except that he presumably gets additional increments for performing the duty of the rank.[7]

More than a half of the conscripts are Great Russian and about seventy per cent of the draft usually comes from West or Central Russia. The conscripts are generally physically fit, or soon become so, and it is said of them that they still have the age-old patience, stamina and hardiness of their forebears. Generally they tend to be shorter and stockier than the youth in the west. No recruit to the tank or motor rifle arms is supposed to need glasses. But there has come a great social change in the pattern of the Soviet peoples, even since 1941, for with the movement to the towns that has been taking place since the last century, it is very doubtful whether the population can be described any longer as being predominantly rural, and the balance in fact has shifted to the urban. Whether the new soldier has what were said to be the innate countryman's skills of his grandfather, skills that in any event were perhaps more praised than real, is unknown, but such a deficiency, if it exists, is probably compensated for by the modern soldier's improved education: that the soldier retains the old capability to improvise is likely and, in addition, he often has some technical aptitude. Yet there is much about him that shows that he is not so very different from the tsarist recruit, for he is primitive, brutal, passive and easily led.

The Russian conscript is very credulous by western standards, and has a completely distorted picture of current affairs and of the world outside of, and sometimes within, the barrier walls of the Soviet Union. For he, his family and his neighbours, have been subjected to incessant propaganda, much of it without a basis of truth, over the whole of their lifetimes; their parents, too, have never known any rule other than that of the communists; and they live in a country where it has been made impossible to read the foreign press without restriction, and difficult, except perhaps in country areas, to receive foreign broadcasts (though nowadays listening certainly goes on); foreign travel is not allowed without elaborate state precautions against defection, and foreign contacts are often dangerous. By dint of repetition, much of the propaganda, since it cannot be refuted, comes to be accepted by the average Soviet citizen, even by the sceptics. It is true that successive Soviet governments, repressive, corrupt and relatively inefficient though they may be, can point with pride to real and lasting achievements, a pride that is shared by the Soviet man and woman in street or field. Admittedly the brutality, the arrests, the disappearances and the corrective labour camps are still part of Soviet life; and yet, since the death of Stalin and the removal of the recurrent nightmare of the mass purges, Soviet life has become a good deal safer, a little more prosperous, even a little more comfortable, provided only that the citizen does what he is told and does not question the communist way of life or any facet of communist society. In rural areas distant from the big towns even militia, party and KGB controls are remote. Many Soviet citizens have actually come to believe that they are better off than their counterparts in Western Europe and in America: they fear war, particularly nuclear war, but they are already convinced, such is the power of the propaganda to which they are subjected, that if war comes it will be by western aggression against the USSR. Because they hear it so often, they may believe that the Soviet Union is invincible, for there is some resemblance between the situation in the USSR today and that in Nazi Germany in 1939. And this is probably the belief of most Soviet conscripts when they enter the army, a belief held most strongly by the Great Russian but tailing off in its conviction should the recruit be

Ukrainian, Belorussian, Tatar-Turkic, Jewish, Russian-Polish, Russian-Finnish, or from the Baltic, Caucasian or Asiatic minorities.[8]

★ ★ ★

When the conscript arrives at his unit he comes under the immediate control, not only of his officers and sergeants but of the *zampolit* company deputy commander and political leader, probably a lieutenant, the modern descendant of the old-time commissar: political surveillance is continued and political education is intensified, since the communists recognize, as the German Nazi Party did in its day, that compulsory military service provides a most effective means of indoctrinating the young. Political lectures are compulsory and take up to six hours training time a week; in addition there are news and current affairs briefings, quizzes and general knowledge contests, lectures, meetings, slide shows and films, anything that has a propaganda potential, and all is organized by the *zampolit*. This propaganda is meant to reinforce the political instruction that the recruit has received from infancy, at school, with the communist Young Pioneers or with the youth movement Komsomol, or from the talks that formed a compulsory part of the political pre-military part-time training with the military commissariats or DOSAAF. The soldiers' canteens, clubs, reading rooms and Lenin's corners, where all reading material is found by the state, are organized by the staff of the *zampolit*, and this staff notes and reports the names of those conscripts who read, what they read, and the questions that they ask. All soldiers and all youth who belong to party organizations are of course a captive audience, and, by dint of repetition, much of what is being taught is retained in the mind of even the inattentive and the indifferent.[9]

A considerable amount of training time might appear to be wasted in political indoctrination, so that one can see a parallel in the time lost in the tsarist army to the regimental priest with the daily religious services and the multitude of strictly observed religious feast days. But the communist party does not see it in this light. The *zampolit* continues to serve as a check on, and counter-weight to, the officer commander, but his real value today is in his primary task of maintaining morale and reporting on military efficiency, for he serves as the party's representative right down to company level: and he has resources that the officer commander does not have, a reliable and confidential network of his own based on party and Komsomol

207

members, many being dedicated and some being fanatical to their cause. At the lower levels particularly, the *zampolit*, provided that he is up to his job, remains the best informed man in his unit, and this is a far cry from the tsarist army during the First World War, where officers did not know their men and often made little effort to do so. And the party so arranges matters that it keeps the *zampolit* to the forefront in the public's and in the soldier's eyes: if there is any credit or popularity to be gained by investigating and righting wrongs, or by assisting the soldier with personal or welfare problems, the *zampolit* is sure to have it. A good *zampolit* is often respected by the rank and file: a fanatical *zampolit* can be hated by all.

The conditions for the conscript are said to be tough even by Soviet standards. Messing is barely sufficient and there are complaints that the cooking is bad and the diet is monotonous unless the regiment supplements it with its own livestock and gardens. The living huts or barracks are adequate, and training accommodation is generally good, though most training is done in the open, for many units move out of their permanent winter quarters to tented camps for the summer.[10] Daily duty and training hours are long, a good deal of training is done by night, and, since supervision is close and time for leisure so rare, there is little opportunity for boredom during the conscripts' service; yet absenteeism, desertion and drunkenness still remain the principal offences. Brutality is fairly widespread; the sergeants appear, as of old, to strike the conscripts with impunity, nor is it apparently unknown for officers to use their fists on the rank and file.[11] Soldiers in guardroom arrest, usually for minor offences such as drunkenness, even though insensible and harmless, can be savagely kicked or beaten by their guards.

After the initial one-month induction period, all further conscript training continues to take place with the soldier's unit. This means that all formations and regiments, including those in operational first-line readiness such as the Group of Forces in Germany, are also training units, about a quarter of their total strength at any one time being made up of men who are either raw recruits or barely out of the recruit stage. The non-commissioned officers who command and train these recruits are, for the most part, conscripts themselves, junior sergeants or sergeants who have been selected and promoted from the intake after such additional training as the unit can afford or, more usually, after a six months' course for potential sergeants in a training division immediately after call-up.[12] These sergeants, when called upon to command and train the men, have at the most from eight to eighteen months' service, very little by any standards, particularly when one takes into account their responsibilities and the advanced complicated equipment they are now called upon to handle. Russian non-commissioned officers tend to be indifferent and slack and are generally not as good as those from the ethnic minorities.[13] Tatars that are literate in Russian make the best sergeants because of their soberness and reliability, their honesty and attention to detail, since these are the centuries-old characteristics of their race. Long-service men form a very small proportion of the corps of non-commissioned officers, for few Soviet conscripts have any wish to extend their service voluntarily beyond the statutory period of two years.

The shortness of army service and the highly technical duties performed by many Soviet troops such as signalmen, vehicle and plant operators, engineers and, more particularly, members of a tank, armoured carrier combat vehicle or gun crew, make it difficult to train the soldier to a really high standard. Some specialists, and these include most tankmen, are sent to specialist schools, but the rest, the vehicle crews, the signallers and motorized riflemen, have to learn their duties with the unit; in the limited time available the man can generally be taught one function only, although efforts are supposed to be made within units to teach the soldier to deputize for his comrade.[14] This situation could create serious problems in that if one man in a tank crew of three or four cannot undertake another's duties, the loss of one man could put a tank out of action. A tank's effectiveness, even its life in battle, depends largely on training, co-ordination and team-work, for the tank that survives is often the one with a crew that knows how to use ground and can first fire a single accurately placed round: without this team-work and crew expertise the most modern high-quality tank will be knocked out by a decidedly inferior model.[15]

The Soviet ground forces are thought to be very economy-conscious in terms of money and equipment. There is a widespread use of simulators rather than actual weapons, and the little equipment that is used for training is often of obsolescent pattern and different from the unit war equipment that is held in preservation in hangars and in store.[16] Much driving is done on simulators or by 'walking the ground', and sub-calibre shooting has to take the place of firing with full-round live ammunition. All of the first-line equipment can be taken out of preservation within a day's notice, but this only happens perhaps once or twice a year just before a major exercise such as the autumn manoeuvres. But if the ground forces were to go to war, they would, ideally, need a shake-down period to accustom themselves to team-work, and to familiarize themselves with their war equipment. In peacetime the battle-efficiency of the conscript Soviet ground forces, tank for tank, may be lower than that of the American and British long-service regular army: too much should not be made of this, however, for it is a defect that can be overcome immediately on mobilization, with just a little extra time for additional training: and the Soviet Army has an abundance of tanks and equipment and, with its enormous war reserve, more than a sufficiency of trained men.

The two-year training cycles are continuous and a new basic training course begins every six months. The keyboard to Soviet training is simplicity, geometrical tactics that can be first taught from diagrams and map tables, relatively uncomplicated equipment, and unsophisticated training methods that do not aim too high and that are based on repetition.[17] The standard of formation and unit training is repeatedly assessed by visiting inspecting boards convened from other military districts.[18]

Conscript non-commissioned officers or specialists who, near the end of their service, elect to re-engage, can, if accepted, extend for two, four or six years, and the scheme is also open to former conscripts who have gone to civilian life but then wish to return to the army. These re-engaged men are meant to form the long-service corps of non-commissioned officers, and the scheme differs little from that used by the tsarist conscript army before 1914. Re-engaged men are set apart from the conscripts in that they receive particularly good rates of pay and privileges; and yet the numbers of time-expired conscripts that elect to remain is very small, less than two per cent a year, and these are not always of the required quality.[19]

In 1971 it appeared that this extended-service scheme would be replaced by another of the same kind, when a rank of warrant officer was introduced, this to be known as *praporshchik* in the army and *michman* (midshipman) in the navy, each warrant to be issued initially for five years. The intention was to create a corps of officers' deputies who would occupy the highest non-commissioned ranks, wearing a special uniform and, except in immediate promotion prospects, having privileges and a status little below those of officers. This innovation was based on the tsarist pattern, although it was intended to cure a different ill, for the tsarist *praporshchik* and *michman* had the status of candidate-officers and were meant to form a reserve of potential officers for war. The Soviet *praporshchik* is a warrant, not a commissioned, officer. At the outset of this Soviet scheme, the *praporshchiki* were recruited from the best of the senior extended-servicemen, and the extended-service programme was then suspended in 1972; as far as is known, those long-service non-commissioned officers not selected as *praporshchiki* were put under notice for phasing out, in what may have been a move to rid the army of unwanted dead wood. For the Soviet extended-service scheme had not been an unqualified success. The next year, however, the extended-service scheme was resuscitated and now appears to be open again both to time-expired conscript non-commissioned officers and to high-grade specialists.[20]

*　　*　　*

As in the pre-1914 imperial army there is no shortage of soldiers in the lower ranks either in peace or in war, for about 700,000 trained conscripts are sent to the reserve each year: but the Soviet Army has the same problem that the tsarist army had in its lack of a corps of long-service senior non-commissioned officers in peace, and a total absence of any such reserve to meet an expansion in war. As in the tsarist conscript army of the last of the Romanovs the commissioned officer corps forms the only stable and continuous element in peace, the professional core around which the whole of the Soviet Army is built. Just as the old imperial army disintegrated when its peacetime officer corps had become casualties in the First World War, so the present Soviet ground forces could not exist in peace or war without their regular officers, an officer corps that is probably nearly 300,000 strong, six times as large as that of the tsarist army. Officers serve for their active life and, as was the case in the tsarist army, there is practically no reserve of trained and experienced officers to replace casualties in war, even though a reserve officer training scheme does exist in peacetime.

Regular officers entering the army may have had a general education at a Suvorov military school, the modern equivalent of a tsarist cadet school: then all aspirants have to attend secondary or higher officers' schools, that are in effect military colleges, for courses from three to five years in duration, at the end of which they are commissioned and are awarded either a technical or an engineering degree. There are said to be over 140 such military colleges in the Soviet Union, each housing about 1,000 students, and, since these are the main source from which the Soviet Army corps of 450,000 officers is maintained, it can be computed that these probably train more than 20,000 graduates a year.[21]

The Soviet authorities have in this way established a privileged and select officer class, select mainly by virtue of its education, a class that, by and large, has never served in the ranks and that takes relatively few of its intake from the ranks. What it does do, however, is to put all its military college students through a six-month intensive and rigorous training course with a training division, as a formed body of students ranking as private soldiers, a course similar to those for junior conscript sergeants; and the potential officers have to qualify on this course before they begin their academic instruction, the few failures at this stage who are considered unlikely to make officers being sent to field units as junior sergeants to complete their two years' conscript service.[22]

The few other-rank conscripts who aspire to become regular active officers must extend their service to become, firstly extended-service men, and then warrant officers; after that they have to pass the reserve commission examination before they can be given an active commission with officer rank. Should the warrant officer not pass this qualifying examination then he may have to wait for direct commissioning after ten years' service.

It is highly probable that the Soviet high command would prefer to fight short sharp wars in the early Hitler fashion, using all its armed resources in surprise and savage offensives, so that wars might be won in single campaigns that can be measured in weeks, perhaps even in days. Such wars, if successful, are not usually costly in casualties, and to wage this type of short war the Soviet Army would not be hampered by the lack of a reserve of trained and experienced officers.[23] But for longer wars and to replace mounting casualties Moscow needs some form of officer reserve, particularly a reserve of young officers: and so it has followed the tsarist army example of creating a reserve officer (or potential officer) corps, and has done so in exactly the same way, in that it offers a reserve second-lieutenant's commission to all suitable time-expired conscripts who have higher or secondary education and can pass the reserve commissioning examination. Reserve commissions are also awarded to recommended graduates of certain Soviet universities and civil colleges who have completed some part-time military training instead of conscript service: this particular category of reserve second lieutenants that has not done two years' conscript service is liable for three years' active duty call-up, although in practice this rarely happens. Both of these categories of reserve second lieutenants, those that have done conscript service and those that have not, like the tsarist *praporshchiki*, have little or no military service and absolutely no experience of command as officers.

Military officers are a privileged class in Soviet society and enjoy a relatively high standard of living that is reflected in their pay, accommodation, rations and the luxury goods that they are allowed to buy. The pay code follows the old tsarist pattern, with an enormous difference between that of a junior officer and an other-rank conscript, but relatively little differential between the basic pay of the commissioned ranks, except that the difference is widened by the other pay elements, length of service and appointment pay.[24] Full pensions are normally payable after twenty-five years of service and are based roughly on half of the rate of pay at the time of retirement.[25] Promotion in the middle and senior regimental ranks, unlike that for the line regiments in the days of the empire, can be fairly rapid, so that an officer can be a major before he is thirty and a lieutenant-colonel before he is forty.[26] On the other hand, since all marshals and generals of the army are exempted from mandatory age limits for retirement, and since any general or colonel may, at the discretion of his seniors, serve for ten years beyond his prescribed retirement age, there are a very large number of senior officers still on the active list who must on this account be blocking the promotion of those below them. The extent to which the age and outlook of these elderly, sometimes very elderly, senior officers acts as an obstacle to military innovation and progress cannot be determined: it is to be noted though that whereas the marshals of the Second World War were in their forties, today's marshals are often in their seventies.

Officer training and the gaining of academic qualifications are probably crucial to promotion and career prospects, and are emphasized to such an extent that they tend to become an obsession.[27]

In consequence vacancies at officers' schools are eagerly sought since the lack of qualification can be a bar to promotion.

The young officer can normally expect to remain at regimental duty, possibly for three years or so after leaving his commissioning school. He is then required to attend a series of arms courses for junior officers, each of them lasting from a few months to a year; these give him the course qualifications needed before he can receive his next step in promotion. Further education is available by military correspondence courses, usually in preparation for entry into one of the many military academies, normally for captains and majors, either for the general staff (the all-arms Frunze) or for the academies that have an arms bias, the courses there lasting from three to five years. The officer may then attend a variety of other command or specialist schools, and finally, if he is so fortunate, a two-year course at the Voroshilov senior academy of the general staff of the armed forces, by which time he is likely to be a colonel or on the general list.[28] In all this, the Soviet Army is very far removed from the old imperial army, where the only worthwhile instruction for the few talented or lucky junior and middle-rank officers was to be found at the Nicholas general staff academy, and where Kuropatkin's twentieth-century attempts to introduce some instruction for the more senior officers was regarded as 'an affront to their grey hairs'.

The present-day Soviet Army attaches the greatest of importance to the study of military history, and in this respect is similar to the Prussian and German Army before 1939.[29] Military officers, however, have neither the time nor the facilities to conduct their own research and seek out prime sources, and they are obliged to accept what they are given in the way of second- or third-hand printed material, the value of which must depend on the knowledge, judgement and impartiality of the writer or editor. In consequence the officers' studies are much flawed since Soviet historical literature is of the most biassed kind, sometimes bordering on the absurd, for the ideological proselytizer calls the tune; the literature contrives, for example, to end the Napoleonic Wars in the 1812 campaign and the 1813 Battle of the Nations (at which Russian troops were present), but without even a mention of 'the hundred days' or the battle of Waterloo.[30] The Second World War is written up in the same vein, fought and won almost entirely by the Red Army and Red Fleet, and is distorted by much political matter, for the writing of any history in the Soviet Union is little more than an exercise in propaganda.

There is little to suggest that ethnic, and certainly not social, origin plays any great part either in the recruitment or the advancement of officers; but the same can be said of the army of Nicholas II. There may be some lingering prejudices against minority nationals serving as officers but these are not likely to be felt as strongly as they are among the rank and file: the young Great Russian officer may have some advantage in that he speaks and has been educated since infancy in his mother tongue, but there seems to be little reason why a minority national of comparable education and fluency in the Russian language should not do as well in advancement and promotion. These things being equal, the decisive factor would appear to be that of judged political reliability, loyalty to communism, and to the Soviet Union as a political entity. Any hint of separatist sympathies or interest, racial pride or loyalties, could prove most prejudicial to such an officer's career prospects. Jews are certainly at a grave disadvantage and have been purged from key and sensitive posts, particularly in the GRU, not merely because of old-Russian prejudices but on account of suspicion of Zionist or Israeli leanings, and because Jews are seen to form a world-wide community.[31] Nor could one imagine that a practising Moslem, or indeed an officer of any other strong religious persuasion, could be among the favoured, since any faith is an anathema to communism.

Much in the philosophy and mentality of the present-day Soviet officer corps, and the aspirations and methods of the Russian communism that directs it, are a continuation or a reflection of the imperial past.[32] Moscow's leaders have become Russians first and communists afterwards, and international communism means little to them except as a lever to buttress the USSR, weaken the capitalist world and extend the Soviet Union's interests and territories; its own communist satellites and allies are to be kept in a state of moral, military and economic subordination to Moscow. The Soviet Union preaches peace but its policies are aggressive and its aims are expansionist, differing little, even in its methods, from those of Ivan III, Ivan the Terrible, Peter the Great, Catherine the Great, Nicholas I and the late Romanovs, except that pan-Slavism and the protection of the Orthodox Church were usually *their* excuse for aggression. Russian officers, from the tsar downwards, tended to be arrogant, bullying, bigotted and chauvinistic, without any understanding of matters or points or view that were not Russian, attaching a very exaggerated importance to rank, their own rank and that of others, using this rank to conceal their ignorance and deficiencies; the same could be said of the imperial civil service. All of this can still be seen in the Soviet officer corps and representatives of government today.[33] General officers in particular are often corrupt. As for the regimental officers, vodka and cards are too frequently their scripture and evening prayers.[34] And the whole system remains, as it was before, entirely repressive and brutal, based on fear, fear of one's superiors, fear of denunciation and fear of responsibility.

There is, moreover, an inability to appreciate the mentalities and characteristics of those peoples and political systems that are outside of the Russian communist orbit, and this too was common to tsardom: for what the communists cannot achieve by aggression, intrigue or subversion, they seek to obtain by bluster and threats, and by playing on the fears of their neighbours, as the tsars did before them. And notwithstanding their vast world-wide KGB and GRU spy network that includes many able and dedicated operators, a network that by its very ubiquity must have had some extraordinary successes in collecting information, the final political-military picture that the Soviet Union has drawn up of the capitalist world tends to be not so much inaccurate in its detail as distorted, even quite wrong, in its interpretation of the general situation and important issues, these distortions showing a lack of a basic understanding of the mentality and the working of the free world.[35] This is reflected in the Soviet officer corps of today.

Then again, it is surprising how ignorant and naive in their understanding of the outside world even the privileged Soviet classes can be. Soviet military officers are provided with a series of official companion reference books, one of the most interesting of which is the *Spravochnik Ofitsera*. This volume is intended for an intelligent readership, indeed, by tsarist standards, an educated one: it tells these men, most with a higher education and many of them graduates of universities, that the world's wondrous inventions were all the work of Russians, giving names, places and dates: radio in 1895, rocketry and rocket dynamics about 1899, the first Russian experimental tank in 1915, the jet engine in 1929; and that radar was in use in Russia in 1938.[36]

In the old days, before the revolution, tsarist military writings were exemplified by meaningless pedantry, and this was a phenomenon of the late nineteenth and early twentieth century that was not found anywhere else in the world; the French and Americans had no trace of it and theory without practicability meant nothing to the Prussians and Germans, and what they wrote could be clearly understood by all. Tsarist military theorists, on the other hand, restated and embellished the obvious and republished it in the form of pretentious, long and muddled treatises that had neither relevance nor application to the problems of the day.

There was some improvement after the revolution, for, except in the occasional essays of Svechin and the few other relics of the old army that remained in the Bolshevik service, and in the writings of the 'politicos', such as Frunze, who tried to dress military matters in a communist garb, this pedantry was not so much apparent in the Red Army in the period between the two world wars, since its leaders were preoccupied with trying to pick up the military ideas of the foreign powers. In the successful war years, from the end of 1942 until 1945, the Soviet counter-offensives were based not on the readings or teachings of abstract communist theorists but on factual situations and practicabilities: the availability of air power, tanks, guns, men and equipment, on terrain, communications and climate; the method by which they were to be used was dictated by the lessons of experience, the lessons of the defeats inflicted on them by the Germans. Stalin and his little military team were practical and down to earth.

With the peace, however, there was a reversion to the ways of long ago. Exhilarated by victory, intoxicated by success, the Soviet leadership and the communist party again turned to the rewriting of history in an attempt to prove to the world that the Soviet Union was the sole victor over Nazi Germany and imperialist Japan, and that the victory represented that of a superior socialist system over capitalism. It could not be admitted by Moscow that the successes of the Red Army owed anything to what had been copied from the Germans, and so the leadership set to work to produce a most elaborate thesis, the Soviet theory of war that was so superior to all others and had brought the USSR to victory.

This newly found branch of military knowledge, decked out with an academic terminology hardly understandable by those who are not politico-military theorists, was convenient to the communist leadership in that it enabled the party to take the directing hand and secure the laurels. Before 1953, Stalin's personality cult required that he should have most of the credit, the party taking second place, but the researchers also resurrected and improved the writings of Marx, Engels and Lenin, for these three had always been regarded as superior in most knowledge, even between the two world wars. Eventually, even tsardom and the old imperial army came in for some credit. On this basis a whole Soviet military science came to be invented that owed nothing to foreigners – except Marx and Engels: and Stalin's role was revalued, in fact undervalued, by his successors. The result is comprehensive in its scope and is very exact, in that everything is rigorously defined and precisely tabulated. To the layman it may appear very learned. What it really signifies and whether indeed it has significance or application, is, however, another matter. Much of it has all the appearances of a revival of tsarist Russian military pedantry.

So it comes about that *Soviet military doctrine* is defined as being 'associated with the scientific determination and calculation of the present stage of world conditions and development' and 'the state's views and instructions on the nature of war, the definition of the military tasks and the forms of solving these tasks': what it really means, quite simply, is – the accepted politico-military policy at the highest level. Or, '*military science* is the sum of all material and psychological phenomena of armed combat, analysed and studied for the achievement of victory in war;' in other words – the study of war. And again, 'the *theory of military art* is the most important element of military science involving the actual method and forms of armed combat;' that is to say – armed conflict. In the new Soviet terminology, training becomes 'military *pedagogy*' and this in its turn is hived off into three compartments, 'formal education', 'ideological [political] education' and 'military training'.[37]

The military literature that is meant to be read by the more senior commander and staff officer and is intended for their instruction in the theory and the higher conduct of war, is of course largely political ideology and is usually tedious and of little practical application. But the officer under instruction is obliged to absorb it and reproduce it in his own work. There are grounds for believing, however, that the Soviet generals and the officer corps are essentially practical men and that this politico-military literature is regarded far less seriously by them than it is by the military analysts in the university faculties in the western world. For many decades these generals and senior staffs have been planning strategic and tactical operations, directing exercises and formulating training methods that have been built up mainly on the experiences of the Second World War and the military basis unwillingly bequeathed to them by Hitler's generals. The Soviet military leaders have applied these, as time went by, to the anticipated conditions of nuclear warfare, and probably with success. And it must be noted that some of the literature designed as a practical aid to the junior Soviet regimental officer in the training of conscripts, is both thoughtful and very well done.

Since 1960 the Soviet Army has entered the world of military cybernetics, new methods of command and control based on electronics, and particularly on computer-technology, probability and human-reaction. Although cybernetics were condemned in the 1953 Soviet military journals as 'a *bourgeois* false science', at the same time the GRU was instructed to intensify its efforts to amass information on the subject – initially from its reading of the western press. In 1959 a scientific cybernetics research branch and faculty were set up in the Frunze academy. Since then the Soviet Union has made great strides in this science, although still well behind the standards of the United States forces.

*　　*　　*

The Soviet Army today is a curious mixture of the very modern and the archaic, of achievement and inefficiency, and, like the Russian Army before it, it lacks uniformity, so that it is impossible to generalize, at least with any degree of accuracy, on its performance or its capabilities. It is striving to make its officer corps the most forward looking, the best trained and the most professional in the world, and, to some extent, it is well advanced towards this goal. Yet, side by side with its insistence on up-to-date and highly sophisticated equipment and its demanding training system, there is still an element of reluctant conservatism and it is continually delving back into the past to salvage some of the more antiquated aspects of tsarist ceremonial and army life.

Many features of the modern Soviet Army parades and ceremonial have come down from tsarist times, and are encouraged because they are regarded as typically and traditionally Russian: the wonder is that they have not forbidden the German command '*Marsh!*' introduced by mad emperor Paul, and replaced it by the earlier Russian word '*Stupai!*' The old Russian form of the Prussian goose-step (popular also with other European armies in the early nineteenth century) has certainly been reintroduced. In a move to bolster the morale, professionalism and the sense of exclusiveness of the Russian officer corps, or, as they express it, 'to maintain the honour, dignity and the high calling of the Soviet officer and to inculcate in him superior moral, political and military qualities', the old tsarist institution of officers' courts of honour has been revived, having the same composition and functions as those of tsarist days. Within the regiment the body of officers elect, from among their own number, seven or more officer members to form the 'officers' comradely courts of honour', and these elected members choose their own president; the members are re-elected, so it is believed, annually, in the old tsarist fashion. The business of the courts is to settle serious personal disputes between officers, including 'property claims against each other for up to 100 rubles', and to try 'misdemeanours unworthy of an officer or detrimental to military honour and *incompatible with the principles of communist morality* [emphasis inserted]', together with other infringements of military discipline and public order. The disciplinary functions of such a court, like those of the tsarist original, are considerable, sentences being either a comradely (non-public) admonishment, a public censure or reprimand, a recommendation that the defendant should lose seniority or rank, or a recommendation for dismissal. The findings of such courts are then acted upon by the military authorities and are either confirmed or set aside; the regulations permit appeals against the finding and sentence.[38]

In reality these courts do not amount to very much beyond window-dressing, a sop to the body of officers, giving it the illusion that it is self governing, admitting and expelling its own members as was done by the old Russian guard regiments and the Prussian officer corps. Soviet judicial and disciplinary systems, and indeed the party system, have powers enough to discipline or remove any officer, with or without good cause. The existence of these courts does not and can not protect the officer from military arrest, and certainly not from arrest by the KGB, where, once arrested, the military officer has no rights as an officer – or as a citizen – for he can be detained, beaten or otherwise ill-used, at the will of the jailers. The exclusiveness of the comradely courts has been somewhat diluted by the more recent extension of the institution so that warrant officers, and indeed extended-service men in the rank and file, enjoy the same rights of selecting *their* own comradely courts to try the peccadilloes of their corps.[39]

Another aspect of the military disciplinary code in so far as it affects Soviet officers, an aspect that surprises some western observers when they first become aware of it, is the detaining and punishment of officers by close-arrest. In many of the garrison headquarters, cells are put aside to hold detained officers, the principal reason for such detention probably being drunkenness or disorderly conduct.[40] But the Soviet system is such that an officer can still be ordered by his superior into guardroom arrest as a routine punishment for a minor, almost trivial, misdeed. In this there is a history of Red Army officer punishment battalions or companies, particularly in the Second World War, these officers having been reduced to the ranks, often summarily by the personal order of a commissar or superior – and often without cause: in the early nineteenth century, tsarist officers could similarly be reduced to the ranks by the order of a senior officer; in the late empire, guardroom arrest was a usual punishment for officers, that punishment that had been so roundly denounced by the tsarist general Meves 'as shameful and degrading to the Russian officer corps', Meves' reasoning being that the officer who is fit for the guardroom is not fit to be an officer. Yet the present-day Soviet Army, so careful, so it says, that its officers should protect their own honour and dignity, can apparently see nothing degrading in this practice.

Whatever the standard of the Soviet officer's training and however efficient he may be, his effectiveness is very much curtailed by the arbitrariness of his seniors, whose overbearing attitudes, usually fomented by their own ignorance and inadequacies, are a reflection of Russian character and military custom; for rank and face-saving are considered to be most important in that country. The Soviet officer has, moreover, an inherent reluctance to show initiative or accept responsibility, and this was common in Russia long before the coming of the Bolsheviks.

*   *   *

The defence ministers and marshals of today demand, in an army where nearly all the officers are communist party members, that the officer 'must be ideologically convinced and an active protagonist and champion of party policy.' The high command is endeavouring, so it says in its literature, to inject and encourage a spirit of initiative, responsibility and self-confidence in its leaders down to the lowest levels. And yet the actions, even the thoughts, of the officer continue to be monitored by his shadow, the accompanying *zampolit*.

We have already recounted how, from time to time during its history, the independent commissar system has given way to the *zampolit* political deputy substitute, and, so say the communists, 'one-man command' has been restored to the officer commander: and this positive statement has been accepted by some western readers. But 'one-man command' has never been a reality in the Soviet armed forces whether the shadow be called a commissar or a *zampolit*, for no officer would choose to act on his own responsibility without political approval.[41] From 1929 to 1933, long before Stalin's mass purges and at a time when ninety per cent of the commanders were said to have been given sole command, German officers reported not just the deference, but the awe, even fear, with which the most senior Red Army officers regarded their assigned deputies. When a question had to be answered, the officer left the answering to the *zampolit*. The British officers who saw the Red Army between 1943 and 1946 (when the commissar had again become the *zampolit*) said the same, for the officer in the presence of the *zampolit* was self-effacing. Officers of the highest rank who were in close touch with Stalin (Zhukov and Vasilevsky among them) were deferential to the commissar members of the council, because they knew that their every action and word could be reported to the head of the PUR and thence to Stalin. In 1945 Zhukov was much subdued in the presence of Vishinsky and the group of political shadowers detailed to accompany him 'as his staff and bodyguard' and to sit in on his meetings with western commanders. For, as Grigorenko has said, if Stalin had regarded Zhukov as a possible threat to himself or to the system, Zhukov would have soon disappeared, not just from the army but from the world: and anyone who thinks otherwise has little understanding of the personalities involved or of the Soviet system.

If the communist party is to be believed, the difference between the commissar and the *zampolit* is that while the former 'supervised', the latter 'helps'. In fact the *zampolit* continues to keep a check on the reliability of the officer and on the morale and efficiency of the unit and he is also responsible for propaganda and political indoctrination;

these activities have both merit and demerit – merit in so far as it is a safe party check on the reliability and morale in the ranks and in that it goes some way to fostering communist *esprit de corps* and countering any suspicion of officer indifference or neglect – demerit in so far as it is wasteful in training time, tiring to the men, and interferes with the proper function of the commander, that of personal command.

But the communist party and the party-political organization in the armed forces do not intend that the *zampolit* should restrict himself to these two functions of counter-weight and propaganda, for the *zampolit* is expected to concern himself with every facet of military life, indeed 'there is no military activity in which the *zampolit* should not be interested.' The *zampolit* is expected to acquaint himself with everything that is going on and, ideally, should be able to drive a tank, man a gun, parachute, and so on, and, in the event of the commander becoming a casualty, take over operational command.[42]

One remains therefore with the conclusion that the units of the Soviet ground forces operate very much as they have always done, that is to say under a duumvirate: the two commanders, the military and the political, are tied together as in a marriage, for better or for worse, and how they get on and the efficiency of their joint command depends largely on their experience and training, and, more particularly, on their temperaments and personalities: on all of these will depend the relationship and the nature of the command.[43] A *zampolit* who can never get on with any commander to whom he is accredited, will lose his job. Yet the *zampolit*, by virtue of the organization that he has behind him, is usually, perhaps always, the senior partner.

This was how the Red Army functioned, and in a large measure successfully, in the closing days of the Second World War, and those westerners who had any contact with the Red Army in the field knew that the *zampolit* was not only the dominant but also the most offensive type of officer to be met, aggressive against western observers and arrogant with his own officers and men. Most of them were fully occupied, not with running around exhorting and quizzing their activists and the rank and file, but in taking a full and often commanding part in planning and control. In 1944 when Lieutenant-General Burrows, in company with Vasilevsky, visited Cherniakhovsky's front in Belorussia, he listened to Makarov's lengthy dissertation on the battle situation, the other generals present being silent: Makarov was in a general's uniform and his detailed knowledge and activities were such that Burrows assumed him to be Cherniakhovsky's chief of staff, and he described Makarov as such in his report to London.[44] In fact Makarov was the *zampolit*, or to give him his correct title at that time, the *chlen*, the political commissar member of the military council.

26 A road-truck with rail-rollers, towing a section of a bridge into position (1965)

27 A mechanical BTM trench-digger made up of a ETR-409 trenching-machine mounted on an artillery tractor (see the full equipment in the background)

28 T 55 A tanks on the Moscow parade

29 Airborne forces *Frog* mobile surface-to-surface rocket-launchers being
unloaded from an An-22 *Cock* air transport

30 An SA-2 *Guideline* on its transporter: for many years this was a principal surface-to-air rocket in the ground forces and in the *PVO Strany* (home anti-aircraft command)

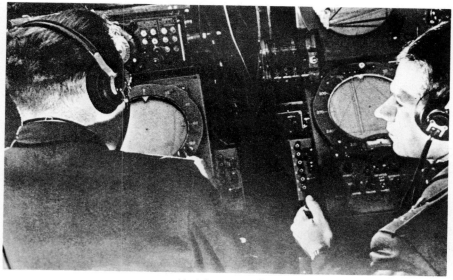

31 Air defence controllers

32 The SA-4 *Ganef* surface-to-air missile in service with the ground forces

33 An SS-X-14 (sometimes called *Scamp*) intermediate missile on a tracked transporter

CHAPTER NINE

The Eighties

Brezhnev gave way as party and state leader to Andropov, who was shortly succeeded by Chernenko, and then by Gorbachev. Brezhnev's minister of defence Grechko became a Politburo member, as did his successor Ustinov, who took over the post in 1976. Marshal of the Soviet Union Ustinov, born in 1908, was not a soldier, however, for most of his active life had been spent in the defence industry and civil economy. On his death in 1984 at the age of seventy-six, he was replaced by Sokolov, a professional soldier who had been a deputy minister of defence for the previous seventeen years. Sokolov, at that time seventy-three years of age and a member of the Central Committee, is credited with the planning for the occupation of Afghanistan.

In recent times the appointment of chief of general staff of the armed forces has been held by Kulikov from 1971 to 1977, Kulikov then becoming the commander-in-chief of the Warsaw Pact forces. Kulikov was succeeded as chief of general staff by Ogarkov, a fifty-nine year old former engineer officer; in 1985 Ogarkov's career pattern followed that of Kulikov when he replaced him as commander-in-chief of the Warsaw Pact forces. The 1985 chief of general staff is Akhromeev who is sixty-one years of age.

The present-day political, foreign and military policy is controlled, as it has always been, by the Politburo, and in particular by the party leader. The minister of defence may, or may not, be a full or candidate member of the Politburo, and Sokolov has only just been admitted to the circle of the chosen. But defence and military business is dealt with more closely by a defence council, that is, in reality, a section of the Politburo, chaired by the first party secretary (Gorbachev) and made up of the few principal Politburo members directly concerned with defence, and attended by the minister for defence and such other party, government and military heads that are co-opted at the time. This defence council approximates to Lenin's and Stalin's GKO, and decides all broader aspects of defence and military policy.[1]

The defence minister has the task of implementing this policy and is also primarily concerned with the direction and leadership of the armed forces in times of peace. To assist him he has a main military council (GVS) that is sometimes attended or chaired by the first party secretary, as it was in Stalin's time: its members are, however, mainly military men. In the absence of the party secretary the council is chaired by the defence minister and has among its permanent representatives the three first deputy ministers of defence (these including the chief of general staff and the commander-in-chief of the Warsaw Pact forces), together with the chief of the PUR main political directorate (who still retains his direct responsibility to the Central Committee and to the party leader), the chief of the Rear Services and all other deputy ministers for defence (the commanders-in-chief of the strategic rocket forces, ground forces, air forces, air defence forces, naval forces, the inspector-general, and the deputies for armaments, civil defence, construction and billeting and so on). In war time it is possible that a nucleus of this main military council would be reformed as a *Stavka*, similar to that of the Second World War.

The Warsaw Pact was set up in 1955, according to Moscow as a political and military counterweight to NATO, and in the west it is sometimes considered that the Pact is similar in its function to the NATO organization. In fact there are very important differences. The Warsaw Pact planning and controlling organization is sited in Moscow and is staffed largely by Soviet officers, and is little more than a part, or extension, of the Soviet ministry of defence, its commander-in-chief being directly subordinate to the Soviet defence minister. The description of its military head (who is always from the Soviet Army) as the 'commander-in-chief of the Warsaw Pact forces' is so very misleading that western press commentators sometimes assume that Ogarkov actually commands the Soviet forces in Central Europe together with the many field divisions that will be found by the communist satellite states, a total peacetime command that these commentators compute as about 1,000,000 men. In fact Ogarkov commands nothing at all in peacetime, certainly not the Soviet groups of forces in Europe nor even the communist satellite divisions that will be brought under direct Soviet Army control in wartime, for Ogarkov's designation of commander-in-chief is merely honorific.[2] Ogarkov's principal task, and a very important one it is, is that of co-ordinating and standardizing the training and equipping *of the other* Warsaw Pact forces, of liaison with the satellite governments and defence ministries and ensuring that the Soviet military requirements are carried out. His real orders come from the Soviet Politburo through the Soviet defence minister, although Ogarkov is theoretically subject to the control of a political consultative committee (of the first secretaries, premiers and foreign ministers of the member states) and a second committee of defence ministers. It is virtually certain that Ogarkov's headquarters would have no command role in the event of war since all Warsaw Pact forces would come directly under the command of the Soviet Army field headquarters to which they had been allotted, while the Soviet groups of forces would be controlled from Moscow through the Soviet general staff of the armed forces.

In 1980 General of the Army Petrov, fresh from his success in Ethiopia where he acted as the military adviser to that country during the Somalia Ogaden war, replaced Pavlovsky as the commander-in-chief of the Soviet ground forces. But he, too, exercises no direct command in peace or in war. Petrov is now sixty-eight years of age. Marshal Epishev, the head of the main political directorate (PUR) has just been retired in 1985 aged seventy-seven years, and has been replaced by Lizichev, the former political commissar with GSFG in East Germany.

*　　*　　*

In the last few years the size and format of the Soviet ground forces has been little altered. The 1984 estimates put the peacetime field strength at 194 active field divisions, of which thirty are in Central Europe, sixty-five in the Western USSR that would be immediately available to move into Germany and Czecho-Slovakia, twenty in the Caucasus, and fifty-two divisions in the Far East. The six Warsaw Pact allies have a further fifty-five divisions.[3] The Soviet armoured force is estimated to hold more than 50,000 modern tanks, and the newest model, the T 80, is already in general service in East Germany.[4]

The Soviet Army can keep this large number of active divisions in existence with a peacetime manpower of less than two million men, simply by manning the formations at different categories A, B or C (sometimes known as 1, 2 or 3), the category A being at eighty per cent of full strength, B something over thirty while C are at five to ten per cent: on mobilization all these divisions can be brought to full strength, and the active strength of the ground forces would be immediately doubled. Certain key units, particularly signal troops and rocket batteries in category C divisions, may be manned at B or even A levels. War equipment is prestocked and the reservist rolls are kept up to date in peace by the military commissariats and formation headquarters.[5]

In addition to the 194 active divisions there is understood to be a very large order of battle of reserve field divisions, and this reserve system, that has been in use in the USSR since the thirties, is a replica of the 1934 German Army reserve system; on the first day of mobilization, all the static and field headquarters, the military districts, armies and divisions, and every unit and sub-unit in the active field force from regiment to battalion, loses its deputy commander and a small staff or nucleus cadre. These deputies become the commanders of second-line reserve formations or units, and the personnel that make up the body of this new shadow army is posted in from reservists.[6] The equipment, that is probably obsolescent or obsolete, is presumably stocked in peacetime in depots ready for use. The number of field formations that would be formed shortly after mobilization by this means would probably be about 200 divisions.

There has been some increase in the size of the peacetime naval infantry force to about 10,000 men, but this takes second place in importance to the raising of special purpose army forces (*spetsnaz*) designed for covert and overt missions, in peace and in war, usually at GRU or KGB direction; one of these missions was apparently the 1979 assassination of the Afghan president Hafizullah Amin. These *spetsnaz* forces, that operate in small but numerous parachuted or helicopter-borne teams far in the enemy rear, were active in the 1968 invasion of Czecho-Slovakia and have been operational in Afghanistan. They are specially trained in infiltration, sabotage, arson, assassination and murder tactics, and their targets are likely to include enemy political or military leaders, nuclear sites, headquarters and communication centres. *Spetsnaz* troops wear the same uniform as airborne troops but have no connection with them.[7]

Whereas the *spetsnaz* troops are specialized diversionary and secret mission forces operating in small groups, a new category of airborne assault troops has reportedly been raised; these also wear airborne troops uniform, but are quite distinct from the *spetsnaz* and airborne troops of the airborne parachute divisions.[8] These assault troops are said to be part of the ground forces and are regularly formed bodies of up to the strength of brigades and are under command of the fronts; they are not parachute troops but are helicopter-borne, and are likely to be used, in a strength of a battalion or more, to storm airfields, rocket sites, and other defended localities in the enemy rear.

Helicopters, though still part of the Soviet air forces, figure prominently in the tactics of the Soviet ground forces, for Soviet doctrine professes that the helicopter is more related to the tank than to fixed-wing aircraft and can dominate, even seize, ground, exactly as a tank can.[9] Helicopters normally form part of regiments under front control, but are allotted to divisional support. Soviet combat helicopters are amongst the most heavily armed in the world and new and more powerful craft are continually being taken into use.

Success in the ground battle must necessarily depend on who controls the tactical air space. The Soviet tactical air forces, though they may lack the quality of some US and NATO aircraft and aircrew, are particularly formidable in numbers. A significant development over the last few years has been the reorganization and merging of strategic, tactical and air defence air formations in most land border areas of the USSR and the transfer of the control of what were the PVO air forces to the air forces of the military district ground force commander. There are no longer two distinctly separate air forces under two commands, and the unified air forces of the military districts now include all air formations within their boundaries except those of the strategic long range air force and transport aviation. This has resulted in a centralized and yet more flexible command organization and in an increased fighter offensive and defensive potential, in that the PVO can call on greater assets and, at the same time, the military district ground force commander has a greater offensive force that he can make available to support the groups of forces fighting beyond his periphery boundaries.[10]

* * *

The future is of course uncertain, though the study of history still gives some guidance as to possible trends and developments, for in some respects Russia and its communist leadership have changed remarkably little in the last seventy years. But there are major differences that must be taken into account and, in this age of dictatorships, centralization, instant communication and push-button nuclear warfare, there are factors that cannot be predicted.

It is entirely against Moscow's interest to begin a nuclear war since the risks to itself are too great. One may assume, with some certainty, that the Soviet Union would not wittingly initiate a nuclear war, though it would certainly threaten to do so if threats alone could secure its object and if the country that it threatened were without nuclear weapons of its own or allies that had them.[11] It is for this reason that unilateral nuclear disarmament by any free western nation would be an act of folly.

The most serious danger of nuclear war could be in a situation where the Soviet Union (or for that matter the United States of America) should believe itself in imminent peril of being the target of a massive pre-emptive nuclear strike, since this might tempt it to get its blow in first. The immediate danger of such a situation may be lessened appreciably by the increase in the numbers of submarine nuclear-missile launchers deployed by both super powers, and possibly by a star wars project: though where this will end there can be no telling. The obvious alternative to such an increase in nuclear and rocket weaponry is a verifiable total nuclear disarmament by all nations. At the moment this happy state of affairs seems as far away as ever.

But the abolition of all nuclear weapons would not necessarily make the world a peaceful place to live in, for the communist bloc continues its aggression by proxy, by infiltration and subversion. The Soviet Union is armed to the teeth and its leaders would have little compunction in putting its great preponderance of air, armoured and naval forces to use in the furtherance of its political and territorial expansion if it could safely do so. These Soviet conventional forces permit Moscow great political and military flexibility.

Even in this nuclear age, with conditions as they are, Soviet political and military thought is tending to become polarized so that a general war of the future is viewed in the probabilities of one of two options: the first, and the most unlikely, is the world nuclear war based on the pre-emptive first nuclear strike, in which the great strategic missiles will be rained down on the American continent, simultaneous attacks being made against Western Europe and other border states: the second option is the waging of air and land-based wars, launched by surprise on areas peripheral to the Soviet Union, by what used to be called 'conventional forces', that is to say air fleets and ground armies, probably with limited strategic objectives, such as the occupation of the whole or part of Iran, Pakistan, Turkey, Greece, Yugoslavia, the Federal German Republic or even Western Europe.[12] The rapid occupation of Afghanistan should provide an object lesson to the free world, for it is somewhat doubtful that Moscow will relinquish its hold over this area that has brought Russian arms to within 300 miles of the Indian Ocean. It is possible that Afghanistan will eventually have a status, similar to that of Outer Mongolia, as a Soviet dependent territory garrisoned by Soviet troops.

The best safeguard for Western Europe is the pledge of United States involvement, the presence of American troops in Germany in time of peace. But if the USSR did attack Western Europe in isolation, it is unlikely that Moscow would resort to the use of nuclear weapons, since this would be against Soviet interests and in any case it would consider the use unnecessary. Moscow would, moreover, do everything in its power to frighten off its NATO opponents from using American tactical nuclear missiles in the land battle.

The NATO political and military leaders may, conceivably, find themselves on the horns of a particular dilemma if faced with a surprise invasion from East Germany and Czecho-Slovakia, by ground forces controlled by a Soviet leadership that has renounced 'the first use' of nuclear weapons. A delay in the decision to use NATO tactical nuclear weapons may put the ground forces of the west at a disadvantage when faced with the numerically stronger Warsaw Pact powers: yet an immediate use of American tactical nuclear weapons invites a rapid response in kind: and the homeland of the West German allies, who are finding a very large proportion of the defending ground troops, makes up much of the battle and target area, from whichever direction the missiles arrive. Flexibility of NATO action can only be restored by conventional forces, for, irrespective of whether or not tactical nuclear missiles are used, air forces and ground troops, particularly armour, are going to be needed by NATO in great numbers if a Soviet invasion is to be repulsed. And a Soviet invasion of Western Europe can be best defeated by the offensive counter-action of highly mobile NATO armoured forces striking deep into the enemy vitals. In no circumstances can the Soviet ground forces be destroyed, whether tactical nuclear missiles are used or not, by the passive defence of borders, for he whose defence is based on the holding of ground must himself be destroyed. The German tankmaster's adage *Bewegung ist Sieg, Halten ist Vernichtung* was a lesson of the last world war and will apply even more forcibly to the next.

Appendices

SOVIET TANK MODELS

Type	Year	Wt tons	Power/wt ratio BHP/tons	Road speed mph	Road range miles	Armament mm Gun	Armament mm MG	Armour mm max	Armour mm min	Crew	Notes
LIGHT TANKS 1919–1939											
M 17 (Renault)	1919	7	5	6	40	37	7.62	16	8	2	
T 18	1927	7	6	9	40	37	7.62	16	8	2	
T 23	1927	4		20	50		7.62	16	8	2	
T 27 (Carden-Lloyd)	1930	3	14	25	100		7.62	8	4	2	Ford engine
T 26 series	1931/7										based on Vickers 6 tone Whippet
T 26 c	1937	9	9	17	120	45	7.62 (2)	14	6	3	with single or twin turrets
T 37 (amphib)	1933	4	12	22	120		7.62	11	4	2	Meadows engine
T 38 (amphib & AB)	1936	4	12	25	140		7.62	9	4	2	Carden-Lloyd suspension
T 46											based on US Christie tank
BT 2	1931	10	33	25	100	37	7.62	20	6	3	Liberty V12 engine
BT 5	1933	12	30	40	100	45	7.62 (2)	20	6	3	capable of road movement
BT 7	1935	14	30	30	200	45	7.62 (2)	22	6	3	without tracks
											all BT had Christie suspension and
BT 8	1935	14	30	30	200	76 how	7.62 (2)	22	6	3	drive and were forerunners of T 34
MEDIUM AND HEAVY TANKS 1919–1939											
T 24	1927	20	14	12	100	45	7.62 (4)	20	8	5	
T 28	1932	28	18	25	100	76 how	7.62 (4)	26	20	8	
T 32 & T 35	1932	40	10	15	100	76 how / 45 (2)	7.62 (5)	44	16	10	based on British Independent AIEI

Name											Notes
T 46	1937	28	10	15	100	45	7.62 (2)	60	10	5	copy of Vickers Independent
M 1	1938	33	8	10	100	37	7.62 (3)	35		6	
M 2	1938	36	10	10	100	76 how 37 (2)	7.62 (2)	25		12	

LIGHT TANKS 1940–1945

Name											Notes
T 40 (amphib)	1940	6	15	30	200		12.7 7.62	12	6	2	Carden-Lloyd suspension
T 60	1941	6	12	25	200	20	7.62	20	15	2	
T 70	1942	9	15	27	200	45	7.62	45	10	2	improved T 60
T 80	1942	12	12	25	200	45	7.62 (2)	60	16	3	

MEDIUM AND HEAVY TANKS 1940–1945

Name											Notes
T 34/76	1940	28	18	30	180	76	7.62 (2)	75	16	4	wide tracks Christie suspension
T 34/85	1944	32	16	30	200	85	7.62 (2)	90	16	5	
T 44	1944	32	16	30	150	85	7.62 (2)	90	15	4	not Christie suspension
KV I or KV/76	1940	48	14	20	180	76	7.62 (3)	90	30	5	
KV 2	1943	50	12	15	200	152 how	7.62 (3)	110	35	5	
KV/85	1944	46	13	20	180	85	7.62 (3)	76	30	5	
JS 1	1943	45	14	20	100	85	7.62 (3)	160	20	4	
JS 2	1944	45	14	20	100	122	7.62 (3)	160	20	4	
JS 3	1945	47	14	20	100	122	7.62 12.7	200	30	4	

LIGHT TANKS 1946–1980

Name											Notes
PT 76 (amphib)	1952	14	30	30	160	76	7.62	15	11	4	twin water-jet propelled

MEDIUM AND HEAVY TANKS 1946–1980

Type	Year	Wt tons	Power/wt ratio BHP/tons	Road speed mph	Road range miles	Armament mm Gun	Armament mm MG	Armour mm max	Armour mm min	Crew	Notes
T 54/55	1954	36	14	30	150	100	7.62	200	80	4	T 44 torsion bar suspension
T 10	1957	50	14	28	100	122	12.7 (2)	200	30	4	
T 62	1965	38	19	30	200	115	7.62 / 12.7	170	20	4	
T 64/T 64A	1974	38	20	40	200	125 smooth	7.62 / 12.7	210+	20	3	+ armour basis
T 72	1975	41	20	40	300	125 smooth	7.62 / 12.7	210+	20	3	+ armour basis
T 80	1980	42		40		125 smooth					

TANK-DESTROYERS (SUs) 1943–1980

Type	Year	Wt tons	Power/wt ratio BHP/tons	Road speed mph	Road range miles	Armament mm Gun	Armament mm MG	Armour mm max	Armour mm min	Crew	Notes
SU 76 (on T 70 chassis)	1943	11	11	28	200	76		25	10	4	
SU 85 (on T 34 chassis)	1945	30		34	150	85				4	54 cal gun
SU 100 (on T 34 chassis)	1945	30		34	150	100		78	47	5	43 cal gun
JS 122 (on JS chassis)	1945	45	45	20	120	122	12.7	90	60	5	29 cal gun/how
JS 152	1945	45	45	20	120	152	12.7	90	60	3	air portable open topped
ASU 57	1957	5	5	25	200	57		12		4	air portable but not amphib
ASU 85 (on PT 76 chassis)	1962	12	12	30	160	85		40			
SU 122 (D74) (on T 54 chassis)	1980	} the existence of these new patterned SUs is unconfirmed
SU 130 (M46) (on T 62 chassis)	1980	

Note: with modern external fuel tanks all road ranges can be increased to 300 miles

SOVIET ARMOURED CARS, APCS AND ACVS (INFANTRY)

Type	Year	Wt tons	Wheeled or Tracked	Road speed mph	Water speed mph	Armament mm Gun	MG	Armour mm max	min	Crew	Passengers	Notes
ARMOURED CARS (1930–1940)												
BA 10 (Ford)			6 whld									
BA 27 & BA Broniford			4 whld									
BA 64 (recce)			4 whld									
BA amphib		3	4 whld	50			7.62			2		
ARMOURED PERSONNEL CARRIERS & INFANTRY COMBAT VEHICLES												
BTR 40	1946	5	4×4 whld	50			7.62	14	9		8	open topped
BTR 152	1947	9	6×6 whld	50			7.62	14	9		16	open topped
BTR 50 (amphib)	1957	14	tracked	27	4			20			12	+ varied armament
BTR 60/70 (amphib)	1961	10	8×8 whld	50	6	14.5+	7.62	7	7	2	14	+ varied armament
BRDM (amphib recce)	1959	6	4×4 or 8×8 whld	50	6		7.62+	7	7	2	4	+ armament
BMD (airborne amphib)		10	tracked	37	6	73+ smooth		19	7	3	8	+ also *Sagger* Atk GM has turret
BMP (amphib)	1967	13	tracked	37	6	73+ smooth		19	7	3	8	+ also *Sagger* Atk GM has turret

UNARMOURED CARGO CARRIERS

Type	Year	Wt tons	Wheeled or Tracked	Road speed mph	Water speed mph	Armament mm Gun	MG	Armour mm max	min	Crew	Passengers	Notes
BAV 6 (amphib)		2½ ton payload	6×6 whld	35	6					2	20	copy of US DUKW
K 61 (amphib)	1955	5 ton payload	tracked	25	6					2	25	
PTSM (amphib)	1968	7 ton payload	tracked	25	6					2		

SOVIET ANTI-TANK WEAPONS

Type	Year	Maximum Effective Range yards	Minimum Effective Range yards	Propellant	Guidance or Bore	Warhead	Penetration	Notes
GUIDED WEAPONS								
AT 1 *Snapper*	1962	2,500	500	Solid rocket	wire	chemical	350 mm	vehicle mounted
AT 2 *Swatter*	1962	3,800	500	"	" radio	HEAT	400 mm	vehicle mounted
AT 3 *Sagger*	1965	3,000	300	"	" wire	HEAT	400 mm	manpack or vehicle mounted warhead armed on firing
AT 4 *Spigot*	1977	2,500	25	"	" semi-auto line of sight	HEAT	500 mm	manpack or vehicle mounted
AT 5 *Spandrel*	1977	4,500	25	"	" semi-auto line of sight	HEAT	500 mm	manpack or vehicle mounted
AT 6 *Spiral*	1977	7,000		"	" laser?	HEAT		
ANTI-TANK GUNS								
20 mm	1934	1,000	nil	fixed charge	rifled	AP shot	24 mm at 300 yards	
37 mm	1942	1,000		"	"	AP & HE	45 mm at 300 yards	
45 mm M 42	1943			"	"	AP	100 mm at 300 yards	
57 mm M 43		2,000		"	"	AP & HE	150 mm at 300 yards (AP)	
76 mm Fd/Atk M 42	1942	2,000		"	"	AP, HE, HEAT	100 mm at 300 yards (AP)	
85 mm Fd/Atk M 45	1945	2,000		"	"	AP, HE, HEAT	150 mm at 300 yards (AP)	

Type	Year	Maximum Effective Range yards	Minimum Effective Range yards	Propellant	Guidance or Bore	Warhead	Penetration	Notes
100 mm Fd/Atk M 44 & M 55	1944	2,000		"	"	AP, HE, HEAT	160 mm at 300 yards (AP)	
	1955	2,000		"	"	APFSDS	250 mm at 300 yards (AP)	
100 mm T 12	1983			"	smooth-bore	APFSDS, HEAT	400 mm at 1,000 yards	a/k only – does not have field role
Inf Atk launcher SPG 82		400				HEAT		
82 mm launcher B 10	1955	500			smooth-bore	HE, HEAT	240 mm any range	
107mm recoilless, B 11	1955	1,200			"	HEAT	380 mm any range	
SPG-9 73 mm recoilless	1969				"	HEAT	rocket-assisted projectile	

SOVIET GROUND ARTILLERY

Type	Year	Calibre mm	Shell Wt lbs	Shell Type	Max Range yards	Notes
76 mm gun 1902, 13, 27, 33 and 39	1902/39	76	14	HE	9,000/ 11,000	
76 mm gun M 42	1942	76	14	HE, AP, HEAT	14,000	also anti-tank & in SU 76
85 mm gun M 44, 45 and 48	1944/48	85	20	HE, AP	17,000	also anti-tank & in SU 85
100 mm gun M 44 and M 55	1944/55	100	35	HE, AP	22,000	also anti-tank & in SU 100
107 mm gun 1910, 30	1910/30	107	36	HE	13,000	
122 mm how 1909, 10, 30	1909/30	122	50	HE	8,400	
122 mm how 1938	1938	122	50	HE, HEAT	13,000	
122 mm gun 1931/37	1931/37	122	55	HE, AP, HEAT	22,000	also in SU 122
122 mm gun M 54/55 and 74	1954/74	122	55	HE, AP, HEAT	28,000?	
122 mm gun/how D 30	1963	122	55	HE, AP, HEAT	16,000	360 degree traverse on three-trail platform
SAU 122 M 1974 (Gvozdika)	1974	122	55	HE, AP, HEAT	15,000/ 21,000	tracked SP artillery also rocket-assisted projectile
130 mm gun M 46	1954	130	70	HE, AP	27,000	
152 mm gun M 1935	1935	152	110	HE, AP	29,000	
152 mm how 1910	1910	152	90	HE	11,000	
152 mm how M 43 (D 1)	1943	152	90	HE, AP	13,000	
152 mm how M 55	1955	152	90	HE, AP	16,000	
152 mm gun/how M 1937	1937	152	100	HE, AP	17,000	also in SU 152
M 1955 (D 20)	1955	152	100	HE, AP	19,000	
SAU 152 (D 20 gun/how) M 1973 (Akatsiya)	1973	152	100	HE, AP and nuclear	24,000/ 37,000	tracked SP artillery; also rocket-assisted projectile said to have nuclear capability

Type	Year	Calibre mm	Shell Wt lbs	Shell Type	Max Range yards	Notes
180 mm gun/how S 23	1980	180	200	HE, AP	30,000/43,000	also rocket-assisted projectile
203 mm gun/how M 1931	1931	203	250	HE	28,000	
203 mm gun SP	1980	203		HE & nuclear		on SP mounting

MULTIPLE ROCKETS

Type	Year	No. missiles	Missile Calibre mm	Features	Range yards	Notes
BM 8	1940	possibly 24		possibly 24 girder rails in two tiers	5,000	truck-mounted
BM 13	1941	16	132	8 girder rails 8 missiles above and below	9,000	truck-mounted (*Katyusha*)
BM 14 (16 or 17 missiles)	1954	16	140	2 banks of 8 tubes	9,000	truck-mounted
BM 14 (8 missiles)	1963	8	140	2 banks of 4 tubes	9,000	on airborne trailer
BM 21	1964	40	122	4 banks of 10 tubes	15,000	called *grad* (hail)
BM 24	1957	12	240	2 banks of 6 tubes	7,000	on tracked carrier
BM 31	1944	12	300	2 banks of 6 in long frame	4,000	truck-mounted
BMD 20	1954	4	200	1 bank of 4 in long frame	19,000	truck-mounted
BMD 25	1957	6	250	2 banks of 3 in long frame	23,000	truck-mounted
new	1978	16	220			

MORTARS (artillery and infantry manned)

Type and calibre	Bore	Loading	Bomb (lbs)	Range yards	Notes
82 mm M 37/41	smooth	muzzle	7 lbs	3,000	man portable (and with wheels)
82 mm automatic					recent addition
120 mm M 38/43	smooth	muzzle	35 lbs	6,000	wheeled and towed
160 mm M 43/	smooth	breech	85 lbs	5,000	wheeled and towed
M 53	smooth	breech	85 lbs	8,000	
240 mm M 52	smooth	breech	200 lbs	10,000	wheeled and towed
240 mm SP					self-propelled recent addition

SOVIET GROUND FORCES TACTICAL SURFACE TO SURFACE ROCKET MISSILES

Type	Year	Range miles	Warhead	Motor	Launcher	Guidance	Notes
Frog (1 to 7)	1957/1965	about 40	HE, CW or nuclear	solid fuel single stage	from rail on modified tracked PT 76 or whld transporter	none-free flight slow-spin stabilized	held in line divisions 30 mins to reload
Scud A and B	1957/1965	about 150	HE, CW or nuclear	liquid single stage	on modified JS tracked or whld transporter erector	inertial	armies or fronts 60 mins to reload
Scaleboard (SS 12) to be replaced by SS 22	from 1969	about 550	nuclear	liquid	on whld transporter erector	inertial	armies or fronts 3 hrs to reload
SS 21 replacing Frog 7		about 75					
SS 23 replacing Scud		about 300					

SOVIET GROUND FORCES ANTI-AIRCRAFT WEAPONS

Type	Year	Ceiling feet	Warhead	Motor	Launcher	Guidance	Notes
SURFACE TO AIR ROCKETS							
SA-2 Guideline	1957	70,000	HE or nuclear proximity fuse	two stage solid and liquid	whld transporter fired from rail on cruciform platform	radio command	with fronts and armies and PVO Strany

	Year	Altitude	Warhead	Propulsion	Launch/mounting	Guidance	Notes
SA-3 *Goa*	1964	medium level 35,000	HE or nuclear	two stage solid	whld truck mounted fired from ground launcher in pairs	command and homing	supplements SA-2
SA-4 *Ganef*	1964	70,000	HE proximity fuse	ramjet with solid boosters	twin mounted and fired from tracked carrier	command	with fronts and armies will be supplemented or replaced by SA-X-12
SA-5 *Gammon* (or *Griffon*)	1963	120,000	HE	two stage solid	whld transporter fired from static rail	command and homing	possibly only with *PVO Strany*
SA-6 *Gainful*	1967	medium level 50,000	HE	ramjet with solid boosters	triple mounted on tracked carrier	homing	with divisions – supplements SA-2 and replaces 57 mm gun
SA-7 *Grail*	1966	low level	HE	two stage solid	man portable shoulder launched	infra red homing	copy of US *Redeye* with units
SA-8 *Gecko*	1974	low level 9,000	HE	dual-thrust solid	in fours on a 6×6 whld amphib	command and homing	with divisions
SA-9 *Gaskin*	1974	low level 10,000	HE	solid	fired in pairs on amphib whld BRDM	infra red homing	with units
SA-11		medium					SA-11 with divisions
SA-13		low					SA-13 with regiments

Type	Year	Ceiling feet	Warhead	Motor	Launcher	Guidance	Notes
LIGHT ANTI-AIRCRAFT GUNS							
Quadruple 23 mm ZSU 23–4 (*Shilka*)		9,000	HE & ball		mounted on semi-armd tracked chassis		cyclic 4,000 rpm with regiments
Dual 57 mm ZSU 57–2		13,000	HE		on modified T 54 tracked chassis		cyclic 540 rpm in tank regiments
MEDIUM AND HEAVY ANTI-AIRCRAFT GUNS							
Various 40 mm and 80 mm Bofors and Vickers, and old pattern 76 mm and 105 mm guns	1920/1939						
85 mm KS 12	1939	25,000	HE proximity fuse				
85 mm KS 18	1944	25,000				with FC radar	
100 mm KS 19	1949	35,000		fixed charge separate ammunition	towed		
130 mm KS 30	1955	50,000					

SOVIET SMALL-ARMS AND INFANTRY WEAPONS

Type	Approx Year	Action	Calibre mm	Magazine rds	Effective Range yds	Practical Rate of Fire	Notes
RIFLES AND CARBINES							
Mossin-Nagant 91/30 rifle also 1938 and 1944 carbine	1891 1938 1944	bolt	7.62	5	450	10	on some models bayonet fixed or folded
Tokarev M 40 rifle	1940	SL gas	7.62	10	450	75	
SMG PPSh M 41 carbine	1941	auto BB	7.62	35/70	300	100	
SMG PPS M 43 carbine	1943	auto BB	7.62	35	200	100	
Stechkin pistol machine pistol APS	1955	auto BB	9.00	8	20/50	20	a hand-pistol with wooden butt-holder
SMG Kalashnikov (AK) later improved as AKM	1947	auto gas	7.62	30	300	100	wooden or metal folding butt. A modified AKM becomes the RPK LMG
Simonov (SKS) rifle	1955	auto gas SL gas	7.62	10	450	75	with folding bayonet
Dragunov (SVD) Sniper rifle	1966	SL gas	7.62	10	1,200	10	
AKS or AK 74	1977	auto gas	5.45	30	300		new small calibre weapon
LIGHT MACHINE-GUNS							
DP or as DT or DTM DPM	1928 1929 1944	auto gas auto gas	7.62 l 7.62 l	50 drum	800	100	on bipod with folding butt modified DP

Type	Approx Year	Action	Calibre mm	Magazine rds	Effective Range yds	Practical Rate of Fire	Notes
RPD	1954	auto gas	7.62 s	100 drum	700	100	on bipod
RP 46 (M 46)	1946/ 1954	auto gas	7.62 l	50 belt or drum	1,200	200	on bipod
RPK (AKM on bipod)		gas	7.62 s	50/100 drum	800	100	on bipod
RPK 74		gas	5.45				as AKS 74
MEDIUM MACHINE-GUNS							
Maxim M 10	1910	recoil	7.62 l	250 belt	2,000	250	on Sokolov whld tripod mount
Goryunov M 43 (SG & SGM)	1943	gas	7.62 l	250 belt	1,500	250	on Sokolov whld or tripod
PK (bipod) PKS (tripod)	1966	gas	7.62 l	100 belt	1,000	100–200	on bipod or tripod
HEAVY MACHINE-GUNS							
DShKM M 38 & M 46	1938	gas	12.7	50 belt	1,500	100	on whld tripod or AA
KPV			14.5	belt	1,500		

SOURCE NOTES

Titles have been included only if the quoted author has more than one work included in the bibliography of this book; in these and other cases the reader should refer to the bibliography for the full description of the source.

CHAPTER I (pages 4 to 25)

1. Descriptions of the tsarist army before 1840 are based mainly on Viskovatov.
2. Meshcheriakov, Vol. 1, p. vi.
3. Cit., Mosse, pp. 125 and 128.
4. Greene, *Russian Campaigns*, p. 45.
5. Kuropatkin, Vol. 1, p. 103.
6. Wellesley, pp.13, 17, 36–7, 71, 110.
7. Greene, *Sketches*, pp.17–29.
8. Wellesley, p. 134.
9. Kuropatkin, Vol. 1, pp. 14–15, 16–23 and 101.
10. Sokolovsky, *Military Strategy*, p. 111; Rotmistrov, Vol. 1, pp. 236–240.
11. Kuropatkin, Vol. 2, pp. 66 and 112.
12. Denikin, *Career*, pp. 55–6 and 64.
13. This is freely admitted in serious Soviet specialist works: see *O Sovetskoi Voennoi Nauke*, pp. 165 and 170.
14. Shaposhnikov, *V. Ist. Zh.*, 8/1966, pp. 75–84, and 9/1966, p. 73.
15. Ibid., *V. Ist. Zh.*, 8/1966 describes the 1907 general staff course.
16. Kuropatkin, Vol. 2, pp. 3, 63–8.
17. Denikin, *Career*, p. 177.
18. Ibid., pp. 202–3.
19. Greene, *Sketches*, p. 22; Denikin, *Career*, p. 83.
20. Wellesley, p.16; also (30 years later) Hodgson, p. 77.
21. Greene, *Russian Campaigns*, pp. 101–3.
22. Denikin, *Career*, p. 76.

23. Lenin, *Sbornik*, XXXVII, p. 200 (still quoted in full as authentic in the 1971 *Officer's Handbook* (*Spravochnik Ofitsera*), p. 147); also *Soch*. Vol. 8, p. 35; a totally different and correct account is given in Rotmistrov, Vol. 1, p. 212; and Zaionchovsky, *V. Ist. Zh.*, 3/1973, pp. 42, 45–7.
24. Shaposhnikov, *V. Ist. Zh.*, 1/1967, pp. 77–8.
25. Knox, Vol. 2, p. 496.
26. In particular *Poedinok* and other tales from *Povosti i Rasskazy*.
27. Knox, Vol. 1, p. xxvii.
28. Zaionchovsky, *V. Ist. Zh.*, 3/1973, p. 42 et seq.; Greene, *Russian Campaigns*, Vol. 1, p. 109; Russian Army Order No. 1, 14 Jan 1909 (Increase in Officers' Pay).
29. 5,000 understrength in 1910 (Knox, Vol. 1, p. xxvi), and 3,000 in 1914 (Golovin, p. 29).
30. See also Zaionchovsky, *V. Ist. Zh.*, 8/1971, pp. 39–43.
31. Kuropatkin, Vol. 2, p. 63; Knox, Vol. 1, p. xxix.
32. Golovin, p. 20; Denikin, *Career*, p. 83; by 1914 the literate had risen to 60%.
33. Forbes, p. 11.
34. Tumanov, cit. Knox, Vol. 2, p. 670.
35. Denikin, *Career*, p. 81.
36. Wellesley, p. 15; an opinion shared by Knox (in 1915), Vol. 1, p. 154, and Williamson (in 1918), p. 8.
37. Greene, *Sketches*, pp. 19, 24–9 and 221.
38. Kuropatkin, Vol. 2, p. 50.
39. Von Löbell, 1907 Sect X, p. 200, and 1912 Sect IX.
40. Golovin, pp. 1–7.
41. Ibid., pp. 203, 206–8.
42. Denikin, *Career*, pp. 202–3; Hodgson, p. 72.
43. Knox, Vol. 1, p. xix.
44. Kuropatkin, Vol. 2, p. 26.
45. Knox, Vol. 2, p. 630; Golovin says much the same, p. 275.
46. Ibid., pp. 11–20.
47. Ibid., pp. 202, 206; also Knox, Vol. 2, p. 606.
48. Confirmed also by Ironside, pp. 29 and 41.
49. Golovin, pp. 26–7, 202, 206–8; Hodgson, p. 60.
50. Kuropatkin, Vol. 2, p. 119 et seq.
51. Golovin, p. 11.

CHAPTER 2 (pages 26 to 56)

1. Golovin, pp. 201–2.
2. Knox, Vol. 1, pp. 143 and 190.

3. Golovin, p. 218; Knox, Vol. 2, p. 349.
4. Knox, Vol. 1, p. 304.
5. Ibid., Vol. 1, p. 217, Vol. 2, p. 350.
6. Ibid., Vol. 1, p. 52.
7. Ibid., Vol. 1, p. 229; also Hodgson, p. 11 and Williamson, pp. 38, 87 and 107; Martel, pp. 47–50; Teske, (*Köstring*), p. 68.
8. Golovin, p. 206; Knox, Vol. 1, pp. 229, 276 and 279; Wollenberg says much the same.
9. Hodgson, p. 179; Williamson, pp. 40 and 81.
10. Knox, Vol. 1, xxxiv, Vol. 1, p. 350; Golovin, p. 236, and 1913 German general staff reports.
11. Knox, Vol. 1, p. 334.
12. Ibid., Vol. 1, pp. 264 and 318 and Vol. 2, pp. 389 and 452; White, p. 48.
13. Denikin, *Career*, pp. xii, 271–3; also Knox, Vol. 1, p. 331.
14. Golovin, p. 245.
15. Ibid., pp. 258 and 267; and White, pp. 11–15.
16. *Prot. Ts. Kom. RSDRP (29)*, p. 124; Trotsky, *Stalin*, pp. 232–4.
17. *Arm. Sov.*, p. 18.
18. Cf., Ulam, Ch. 1.
19. *Trotsky Papers*, Vol.2, doc. 444, p. 21.
20. Podvoisky, *V. Ist. Zh.*, 12/1968, pp. 12–17 and 6/1968, pp. 3–12; *Dekr. Sov. Vlast.*, Vol. 1, pp. 20–65, 352 and 522; *Arm. Sov.*, pp. 18–22; *50 Let*, p. 17.
21. *50 Let*, pp. 17 and 44 note 1.
22. Ibid., pp.18 and 33.
23. Ibid., p. 20.
24. Ibid., p. 33 note 3.
25. *Arm. Sov.*, p. 25; Lenin, *Soch.*, Vol. 35, p. 222.
26. *Arm. Sov.*, p. 27; *50 Let*, p. 22.
27. Ibid., pp. 24–7.
28. *Arm. Sov.*, p. 31; Borisov, p.22.
29. *Arm. Sov.*, p. 28; *50 Let*, p. 30.
30. *Bazhanov*, pp. 48, 55 and 61; Lenin's views in Souvarine, pp. 120 and 132.
31. *Arm. Sov.*, p. 32; *50 Let*, p. 33.
32. Ibid., p. 35.
33. Ibid., p.42.
34. Ibid., p. 35.
35. *V. Ist. Zh.*, 6/1967, p. 79.
36. Littauer, pp. 246–7.
37. Denikin, *White Army*, p. 159.
38. Trotsky, *Stalin*, p.278; Lenin, *Soch.*, Vol. 39, p. 313.

39. Trotsky, *Kak Voor. Rev.*, Vol. 1, pp. 17 and 151; *Trotsky Papers*, Vol. 1, pp. 148 and 544.
40. *Arm. Sov.*, p. 31.
41. Rotmistrov, Vol. 1, p. 377. Tsarist divisions normally had two brigades; the three brigade division was a Red Army experiment.
42. Ibid., p. 378.
43. Rotmistrov, Vol. 1, p. 422.
44. Souvarine, pp. 112–4; Vereshchak cit., *Pravda*, 7 Feb 28 and 20 Dec 29; Yaroslavsky, p. 72; Trotsky, *Stalin*, p. 232.
45. *V. Ist. Zh.*, 9/1971, p. 118 et seq.
46. *Hist. Civ. War in USSR*, Vol. 2, p. 41.
47. *Iz Ist. Grazhd. Voin.*, Vol. 1, p. 231; *V. Ist. Zh.*, 2/1971, p. 47.
48. Voroshilov, *Stalin i Kr. Arm.*, pp. 13–14; *Grazhd. Voin.*, Vol. 1, p. 20; Stalin, *Soch.*, Vol. 4, pp. 122–4.
49. *Iz Ist. Grazhd. Voin.*, Vol. 1, p. 494; Stalin, *Soch.*, Vol. 4, p. 453.
50. *Dir. Kom. Front.*, Vol. 1, pp. 336 and 345; Rotmistrov, Vol. 1, p. 386; *Trotsky Papers*, Vol. 1, pp. 135 and 140.
51. *50 Let*, pp. 47–51.
52. *Iz Ist. Grazhd. Voin.*, Vol. 1, note 116.
53. *Dir. Glav. Kom.*, p. 118; *Trotsky Papers*, Vol. 1, p. 116.
54. Voroshilov's partisan school; cf., *50 Let*, p. 53.
55. *KPSS v Rez. i Resh.*, Pt 1, p. 446; Lenin, *Sbornik, XXVII*, pp. 135–40; *V. Ist. Zh.*, 4/1972, p. 4.
56. Trotsky-Markhlevsky correspondence – *Trotsky Papers*, Vol. 1, p. 764.
57. Kameneva, *Nov. Mir*, 3/1969, p. 169; *V. Ist. Zh.*, 4/1971, pp. 56–8.
58. Kameneva, *Nov. Mir*, 3/1969, pp. 173–7; Kamenev, *Vosp. o Lenine*, Vol. 2, pp. 255–61.
59. *Trotsky Papers*, Vol. 1, pp. 442–4.
60. Ibid., Vol. 1, p. 482.
61. Ibid., Vol. 1, pp. 578–80; Trotsky, *Stalin*, pp. 313–4; *V. Ist Zh.*, 6/1967, p. 116.
62. *Trotsky Papers*, Vol. 1, p. 594.
63. Denikin, *White Army*, pp. 279–80.
64. Trotsky, *My Life*, p. 387 and *Stalin*, pp. 314, 322–3; Voroshilov, *Stalin i Kr. Arm.*, p. 31.
65. *Iz Ist. Grazhd. Voin.*, Vol. 2, pp. 521–3 and note 206; Rotmistrov, Vol. 1, p. 414; *Dir. Glav. Kom.*, doc. 454, p. 475 et seq.; *50 Let*, pp. 93–8.
66. Denikin, *White Army*, p. 159.
67. Voroshilov, *Stalin i Kr. Arm.*, pp. 33–4; Trotsky, *Stalin*, pp. 274–5; Budenny, Vol. 1, pp. 321 and 335; Rotmistrov, Vol. 1, p. 422.
68. *V. Ist. Zh.*, 2/1966, p. 5 et seq.
69. *50 Let*, pp. 128–9.

70. Todorsky, pp. 13–47; *V. Ist. Zh.*, 1/1969, p. 45.
71. Budenny, Vol. 1, pp. 434–6, 'he was just a youngster, his aggression being only a cloak . . . he felt strangely out of place in such an exalted position'.
72. *Grazhd. Voin. na Ukr.*, Vol. 3, p. 306; Lenin, *Sbornik*, XXIV, pp. 333–4; *Iz Ist. Grazhd. Voin.*, Vol. 3, pp. 329, 336, 338–9, 341–3 and 346; *Trotsky Papers*, Vol. 2, p. 240; Budenny, Vol. 2, pp. 288–9 and 306.
73. *Iz Ist. Grazhd. Voin.*, Vol. 3, pp. 348–9; *Dir. Glav. Kom.*, p. 709.
74. Ibid., p. 711; *Iz Ist. Grazhd. Voin.*, Vol. 3, p. 351.
75. No. 0361/SEK of 15 Aug; Budenny, Vol. 2, pp. 309–11; *V. Ist. Zh.*, 8/1966, p. 85 et seq.
76. *Iz Ist. Grazhd. Voin.*, Vol. 3, pp. 355 and 361–2.
77. Lenin, *Soch.*, Vol. 32, p. 149 and Vol. 51, pp. 254–5 and 258.
78. Trotsky, *Stalin*, pp. 296 and 329.
79. Tukhachevsky, *Izb. Proizved.*, p. 162.
80. Todorsky, p. 66; Rotmistrov, Vol. 1, p. 426; *V. Ist. Zh.*, 9/1962, p. 62.

CHAPTER 3 (pages 57 to 89)

1. Cf., Akhmedov, p. 34.
2. Bazhanov, pp. 29–30.
3. Trotsky, *Stalin*, p. 374; Rigby, p. 27.
4. Svetlana, p. 27.
5. Bazhanov, pp. 17–22.
6. Ibid., pp. 22–5.
7. Ibid., pp. 40, 45, 91–2, 133–4.
8. Akhmedov, p. 108.
9. Bazhanov, pp. 27, 32–4, 94–5.
10. *Arm. Sov.*, p. 94.
11. Cf., White, p. 114.
12. Ibid., p. 85.
13. Ibid., pp. 159–60 and 191.
14. *50 Let*, p. 24.
15. White, pp. 158–60.
16. Ibid., p. 176.
17. Trotsky, *Mil. Writ.*, pp. 28, 54, 59, 63–9 and 70–93.
18. *Ross. Komm. Part. IX S'ezd*, 351 et seq.
19. *KPSS v Rez. i Resh.*, p. 569; Wollenberg, p. 171.
20. Stalin himself summed up the situation in his 1925 speech to the plenum of the Central Committee: Stalin, *Soch.*, Vol. 7, p. 11.
21. White, p. 80.
22. Voroshilov, *Stat. i Rech.*, pp. 281 and 563.
23. *Arm. Sov.*, p. 105.

24. Ibid., p. 106.
25. Cf., White, p. 66.
26. Bazhanov, p. 72; Voroshilov, *Stat. i Rech.*, p. 8; Wollenberg, p. 164.
27. Barmine, p. 219.
28. *Docs Germ. For. Policy*, C, Vol. 2, p. 333.
29. *Sov. Arm.*, p. 106; *50 Let*, p. 173.
30. White, p. 264; Wollenberg, p. 182.
31. White, p. 275.
32. Ibid., p. 274.
33. Wollenberg, pp. 181–2.
34. White, p. 224.
35. Ibid., p. 233; also Wollenberg, p. 69.
36. Cf., *Arm. Sov.*, p. 115 (single command said to date from 1925); also White, p. 235.
37. Wollenberg, p. 188.
38. *Arm. Sov.*, pp. 107–8; Frunze, *Izbr. Proiz.*, p. 215; White, p. 285.
39. Ibid., p. 260.
40. Ibid., pp. 297–304.
41. Soloviev, pp. 16–25.
42. White, p. 348.
43. Samoilo, still said to be alive and free in the Soviet Union in 1961 and enjoying a lieutenant-general's pension.
44. Also Wollenberg, p. 259.
45. Soloviev, pp. 26 and 119.
46. Pilsudsky, pp. 58, 79 et seq; also Wollenberg, p. 129.
47. Ibid., pp. 191 et seq. and 271. Tukhachevsky urged that organization and method should be learned from the Germans, artillery from the French and aviation from the Americans.
48. Voroshilov, *Stat. i Rech.*, p. 601; White, p. 277, citing Chamberlin's 1934 account of vast industrial growth in the Urals and Western Siberia; Wollenberg, p. 207.
49. Cf., *O Sov. Voen. Nauk.*, pp. 170–8; Kolganov, p. 9; Hilger, p. 207.
50. *Arm. Sov.*, p. 109.
51. Cf., von Seeckt, Vol. 2, pp. 308–9.
52. Such a view also in Wollenberg, p. 237.
53. Carsten, p. 237.
54. Castellan, pp. 191–3; and in *Les Relations Germano-Soviétiques 1933–39*, (ed. Duroselle), p. 183 et seq: Carsten, pp. 236–7, cit. Speidel; and Carsten in *Survey*, 10/1962, pp. 114–32.
55. Cf., Teske, *Köstring*, pp. 46–50 and 140–66; Rainer Wohlfeil/Hans Dollinger, *Die deutsche Reichswehr Zusammenarbeit mit der Roten Armee*, p. 182 et seq; we are also indebted for other printed sources indicated to

us by Colonel Hans Roschmann and by the Bundesarchiv-Militärarchiv and the Militärgeschichtliches Forschungsamt, Freiburg.

56. In 1942 the Soviet Navy in Murmansk and Archangel was regarded as very small fry and its capabilities were not at all highly regarded: from information given to the authors by Admiral Sir Geoffrey Miles and Captain S.W.Roskill RN; we are also indebted for other material from Captain R.C.S. Garwood RN, a Russian-speaking officer attached to the Black Sea Fleet in the war years.

57. Von Manstein, *Aus einem Soldatenleben*, pp. 140–3.

58. Cf., *50 Let*, pp. 200–2; Rotmistrov, Vol. 1, p. 479.

CHAPTER 4 (pages 90 to 116)

1. See also Erickson, p. 266 et seq.

2. Von Manstein, *Aus einem Soldatenleben*, pp. 140–2.

3. Von Blomberg: '*Voroshilov hat die Armee zweifellos fest in der Hand*'; the same wording was used by Trotsky on 27 Oct 1918, '*dovol'no tverdaia ruka*' (*Trotsky Papers*, Vol. 1, p. 164).

4. Cit., Erickson, p. 267; also Carsten, pp. 281–2.

5. Cit., Erickson, p. 272.

6. Von Manstein, *Aus einem Soldatenleben*, pp. 149–58.

7. Teske, *Köstring*, p. 327.

8. Hilger, p. 207.

9. Teske, *Köstring*, p. 104.

10. Ibid., pp. 315 and 318.

11. Martel, pp. 23–7.

12. Ibid., pp. 14–20.

13. Ibid., p. 51.

14. Stalin, *Leninism*, p. 541.

15. *50 Let*, pp. 195–200; also White, p. 358 et seq.

16. Kuznetsov, *Oktiabr'*, 9/1963, p. 174.

17. On Shaposhnikov's character see Vasilevsky, p. 110; Golikov, *V. Ist. Zh.*, 5/1966, p. 65; Knox, Vol. 1, pp. 107 and 137; Konev, cit., Djilas, p. 55.

18. Hilger, pp. 290 and 301–3.

19. Meretskov, pp. 168–9.

20. Grabin, *Oktiabr'*, 11/1973, p. 151 and 12/1973, p. 123.

21. Voronov, p. 45.

22. Ibid., pp. 115–6; Samsonov, *V. Ist. Zh.*, 5/1969, pp. 52–4.

23. Zhukov, pp. 214, 217 and 307.

24. Vannikov, *V. Ist. Zh.*, 2/1962, pp. 78–86.

25. Ibid., 6/1973, p. 79; Kolganov, p. 320.

26. Sherwood, Vol. 1, p. 329.
27. Emelianov, *Nov. Mir*, 2/1967, p. 85.
28. *Pravda*, 18 Jul 48.
29. Iakovlev, p. 192.
30. Rotmistrov, Vol. 1, pp. 377, 479–81 and Zakharov, *V. Ist. Zh.*, 2/1971, p. 40.
31. *Sobr. Zakon. R.K.*, 27/5 No. 34.
32. Akhmedov said that 'we in the GRU were told that Litvinov's harping on peace was diplomatic eyewash,' p. 86.
33. Meretskov, p. 179; Vasilevsky, p. 100.
34. Rotmistrov, Vol. 1, p. 499.
35. Shtemenko, Vol. 1, p. 18.
36. *Ist. Vel. Ot. Voin.*, Vol. 1, p. 277.
37. *Voennaia Mysl'*, 6/1940, p.3, cit., White, p. 421.
38. *KPSS o Voor. Sil*, p. 298; *Sots. Vest.*, 25 Feb 41, p. 47.
39. Krupchenko, *V.Ist. Zh.*, 5/1968, p. 42.
40. Rotmistrov, Vol. 1, p. 479.
41. Zhukov, pp. 181–3.
42. Vasilevsky, p. 107; Meretskov, p. 195, 198–200; Zhukov, p. 197; Kazakov, p. 56; Eremenko, *V Nach. Voin.*, p. 45.
43. Kuznetsov, *V. Ist. Zh.*, 9/1965, p. 73; *Oktiabr'*, 11/1965, pp. 146–7, 162–71; Zhukov, pp. 233, 244, 245 and 247; Tiulenev, p. 42; Voronov, pp. 171 and 175; Rigby, pp. 53 and 55.
44. *50 Let*, p. 235; Zhukov, p. 250.
45. Bagramian, *V. Ist. Zh.*, 1/1967, p.56.

CHAPTER 5 (pages 117 to 147)

1. Von Bock, *Tagebuch*, 8 Jul 41 and 5 Aug 41.
2. Hubatsch, pp. 145, 148–9; and *KTB des OKW*, Vol. 1, p. 661.
3. Hubatsch, op. cit., p. 150.
4. *KTB des OKW*, Vol. 1, p. 702.
5. Kuznetsov, *V. Ist. Zh.*, 9/1965, p. 73; Zhukov, pp. 233, 244–5, 249.
6. Vasilevsky, *V. Ist. Zh.*, 6/1974, p. 124; Zhukov, pp. 273 and 283; Boldin, *V. Ist. Zh.*, 4/1961, p. 67; Bagramian, *Gorod-Voin*, p. 140, and *V. Ist. Zh.*, 3/1967, p. 52.
7. *Ist. Vel. Ot. Voin.*, Vol. 2, p. 62.
8. Cf., Gorbatov, *Gody i Voiny*, *Nov. Mir*, May 1964 (Eng. trs., pp. 163–5).
9. Platonov, p. 187; *Ist. Vel. Ot. Voin.*, Vol. 2, p. 18; all fighting ceased on 29 Jun, cf., von Bock, *Tagebuch*, 4 Jul 41 and Halder, *KTB*, Vol. 3, p. 22.
10. Cf., Zhukov, p. 297; Platonov, p. 212; Vorobev, p. 92; Vasilevsky, *Bitva*

za Moskvu, p. 12.

11. Guards titles were introduced on 18 Sep 41, being awarded in the first instance to four rifle divisions.

12. Cf., *Die Kriegswehrmacht der UdSSR (Fremde Heere Ost (II))*, issued 15 Jan 41.

13. Teske, *Köstring*, pp. 234, 267 and 315; Feis, pp. 10–11; Woodward, p. 150 and footnote; Sherwood, Vol. 1, pp. 328–43.

14. Halder, *KTB*, Vol. 2, p. 86: the Köstring-von Tippelskirch 1940 correspondence; also *Fremde Heere Ost 20/001/geh Ausl XXIb* dated 17 Oct 40.

15. Halder, *KTB*, Vol. 3, pp. 326, 328 and 331; Guderian, *Panzer Leader*, p. 252; von Bock, *Tagebuch*, 7 Dec. 41; also *KTB des Oberkommandos der Heeresgruppe Mitte*, p. 1008.

16. Cf., The Stalin-Eden conversations, Eden, pp. 289–99.

17. Zhukov, pp. 362–6, and *Bitva za Moskvu*, p. 76; Sokolovsky, *Razgrom . . . pod Moskvoi*, pp. 30 and 67–78; also *V. Ist. Zh.*, 3/1967, p. 70; Golikov, *V Moskovskoi Bitve*, pp. 11–28.

18. Cf., Kesselring, p. 120.

19. Halder, *Hitler as Warlord*, p. 51.

20. From whence the fanatical 'stand and fight' order of 20 Dec 41 *(OKH Gen St d H. Op Abt (1) Nr. 32061/41 g. Kdos)*.

21. German casualties from Nov 41 to Mar 42 in dead and missing were variously computed at between 108,000 (Halder) and 151,000 (Mueller-Hillebrand); the German wounded were put at 268,000 and the daily sick at 61,000. The overall Red Army losses in prisoners alone were over three million by Jan 42.

22. *Pravda*, 1 Jul 41; Stalin, *On the Great Patriotic War*, p. 50; Kuznetsov, *V. Ist. Zh.*, 9/1955, p. 65; Vasilevsky, p. 122.

23. Starinov, p. 210.

24. *KPSS o Voor. Sil.*, p. 305.

25. Shtemenko, Vol. 1, p. 31.

26. Zhukov, p. 318; Vasilevsky, p. 141; Bagramian, *So Begann der Krieg*, p. 274; *Ist. Vel. Ot. Voin.*, Vol. 2, p. 104.

27. *KTB des OKW*, Vol. 1, p. 702.

28. Rokossovsky, *Sold. Dolg*, pp. 52–61.

29. Konev, *V. Ist. Zh.*, 10/1966, p. 56.

30. Sbytov, *Bitva za Moskvu*, pp. 402–4.

31. Zhukov, pp. 345–52.

32. Konev, *V. Ist. Zh.*, 10/1966, p. 65.

33. Werth, p. 234; Birse, p. 79.

34. Pronin, *Bitva za Moskvu*, p. 465; Telegin, *Vopros. Ist.*, 9/1966, p. 104.

35. Zhukov, pp. 362–6.

36. Vasilevsky, *Bitva za Moskvu*, p. 23.
37. Shelakhov, *V. Ist. Zh.*, 3/1969, pp. 56–9.
38. Shtemenko, Vol. 1, pp. 30–2 and Vol. 2, p. 7; Vasilevsky, pp. 124–6.
39. Vasilevsky, p. 126; Shtemenko, Vol. 2, p. 39; Zhukov, pp. 305–8 and p. 289.
40. Shtemenko, Vol. 1, pp. 44, 47–8; and Voronov, p. 180.
41. Cf., Sherwood, Vol. 1, pp. 328–47; 'It was nauseating,' said Ismay, 'to see brave men reduced to such servility.' Ismay, p. 233; also Rotmistrov, Vol. 2, pp. 52, 57 and 104; and Gorbatov, pp. 104–7 and 169.
42. Vasilevsky, p. 190 and *Stalingrad. Ep.*, p. 75; Zhukov, p. 396.
43. *KTB des OKW*, Vol. 2, p. 391.
44. Vasilevsky, *V. Ist. Zh.*, 8/1965, p. 3.
45. Stalin's 'standstill order' No. 227 of 28 Jul 42 having had no effect.
46. Rotmistrov, Vol. 2, pp. 160–1 and *Stalingrad. Ep.*, pp. 605–7; *Ist. Vel. Ot. Voin.*, Vol. 2, pp. 420–1; Kazakov, p. 130; Rokossovsky, *Sold. Dolg*, pp. 128–30.
47. *KTB des OKW*, Vol. 2, pp. 1305–7; Greiner, pp. 401–2.
48. Zhukov, pp. 407 and 413–4; *Ist. Vel. Ot. Voin.*, Vol. 3, p. 17 et seq.; Rokossovsky, *Sold. Dolg*, pp. 139–42; Moskalenko, *Stalingrad. Ep.*, pp. 222–3 and Vasilevsky, p. 83.
49. Rotmistrov, Vol. 2, p. 197; *Ist. Vel. Ot. Voin.*, Vol. 3, p. 18; Eremenko, *Stalingrad*, pp. 326–9; Vasilevsky, *Stalingrad. Ep.*, p. 85; Zhukov, pp. 433–4.
50. Vasilevsky, *Stalingrad. Ep.*, p. 116; Zhukov, pp. 453–4; Samsonov, *Stalingrad. Bit.*, p. 484.
51. *KTB des OKW*, Vol. 3, p. 1482; Mueller-Hillebrand (Vol. 3, Ch. 12) calculates 6 German Army losses from 23 Nov to 2 Feb as 209,500.
52. Cf., Schlauch; Stettinius, *Lend-Lease*; *Command Decisions*, pp. 154–81; Jacobsen, p. 568.
53. *KTB des OKW*, Vol. 3, pp. 213, 1531–2; Klink, pp. 57–9; von Manstein, *Lost Victories*, p. 443; Guderian, *Panzer Leader*, pp. 306–8.
54. Mueller-Hillebrand, Vol. 3, Tables 48–50.
55. Shtemenko, Vol. 1, pp. 146–8; Zhukov, pp. 483–92; *V. Ist. Zh.*, 6/1968, pp. 67–8 and 7/1968, pp. 79–92; *50 Let*, p. 492; *Ist. Vel. Ot. Voin.*, Vol. 3, pp. 245–8 and 269.
56. Stalin's words quoted in Deane, pp. 145–7.
57. Martel, p. 56; Burrows, *PRO WO 106/3272 Sitreps 4 Nov to 19 Dec 43 Appx K/1*.
58. Shtemenko, Vol. 1, pp. 138–9.
59. Ibid., p. 139.
60. Vasilevsky, p. 273; Rokossovsky, *Sold. Dolg*, p. 192.
61. *Soviet Military Review*, 5/1965, actually predates the SU to 1931!

62. Cf. Voronov, p. 202.
63. Rotmistrov, Vol. 2, p. 187 et seq.
64. Martel, pp. 47–50 and 51–2.
65. Shtemenko, Vol. 1, pp. 232–5.
66. *KTB des OKW*, Vol. 4, p. 858.
67. German losses in the east from June to September, both months inclusive, were 215,000 dead and 627,000 missing. Mueller-Hillebrand, Vol. 3, p. 171.
68. Matsulenko, p. 103; Biriuzov, *Surov. God.*, p. 423.
69. Shelakhov, *V. Ist. Zh.*, 3/1969, pp. 56–9; Shtemenko, Vol. 1, pp. 334–7; Vasilevsky, *V. Ist. Zh.*, 6/1967, pp. 82–3.
70. Shtemenko, Vol. 1, p. 359; Vasilevsky, *V. Ist. Zh.*, 6/1967, p. 86; Deane, pp. 272–4.
71. Cf., Deane, pp. 275–6; also Shtemenko, Vol. 1, pp. 359–61.

CHAPTER 6 (pages 148 to 177)

1. *O Sov. Voen. Nauk.*, pp. 200 and 202 et seq.
2. Voroshilov, *Stalin and the Armed Forces*, p. 144; in 1958 (after Stalin's death), however, Voroshilov momentarily changed his tune in a radio talk describing the annihilating effect of nuclear weapons – a remark that was not subsequently reported.
3. Burrows, *(PRO) War Office report 106/3273 Appx B/2*.
4. Cf., Sokolovsky, *Military Strategy*, (Engl. tr.), p. 56; also (at some length) in Zaletny's *Militarizatsiia FRG*, Moscow 1969.
5. Cf., Garthoff, p. 41.
6. Garthoff, pp. 42–6.
7. Ibid., pp. 48–50.
8. *O Sov. Voen. Nauk.*, pp. 201–2; also Garthoff, p. 57.
9. See also Garthoff, p. 54 et seq.
10. Miller, p. 141.
11. Cf., V. Suvorov, p. 263 et seq.
12. Djilas, pp. 146 and 169; also Anders, p. 83.
13. Cf., Shtemenko, Vol. 2, pp. 279, 300 and 499.
14. Shtemenko, Vol. 2, p. 500.
15. Voroshilov, *Stalin and the Armed Forces*, pp. 105–14.
16. Lenin, *Soch.*, Vol. 24, p. 544.
17. It is remarkable that the principles of war set out under Khrushchev (1964) in fact differ little from Stalin's; cf., *O Sov. Voen. Nauk.*, pp. 292 and 296.
18. Shtemenko, Vol. 2, p. 505.
19. Shtemenko, *V. Ist. Zh.*, 2/1971, p. 39.

20. Vasilevsky, p. 529.
21. Djilas, p. 159.
22. Montgomery, p. 415.
23. Vasilevsky, pp. 530–1.
24. Cf., Konev, *Nov. Mir*, 7/1965, p. 134 et seq; Voronov, p. 202.
25. Shtemenko, Vol. 2, p. 77.
26. Djilas, p. 106.
27. Ibid., p. 138.
28. Rigby, p. 81.
29. The armed forces had been mobilized so that the 1948 strength of 2,874,000 rose rapidly to near the six million mark. Even in 1955 the strength was 5,763,000. *O Sov. Voen. Nauk.*, pp. 201–2; see also Garthoff, p. 20.
30. Rigby, p. 67; also Garthoff, pp. 19 and 20.
31. Cf., Garthoff, 'on the legacy of Stalinist stagnation' p. 63 et seq.

CHAPTER 7 (pages 178 to 202)

1. Garthoff, pp. 18, 21 and 22; Penkovsky, p. 280.
2. Lugansky on Malenkov, *Na Glubokikh Virazhakh*, Alma-Ata, 1966, p. 83 et seq, cit., Bialer, p. 454 et seq.
3. Dinerstein, p. 18.
4. Garthoff, pp. 22–3.
5. Ibid., pp. 26–7; also Dinerstein, op. cit., p. 18.
6. Penkovsky, pp. 50 and 310; Artemev was commanding in Moscow in 1941 see Bialer, p. 305 et seq.
7. Penkovsky, p. 206.
8. Garthoff, pp. 28–32.
9. Also V. Suvorov, p. 24; Garthoff, pp. 30–1.
10. Garthoff, pp. 34 and 48; Penkovsky, p. 235.
11. Cf., Penkovsky, pp. 233 and 310.
12. Garthoff, p. 42.
13. Ibid., p. 44; *Handbook on the Soviet Armed Forces*, Sect. 12, p. 1; Borisov, p. 77 et seq; the KGB, however, are responsible for the security and custody of nuclear missiles. Cf., Penkovsky, p. 331.
14. Garthoff, p. 57; *O Sov. Voen. Nauk.*, pp. 201–2.
15. Cf., *Handbook on the Soviet Armed Forces*, Sect. 8.
16. See *inter alia:* Garthoff, p. 75; Erickson and Feuchtwanger, p. 49 et seq.
17. Cf., V. Suvorov, p. 90 et seq.
18. Equipment detail from Arndt.
19. Zhukov's speech to the 20th Party Congress; also Krasilnikov's 1956 anthology, cit., Dinerstein, p. 215 and Garthoff, pp. 78–9.

20. Cf., Kosorukov and Matsulenko, *Voen. Vest.*, 7/1955, p. 92, cit., Garthoff, p. 107; also V. Suvorov, p. 161.
21. Cf., Dinerstein, p. 257; Garthoff, pp. 80, 98–9 and 103.
22. Even Zhukov hinted at the possibility of some change in March 1957: cit. Dinerstein, p. 219 and Garthoff, p. 88.
23. Penkovsky's evidence of the 'Special Collection' and Gastilovich's views, p. 227 et seq.
24. Television record of his New York address to the United Nations; Penkovsky, pp. 212, 228 and 230.
25. Cit., Dinerstein, pp. 232–5.
26. Khrushchev's Jan 1960 speech to the Supreme Soviet in which it is said that he put forward the slogan '[nuclear] firepower for manpower': Penkovsky, p. 223.
27. The savings to be used on nuclear rocketry – what Penkovsky called 'more rubble for a ruble', p. 223 et seq; and 240–3.
28. Penkovsky, p. 232 and V. Suvorov, p. 270.
29. Penkovsky, p. 225.
30. V. Suvorov, p. 270.
31. Penkovsky, p. 248.
32. *Handbook on the Soviet Armed Forces*, Sect. 8, p. 13; Isby (p. 30) and V. Suvorov (pp. 72–3) put the present strength at above 50,000 tanks.
33. A Soviet tank battalion has consisted of thirty fighting tanks for nearly half a century (with an addition of one or two command tanks). Isby believes (p. 71) that the high category motor rifle divisions now have tank battalions of fifty tanks; V. Suvorov (p. 72) says that this new organization is used only in the commander's reserve independent tank battalion at divisional level and above.
34. Isby, pp. 20–1. For a British variant see 1977 *RUSI Journal* article by Maj.-Gen. F. Kitson, the commander of a BAOR armoured division at that time.
35. Equipment information based on, *inter alia*, information in Arndt and Isby and in the *Handbook on the Soviet Armed Forces* and *Soviet Military Power* (1983 and 1984).
36. Isby, pp. 76–100 et seq.
37. V. Suvorov, p. 207.

CHAPTER 8 (pages 203 to 224)

1. Cf., Goldhamer, pp. 4–6.
2. V. Suvorov, p. 220.
3. Ibid., pp. 252 and 263.
4. *Handbook on the Soviet Armed Forces*, Sect. 5.

5. V. Suvorov, p. 217.
6. The wording of the present oath is given in *Handbook on the Soviet Armed Forces*, Sect. 5, p. 2; also Borisov, p. 103.
7. At the time V. Suvorov did his initial service it was three rubles a month.
8. One battery (of about 200 men) was said to have twenty-four different nationalities among its intake, *Krasn. Zvezd.*, 20 Dec 69, p. 3, cit., Goldhamer, p. 187: V. Suvorov says that some of these have never even heard the Russian language until they enter the army.
9. Isby, p. 70; V. Suvorov, p. 229; *Handbook on the Soviet Armed Forces*, Sect. 5, p. 9.
10. Ibid., Sect. 6, pp. 8-10; Isby, p. 65.
11. V. Suvorov, pp. 223-9 and 252.
12. Ibid., p. 233.
13. Ibid., p. 234.
14. Maps (of the USSR) are restricted documents and, so V. Suvorov says, 'map reading is taught only to those who need to know!', p. 233.
15. Ibid., pp. 76 and 97. Isby says (at p. 100) that 'the T 72 tank ended, at least temporarily, the US qualitative lead in tanks'.
16. Isby, pp. 65 and 75.
17. Ibid., p. 79.
18. V. Suvorov, p. 250.
19. Isby, p. 64; *Handbook on the Soviet Armed Forces*, Sect. 5 p. 6.
20. Goldhamer, pp. 10-21; *Handbook on the Soviet Armed Forces*, Sect. 5, p. 6. Korkeshkin, p. 29 et seq.
21. *Handbook on the Soviet Armed Forces*, Sect. 6, p. 4, gives the annual total as approximately 60,000 for the whole of the Soviet Army. This may be so, though the figure seems high.
22. V. Suvorov, p. 270 et seq.
23. Penkovsky, pp. 258-9.
24. *Handbook on the Soviet Armed Forces*, Sect. 5, pp. 8-9.
25. *The Officer's Handbook (Spravochnik Ofitsera) 1971*, p. 203; Borisov, p. 129.
26. V. Suvorov, p. 278 et seq.
27. Isby, pp. 65 et seq; *Handbook on the Soviet Armed Forces*, Sect. 6, p. 4; V. Suvorov, p. 283.
28. V. Suvorov, p. 283 et seq.
29. Isby, p. 30.
30. Rotmistrov, Vol. 1, p. 526 (and Admiral Ushakov, p. 154).
31. Jewish officers have been discriminated against since about 1950 and, according to Penkovsky, none are now allowed in the intelligence service. Penkovsky, p. 358.
32. This was already the case in the thirties; see Wollenberg, p. 301.

33. *Handbook on the Soviet Armed Forces*, Sect. 6, p. 9, para 16f.; also Goldhamer, p. 178 et seq.
34. V. Suvorov, pp. 252 and 286–7.
35. Penkovsky, p. 255; it is also apparent in *The Officer's Handbook (Spravochnik Ofitsera) 1971.*
36. Ibid., pp. 147, 277–8 and 283 (rockets, jets, radio, radar and the tank).
37. Kolganov, p. 74 et seq; Reznichenko, p. 6 et seq; Rotmistrov, Vol. 1, p. 354 et seq; *The Officer's Handbook (Spravochnik Ofitsera) 1971*, pp. 48–61; also summarized in *Handbook on the Soviet Armed Forces*, Sect. 4; and Isby, p. 11 et seq.
38. *The Officer's Handbook (Spravochnik Ofitsera) 1971*, p. 206 et seq; Grechko, *Armed Forces of the Soviet Union 1977*, p. 231, talks of 'the most noble moral qualities of Soviet man.'
39. Goldhamer, p. 10.
40. Ibid., p. 149, quoting *Smena*, No.6 (1972), pp. 3–5.
41. Ibid., p. 299.
42. Khmel, p. 50.
43. Ibid., p. 185 et seq.
44. Burrows, *(PRO War Office report 106/3273 Appx M/2.*

CHAPTER 9 (pages 225 to 232)

1. Cf., *Handbook on the Soviet Armed Forces*, Sect. 2; Isby, p. 15; *Soviet Military Power (1984)*, pp. 7–9.
2. Cf., V. Suvorov, p. 20; *Handbook on the Soviet Armed Forces*, Sect. 3, p. 2.
3. *Soviet Military Power (1983)*, p. 37 and *Soviet Military Power (1984)*, pp. 13, 14 and 58 et seq.
4. Isby, p. 71; V. Suvorov, p. 72; the US 1983 estimate shows 42,000 main battle tanks.
5. V. Suvorov, p. 138 et seq; Isby, p. 28.
6. *Handbook on the Soviet Armed Forces*, Sect. 5, p. 13; V. Suvorov, p. 138 et seq.
7. *Soviet Military Power (1984)*, pp. 69–70.
8. V. Suvorov, p. 74 et seq.
9. V. Suvorov, p. 191; *Soviet Military Power (1983)*, pp. 40–3; Isby, p. 76.
10. *Soviet Military Power (1984)*, p. 55.
11. Cf., Dinerstein, pp. x and xii.
12. A long war, even a 'conventional' long war, would not be intended though it might result from miscalculation: Penkovsky, p. 258.

BIBLIOGRAPHY

BOOKS

Akhmedov, I. *In and Out of Stalin's GRU*. University Publications of America, Inc., 1984.

Alliluyeva, S. *Twenty Letters to a Friend*. Hutchinson, London 1967.

Anders, W. *An Army in Exile*. Macmillan, London 1949.

Arndt, R. F. *Waffen und Gerät der Sowjetischen Landstreitkräfte*. Walhalla u. Praetoria Verlag, Regensburg 1971.

Bagramian, I. Kh. *Gorod-Voin na Dnepre*. Moscow 1965. *So Begann der Krieg*. Militärverlag, Berlin 1972.

Barker, A.J. and Walter, J. *Russian Infantry Weapons of WW II*. Arco Publishing Co. Inc., New York 1971.

Barmine, A. *Memoirs of a Soviet Diplomat*. Lovat Dickson, London 1938.

Batov, P. I. *V Pokhodakh i Boiakh*. Moscow 1962.

Bazhanov, B. *Stalin – Der Rote Diktator*. Aretz, Berlin 1931.

Bialer, S. *Stalin and his Generals*. Souvenir Press, London 1970.

Biriuzov, S. S. *Surovye Gody*. Moscow 1966. *Kogda Gremeli Pushki*. Moscow 1961.

Birse, A. H. *Memoirs of an Interpreter*. Michael Joseph, London 1967.

Blumenthal, F. *Politicheskaia Rabota v Voennoe Vremia*. Moscow 1929.

Bryant, A. *The Turn of the Tide*. Collins, London 1957. *Triumph in the West*. Collins, London 1959.

Borisov, B. and Ryabov, V. *The Soviet Army*. Moscow 1961.

Budenny, S.M. *Proidennyi Put'*. (Two Vols). Moscow 1958–65.

Bychevsky, B. V. *Gorod-Front*. Moscow 1963.

Carsten, F. L. *The Reichswehr and Politics 1918–1933*. OUP, London 1966.

Castellan, G. *Le Réarmement Clandestin du Reich 1930–1935*. Librairie Plon, Paris 1954.

Chamberlin, W. H. *The Russian Revolution 1917–21* (Two Vols). Macmillan, London 1935.

Danilevsky, A. F. *V. I. Lenin i Voprosy Voennogo Stroitel'stva na VIII S'ezde RKP (b)*. Moscow 1964.

Deane, J. R. *The Strange Alliance*. Murray, London 1947.

Denikin, A.I. *The Career of a Tsarist Officer – Memoirs 1872–1916*. University of Minnesota Press, Minneapolis 1975. *The White Army*. Cape, London 1930.

Deutscher, I. *Stalin – A Political Biography*. OUP, London 1967.

Dinerstein, H. S. *War and the Soviet Union*. Praeger, New York 1962.

Djilas, M. *Conversations with Stalin*. Rupert Hart-Davis, London 1962.

Eden, A. *Memoirs – The Reckoning*. Cassell, London 1965.

Egorov, A.I. *Razgrom Denikina*. Moscow 1936.

Eremenko, A.I. *Stalingrad*. Moscow 1961. *V Nachale Voiny*. Moscow 1964. *Pomni Voinu*. Donbass 1971.

Erickson, J. *The Soviet High Command 1918–1941*. Macmillan, London 1962. *Soviet Military Power* supplement to *Strategic Review*. Washington D.C., Spring 1973.

Erickson, J. and Feuchtwanger, E. J. *Soviet Military Power and Performance*. Archon, New York 1979.

Fediuninsky, I. I. *Podniatie po Trevoge*. Moscow 1964.

Feis, H. *Churchill, Roosevelt, Stalin*. Princeton UP, 1966.

Forbes, A. *Souvenirs of Some Countries*. Macmillan, London 1885.

Frunze, M.V. *Sobranie Sochinenii*. (Three Vols). Moscow 1929. *Izbrannye Proizvedeniia*. (Two Vols). Moscow 1957.

Garthoff, R.L. *Soviet Strategy in the Nuclear Age*. Praeger, New York 1962.

Goldhamer, H. *The Soviet Soldier*. Crane, Russak & Co. Inc., New York 1975.

Golikov, F. I. *V Moskovskoi Bitve*. Moscow 1967.

Golikov, S. *Vydaiushchiesia Pobedy Sovetskoi Armii v Velikoi Otechestvennoi Voine*. Moscow 1954.

Golovin, N. N. *The Russian Army in the World War*. OUP, London 1931.

Gorbatov, A. V. *Years off my Life*. Constable, London 1964.

Grechko, A. A. *Bitva za Kavkaz*. Moscow 1967. *Cherez Karpaty*. Moscow 1970. *Osvodobitel'naia Missiia Sovetskikh Vooruzhennykh Sil vo Vtoroi Mirovoi Voine*. Moscow 1971. *The Armed Forces of the Soviet Union*. Moscow 1977.

Greene, F. V. *Russian Campaigns in Turkey 1877–8*. (Two Vols). D. Appleton & Co., New York 1879. *Sketches of Army Life in Russia*. New York 1880.

Greiner, H. *Die Oberste Wehrmachtführung*. Limes Verlag, Wiesbaden 1951.

Grigorenko, P. *Grigorenko Memoirs*. W.W. Norton & Co., New York 1982.

Guderian, H. *Panzer Leader*. Michael Joseph, London 1952. *Die Panzerwaffe*. Union Deutsche Verlag, Stuttgart 1943.

Halder, F. *Kriegstagebuch*. (Three Vols). Kohlhammer, Stuttgart 1962. *Hitler as Warlord.* Putnam, London 1950.

Hilger, G. *The Incompatible Allies.* Macmillan, New York 1953.

Hodgson, J.E. *With Denikin's Armies.* Lincoln Williams, London 1932.

Hubatsch, W. *Hitlers Weisungen für die Kriegführung 1939–1945.* Bernard u. Graefe, Frankfurt 1962.

Iakovlev, A. S. *Tsel' Zhizni.* Moscow 1966.

Ironside, E. *Archangel 1918–19.* Constable, London 1953.

Ismay, H. L. *The Memoirs of General the Lord Ismay.* Heinemann, London 1960.

Isby, D. G. *Weapons and Tactics of the Soviet Army.* Jane's Publishing Co. Ltd, London 1981.

Jacobsen, H. A. *Der Zweite Weltkrieg in Chronik und Dokumenten.* Wehr u. Wissen Verlagsgesellschaft, Darmstadt 1961.

Kamenev, S. S. *Vospominaniia o V. I. Lenine.* Moscow 1957. *Zapiski o Grazhdanskoi Voine i Voennom Stroitel'stve.* Moscow 1963.

Kazakov, M. I. *Nad Kartoi Bylykh Srazhenii.* Moscow 1965.

Kesselring, A. *Soldat bis zum letzten Tag.* Athenäum, Bonn 1953.

Khmel, A. *Education of the Soviet Soldier.* Moscow 1972.

Klink, E. *Das Gesetz des Handelns 'Zitadelle' 1943.* Deutsche Verlags Anstalt, Stuttgart 1966.

Knox, A. *With the Russian Army 1914–17.* (Two Vols). Hutchinson, London 1921.

Kolganov, K. S. *Razvitie Taktiki Sovetskoi Armii v Gody Velikoi Otechestvennoi Voiny 1941–5.* Moscow 1958.

Konev, I. S. *Zapiski Komanduiushchego Frontom 1943–4.* Moscow 1972.

Korkeshkin, A. *The Soviet Armed Forces.* Moscow 1975.

Korolivsky, S.M. *Grazhdanskaia Voina na Ukraine 1918–20.* Moscow 1968.

Kravchenko, G.S. *Voennaia Ekonomika SSSR 1941–45.* Moscow 1963.

Krivitsky, W.G. *I was Stalin's Agent.* Hamish Hamilton, London 1939.

Kurochkin, P.M. *Pozyvnye Fronta.* Moscow 1969.

Kuropatkin, A. N. *The Russian Army and the Japanese War.* (Two Vols). John Murray, London 1909.

Kuznetsov, N.G. *Nakanune.* Moscow 1966.

Leliushenko, D. D. *Zaria Pobedy.* Moscow 1966. *Moskva-Stalingrad-Berlin-Praga.* Moscow 1970.

Lenin, V. I. *Leninskii Sbornik.* Moscow XXIV (1942), XXVII (1942), XXXIV (1942), XXXV (1945), XXXVI (1959), XXXVII (1970). *Voennaia Perepiska (1917–20).* Moscow 1956. *Polnoe Sobranie Sochinenii.* (5th Ed.). Vols 8, 24, 29, 30, 32, 35–7, 39, 40, 50–1, 54–5.

Littauer, V. S. *Russian Hussar.* Allen, London 1965.

Livshits, Ia. L. *Pervaia Gvardeiskaia Tankovaia Brigada v Boiakh za Moskvu.* Moscow 1948.

Lugansky, S. D. *Na Glubokikh Virazhakh*. Alma-Ata 1966.

Lunacharsky, A. V. *Revoliutsionnye Siluety*. Moscow 1923.

Lyons, M. *The Russian Imperial Army*. Stanford University, California 1968.

Malinovsky, R. Ia. *Final*. Moscow 1966. *Budapest-Vena-Praga*. Moscow 1969.

Manstein, E. von. *Aus einem Soldatenleben*. Athenäum, Bonn 1958. *Lost Victories*. Methuen, London 1958.

Martel, G. *The Russian Outlook*. Michael Joseph, London 1947.

Matsulenko, W. A. *Die Zerschlagung der Heeresgruppe Südukraine*, Berlin 1959.

Mayer, S. L. *The Russian War Machine 1917–1945*. Bison Books – Arms and Armour Press, London 1977.

McNeal, R.H. *Stalin's Works (Bibliography)*. Stanford UP 1967.

Melikov, V. A. *Geroicheskaia Oborona Tsaritsyna 1918*. Moscow 1938.

Meretskov, K.A. *Na Sluzhbe Narody*. Moscow 1970.

Meshcheriakov, G. P. *A. V. Suvorov*. (Four Vols). Moscow 1949.

Miliukov, P. *Rossiia na Perelome*. Paris 1927.

Miller, W. *Russians as People*. Phoenix, London 1960.

Molotov, V. *Stalin and Stalin's Leadership*. Moscow 1950.

Montgomery, B. L. *Memoirs*. Collins, London 1958.

Moskalenko, K. S. *Na Iugo-Zapadnom Napravlenii 1943–45*. Moscow 1972.

Mosse, W. E. *Alexander II*. English University Press, London 1964.

Mueller-Hillebrand, B. *Das Heer 1939–1945*. (Three Vols). Mittler, Frankfurt.

Nepomniashchy, K. *Polki Idyt na Zapad*. Moscow 1964.

Novikov, A. A. *V Nebe Leningrada*. Moscow 1970.

Penkovsky, O. *The Penkovsky Papers*. Avon, New York 1966.

Peresypkin, I. T. *Radio-Moguchee Sredstvo Oborony Strany*. Moscow 1948. *Sviaz' v Velikoi Otechestvennoi Voine*. Moscow 1973.

Perrett, B. *Fighting Vehicles of the Red Army*. Arco, New York 1969.

Petrov, Iu. P. *Partiinoe Stroitel'stvo v Sovetskoi Armii i Flote*. Moscow 1964. *Stroitel'stvo Politorganov, Partiinykh i Komsomol'skikh Organizatsii Armii i Flota (1918–1968)*. Moscow 1968.

Petrovsky, D. A. *Voennaia Shkola v Gody Revoliutsii*. Moscow 1924.

Pilsudsky, J. *Year 1920*. Pilsudsky Institute 1972.

Platonov, S. P. *Vtoraia Mirovaia Voina*. Moscow 1958.

Pokrovsky, M. *Ocherki po Istorii Oktiabr'skoi Revoliutsii*. (Two Vols). Moscow 1927.

Reznichenko, V. G. *Taktika*. Moscow 1966.

Rigby, T. H. (ed.) *The Stalin Dictatorship*. Sydney UP, Sydney 1968.

Ritter, G. *Das Kommunemodell und die Begründung der Roten Armee im Jahre 1918*. Osteuropa-Institut, Berlin 1965.

Rokossovsky, K. K. *Velikaia Pobeda na Volge*. Moscow 1965. *Soldatskii Dolg*. Moscow 1968.

Rotmistrov, P. A. *Istoriia Voennogo Iskusstva*. (Two Vols). Moscow 1963.

Samsonov, A. M. *Die Grosse Schlacht vor Moskau*. Militärverlag, Berlin 1959. *Stalingradskaia Bitva*. Moscow 1968.

Sandalov, L. M. *Perezhitoe*. Moscow 1961.

Schlauch, W. *Rüstungshilfe der USA an die Verbündeten im Zweiten Weltkrieg*. Wehr u. Wissen Verlagsgesellschaft, Darmstadt 1967.

Scott, H. F. and W. F. *The Soviet Art of War*. Westview Press, Boulder, Colorado 1982. *The Armed Forces of the USSR*. Westview Press, Boulder, Colorado 1981.

Seaton, A. *The Russo-German War 1941–45*. Arthur Barker, London 1971. *The German Army 1933–45*. Sphere (London) and Meridian, New York 1985. *The Horsemen of the Steppes* (Cossacks). The Bodley Head, London 1985.

Seeckt, H. von. *Aus meinem Leben* (Ed. von Rabenau) (Two Vols). Hase u. Kohler, Leipzig 1940.

Shaposhnikov, B. M. *Na Visle*. Moscow 1924. *Mozg Armii*. Moscow 1927.

Sherwood, R. E. *The White House Papers of Harry Hopkins*. (Two Vols). Eyre and Spottiswoode, London 1948–9.

Shtemenko, S. M. *General'nyi Shtab v Gody Voiny*. (Two Vols). Moscow 1968–73.

Sokolovsky, V.D. *Voennaia Strategiia*. Moscow 1963: in English translation as *Military Strategy*. Pall Mall Press, London 1963. *Razgrom Nemetsko-Fashistkikh Voisk pod Moskvoi*. Moscow 1964.

Soloviev. M. *My Nine Lives in the Red Army*. David McKay Co. Inc., New York 1955.

Souvarine, B. *Stalin*. Secker and Warburg, London 1939.

Stalin, J. V. *Na Putiakh k Oktiabriu*. Leningrad 1925. *Leninism*. Lawrence & Wishart, London 1940. *On the Great Patriotic War*. Hutchinson, London 1947. *Sochineniia*. (Thirteen Vols). Moscow 1946–51. *Stanford Sochineniia*. (Three Vols). Ed. R. H. McNeal. Stanford UP 1967. *Economic Problems of Socialism in the USSR*. Moscow 1952. *Stalin – Kratkaia Biografiia*. Moscow 1950.

Starinov, I. T. *Miny Zhdut Svoego Chasa*. Moscow 1964.

Stewart, G. *The White Armies of Russia*. Macmillan, New York 1933.

Sukhanov, N. N. *Zapiski o Revoliutsii*. Moscow 1922. *The Russian Revolution 1917*. OUP 1955.

Suvorov, Viktor. *Inside the Soviet Army*. Hamish Hamilton, London 1982.

Svechin, A. A. *Strategiia*. Moscow 1927.

Sverdlov, Ia. M. *Izbrannye Proizvedeniia*. Moscow 1960.

Teske, H. *General Ernst Köstring*. Mittler, Frankfurt a.M. 1966.

Tiulenev, I.V. *Cherez Tri Voiny.* Moscow 1960.

Todorsky, A. I. *Marshal Tukhachevskii.* Moscow 1963.

Trotsky, L. D. *Kak Vooruzhales' Revoliutsiia.* Moscow 1924. *My Life.* Butterworth, London 1930. *The History of the Russian Revolution.* (Three Vols). Gollancz, London 1932–3. *Stalin.* Harper, London 1946. *Military Writings.* (Ed. Breitman). Merit, New York 1969.

Tukhachevsky, M. N. *Voina Klassov.* Moscow 1921. *Manevr i Artilleriia.* Moscow 1924. *Izbrannye Proizvedeniia.* (Two Vols). Moscow 1964.

Ulam, A. B. *The Bolsheviks.* Macmillan – Collier, New York 1968.

Vasilevsky. A. M. *Delo Vsei Zhizni.* Moscow 1974.

Viskovatov, *Istoricheskoe Opisanie Odezhdy i Vooruzhenniia Rossiiskikh Voisk.* (Nineteen Vols). St Petersburg 1841–8.

Vorob'ev, F.D. and Kravtsov, V. M. *Pobedy Sovetskikh Vooruzhennykh Sil v Velikoi Otechestvennoi Voine.* Moscow 1953.

Voronov, N. N. *Na Sluzhbe Voennoi.* Moscow 1963.

Voroshilov, K. E. *Stat'i i Rechi.* Moscow 1937. *Stalin i Krasnaia Armiia.* Moscow 1938. *Stalin and the Armed Forces of the USSR.* Moscow 1951.

Wellesley, F.A. *With the Russians in Peace and War.* Eveleigh Nash, London 1904.

Werth, A. *Russia at War.* Barrie and Rockcliff, London 1964.

White, D. *The Growth of the Red Army.* Princeton UP 1944.

Wildman, A. K. *The End of the Russian Imperial Army.* Princeton UP, New Jersey 1980.

Williamson, H. N. H. *Farewell to the Don.* Collins, London 1970.

Wollenberg, E. *The Red Army – A Study of the Growth of Soviet Imperialism.* Martin Secker and Warburg, London 1940.

Woodward, E. L. *British Foreign Policy. History of the Second World War.* HMSO, London 1962.

Yaroslavsky, E. *Landmarks in the Life of Stalin.* Lawrence and Wishart, London 1942.

Zakharov, M. V. *Osvobozhdenie Iugo-Vostochnoi i Tsentral'noi Evropy Voiskami 2go i 3go Ukrainskikh Frontov.* Moscow 1970.

Zaletny, A. F. *Militarizatsiia FRG.* Moscow 1969.

Zhukov, G. K. *Vospominaniia i Razmyshleniia.* Macdonald, London 1969.

ANTHOLOGIES, EDITED WORKS, PRINTED DOCUMENTS, OFFICIAL PUBLICATIONS AND REFERENCE BOOKS

Armiia Sovetskaia. Moscow 1969.

Bitva za Moskvu. Moscow 1968.

Bitva za Stalingrad. Volgograd 1973.

Bol'shaia Sovetskaia Entsiklopediia. (Three Eds.). Moscow 1926–70.

Command Decisions. Department of the Army, Harcourt Brace, New York 1959.

Das Deutsche Reich und der Zweite Weltkrieg – Band 4. Deutsche Verlags-Anstalt, Stuttgart 1983.

Dekrety Sovetskoi Vlasti. (Five Vols). Moscow 1957–71.

Direktivy Glavnogo Komandovaniia Krasnoi Armii (1917–1920). Moscow 1969.

Direktivy Komandovaniia Frontov Krasnoi Armii (1917–1920). (Two Vols). Moscow 1971–2.

Documents of German Foreign Policy, HMSO, London.

Dokumenty o Geroicheskoi Oborone Petrograda v 1919 g. Moscow 1941.

Dokumenty o Geroicheskoi Oborone Tsaritsyna v 1918 g. Moscow 1942.

German (WW2) diaries, war diaries and documents held in the Militär-Archiv, Freiburg.

Grazhdanskaia Voina (Vols 2 and 3). Moscow 1928–30.

Grazhdanskaia Voina. (2nd Ed. Four Vols). Moscow 1953–9.

Grazhdanskaia Voina na Ukraine. (Four Vols). Kiev 1967.

Handbook on the Soviet Armed Forces. DDB-2680–40–78. US Defense Agency, 1978.

Istoriia Kommunisticheskoi Partii Sovetskogo Soiuza. (Vol. 3). Moscow 1968.

Istoriia Velikoi Otechestvennoi Voiny Sovetskogo Soiuza. (Six Vols). Moscow 1961–5.

Iz Istorii Grazhdanskoi Voiny v SSSR. (Three Vols). Moscow 1960–1.

KPSS o Vooruzhennykh Silakh Sovetskogo Soiuza (Dokumenty 1917–68). Moscow 1969.

KPSS v Rezoliutsiiakh i Resheniiakh. (Vol. 2). Moscow 1970.

Kriegstagebuch des Oberkommandos der Wehrmacht. (Four Vols). Bernard u. Graefe, Frankfurt.

Löbell, von. *Jahresberichte über das Heer und Kriegswesen.* 1907 and 1912.

Malaia Sovetskaia Entsiklopediia. (3rd Ed.). Moscow 1958.

Nastavlenie po Postoiannym Liniiam Sviazi 1943 g. Moscow 1945.

Nazi-Soviet Relations 1939–41. Department of State Publication 3023.

O Sovetskoi Voennoi Nauke. Moscow 1964.

Osnovy Sovetskogo Voennogo Zakonodatel'stva. Moscow 1966.

Pogranichnye Voiska v Gody Velikoi Otechestvennoi Voiny. Moscow 1968.

Protokoly Tsentral'nogo Komiteta RSDRP (1929).

Russian Military Power (Ed. Menaul). Salamander Books Ltd 1980. (US edition *The Soviet War Machine* (Ed. Bonds). Chartwell – St Martins Press, 1976).

Sluzhba Sviazi. (uchebnik dlia shkol RKKA). Moscow 1935.

Sobranie Zakonov i Rasporiazhenii RK Pravitel'stva SSSR, 27/5 1937, No. 31.

Spisok General'nago Shtaba. St. Petersburg 1913.

SSSR v Velikoi Otechestvennoi Voine (1941–45) (Kratkaia Khronika). Moscow 1964.

St Petersburg Army Orders (from 1909).

Stalingradskaia Epopeia. Moscow 1968.

The History of the Civil War in the USSR. (Vol. 2). Lawrence and Wishart, London 1947.

The Officer's Handbook (Spravochnik Ofitsera), Moscow 1971. A Soviet View – Soviet Military Thought No. 13, published under the auspices of the US Air Force.

The Red Army Today. Moscow 1939.

The Trotsky Papers (1917–21). (Ed. Meijer – Two Vols). Mouton, The Hague 1964–71.

Ukrains'ka Radians'ka Entsiklopediia. Kiev 1959.

Velikaia Otechestvennaia Voina Sovetskogo Soiuza 1941–1945 (Kratkaia Istoriia). Moscow 1965.

Voprosy Strategii i Operativnogo Iskusstva v Sovetskikh Voennykh Trudakh (1917–1940). Moscow 1965.

50 Let Vooruzhennykh Sil SSSR. Moscow 1968.

50 (Piat'desiat) Let Sovetskikh Vooruzhennykh Sil Fotodokumenty. Moscow 1967.

PERIODICALS

Bol'shevik
Istoriia SSSR
Kommunist
Kommunist Vooruzhennykh Sil
Novaia i Noveishaia Istoriia
Novyi Mir
Oktiabr'
Proletarskaia Revoliutsiia
RUSI Journal
Sotsialisticheskii Vestnik
Soviet Military Power
Soviet Military Review
Strategic Review
Survey
The New Yorker
Voenno-Istoricheskii Zhurnal
Voennyi-Vestnik
Voprosy Istorii

INDEX

This index is in three parts, Name Index, Place and Peoples and Subject Index and Glossary

NAME INDEX

All entries of particular interest are accompanied by a few words giving titles, official positions and ranks. Tsarist and White Russian ranks are shown thus: (Gen.). Where officers held in turn tsarist and Soviet ranks, only the Soviet ranks have been shown. Soviet ranks are shown without parenthesis and are usually those held in final appointments, it being noted that some officers, e.g. Kulik, Mekhlis and Shtemenko, were at times demoted. Marshal of the Soviet Union is shown as: M of SU. The military ranks of foreigners are distinguished by the suffixes (US) (Brit) (Fr) (Germ) etc.

Akhromeev, S. F., M of SU, chief of general staff of armed forces 1984, 225

Akopov, S. A., commissar for motor industry, 106

Alexander I, tsar and emperor 1801–1825, 8

Alexander II, tsar and emperor 1855–1881, 8, 9, 10, 13, 171

Altfater, V. M., (Rear-Adm.), 38

Andropov, Iu. V., head of KGB, party secretary and de facto head of state, 165, 225

Antonov, A. I., Gen., praporshchik 1916 and later deputy and chief of Red Army general staff, 144, 150, 167

Antonov-Ovseenko, V. A., officer cadet 1904, revolutionary and Trotskyite, head of PUR 1922–24, 35, 36, 68

Apanasenko, I. R., Gen., Red Guard and cavalry leader under Budenny, in Far East until 1943, 76

Artemev, P. A. Lt-Gen., head of Moscow military district, 179, 180

Bagramian, I., Kh., M of SU, Armenian praporshchik 1915, Red Army cavalry from 1921, WW II army and front commander, head of Rear Services, 168, 180

Barmine, A., Soviet defector, 70

Bazhanov, B., Soviet defector— secretary to Politburo, 58, 59, 60

Beck, L., Col-Gen. (Germ), chief of German army general staff, 88, 129

Benes, Eduard, president of Czecho-Slovakia, 100

Berens, E. A. (Capt. 1st Cl), became chief of staff Red Navy, 38

Beria, L. P., titular M of SU, head of NKVD then MGB/MVD, 114, 164, 165, 178, 179, 180

Bessonov, N. I., military commissar, 39

Biriuzov, S. S., M of SU, Red Army 1922, chief of staff of armies and fronts in WW II, then C-in-C Central Group, PVO and rocket forces, 80

Birse, A. H., Maj. (Brit), British embassy Moscow, 44

Blomberg, W. von, FM (Germ), German minister of defence and war, 91

Blyukher, V. K., M of SU, also known as Medvedev and Galin, former NCO and Old Bolshevik, division commander in Civil War, army commander in Far East from 1929, 90, 96, 99

Bock, F. von, FM (Germ), C-in-C army groups centre and south, 126

Bonch-Bruevich, M. D., (Gen.), 1917 chief of staff to revolutionary high command, 36, 38, 78

Brezhnev, L. I., titular M of SU, military commissar in WW II, subsequently party secretary and de facto head of state, 43, 191, 225

Brooke, A., FM (Brit) Viscount, chief of imperial general staff, 144

Bubnov, A. S., Old Bolshevik, military commissar in Civil War, later head of PUR, 68

Budenny, S. M., M of SU, a cavalry OR extended-service man since 1903 and a sergeant in 1917, Civil War cavalry army commander, an associate of Stalin, then inspector of cavalry, commander Moscow military district, in WW II commander of fronts and theatres, 46, 51, 52, 53, 54, 55, 60, 61, 68, 76, 79, 80, 90, 93, 96, 99, 102, 114, 115, 118, 125, 126, 144

Bukharin, N. I., Politburo member, 58, 61

Bulganin, N. A., titular M of SU, Old Bolshevik, Cheka member and military commissar in Civil War and WW II, minister of defence and prime minister, 125, 127, 150, 151, 167, 179

Burrows, M. B., Lt-Gen. (Brit), head of British military mission in Moscow, 140, 144, 223, 224

Catherine (II) the Great, tsarina and empress 1762–96, 7, 8, 215

Chernenko, K., Politburo member, first secretary and de facto head of state, 225

Cherniakhovsky, I. D., Gen., entered Red Army 1924, artillery then tanks, WW II front commander, 223, 224

Chuikov, V. I., M of SU, entered Red Army 1918, between 1920–42 intermittent service in Far East and China, army commander in WW II, then commander GSFG and military districts and C-in-C ground forces, 168, 180, 181, 192

Clausewitz, Carl von, Gen. (Prus), military theorist and writer, 53, 69

Danilov, (Gen.), assistant chief of general staff, 23, 26

Deane, J. R., Maj.-Gen. (US), US military mission in Moscow, 144

Denikin, A. I., (Gen.), imperial general staff officer and White leader, 2, 10, 15, 16, 20, 22, 40, 44, 50, 51

Diebitsch, H. K. F. A., (FM) Count von, 9

Djilas, M., Yugoslav revolutionary partisan and politician, 166, 169

Dubenko, P. E., Army Comd 2nd Cl., 1911 naval rating and Bolshevik, revolutionary leader of ground forces in Civil War, later commander Leningrad military district, 35

Dudorov, N. P., head of MVD, 165

Dukhonin, (Gen.), last imperial chief of staff and C-in-C at the Mogilev Stavka, 36

Dzerzhinsky, F. E., Polish revolutionary and associate of Stalin, head of Cheka—GPU, 50, 52, 60, 102

Eden, Sir Antony, British foreign minister, 144

Egorov, A. I., M of SU, tsarist officer from 1905, entered Red Army 1918, became front commander and associate of Stalin, later chief of Red Army general staff, 39, 52, 53, 54, 55, 62, 91, 93, 96, 99, 103

Emelianov, V. S., a defence industries official, 106

Engels, Friedrich, German socialist and collaborator of Marx, 218

Epishev, A. A., Gen., chief of PUR and military commissar, 227

Eremenko, A. I., M of SU, a tsarist

cavalry NCO, later a Red cavalry corps commander, WW II commander of armies and fronts, then of military districts, 76, 125, 126, 180

Fedorenko, Ia. N., Chief Marshal of Armoured Troops, 1915 naval rating entered Red Guards and armoured trains, from 1940 in armoured directorate of high command, 106
Frederick the Great, King of Prussia 1740–1786, 5, 7
Frederick William, Great Elector of Brandenburg 1640–1688, 4
Frederick William I, King of Prussia 1713–1740, 5
Fritsch, W. T. L., Col-Gen. (Germ), Freiherr von, C-in-C German Army, 129
Frunze, M. V., Army Commander, Old Bolshevik and revolutionary, in Civil War military commissar and commander armies and fronts, 1925 minister for army and naval affairs, 62, 65, 66, 67, 68, 69, 70, 71, 72, 74, 79, 80, 102, 217

Gaulle, Charles de, Gen. (Fr), armoured theorist, 84
Gittis, B. M., (Col), tsarist officer then Red Army front commander, 53
Golikov, F. I., M of SU, entered Red Army through Red Guards, military commissar until 1931 then command appointments, in 1940 headed GRU, 1941 headed mission in UK and USA, WW II front commander, later head of PUR, 132, 133
Golovko, A. G., Adm., headed Northern Fleet in WW II, 144
Gorbachev, M., Politburo member and party secretary and de facto head of state, 225
Gordov, V. N., army and front commander in WW II, 167
Gorshkov, S. G., Adm. of Fleet of SU, in WW II served on Black Sea, then chief of naval forces from 1956–86, 144
Govorov, L. A., M of SU, tsarist artillery officer with Kolchak's

Whites, joined Red Army 1919, in WW II front and group commander, not accepted into party until 1942, later inspector-general and head of PVO, 150, 168, 170
Grabin, V. G., Col-Gen. of Technical Troops, 104
Grechko, A. A., M of SU, entered Red Army 1919, army commander in WW II, commander GSFG, then C-in-C ground forces and minister of defence, 180, 181, 192
Greene, F. V., Lieut US Engineer Corps, attached to tsarist army, 13, 17, 20, 94
Grigorenko, P., Maj.-Gen., Ukrainian Red Army engineer and staff officer, formation commander in WW II, instructor at Frunze, now in USA, 222
Guchkov, A. I., minister of war in provisional government 1917, 31
Guderian, H., Col-Gen. (Germ), major of Reichsheer motor transport corps, then panzer commander and inspector-general of panzer troops, 84, 85, 87, 88, 108, 124, 138, 149
Gusev, S. I., Old Bolshevik, military commissar in Civil War, later head of PUR, 36, 49, 65, 66

Harpe, J., Col-Gen. (Germ), major of Reichsheer motor transport corps, then panzer and army group commander, 84
Harriman, W. A., US ambassador to Moscow, 147
Heydrich, R., SS and chief of German security service, 100
Hilger, G., German embassy staff in Moscow, 103, 104
Hindenburg, Paul von, FM (Germ), chief of general staff of field army 1916–19, German president 1925–34, 97
Hitler, Adolf, Austrian and naturalized German, leader of Nazi party, chancellor and Führer, C-in-C Wehrmacht 1938, C-in-C Germany Army 1941, 84, 88, 92, 97, 100, 101, 105, 111, 117, 119, 123, 124, 125,

Hitler – cont.
129, 130, 134, 135, 136, 137, 138,
139, 142, 145, 164, 165, 212, 219
Hopkins, H. L., US presidential
emissary, 2, 105

Iakovlev, A. S., Soviet aircraft
designer, 106, 107
Ignatev, (Maj.-Gen.) Count, former
tsarist officer in Red Army employ,
18, 92, 162
Ironside, E., FM (Brit) Lord, in
command British forces at Archangel
in 1919, 94
Ismay, H., Gen. (Brit) Lord, chief staff
officer to Churchill, 144
Ivan (IV) the Terrible, tsar of Muscovy
1533–1584, 4, 215

Kaganovich, L. M., Politburo member
and associate of Stalin, 59, 178, 180
Kamenev (Rosenfeld), L. V., Old
Bolshevik and Politburo member,
58, 61, 62, 99
Kamenev, S. S., (Col), tsarist officer,
joined Red Army in 1918, front
commander and then C-in-C and
inspector, 49, 50, 51, 52, 53, 54, 55,
69, 78
Kennan, George F., US ambassador to
Moscow, 1
Kerensky, A. F., lawyer, member and
then prime minister of provisional
government 1917, 30, 31, 32, 41
Khrulev, A. V., Gen., from Red
Guards to Red Army, military
commissar 1918–29, with cavalry, in
army rear services from 1941, 150
Khrushchev, N. S., Lt-Gen., a protégé
of L. M. Kaganovich, joined party in
1918, became party official and rose
to Politburo, in WW II being a
military commissar with fronts:
eventually ousted Malenkov to
become party secretary and de facto
head of state, 43, 56, 100, 125, 148,
150, 169, 170, 171, 178, 179, 180,
181, 189, 190, 191
Kirov, S. M., Old Bolshevik, military
commissar from 1919 and then
Politburo member, 99
Kirponos, M. P., Col-Gen., Red Army

since 1918, commander of military
districts and fronts, 113, 114, 115,
117, 126
Knox, A. W. F., Maj.-Gen. (Brit),
military attaché St Petersburg 1911–
14, then with military mission 1914–
17, 18, 21, 23, 24, 26, 27, 28, 94,
143
Kolchak, A. V., (Adm), White leader
in Siberia, 49
Konev, I. S., M of SU, tsarist NCO,
military commissar from 1918–27,
then command appointments, in
WW II army and front commander,
then C-in-C ground forces, inspector-
general, military districts and
Warsaw Pact, 110, 126, 127, 138,
150, 167, 168, 170, 178, 180, 181
Köstring, E. A., Gen. (Germ), German
military attaché to Moscow, 91, 92,
103, 120, 121
Kovalev, M. P., Col-Gen., 1915
praporshchik, military district and
front commander, 112
Kruglov, S. N., Lt-Gen., head of
MVD, 165
Krylenko, N. V., Old Bolshevik and
revolutionary, 35, 36
Kühlenthal, Col (Germ), head of
Reichsheer military intelligence, 91,
94
Kulik, G. I., M of SU, tsarist NCO, in
Red Army 1918 with Budenny, then
to command and artillery
appointments, subsequently
promoted and demoted, 115
Kulikov, V. G., M of SU, with tank
units in WW II, then commander
armies and military districts, GSFG,
chief of general staff and C-in-C
Warsaw Pact, 225
Kuprin, A. I., tsarist junior officer and
novelist, 18
Kuropatkin, A. N., (Gen.), minister of
war 1898–1904, 14, 15, 16, 21, 23,
24, 214
Kutuzov, M. I., (FM), Prince of
Smolensk, C-in-C 1812, 8
Kuznetsov, F. I., Col-Gen.,
praporshchik 1915, WW II military
district and front commander, 115
Kuznetsov, N. G., Adm. of Fleet of

SU, naval rating Red Fleet in Civil War, commander Pacific Fleet 1937, then C-in-C Navy, 103, 105, 167, 170

Lashevich, M. M., Old Bolshevik, military commissar in Civil War, 70
Lebedev, P. P., (Maj.-Gen.), to Red Army 1918, chief of staff to fronts and to C-in-C, 49, 53, 69, 78
Leer, G. A., (Gen.), professor and head of tsarist staff academy, 14, 15
Lenin (Ulianov), V. I., a lawyer and revolutionary of Kalmyk and Volga-German antecedents, a former associate of Plekhanov and Trotsky, then Bolshevik leader, 17, 32, 34, 35, 36, 37, 38, 40, 43, 44, 45, 46, 47, 48, 49, 51, 55, 56, 57, 58, 59, 60, 61, 62, 64, 65, 67, 71, 73, 79, 81, 97, 102, 125, 140, 141, 166, 218, 226
Liddell-Hart, Sir Basil, British military writer, 84
Littauer, V. S., (Capt of Sumsky hussars), 39
Lizichev, A. D., Gen., military commissar, 227
Lutz, O., Gen. (Germ), Reichsheer motor transport corps then panzer general, 87, 88
Lvov, G. E., Prince and first head of 1917 provisional government, 30

MacArthur, D., Gen. (US), 147
Makarov, V. E., Lt-Gen., military commissar in WW II, 223, 224
Malenkov, G. M., military commissar in Civil War, party official and Politburo member, later party secretary and de facto head of state, 127, 178, 179, 180
Malinovsky, R. Ia., M of SU, tsarist NCO in Red Army from 1920, army and front commander in WW II, then C-in-C ground forces and minister of defence, 146, 168, 181, 191, 192
Manstein, E. von, FM (Germ), staff officer and army group commander, 86, 91, 94, 135, 143

Martel, G. LeQ., Lt-Gen. (Brit), tank designer WW I and armoured director, headed mission to Moscow, 92, 93, 94, 140, 143, 144
Marx, Karl, philosopher and political writer, 218
Mekhlis, L. Z., Col-Gen., military commissar in Civil War and WW II, editor of Pravda, head of PUR, 113, 114, 116
Meretskov, K. A., M of SU, Red Guard, then Red cavalry, chief of Red Army staff then army and front commander in WW II, 104, 112, 113, 114, 147, 168
Merkulov, M. K., Lt-Gen., head of KGB, 164
Meves, (Gen.), tsarist corps commander, 17, 221
Mikhailov, B. D., party official, 58
Mikhnevich, (Gen.), tsarist military theorist, 14, 15
Mikoyan, A. I., Politburo member responsible for heavy and light industry, 169
Miles, Adm (Brit), Sir Geoffrey, head of military mission in Moscow, 144
Miller, E. K., (Gen.), White leader, 99
Molotov (Skriabin), V. M., party official and associate of Stalin, later prime minister and foreign minister, 58, 59, 60, 95, 96, 97, 103, 104, 124, 127, 147, 169, 178, 180
Montgomery, B. L., FM (Brit) Lord, army group commander in WW II, 167
Moskalenko, K. S., M of SU, in Red Army artillery, army commander in WW II, then commander of Moscow military district, C-in-C strategic rocket forces and inspector-general, 180
Muralov, N. I., Old Bolshevik and revolutionary commander, 69
Muravev, M. A., (Col), a Left-Socialist revolutionary, 36

Napoleon Bonaparte, 1, 5, 8, 41, 70
Nelson, Horatio, Adm. Lord, 1
Neznamov, A. A., (Gen.), tsarist professor of strategy, 50

Nicholas I, tsar and emperor 1825–1855, 8, 10, 11, 215

Nicholas II, tsar and emperor 1894–1917, 23, 24, 25, 28, 140, 215

Novikov, A. A., Chief Marshal of Aviation, a school teacher, entered Red Army 1919 and party in 1920, commander and military commissar, went to air force after 1927, then head of army aviation, 167

Novitsky, F. F., (Gen.), Red Army adviser in 1918, 28, 69

Ogarkov, N. V., M of SU, engineer troops WW II, staff officer and formation and military district commander, chief of general staff of armed forces and C-in-C Warsaw Pact, 225, 226, 227

Ordzhonikidze, G. K., Old Bolshevik and military commissar in Civil War, responsible for heavy industry from 1932, then persecuted by Stalin, 46, 53, 62

Paul I, tsar and emperor 1796–1801, 8, 131, 220

Paulus, F., FM (Germ), major of Reichsheer motor transport corps, later panzer and staff officer and army commander, 84, 88, 136

Pavlov, D. G., Gen., Red Army tank officer in Spain, chief of armoured vehicle directorate and front commander in WW II, 108, 113, 114, 117, 125, 126

Pavlovsky, I. G., Gen., with staff and troops in WW II, commander of military districts, C-in-C ground forces, 192, 227

Peter (I) the Great, tsar and emperor 1689–1725, 4, 215

Petrov, V. I., Gen., staff and commander in WW II, then commander of military districts and C-in-C ground forces, 227

Pilsudsky, J., Marshal (Pol), Polish revolutionary and soldier, C-in-C republican forces, 80

Plekhanov, G. V., Marxist philosopher, 59

Podvoisky, N. I., first commissar for war 1918, 37

Purkaev, M. A., Gen., a Mordvin praporshchik in 1916, entered Red Army 1918, commander and staff officer, military attaché Berlin 1939, army and front commander WW II, 147, 168

Radek, K. B., a Bolshevik and Trotsky supporter, member of the Comintern and Central Committee, 71

Ribbentrop, J. von, German foreign minister, 112

Röhm, E., chief of staff of Hitler's SA (brown-shirts), 97

Rokossovsky, K. K., M of SU, tsarist cavalry NCO then commander of Red cavalry formations, imprisoned, army and front commander in WW II, inspector-general, 127, 133, 138, 168

Roosevelt, F. D., US president and war leader, 105

Rotmistrov, P. A., Chief Marshal of Armoured Troops, tank army commander and armoured theorist, 14

Samoilo, A. A., Lt-Gen., former tsarist general in Red Army, 78

Seeckt, H., von, Col-Gen. (Germ), chief of Reichsheer, 82, 83

Semichastny, V. E., head of KGB, 165

Serov, I. A., Lt-Gen., head of KGB and member of GRU, 165, 180

Shaposhnikov, B. M., M of SU, tsarist staff officer in Red Army, deputy and chief of Red Army general staff, 15, 18, 39, 54, 69, 78, 79, 80, 90, 103, 112, 114, 126, 132, 133, 144, 167

Shchadenko, E. A., Ukrainian Old Bolshevik, military commissar in Civil War, then head of PUR and directorate for Red Army personnel, 51, 102, 116

Shchelikov, N. A., Col-Gen., head of MVD, 165

Shelepin, A. N., head of KGB, 165

Shtemenko, S. M., Gen., tank officer employed throughout WW II on general staff in Moscow, then chief of general staff, 166, 170

Skliansky, E. M., deputy to Trotsky as commissar for war, 55, 68

Skoblin, (Gen.), a White general émigré, 100

Smilga, I. T., Old Bolshevik and military commissar in Civil War, 64

Smirnov, P. A., Adm., head of naval commissariat, 103

Snesarev, A. E., (Gen.), tsarist general re-employed in the Red Army, 46

Sokolov, S. L., M of SU, tank officer in WW II, staff officer and commander of military districts, 225

Sokolovsky, V. D., M of SU, in Red Army from 1918, staff officer and front commander in WW II, commander of GSFG, chief of general staff and inspector-general, 14, 127, 170

Soloviev, M., military correspondent of Izvestia, 76

Stalin (Djugashvili), I. V., a Georgian Old Bolshevik and associate of Lenin, in Civil War a military commissar with fronts, became first party secretary and most important member of governing troika, dislodging Trotsky and assuming dictatorship: concentrated on heavy industry and rearmament in successive five-year plans but appeased Hitler's Germany: he was solely responsible for the great purges; in WW II he became defence minister and C-in-C, personally directing the Soviet war effort, this situation not altering until his death: 2, 43, 44, 45, 46, 47, 48, 50, 51, 53, 54, 55, 56, 57, 58, 59, 60, 61, 62, 63, 68, 70, 71, 79, 80, 81, 92, 95, 97, 98, 100, 101, 102, 103, 104, 105, 106, 107, 110, 112, 113, 115, 116, 118, 124, 125, 126, 127, 128, 129, 130, 131, 132, 133, 135, 138, 139, 140, 141, 142, 147, 148, 149, 150, 151, 164, 165, 166, 167, 168, 169, 170, 171, 178, 179, 180, 181, 190, 206, 217, 218, 222, 226

Stogov, N. N., (Gen.), tsarist officer temporarily with the Red Army, 39

Sukhomlinov, V., (Gen.), tsarist minister of war 1905–1915, 23

Suvorov, A. V., (FM), field commander and supremo under Catherine the Great, 7, 8

Suvorov, Viktor, nom de plume of a recent Soviet army officer defector

Svechin, A. A., (Gen.), tsarist military theorist who entered Red Army service, 64, 65, 68, 78, 99

Sverdlov, Ia. M., Old Bolshevik, head of the Vtsik, 33, 38, 53, 58, 68

Sytin, P. P., (Gen.), tsarist general in the Red Army, 47, 63, 99

Tedder, A., Marshal (of the RAF), Lord, 144

Ter-Arutiuniants, M. K., former praporshchik and revolutionary, 36

Thoma, W., Gen. (Germ), Ritter von, former major of Reichsheer motor transport corps, then a panzer leader, 84

Timoshenko, S. K., M of SU, Bessarabian Little Russian and tsarist cavalry NCO, Red cavalry division commander in Civil War, commander military districts and then commissar for defence from 1940: in WW II the commander of fronts and theatres, 46, 79, 112, 113, 114, 118, 124, 125, 126, 132, 141, 144, 168

Tolbukhin, F. I., M of SU, tsarist officer from 1915, joined Red Army in 1919, front commander in WW II, 168

Tomsky, M. P., Old Bolshevik and party official, 58

Trotsky (Bronstein), L. D., early associate of Lenin with whom he quarrelled, accused of being a Menshevik, rejoined the Bolsheviks and took a leading part in the revolution, becoming commissar for foreign affairs and then for war, in which post he was in part a creator of the Red Army: in conflict with Stalin he was dislodged by the Bolsheviks, 17, 31, 32, 37, 38, 39, 40, 41, 43, 44, 45, 46, 47, 48, 49, 50, 51, 55, 57, 58, 59, 60, 61, 62, 64, 65, 66, 67, 68, 69, 70, 79, 80, 90, 102, 119

Tukhachevsky, M. N., M of SU, tsarist second lieutenant who entered Red Army 1918 and became army and front commander in Civil War: he was defeated in the Polish War but then became chief of army staff and a military district commander, 52, 53, 54, 55, 62, 65, 66, 68, 69, 79, 80, 81, 85, 90, 93, 95, 96, 99, 100, 101

Uborevich, I. P., Army Commander, a tsarist NCO and praporshchik who entered the Red Guards and in the Civil War commanded an army: according to Soviet sources, in 1927–8 he 'studied at the Higher Military Academy of the German General Staff [sic]'; he then commanded military districts, 85, 90, 93, 99, 100

Ushakov, (Adm.), commander of tsarist Black Sea fleet 1787–1791, 1, 78

Ustinov, D. F., a titular M of SU, a technical official who in WW II was a commissar of armaments and 'a general of the artillery engineers': he then became a minister of the defence industry and afterwards minister of defence, 225

Vannikov, B. L., a commissar for armaments, 105

Vasilevsky, A. M., M of SU, a former tsarist praporshchik and wartime officer who joined the Red Army in 1919; served in field formations in Civil War and then to the general staff: in WW II he was deputy and chief of general staff and commander of fronts and groups of fronts: later he was minister of defence, 127, 129, 131, 132, 133, 135, 138, 141, 144, 147, 148, 150, 167, 170, 222, 223

Vatsetis, I. I., (Col), a Latvian and former tsarist officer who became the first C-in-C Red Army, 36, 47, 48, 49, 55, 57, 62, 78, 99

Vatutin, N. F., Gen., joined the Red Army in 1920 and was a specialist commander from 1921; he became a deputy chief of general staff in Moscow; in WW II he was both a staff officer and front commander, 138

Vershinin, K. A., Chief Marshal of Aviation, entered Red Army infantry in 1919, to air arm in 1930, in WW II commanded air armies, 106, 150

Vishinsky, A. Ia., Soviet lawyer and procurator, later foreign minister, 222

Voronov, N. N., Chief Marshal of Artillery, joined Red Army in 1918, became head of artillery and deputy head of GAU, in WW II group commander, 104, 113, 114, 131, 141, 144

Voroshilov, K. E., titular M of SU, Old Bolshevik and revolutionary and close associate of Stalin from 1918; he had no military experience or training but commanded an army in Civil War and was also a military commissar; in 1924 was commander Moscow military district and from 1925–40 commissar for war/defence: in WW II he was an occasional commander of groups, 46, 47, 48, 51, 53, 54, 55, 59, 60, 62, 63, 64, 66, 68, 69, 70, 71, 74, 75, 77, 79, 80, 86, 90, 92, 93, 95, 96, 97, 98, 99, 102, 104, 109, 113, 114, 115, 118, 125, 127, 141, 144, 150, 166, 170

Voznesensky, N. A., Politburo member, 167

Wavell, A. P., FM Lord, British wartime C-in-C, 92

Wellesley, F. A., Col (Brit), military attaché in St Petersburg, 13, 20, 94, 143

Williamson, H. N. H., Brigadier (Brit), with the military mission to the Whites, 94, 143

Wilson, R., Gen. (Brit) Sir, with the military mission to the 1812 tsarist field force, 94

Wollenberg, E., a Red Army military specialist commander, 70, 74, 75, 80

Wrangel, P., (Gen.) Baron, 52

Yagoda, G. G., head of NKVD, 164

Yezhov, N. I., head of NKVD, 164

Yumashev, I. S., Adm., C-in-C Soviet Navy, 150

Zakharov, M. V., M of SU, entered Red Army from Red Guards, artillery commander in Civil War with Voroshilov's 10 Army; in WW II a front chief of staff, then inspector-general and commander GSFG, 181

Zhdanov, A. A., Col-Gen., associate of Stalin and Politburo member, military commissar in WW II, 125, 170

Zhukov, G. K., M of SU, a tsarist cavalry NCO who served in Civil War under Timoshenko, then a cavalry and military district commander; he was briefly chief of Red Army general staff under Timoshenko then in WW II a front and group commander and deputy to the supremo: after the war he was C-in-C GSFG and C-in-C ground forces and minister of defence, 104, 114, 115, 126, 127, 131, 135, 138, 141, 144, 166, 168, 170, 178, 179, 180, 181, 191, 222

Zinovev, G. E., a school teacher and Old Bolshevik, associate of Lenin and Politburo member, 59, 61, 70, 99

PLACE AND PEOPLES INDEX

Afghanistan, 193, 225, 228, 231

Amur, R., 147

Arctic, 193

Armenians, a minority people in Caucasus and Turkey, 16, 35, 168

Asia, 43, 49, 134, 204

Asiatic minorities of the empire and USSR, 16, 204, 207

Astrakhan, 34, 128

Austerlitz, 1805 battle of, 8

Austro-Hungarian Empire, 6, 8, 26, 27

Balkans, 111, 145, 146

Baltic States, 16, 33, 48, 111, 145, 207

Bataisk, 45

Belgium, 138, 146, 149

Belgorod, 50

Belorussia, 52, 93, 117, 125, 139, 145, 177, 223

Belorussians, a Belorussian-speaking West Slav minority people, 16, 21, 56, 75, 111, 203, 204, 207

Berlin, 7, 9, 84, 87, 92, 126, 166, 170, 191

Bessarabia, 145

Bessarabians, see Ukrainians (Little Russians)

Bialystok, 52

Borodino, 1812 battle of, 8, 94

Brest (Litovsk), 119

Caucasian minorities of the empire and USSR, 203, 204, 207

Caucasus, 21, 51, 91, 117, 133, 134, 135, 136, 167, 193, 227

China, 136, 182, 192

Cossack minorities of the empire and USSR, 5, 11, 25, 29, 31, 32, 66, 75

Crimea, 9, 51, 52, 133

Czecho-Slovakia, 45, 100, 192, 227, 228, 231

Don Cossacks, Russian-speaking minority and largest of the hosts, 29, 33, 36, 45, 51

Don, R., 133, 134, 135

Don Steppe, 43, 45, 49, 50, 66, 132, 134

Donets, R., 45

Dorogobuzh, 52

East Germany (GDR), 148, 152, 175, 192, 227, 231

East Prussia, 56

Elbe, R., 170

Estonians, a Baltic minority Finnic people, 21

Far East, 115, 122, 128, 136, 146, 147, 227

Federal German Republic, *see* West
 Germany
Finland, 2, 21, 112, 113, 137, 145
Finnish minorities, 16, 168, 207
Finns, 2, 16, 22
France, 5, 108, 112, 120, 123, 138,
 145, 146, 149

Georgians, a Caucasian minority
 people, 16, 35, 45, 46, 107, 169
German Empire, based on Prussia, 22,
 24, 26, 27, 91
German nationals of the Russian
 empire and USSR, 9, 34,
Germany, 56, 82, 84, 88
Germany, the Third Reich, 2, 81, 97,
 98, 99, 100, 101, 103, 106, 111, 117,
 123, 132, 136, 145, 150, 164
Great Britain, 13, 27, 81, 112, 136,
 146
Great Russians, a Russian-speaking
 Slavic majority people of the empire
 and USSR, 5, 6, 7, 16, 20, 22, 23,
 27, 28, 34, 75, 76, 81, 168, 169, 203,
 204, 205, 206, 215
Greece, 231

Hiroshima, 147
Holland, 83, 138, 149
Hungary, 145, 146, 192

Indian Ocean, 193, 231
Iran, formerly Persia, 231
Italy, 145
Izyum, 132, 137, 139

Japan, 2, 23, 98, 112, 136, 146, 147
Jews, 16, 22, 35, 76, 112, 167, 204,
 207, 215

Kalmyk-Mongols, a West Mongol
 minority of the empire and USSR,
 16, 34
Kama, R., site of Reichsheer tank
 school, 83, 84, 85
Kazan, 83, 84
Khalk(h)in Gol, R., 107
Kharkov, 50
Khasan, L., 107
Kiev, 52, 59, 115
Kozlov, 47, 50
Kuban Cossacks, Ukrainian-speaking

and second largest Cossack host, 45,
 51
Kuibyshev, formerly Samara, 127
Kunersdorf, battle of, 7, 94
Kursk, 136, 137, 138, 139

Latvians, a Lettish Baltic minority
 people, 35
Leipzig, Battle of the Nations, 8, 214
Leningrad, formerly Petrograd, 80, 85,
 99, 115, 125, 132, 137
Lipetsk, site of Reichsheer air school,
 83, 85
Lithuania, 56
Lithuanians, a Baltic minority people
 and remnants of a mighty empire,
 21, 22
Little Russians, *see* Ukrainians
Livonia, a former Finnic minority state
 in the area of Estonia, 4
London, 1, 120, 132, 224
Lublin, 53, 54, 55
Lugansk, 46
Lvov, or Lemberg, 54, 55

Mediterranean, 136, 193
Minority peoples of the empires, 16, 31
Minority peoples of the USSR, 75, 203,
 215
Mogilev, 28, 29, 36, 39
Mongolia (Outer), a Soviet
 dependency, 146, 231
Mordvins, a Finnic minority, 168
Moscow, 2, 32, 36, 39, 44, 46, 47, 49,
 50, 53, 55, 60, 66, 69, 91, 92, 117,
 118, 119, 121, 124, 126, 127, 128,
 130, 131, 132, 140, 144, 147, 150,
 162, 167, 170, 173, 175, 177, 178,
 180, 217, 226, 230, 231
Moslems (Islam), 204, 215
Murmansk, formerly Alexandrovsk,
 137

Nagasaki, 147
Netherlands, *see* Holland

Onega, L., 128
Orel, 50
Orenburg Cossacks, a Russian-speaking
 minority, 45

Pacific, 147, 193

Pakistan, 231
Paris, 1, 99, 100
Pearl Harbour, 128
Penza, 53
Perm, 102
Persia, later Iran, 59
Petrograd, formerly St Petersburg, later
    Leningrad, 28, 29, 30, 31, 32, 33,
    35, 36, 39, 41, 57, 102
Poland, 33, 52, 53, 55, 56, 66, 85, 90,
    112, 146, 192
Poles, a Polish-speaking West Slav
    nation, formerly a minority under
    the empire, 8, 16, 21, 22, 35, 207
Polish Republic, 44, 48, 52, 53, 54, 56,
    86, 90, 111, 112
Pripet, R. and marsh, 52, 53
Prussia, later the principal state of the
    German Empire, 4, 5, 6, 7, 8, 9, 11,
    12, 15, 16, 17, 22, 59

Rostov on Don, 45, 131, 137
Rumania, 145
Russia, 1, 2, 10, 12, 13, 18, 21, 23, 25,
    26, 32, 39, 44, 56, 117, 121, 123,
    124, 128, 136, 138, 192, 220, 221

St Petersburg, later Petrograd, 5, 9, 28
Samara, later Kuibyshev, 53
Saratov, 50
Siberia, 21, 31, 33, 39, 45, 48, 49, 66,
    69, 122, 128
Smolensk, 52, 117
Soviet Union, 2, 44, 59, 69, 71, 79, 80,
    81, 82, 84, 85, 86, 87, 89, 91, 97,
    98, 100, 101, 103, 108, 111, 114,
    115, 117, 118, 120, 123, 136, 137,
    138, 144, 146, 147, 148, 149, 150,
    151, 152, 162, 172, 174, 175, 176,
    177, 178, 192, 197, 203, 204, 215,
    216, 217, 229, 230
Spain, 107, 108
Stalingrad, formerly Tsaritsyn, later
    Volgograd, 102, 119, 133, 134, 135,
    136
Sweden, 4, 5, 112

Taman, 52
Tatars, a numerous collection of
    Moslem Turkic minority peoples
    once partly Cossack and nomad, the
    remnants of a mighty empire, 5, 6,
    16, 21, 81, 207
Tikhvin, 130
Tsaritsyn, later Stalingrad, 46, 47, 102
Turkestan, 21, 193
Turkey, 8, 14, 20, 193, 231

Ukraine, 33, 36, 37, 43, 45, 46, 48, 49,
    50, 52, 68, 117, 119, 125, 132, 136,
    139, 145, 177, 180, 192
Ukrainians, a Ukrainian-speaking
    South Slav nation, sometimes under
    Poland or Russia, now a minority
    people of the USSR; also known by
    the tsars as Little Russians to
    distinguish them from Great Russian
    people, 16, 21, 32, 56, 75, 81, 111,
    168, 203, 204, 207
Ural, R. and range, 39, 49, 128
Ural Cossacks, a Russian-speaking
    minority, 45
USA, 81, 124, 136, 147, 148, 175, 190,
    196, 230
USSR, see Soviet Union

Velikie Luki, 137
Vistula, 52
Vladivostok, 137
Volga, R., 39, 46, 83, 133, 134, 135,
    170
Volgograd, see Tsaritsyn and Stalingrad
Voronezh, 133, 134, 165
Vyazma, 126, 127

Warsaw, 52, 54, 80, 102
Washington, 1, 132, 177
Waterloo, 1815 battle of, 1, 214
West Germany (FGR), 231

Yugoslavia, the South Slavs, 231
Yukhnov, 127

SUBJECT INDEX AND GLOSSARY

ACVI, armoured combat vehicle infantry, an APC modified for combat and often equipped with turret-mounted offensive armament

AFV, armoured fighting vehicle

Air forces, Red and Soviet, see under Red Army and Soviet Army

All-Russian Congress of Soviets and its Executive (Vtsik), 31, 33, 38, 53, 57

Anti-aircraft weapons, small-arms, machine-guns, artillery anti-aircraft guns or surface-to-air guided or homing missiles

Anti-Semitism in Russia, 16, 22, 76, 215

Anti-tank weapons, anti-tank grenades or grenade launchers, rifled or smooth-bore guns, or guided missiles

APC, armoured personnel carrier, an armoured tracked or wheeled vehicle to carry troops

Armament industry and technology: Soviet, 81, 86–8, 95, 101, 102, 103, 128, 166, 167, 175, 178–9 tsarist, 13, 25

Armoured assault artillery, German armoured and tracked tank-destroyers, used in a direct-fire role, 142, 157

Armoured car, a wheeled armoured fighting or reconnaissance vehicle

Artillery, may be anti-aircraft, anti-tank or field branch (field, medium or heavy guns, short-range multiple rocket or guided or unguided surface-to-surface missile)

Artillery direct fire, flat trajectory close-range (and usually visually aimed) fire

Artillery indirect fire, usually at distant targets hidden from the guns: trajectory may be low (guns) or high (howitzers and mortars)

Artillery, SP (self-propelled), highly mobile guns (on a self-propelled wheeled or tracked platform) usually used in an indirect-fire role

Austrian Army, 6, 8, 26, 38, 45

Blitzkrieg (lightning war), 124, 149, 189

Bolshevik Party, the so-called majority party led by Lenin after the 1903 split of the Social-Democratic Workers Party away from Plekhanov and the Mensheviks: *see also* Communist, Politburo and Central Committee, 44, 45, 58, 64, 68, 73

Bolshevik (Communist) Party Congresses (that met at very irregular intervals): numbered in sequence:
   8th Party Congress 1919, 48
   10th Party Congress 1921, 55
   11th Party Congress 1922, 66

Bolshevik form of government, 32, 33, 34, 178

Bolsheviks, 23, 25, 29, 30, 31, 32, 33, 34, 35, 36, 37, 38, 39, 40, 41, 42, 45, 47, 48, 50, 52, 54, 57, 58, 59, 64, 65, 99, 221

Border guards (Soviet), also known as border or frontier troops, under NKVD and later KGB and not part of the army, 112, 164, 165, 192

Border guards (tsarist), 10,25

Brest-Litovsk, treaty 1918, 37, 48

Central Committee (of Bolshevik/Communist Party), originally a small elected nucleus theoretically responsible for the direction of the party: from 1919 the permanent Politburo and Orgburo were formed to direct all day to day business when the Central Committee was not in session. From the Orgburo was developed the Secretariat controlled by the first secretary, so that from the early twenties the party was in fact ruled by the party leader (first secretary) and Politburo in their own right, their mandate from the Orgburo and Central Committee being largely fictional, 32, 34, 46, 48, 49, 51, 59, 63, 71, 102, 150, 151, 179, 180, 225

Central Powers, 30, 35, 37

Central Staff (in Moscow), controlling partisans, diversionist wreckers and others, 167

Cheka (Soviet secret police), later called GPU, OGPU and NKVD (which see): now under the KGB, 40, 50, 52, 59, 98, 140, 164

Chemical warfare, 82, 197

Chlen (i.e., the member), the military commissar member of military councils of armies, fronts and military districts who may, or may not, be the head of the formation political department, 151, 224

Citadel, at Kursk 1943, the last German offensive in the east, 138–9

Civil War (Russian) 1918–1920, 23, 33, 45, 50, 65, 69, 102, 113, 127

Comintern, a Moscow organization to coordinate and direct communist activities abroad, 66

Commissar for Navy (from 1937), 97, 103 (amalgamated in MVS in 1946) 150, (separated again in 1950) 167

Commissar for War, later Military and Naval Affairs then Defence (NKO), 37, 43, 68, 69, 70, 96, 97, 104, 113, 124, 125, 128

Commissars, departmental ministers, having no connection with military Red Army commissars (which see), 33, 34, 40, 105

Committee for Defence (Defence Commission), 95, 97

Committee for Military and Naval Affairs (1917), 36

Communist Party, see also Bolshevik Party, Central Committee and Politburo, 221

Cossacks, self-ruling minorities of mixed Russian, Ukrainian and Tartar-Turkic stock, mostly in military cavalry hosts

Council of People's Commissars (Sovnarkom), the governmental executive, 33, 34

Crimean War, 9, 11, 14

Disorders, Russian, civil and military 1905, 12, 21

DOSAAF (that replaced DOSAV, DOSFLOT and DOSARM), a voluntary organization to promote interest in, and to undertake part-time and preparatory training for, the armed forces; (see also Osoaviakhim), 160, 161, 207

Duma, tsarist parliamentary body (of a consultative nature), 30

First World War 1914–1917 (involving Russia) 1914–1918 (involving the Entente), 26 et seq.

Five-Year Plans (Russian), 81, 83, 87, 97

Franco-Prussian War 1870, 12

French Army, 8, 12, 113, 119, 120, 123, 128, 169, 217

Frontier guards see border troops

Frunze general staff (later all-arms) academy, 76, 214

German Air Force see Luftwaffe

German Army, 2, 22, 23, 26, 28, 29, 38, 45, 82–9, 97, 99, 107, 108, 113, 114, 115, 117, 120, 121, 123, 124, 126, 129, 130, 145, 164, 169, 214, 217, 228, 232

German armoured doctrine, 82–9, 107, 108, 114, 146, 155

German army general staff, 83, 88, 90, 91, 101, 129, 130, 145, 155

German military thought, 82–9, 107, 108, 114

German panzer arm, 82–9, 107, 108, 114, 117, 121, 123, 124, 138, 145

Gestapo, German state secret police, 100, 130, 145

GKO, main defence committee: 1918, 124, 226 1941, 124, 127, 128, 226

GPU see Cheka

Great purges 1936–1938, 98–101, 110, 165, 178, 206, 222

GRU, main intelligence directorate of the general staff operating its own world-wide foreign espionage service, 66, 132, 215, 216, 228

GSFG, the group of Soviet forces in (East) Germany

Guerrilla warfare, see Central Staff and partisans

Gun, usually of a calibre/bore of 20mm and upwards, rifled or smooth-bore, firing shot or shell, with a flat or low flight trajectory

GVS, main military council 1985, 226

Heavy industry (Soviet), 81, 95, 97, 101, 167, 178

Higher Military Council see VVS

Howitzer, a rifled bore artillery piece that is usually fired in the upper register: though its range is somewhat limited it fires a large-calibre and heavy shell

Intelligentsia (Russian), 24

Internal security troops NKVD/MVD, responsible for supporting the police and quelling mutinies in the armed forces: they are not part of the army, 111, 112, 164, 165, 178

Izvestia, originally the newspaper of the Petrograd soviet and then the Congress of Soviets of Workers Deputies; now a national paper, 30, 76

Japanese Army, 23, 146, 147

Katyusha, a WW II truck-mounted multiple rocket battery, 142

KGB, secret police, formerly NKVD and OGPU: responsible for political and other espionage abroad and counter-intelligence and security within the USSR: in addition it controls the border guards and other organizations, together with nuclear stockpiles and equipment, and has a powerful influence over the GRU, the armed forces and civil police, 66, 140, 163, 164, 165, 178, 180, 181, 206, 216, 222, 228

Komsomol, the young communist league, 73, 101, 110, 164, 207

Konvoi Cossacks, tsarist Caucasian household troops, 29

Kronstadt naval rebellion, 68, 80

Kwantung Army (Japanese), 147

Left Socialist Revolutionaries, 35, 36, 41, 53, 57

Luftwaffe, German air force, 83, 97, 105, 108, 109, 115, 121, 122, 123, 135, 138, 139, 145

Machine-carbine (MC), fully automatic light carbine or assault rifle formerly known as sub machine-gun

Mensheviks, a so-called minority faction of the Social Democratic Workers Party that split with the Bolsheviks in 1903, 29, 30, 31, 32, 38, 57

Military attachés (foreign) in St Petersburg and Moscow, 2, 13, 14, 17, 20, 21, 23, 24, 26, 27, 28, 92

Ministry of Armed Forces (MVS) from 1946, controlling the Soviet Army and Navy, 150

Ministry for the Navy, from 1950, 167, 170, (returns to Defence Ministry 1953) 181

Ministry of War, the former MVS, from 1950, 167

Ministry of Defence, formerly for War, from 1953, 167, 179, 180, 181, 182, 191, 192

Mortar, a light short-range artillery piece used by artillery and infantry, usually smooth-bored and muzzle-loaded, firing a heavy high-trajectory fin-stabilized bomb

Napoleonic Wars, 1, 2, 5, 214

National (minority) formations in the Red/Soviet Army, 75

NATO, North Atlantic Treaty Organization, 176, 177, 189, 192, 195, 196, 226, 229, 231

NKVD, literally 'the peoples commissariat of internal affairs', including the secret police: see also Cheka, GPU and KGB, 98, 100,

111, 114, 127, 131, 140, 163,
(becomes MVD) 164, 165, 168,
180
Nuclear graduated response, 177, 189
Nuclear limited warfare, 177, 189
Nuclear warfare, 147, 148, 170, 171,
175–6, 188, 189, 197, 206, 230,
231

OGPU secret police, *see* Cheka and
GPU
Operative art, a level of operational
activity between strategy and
tactics, recognized by the German
and Russian (including Soviet)
armies but not in the western
world, 43
Opolchenie, the army reserve, 8, 21, 26
Orgburo (of the Communist party), 58
Orthodox Church, 45, 169, 204, 215
Osoaviakhim, originally a part-time
voluntary organization to train the
population in air-raid and chemical
defence, it also undertook
premilitary training, 152, 160, 161

Partisans, 41, 46, 118, 139, 167
Petrograd Soviet, 30, 31, 32, 33, 41, 57
Polish Army, 52, 54
Politburo of the Bolshevik/Communist
Party, 34, 41, 46, 48, 49, 50, 57,
58, 59, 63, 70, 71, 102, 125, 128,
166, 170, 178, 179, 180, 181, 190,
191, 192, 225, 227
Political members (military commissars)
of military councils, *see also* chlen
Politruk, a low ranking military
commissar usually at company
level
Praporshchik (Soviet), a warrant officer
Praporshchik (tsarist) a candidate
officer
Principles of war, (Soviet from 1942),
166
Provisional Russian government 1917,
30, 31, 32, 41
Prussian Army, *see also* Germany
Army, 4, 5, 6, 7, 8, 9, 11, 12, 15,
16, 22, 78, 214, 217, 220
PUR, the main political (commissar)
directorate of the Red/Soviet
Armies responsible only to the

Central Committee, 68, 99, 113,
116, 133, 150, 151, 180, 222, 226,
227
Purges, *see* the Great purges
PVO (Strany), literally AA defence of
the homeland, a command that
incorporates air force fighter and
army AA artillery of all type; now
known simply as PVO, 3, 109, 150,
151, 152, 181, 182, 184, 226, 229

Radar, 2, 109, 173–4, 216
Radio, 2, 94, 109, 137, 143, 158, 173–
4, 216
Rasputitsa, literally the breaking up of
the roads, periods of thaw or flood
Raznochintsy, the educated section of
tsarist society without rank, station
and often means
Red Army (1918–1946) afterwards the
Soviet Army:
air force, 3, 75, 82, 83, 84, 95, 96,
105, 106, 107, 108, 109, 122,
123, 138, 139, 141
armament and equipment, 42, 67,
77, 80, 86–8, 92, 95, 101, 102,
104, 137, 141
armour/tanks:
general, 75, 81, 82, 84–6, 101,
102, 105, 106, 108, 113, 122,
135, 137, 143, 145
organization, 84–6, 93, 107, 113,
122, 133, 143
theory of warfare, 81, 82, 83, 84–
6, 105, 108, 113
artillery:
general, 71, 75, 79, 81, 101, 104,
105, 108, 115, 122, 142, 145,
146
anti-aircraft, 105
anti-tank, 105
assault, *see* SUs
divisions, 153
multiple rocket, 142
self-propelled, 157
attachés views on, 2, 91, 92, 120,
140, 143, 144
badges of rank, 72, 96, 125, 141
British views on, 2, 92, 93–5, 120,
140, 143, 144, 222, 223, 224
cadres (regular component), 67, 68,
71, 98

Red Army – cont.
  cavalry, 39, 42, 43, 51, 66, 82, 93,
    98
  commissars (military), *see also*
    zampolit and politruk, 40, 41,
    43, 45, 47, 49, 51, 53, 54, 55,
    62, 63, 64, 65, 72, 73, 74, 77,
    90, 99, 101, 110, 111, 113, 125,
    144, 224
  conscription, 38, 39, 41, 55, 61, 68,
    71, 75, 98, 111, 112
  councils (military) at HQ district,
    front and army, 40, 41, 54, 55,
    99, 101, 125, 127
  discipline, 117, 118, 146
  field organization:
    military districts, 109, 118
    theatres, 118
    fronts, 42, 109, 118
    armies, 42, 109, 143
    cavalry armies, 42, 43, 51, 53, 55,
      68
    tank armies, 133, (1943) 143, 145,
      152
    corps, 42, 93, 143
    cavalry corps, 42, 43
    mechanized corps, 87, 93, 107,
      108, 113, (1943) 143, 152
    divisions, 42, 61, 82, 92, 98, 107,
      141, 142, 143
    brigades, 42, 82, 87, 92, 107, 108,
      143
  founding of, 36, 37, 38, 44, 45
  general staff under NKO (earlier Red
    Army staff), 39, 76, 80, 91, 93,
    96, 103, 104, 109, 112, 114
  general staff under Stavka (from
    1941–1946), 125, 126, 128, 130,
    131, 141, 144
  general staff academies, *see* the
    Frunze and the Voroshilov
  German influence on, 78, 82, 83–8,
    91, 92, 108, 114, 146
  German views on, 90, 91, 92, 103,
    120, 222
  guard titles (from 1941), 119, 120
  high command, 38, 47, 49, 50, 54,
    65, 69, 76, 80, 99, 100, 109,
    114, 118, 124, 127–9, 130, 133,
    135, 138, 139, 147
  infantry, 71, 82, 123, 124, 134, 135,
    141, 146

infantry weapons, 105
intelligence, *see* GRU
investigating commissions, 46, 125,
    127, 131
manoeuvres, 90, 93, 94
marshals and generals, 96, 97, 113,
    115, 116, 126, 222
medals and orders, 141
mobilization, 115
non-commissioned officers (NCOs),
    72, 94
officers, *see also* specialist
    commanders, 141, 144
order of battle and strength, 61, 69,
    98, 107, 108, 109, 112, 114,
    115, 128, 138, 142
other ranks (generally), 37, 42, 71,
    72, 91, 93, 94
parachute forces, 80, 94
pay, 37, 72, 74
political control, education, and
    party army organization, *see also*
    PUR, 72, 73, 74, 101, 110, 141
politruk, 73, 110
ranks, 37, 72, 96
rations and messes, 72, 74
rear services, existed as part of the
    Red Army from 1942
secret police (counter-intelligence)
    detachments in, *see under*
    NKVD and KGB specialist
    (military) commanders/officers,
    39, 40, 41, 42, 43, 44, 46, 47,
    48, 49, 53, 61, 62, 63, 64, 67,
    68, 69, 71, 72, 73, 74, 75, 76,
    77, 90, 91, 93, 94, 97, 110, 126,
    141
specialist commanders, summary
    demoting, imprisonment and
    shooting of, 40
tanks, *see under* armour/tanks
technical services, 71, 75
territorial militia, 65, 67, 68, 71,
    98
thought, doctrine, strategy,
    operations and tactics, 42, 43,
    65, 66, 77, 78, 79, 82, 83, 94,
    95, 100, 101, 105, 108, 113,
    117, 118, 217
training, 44, 72, 75, 76, 77, 78, 79,
    91, 94, 100, 101, 109, 115, 117,
    118

Tsaritsyn (guerrilla) group in, 46, 48, 64, 66, 116
women in, 76
zampolit, 74, 110, 224
military districts, theatres, fronts and armies:
Belorussian MD, 112, 114
Kiev MD, 112, 114, 115
Leningrad MD, 80, 112, 114, 115, 125
Moscow MD, 69
Far East Theatre 1945, 147
South-West Theatre 1941–2, 132
West Theatre 1941, 125, 126
Caucasus Front 1919, 53
East Front 1918, 49, 53
South Front 1918, 46, 47, 50, 51, 52, 53
South-West Front 1920, 52, 53, 54, 55, 62
West Front 1920, 52, 53, 55, 79
Bryansk Front 1942, 126
Central Front 1943, 138
1 Far East Front 1945, 147
2 Far East Front 1945, 147
Kalinin Front 1942, 127
Reserve Front 1941, 126
South-West Front 1941, 117, 126 (new) 132
Steppe Front 1943, 138
Transbaikal Front 1945, 146
Voronezh Front 1942, 138
West Front 1941, 117, 125, 126, 127, 128
10 Army 1918, 46, 47
Red Guard, 32, 35, 36, 37, 132
Red Navy, 68, 86, 95, 96, 98, 103, 144, 214
Reichsheer, see also German Army, 82, 83, 84–8
Reichswehr, see also Wehrmacht, 82, 83
Revolution, February 1917, 30, 31
Revolution, October 1917, 30, 32, 38
Revolutionary Military Council of the Republic (RVSR), the directing high command council and successor to the VVS, 47, 49, 50, 63, 64, 65, 69
Revolutionary Military Council (RVS) and successor to RVSR, 69, 95, 96, 98, 104

Riga, treaty 1921, 56
Rocketry and rocket weapons, 2, 142, 146, 148, 181, 216, 230
Russian character and characteristics, 6, 7, 8, 14, 18, 19, 20, 21, 23, 27, 28, 91, 93, 94, 95, 134–6, 137, 146, 162, 175, 194, 215, 216, 219–20, 221
Russian corruption and inefficiency, 14, 15, 19, 23, 27, 175, 203, 206, 215, 216
Russian imperial tsarist army before 1918:
armament and equipment, 9, 13, 26, 100
artillery, 13, 26, 28
cavalry, 4, 5, 18, 29
conscription and recruiting, 6, 11, 12, 13, 19, 20, 21, 23
Cossacks, 18, 25, 29, 31, 66, 75, 98
courts of honour (officers), 17
discipline, 12, 23, 27, 30, 31
dissolution, 33, 35
field organization:
military districts, 39
armies, 16
corps, 16
cavalry corps, 16
divisions, 15, 16, 26
brigades, 15
regiments, 15, 16, 17, 22
foreign attachés views on, 10, 13, 14, 15, 17, 19, 20, 21, 23, 26, 27, 28, 78
general staff, 9, 16, 27, 37
general staff academy (Nikolaevsky), 9, 15, 16, 76, 214
guard cavalry and foot, 9, 10, 11, 13, 14, 18, 29
high command, 8, 9, 23
infantry, 7, 9, 10, 26, 28
general officers, 8, 9, 10, 13, 14, 27, 33, 214
officers, origin and training, 5, 6, 9, 10, 11, 14, 16, 17, 18, 19, 20, 27, 30, 31, 110, 214, 215
officers' reserve, lack of, 12, 19, 27, 28, 29
officers, summary arrest and demoting, 17
officers, candidate, see praporshchik (tsarist), 19, 28, 213

Russian imperial tsarist army – cont.
non-commissioned officers, 12, 28, 61
other ranks, 6, 11, 19, 20, 26
order of battle and strength, 9, 26
pay, 18, 19
Prusso-German influence on, 4, 5, 8, 11, 12, 15, 16, 17, 22, 24, 25, 43, 78
reserve of rank and file, 12, 13, 20, 21, 26
sappers and miners, 21
thought, doctrine, strategy and tactics, 7, 8, 9, 14, 15, 43, 78, 216, 217
training, 7, 8, 9, 10, 12, 29, 109
regiments referred to:
Foot-guards; Litovsky, Pavlovsky, Preobrazhensky, Volynsky, Semenovsky, 5, 29
Dragoons; 1 Moskovsky, 5
Grenadier; 13 Erivansky, 4
Foot; Butyrsky, Moskovsky, 4
Rifles; Caucasian, Finnish, Transcaspian, Turkestan, 17
Russian nobility, 4, 5
Russo-Finnish War 1939–1940, 112, 113
Russo-German War 1941–1945, 23, 115, 117 et seq.
Russo-German military collaboration 1921–1933 and 1939–1941, 82–9, 92
Russo-German treaty and secret protocol Aug/Sep 1939, 111, 112
Russo-Japanese War 1904, 20, 21, 26
Russo-Polish War 1920, 52–6, 79
Russo-Turkish War 1877–1878, 14
RVS and RVSR see revolutionary military councils

Second Front, Anglo-American landings in France, 145
Second World War 1939–1945
Secret police (Soviet) see under Cheka, GPU, OGPU, NKVD and KGB
Secret police (tsarist), 25
Serfdom (Russian), 6,7, 10, 12
Small-arms, infantry light weapons and all soldiers' personal weapons, i.e., pistols, rifles, machine-carbines

and light and medium machine-guns
Socialist-Revolutionaries, 24, 29, 30
Soldiers elected committees 1917, 31, 35, 40, 41
Soviet, literally council, the name taken by the Bolsheviks from the Petrograd and many regional soviets, and the Congress of Soviets
Soviet Army since 1946, formerly the Red Army:
airborne assault troops, 228, 229
airborne forces, 156, 182, 183, 193, 228, 229
air force:
tactical air forces, 3, 149, 150, 156, 171, 182, 184, 190, 226, 229
long range air force, 182
military air transport force, 182
anti-aircraft weapons (incl. GW), 184, 194
anti-tank weapons (incl. GW), 172, 173, 184, 185, 196, 201
amphibious vehicles, 173, 186, 198
armament and equipment, 159, 160, 172, 173, 174, 201, 202, 209, 228
armour/tanks and SUs:
general, 149, 150, 153–7, 158, 172, 173, 193, 195, 197, 205, 209, 210, 216, 227
organization, 183, 193
theory of warfare, 149, 171, 172–4, 175, 177, 182, 187, 188, 189, 191, 193, 212, 219
armoured combat vehicles infantry (ACVIs), 187, 188, 198
armoured personnel carriers (APCs), 172, 173, 176, 186, 187, 188, 198
artillery:
general, 150, 153, 158, 160, 171, 174, 176, 199, 200
anti-aircraft, 153, 184, 194
anti-tank, 153, 158, 172, 173, 201
divisions, 153, 193
multiple-rocket, 153, 159, 174
self-propelled, 157, 196, 197, 200

single rocket, unguided and
guided, 174, 176, 181, 184, 194
nuclear, 174, 189, 190, 200
bridging, 173
cavalry, 156, 170
commissars (military) *see also*
zampolit and politruk, 151, 163,
180, 207, 222
conscription, 12, 160, 161, 192, 203,
204, 205, 206, 207
councils (military) at HQ district,
group, front and army, 151, 163
courts of honour for officers and
praporshchiki, 220
cybernetics (military), Soviet study
of, 219
discipline, 162, 204–5, 208, 220, 221
field organization:
military districts, 151, 182, 210
groups, 152, 182
fronts, 152
mechanized armies, 152, 153, 182
tank armies, 182, 183, 193
combined-arms armies, 182, 183,
193
corps, 152, 153, 182
mechanized divisions, 152, 154,
155, 156, 160, 171, 172
motor rifle divisions, 172, 182,
183, 193
tank divisions, 152, 154, 156, 171,
182, 183, 193
rifle divisions, 152, 153, 156, 160,
171
army general staff, and later general
staff of the armed forces, 150,
151, 167, 170, 181, 182, 225,
226, 227
general staff academies, *see* the
Frunze and the Voroshilov
German influence on, 149, 150, 154,
155, 173, 177, 186, 187, 194,
217, 219, 228
ground forces, HQ and C-in-C, 3,
150, 151, 168, 181, 182, 192,
226, 227
Group of Soviet Forces Germany
(GSFG), 152, 168, 192, 208,
226, 227
guards titles, some historic retention
of, 152
helicopters, 184, 229

high command, 150, 167, 177, 178–
82, 222
infantry, including motorized
infantry, 149, 183, 187, 188,
193, 198, 199, 205, 209
infantry weapons, 159, 174, 201
inspector-general, 150, 168, 170, 226
intelligence *see* GRU
manning and mobilization categories,
227, 228
manoeuvres, 210
marshals and generals, 191, 213, 221
mobilization, 227, 228
night fighting and night-vision
equipment, 185, 186
non-commissioned officers and
extended servicemen, 161, 208,
209, 210, 212
officers, 161, 162, 191, 192, 207,
208, 211, 215, 216, 219, 221,
223
officers, arrest of, 220, 221
officers' reserve, lack of, 211, 212,
213
officers, retirement and pensions,
161, 191, 192, 213
officer schools, 211, 212, 214
officers' status, 162, 191, 192, 212,
213
officers summary demoting,
imprisonment and shooting of,
220, 221
officer training, 211, 212, 213, 214,
215, 216, 219, 221
other ranks, 160, 161, 203, 204, 205,
206
other ranks' reserve, 151, 211
order of battle and strength, 160,
175, 182, 191, 192, 193, 227,
228
pay and conditions, 161, 162, 191,
205, 208, 210, 213
parachute forces, 228, 229
political control, education, and
party army organization, *see also*
PUR, 163, 180, 181, 207, 208,
222, 223
praporshchiki (Soviet), 210, 211,
212, 213
ranks, 161, 162
rations and messes, 161, 208, 210,
213

Soviet Army – cont.
  rear services, 3, 150, 226
  reserve field divisions, 160, 228
  secret police (counter-intelligence)
    detachments in, *see under*
    NKVD and KGB
  spetsnaz, 228, 229
  training, 205, 209, 210
  training divisions, 209, 210
  tanks, *see under* armour/tanks
  tanks, underwater wading, 173, 186
  uniforms, 162, 163
  zampolit, 163, 164, 207, 208, 222,
    223
  military districts:
    Moscow and Volga, 167, 180
Soviet defence council 1985, 225
Soviet defence minister 1985, 221, 225,
  226
Soviet form of government, *see under*
  Bolshevik
Soviet (published) military history, 1,
  2, 43, 66, 67, 69, 70, 77, 78, 79,
  108, 117, 119, 120, 144, 147, 148,
  150, 166, 169, 171, 214, 218, 219
Soviet (Stalin) military science, 166,
  217–19
Soviet Navy, 150, 151, 167, 182, 190,
  192, 226
Soviet naval infantry, 228
Soviet militia, i.e. the civil police, 206
Sovnarkom, *see* Council of People's
  Commissars
Spetsnaz, special purpose airborne
  troops, *see under* Soviet Army
Stavka (tsarist) 28, 29, 30, 36, 125
Stavka 1941, 125, 128, 131, 133
Stavka 1985, 226
Strategic Rocket Forces (Soviet) 3, 81,
  182, 190, 226
Strategy, the art of preparing,
  mobilizing, concentrating moving
  and deploying forces and resources
  world-wide, between theatres of
  war, or within a theatre, with a
  view to success in battle
Streltsy, archers and musketeers in the
  service of Muscovy, 4
SU, literally a self-propelled
  equipment, in reality the 1943
  Soviet copy of the German assault
  artillery tank-destroyer, a tracked

fully armoured turretless tank,
  carrying a gun in the hull; used
  from 1943 to date, 2, 142, 156–7,
  197
Suvorov cadet schools, from about 1945
  originally for children, now for
  adolescents, 163
Swedish Army, 4, 5

Tachanka, a 1918 horse-drawn vehicle
  carrying a Maxim MG
Tactics, the art of fighting a battle
  when in contact with the enemy,
  in Soviet terms usually at the level
  of corps and below
Tank, a tracked and armoured fighting
  vehicle carrying offensive fire
  power, nowadays usually mounting
  a turret and gun as main
  armament; *see under* armour (Red
  and Soviet Armies)
Tank-destroyer, *see* SU
Turkish Army, 14, 20

Versailles, treaty 1919, 82
Voroshilov (senior) general staff
  academy, 214
Vtsik, the executive of the All-Russian
  Congress of Soviets, which *see*
VVS, the higher military council 1918,
  the forerunner of the RVSR, 38,
  47, (reconstituted 1946) 166
VCh, high frequency Soviet telephone
  (later also radio) system used in
  WW II, 141
V weapons, German pilotless bombers
  (V1) and rocket (V2), 146, 148

Waffen SS, the German armed SS,
  totalling about thirty divisions
  by the end of WW II, 111, 155,
  165
Warsaw Pact, the military pact between
  the USSR and its communist East
  European satellites, covering the
  European theatre only, 181, 225,
  226, 227, 231
Wehrmacht, the German armed forces
  1935–1945, 115, 119, 120, 121,
  123, 124, 133
Whites, the anti-Bolshevik Russian
  forces 1918–1920, 40, 42, 44, 45,

48, 49, 50, 51, 52, 53, 61, 65, 66, 69

Women: there were no women in the tsarist army except in the medical services in war (as early as 1853): very few women were taken into the Red Army between the wars except in some specialist and technical appointments: between 1941–1945 there was a large scale recruitment of women, mainly voluntary, as auxiliaries in the signal, traffic control, medical, clerical and administrative services; there were some highly publicized propaganda stories of women aviators, snipers and tank crew, but the employment of women in these posts was rare: women are not conscripted at all into the Soviet Army other than occasionally as doctors, pharmacists or technical specialists; there is, however, a small regular cadre of women officers and non-commissioned officers in peace on which the women's services could be expanded in the event of war. *See also under* Red Army

Young Pioneers, communist organization for schoolchildren; the infants were known as 'the Young Oktiabrists': from the Pioneers the youth passes to the Komsomol

Zampolit, the deputy (political) leader: the zampolit is the name given to the military commissar when officially he no longer has the power of veto over the commander.